Muddy Waters

THE MOJO MAN

MUDDY WATERS

THE MOJO MAN

Sandra B. Tooze

ECW PRESS

We acknowledge the support of the Canada Council
for the Arts for our publishing program.
This book has been published with the assistance
of grants from the Ontario Arts Council.

CANADIAN CATALOGUING IN PUBLICATION DATA

Tooze, Sandra B.
Muddy Waters: the mojo man

ISBN 1-55022-296-1

1. Muddy Waters, 1915–1983.   2. Blues
musicians — United States — Biography.
I. Title.

ML420.M82T66 1997   782.42164'3'092   C96-990102-X

Design and imaging by ECW Type & Art, Oakville, Ontario.
Printed by Printcrafters, Winnipeg, Manitoba.

Distributed in Canada by General Distribution Services,
30 Lesmill Road, Don Mills, Ontario M3B 2T6.

Distributed in the United States by Login Publishers Consortium,
1436 West Randolph Street, Chicago, Illinois, U.S.A. 60607.

Published by ECW PRESS,
2120 Queen Street East, Suite 200,
Toronto, Ontario M4E 1E2.

http://www.ecw.ca/press

PRINTED AND BOUND IN CANADA

For Albert T. Tooze . . .
always loved, always remembered

Eric Clapton and Muddy Waters,
Chicago Stadium, June 1979 (D. Shigley)

FOREWORD

Perhaps the greatest misconception about the blues is that it is simply an opportunity to express sadness or anger about the injustices of life. It surely does contain these emotions, and in fact that's exactly what it does, but it contains them within the essential elements of honesty, humour and humility, creating, in turn, the overall principle of dignity. The blues is not about self-pity or self-indulgence, it is about courage in the face of adversity, the truth of the soul, and the nobility of the spirit in its infinite capacity to suffer and rejoice at exactly the same time. How, you may ask, do I know all this? Because I have listened to Muddy Waters all of my life, and this is what his music taught me.

I eventually met Muddy and got to know him pretty well, and to me he was like a tribal chief, a Buddha, and a naughty boy all rolled into one, but what I remember most about him was his dignity.

In response to his own personal vision, Muddy took the music of the Delta plantation, transplanted it in a Chicago nightclub, surrounded it with an electric band and proceeded to change the course of popular music forever. In doing so, I believe Muddy became one of the most significant links between early Afro-American culture and the global electronics of modern rock 'n' roll as we know it today.

For myself, nothing can compare with the eerie combination of his slide and voice on songs like "Walkin' Blues" or "I Feel Like Going Home." His music changed my life, and whether you know it or not, and like it or not, it probably changed yours, too.

Eric Clapton

CONTENTS

ACKNOWLEDGMENTS

Writing this book has been a personal journey of unequaled self-discipline, elation, frustration and fear. It's taught me about the generosity of others, most of them strangers, who gave freely of their time and memories to help honor a man who exerted a lasting impact on every life he touched. This biography would have been barren without the gracious assistance of the following people. I thank them most sincerely.

Lucy Aubree	Chris Barber
Marcia Beamish	Elvin Bishop
Clive Blewchamp	John Brim
Mojo Buford	R.L. Burnside
Geary Chansley	Marshall Chess
Eric Clapton	Francis Clay
James Cotton	Sherman Darby
Patrick Day	Bo Diddley
Richard Flohil	Roger Forrester
Willie Foster	Andy Grigg
John Hammond	Jamie Harrison
Kathleen Hawkins	Tom Heimdal
Levon Helm	John Lee Hooker
Cilla Huggins	Mick Jagger
Calvin Jones	Mike Kappus
Gary Kendall	B.B. King
Andreas Koch of the	Paul Koch
Music Book Store	Jim Kozlowski
Bob Laul	Sam Lay
S.P. Leary	Lovie Lee
Mark Lipkin	Andrew List

Andy McKaie
Bob Margolin
Margaret Meredith of
the Blues Foundation
Charlie and Henrietta
Musselwhite
Jim O'Neal
Nigel Paul
John Primer
Catherine Reid
Jimmy Rogers
John Ruskey and the staff
of the Delta Blues Museum
Marty Salzman
Joel Spillman
Howard Stovall
Ron Stuart
Rufus Thomas
Dick Waterman
Alexandra Wgnick
Pete Whelan
Early Wright

Magic Dick
Mike Markowitz
Ken Minahan
Tom Moon
Mark Naftalin
Bruce Nemerov
Paul Oscher
Jerry Portnoy
Tom Radai
Andy Robble
Lee Rosenblit
Kathleen Saraceni
of Carnegie Hall
Willie Smith
Jerry Stone
Mrs. W.H. Stovall
Koko Taylor
Gayle Dean Wardlow
Junior Wells
Wendy of the Circuit Clerk's
Office, Rolling Fork
Val Wilmer

Especially rewarding was the opportunity to speak with members of Muddy's own family. I extend my deep appreciation to Elve Morganfield, Joseph Morganfield, Robert Morganfield, Williams Morganfield and Reverend Willie Morganfield.

I must reserve a special expression of gratitude for the extraordinary people I met in Mississippi, who did their utmost to make my visit a successful and most enjoyable one. I am indebted to Joe Garrison, who faced impending danger as I practiced driving on Highway 55, who served as my mojo adviser and who has remained a friend ever since. Thanks, too, to the staff of the Blues Archives at the University of Mississippi, especially Ed Komara, who went far beyond the call of duty by assisting me in every way possible. It's hard to imagine my stay in Clarksdale without the invaluable assistance and friendship of Patty Johnson of Rooster Blues Records, who kept steering me in the right direction, and

Nancy Kossman of the Delta Blues Museum, who escorted me to Rolling Fork and fed me peanut-butter sandwiches. As well, thanks to David "Pecan" Porter for his informative tour of the Stovall Plantation.

Of course, this biography would have been sorely lacking without the essential addition of the discography of Muddy Waters, reprinted with the generous permission of the authors, Phil Wight and Fred Rothwell, as well as Tony Burke of *Blues & Rhythm* magazine. I also appreciate the assistance they provided in other areas of my research.

To my friend Brian Wickham, mere thanks seem insufficient. He was always there to listen to my agonies and ecstasies, to offer invaluable suggestions, to lend me stacks of written material and to share his encyclopedic knowledge of blues. This would have been a lesser book without him.

I owe a deep debt of gratitude to my agent and friend Matie Molinaro, who doggedly stuck by this project for years, always optimistic as she faced what seemed like an impenetrable wall of uninterested publishers. As well, her son Paul maintained the faith and buoyed my spirits. I appreciate, too, the invaluable expertise of my editor, Mary Williams, and my proofreader, Stuart Ross.

Of course, none of this would have been possible without the opportunity of a lifetime, provided by Jack David of ECW Press. It was a pleasure working with his dedicated and enthusiastic staff, including Nicola Winstanley, Jennifer Hale, Jennifer Trainor and Paul Davies. And finally, a special thank-you to my mother, Emily Tooze, for her unstinting support and love.

INTRODUCTION

The air was as soggy and stagnant as a Mississippi swamp on my first night in the Delta. I'd kicked back in the Stackhouse Recording Studio in Clarksdale to enjoy a rehearsal by blues guitarist and singer Lonnie Pitchford, backed by bassist David "Pecan" Porter. Pitchford delivered a searing set of down-home blues born on this very turf. The music spoke of the anguish and aspirations of the rural black experience, evoking all the passion that had been conjured up by bluesmen for close to a hundred years before.

I was in Mississippi to trace the footsteps of a giant, to unearth the rapidly disappearing remnants of the early life of a great bluesman by visiting the places that had imprinted his psyche and by talking to the folks who had known him way back when. Muddy Waters was a titan of the blues and a colossus as a man. I suspected the roots of his preeminence lay buried in the fertile Mississippi mud.

As Pitchford's country blues sliced through the sweltering studio, I was carried back in time, where more than 70 years ago those same songs had tantalized young Muddy, a boy living with his grandmother just outside this very town. These were the sounds that had molded the burgeoning musician, that had determined his life's path and that he would later use to cut a swath through new musical territory. Pitchford's skillful renditions of numbers by Son House and Robert Johnson — the two Delta bluesmen who most influenced Muddy — were eerie reminders of those itinerant musicians who had passed through Clarksdale, inflaming the youth's passion for the blues and stoking the blaze of his ambition.

Two days later I was privileged to bear witness to another fount of Muddy's inspiration, the black Baptist church. Invited to attend a service at the Bell Grove Baptist Church by its pastor — and Muddy's cousin — the Reverend Willie Morganfield, I was warmly welcomed into an experience I will never forget. The church that

Muddy attended outside of town may have been more rustic, but the feeling of community and the love of God, which remained an integral part of Muddy's life, would have been the same. As the children of the Bell Grove choir vocalized from their hearts, swaying and clapping to celebrate their Lord, I was mindful that a similar scene provided young Muddy with his initial taste of singing and that he always credited the church as the place where he cultivated his soulful vocals.

Reverend Morganfield shares many extraordinary attributes with his more famous cousin. A dignified, loving man who garners respect from all who know him, the pastor is also a master musician with many gospel albums to his credit. On the day of my visit, his singing from the pulpit was breathtaking; his voice soared with emotion and praise for the Lord, causing the woman beside me to erupt into bouts of uncontrollable weeping.

Perhaps it was daring fate, but following the cleansing of my soul, I ventured that evening into the devil's territory at Junior Kimbrough's juke joint near Holly Springs, northeast of Clarksdale. As steamy as hell and often as raucous, here, too, was a Delta institution that left a deep imprint on Muddy. Like the church, these shacks were meeting places of the black community. Back when Muddy was a boy, such venues were where a budding musician could garner inspiration and test his wings. The music being cranked out this night owed its origins to Muddy's Chicago blues sound. The master's blues had come full circle, back to the source, where as an impassioned youth in country roadhouses almost seven decades before, he was influenced to set a course that would alter both blues and popular music.

A hundred miles to the south of Clarksdale, through Delta farmland laid flawlessly flat by eons of flooding of the Mississippi River, is the small town of Rolling Fork, the closest settlement to Muddy's country birthplace. Disjointed by the sleepy waters of Deer Creek, the town surrounds a central square containing the Sharkey County Courthouse. And while Muddy lived near here for only the first three years of his life, Rolling Fork remains mindful of its place in blues history. When I visited the town square, a small knot of older men sheltered from the noonday sun in a gazebo built in remembrance of Muddy Waters. In front of it, a plaque proclaims the town's pride in its most famous son.

The following day I headed out to the Stovall Plantation, five miles outside of Clarksdale, where Muddy lived from age three to 28. Fortuitously, I was accompanied by David "Pecan" Porter, who was not only a former resident of Stovall, but lived in Muddy's house after the great bluesman had made his mark in Chicago.

The luxuriant beauty of the Delta countryside surprised me. I'd half expected that the harshness of the white man's domination would be reflected in the landscape. As if to compensate for past injustices, however, nature had burst forth with a profusion of verdant green, speckled with purple wildflowers. While most of Mississippi's original subtropical forest was leveled long ago to accommodate King Cotton, frequent stands of trees were spared to delineate the fields, preventing the stark monotony of a flat, empty vista.

We arrived on Stovall 52 years to the month after Muddy left. There had been a downpour the previous day — as there had been just before Muddy said his final farewell to his grandmother — so my first glimpse of the majesty of Stovall must have been similar to Muddy's parting glance. On this May day, tender shoots of cotton were beginning to climb towards the broad expanse of a blue Delta sky. Scarlet flashes signaled the presence of cardinals and red-winged blackbirds as they darted amongst the sweetgum, cottonwood and sycamore trees. Stovall cattle browsed on a lush carpet of grass and wildflowers, which sloped up to the top of the levee hugging the forested shores of the Old River. As Muddy had done in his youth, local fishermen were casting their lines into the lazy waters of this former Mississippi channel.

Happily, my visit to Stovall occurred before corporate America bought and uprooted one of the most sacred shrines of the blues; the skeleton of Muddy's cabin was still located on the edge of a cotton field, where it had stood since before the Civil War. More than in any other place I visited, this weather-weary, crumbling shack resurrected the ghosts of Muddy's early life. Within its bleached timbers, a bereaved three-year-old began a new life with the grandmother who would shape his existence, a child discovered his insatiable appetite for music, a toilworn adolescent moaned the blues and a seasoned musician showcased his talent in front of his friends.

From this humble structure emerged a proud, determined man who was willing to gamble that Chicago would be his promised land — that there he could unshackle the limitations of the South. Yet no matter how lofty his subsequent success, Stovall remained his anchor, in both his values and his music. This cabin — this culture — had nurtured a bluesman who would conquer the world.

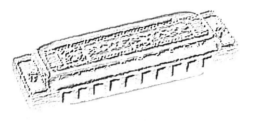

I

I guess I was born with two things — trouble and love for the blues.[1]

On Sunday, 4 April 1915, a newborn baby announced his arrival with a wail that would wake the world.

His name was McKinley Morganfield; the moniker "Muddy Waters" was yet to come. It was coincidental, yet apropos, that he shared his first name with the loftiest peak on the North American continent. As a man he would attain towering heights of his own. Yet back in 1915, he was born at the base of a slippery slope. His was an existence of insurmountable contrasts, of verdant beauty and barbarous cruelty, of cultural riches and aching poverty, of black and white.

He was the second son of Ollie Morganfield and Berta Jones. His parents weren't married, but they may have lived together as husband and wife. Ceremonial formalities were sometimes neglected in the rural South. Berta died when McKinley was only three, and there are no surviving details of her life or character.

A little more is known of Ollie. Originally from Birmingham, Alabama, he settled in a two-room shack outside Rolling Fork, Mississippi, as a sharecropper and cultivated cotton and corn. In order to supplement the meager provisions meted out to croppers, Ollie raised his own chickens and hogs and grew watermelons. It was a life dogged by deprivation, within a system designed to keep the black man down. Nevertheless, Ollie was a man of honor and dignity, described by his son Robert as "the best man I ever knew."[2]

And when Ollie took a break from the drudgery of survival, he found solace in the blues. It was the music of the Delta, born of the black experience, specific to the frustration and pain of the black man, yet it spoke, too, of his hopes and small victories. Although never a professional musician, Ollie sang and played guitar and harmonica at local get-togethers. His avocation infused the infant McKinley with his first shot of the blues.

McKinley was born outside the hamlet of Rolling Fork, although his exact birthplace is unclear. Muddy claimed he was born in Sharkey County on a plantation called Kroger. There was no farm of that name, however; Kroger was the name of the company that ran the Magnolia Plantation at Steel Bayou, about six miles out of Rolling Fork. That was where Ollie lived *after* Berta died. According to Robert Morganfield, McKinley's younger half-brother, McKinley was born on the Cottonwood Plantation in Issaquena County, also near Rolling Fork.

Rolling Fork is located in the southern Mississippi Delta. This delta is not located at the mouth of the Mississippi, but begins nearly 300 miles upriver at Vicksburg and extends in an almond shape almost 250 miles north to Memphis, Tennessee. It's an alluvial plain, formed by eons of flooding of the Mississippi River on the west and to a lesser extent by the Yazoo River to the southeast. This is cotton country, flat as a griddle, yet lush and resplendent, with the gentle hills of central Mississippi demarcating the eastern boundary of the floodplain. Delta summers sizzle and steam, partnered with drenching downpours and the threat of tornadoes. The winters deliver cold rains and occasional ice.

The rich, fertile silt, over 50 feet deep, originally supported a subtropical rain forest, entwined with treacherous swamps and sluggish bayous. Bears and panthers once roamed the dense wilderness; still waters teemed with giant catfish, venomous water snakes and malarial mosquitoes. It took a bold pioneer to do battle with this savage landscape and hack out a farm from the jungle. That's when slavery reared its barbarous head.

The first white settler in what later became the town of Rolling Fork was Thomas Y. Chaney, who bought his tract of land in 1826 while on a government surveying trip. He returned two years later with his family and established the Rolling Fork Plantation along the banks of Deer Creek. Chaney named his home after the rolling waters of a fork in the creek as it cascaded towards its outlet in the Sunflower River, to the east of the site.

In those days Deer Creek wasn't the shallow, babbling brook that some imagine Muddy Waters splashing in as an infant. Unlike the low, narrow stream it is today, it was a navigable river as late as the Civil War. Union gunboats steamed up Deer Creek to Rolling Fork, thwarted only by the felled trees locals had heaved across the embankments.

After the turmoil of the Civil War, King Cotton claimed the Delta for its own. The price was astronomical: incalculable human anguish and environmental devastation. Nature was tamed by massive deforestation and by hemming in the Mississippi with levees, artificial embankments of earth. The emerging Delta farmland needed laborers, and former slaves were enticed to the Mississippi frontier to wrench cotton fields out of timberland. However, any fantasies they harbored that, through hard work, black families could emerge out of misery were quickly quashed.

In the period following Reconstruction, black America was cemented behind social and financial barriers, separate from white society. Sharecropping and segregation were crafted to subjugate blacks and relegate them as close to the former system of bondage as the federal government would permit. Jim Crow laws (named after the character in an 1820s minstrel song and dance, called "Jump Jim Crow") formalized segregation and made black folks jump to the white man's tune. By 1914, the year before McKinley's birth, every state in the South had legislated racial isolation. Through the artifice of literacy tests and poll taxes and by only permitting descendants of previous voters (that is, white voters) to cast a ballot, state governments essentially slammed the ballot box shut on blacks. Society, too, was cleanly split along the color line. With segregated schools, medical facilities, restaurants, theaters, restrooms, streetcars, trains and even cemeteries, the white world could almost deny the existence of black America. It was a stratagem of control and repression.

One convenient rationalization for the yoke of racism — for those whites who required one — was that the black race needed to be taken firmly in hand. David Cohn, a white Delta writer of the period, wrote that blacks were "childlike" and "emotionally unstable," incapable of assuming equality on the unlikely chance it was offered. Ethically, too, Cohn maintained they fell far short of white standards, declaring that for blacks "life is a long moral holiday."[3] He was not alone in his delusions.

Severe economic deprivation stifled the black populace through undernourishment and subsequent ill health and disease. Withholding all but the most basic education was another method. At the time of McKinley's birth, the U.S. senator from Mississippi, James K. Vardaman, was a white supremacist who considered blacks to be less than human. He maintained that to educate blacks beyond the menial level would only frustrate them with unfulfilled dreams. Besides, he reasoned, educating a black "only spoils a good field hand."[4]

And the partner of subjugation was violence. Fear permeated the existence of southern blacks. This was the reality of McKinley's young life. The brutality of the chain gang awaited the slightest infraction or even an unproved accusation. A glance at a white woman could be interpreted as rape. One false move could mean death. It was a life that permitted no easing of one's guard. If the law didn't get you, the Ku Klux Klan — a brotherhood that most southern politicians had belonged to — upheld its prerogative through floggings and lynchings. White crime against blacks, including murder, routinely went unpunished.

An argument could be made that, if it weren't for this history, the blues would not have flourished. The black American would have been out spending his disposable cash, feeling all was right with the world and enjoying the American dream. He wouldn't have been trapped in a sharecropper's shack, with little reason for hope and music as one of the few outlets for his frustration. So when Ollie played the blues to his tiny son, it was more than a catchy tune. It was an intregal part of the black experience and culture of the Delta.

In 1918, before McKinley's third birthday, the bottom fell out of his world. Ollie married Gertrude Crayton on 5 March and went on to father five more sons and five daughters. Presumably he hadn't lived with McKinley's mother, Berta, and their sons for some time. Berta died that year, but whether before or after Ollie's nuptials is not known. The toddler was left an orphan. Most everyone McKinley loved was gone.

But then 39-year-old Della Jones, Berta's mother, entered the scene. His grandmother was to become the single most important influence on McKinley's life. She toted him a hundred miles north, to her cabin on the Stovall Plantation, outside Clarksdale, Mississippi, where Ollie's brother Louis Matthews Morganfield and his family also sharecropped.

Before the influx of its white and black populations, Clarksdale had been home to the Chocktaw nation. But these aboriginals had been coerced westward by a federal government that snatched all the best timberland and farmland for itself. By the time 16-year-old John Clark arrived from New Orleans, about 1839, most of the Chocktaw had found refuge in Oklahoma.

The enterprising teenager was looking for forest to log, but the choice sites along the Mississippi River had been grabbed up as soon as the Chocktaw left. He found a suitable alternative location, however, 12 miles east of the Mississippi, along the banks of the Sunflower River. From there he could just as easily float his logs down to market in New Orleans.

By 1848 Clark had accumulated $126.25, enough to buy 101 acres of this land from the U.S. government, and he set about building a town. Although slavery was the work force of preference, Clark would have none of it. Instead, he brought his laborers, all free men, down from the North. The Civil War, however, forced a suspension in construction. Finally, in 1882, more than 40 years after Clark first swung an ax on the banks of the Sunflower, the site officially became the town of Clarksdale. Over the next few years, Clarksdale began to thrive as the railroad pushed its way through town and cotton fields replaced the wooded wilderness.

At the turn of the century, a local resident became responsible for popularizing the blues and delivering it to a national audience. In 1903 William Christopher Handy, a former minstrel musician, arrived in Clarksdale to serve as conductor of the black Knights of Pythias Band. Returning to town one night from Tutwiler, 14 miles southeast of Clarksdale, he was waiting for an overdue train when a black man sat down beside him in the station and began singing and playing the blues. Excited by the possibilities he heard in this new music, W.C. Handy adapted it for a larger band, and his blues-based compositions subsequently earned him the title "Father of the Blues."

By the time McKinley first set his wide eyes on Clarksdale in 1918, it was a flourishing town of 7,000. Seven-year-old Thomas "Tennessee" Williams was living there with his grandparents, soaking up the ambience for his later dramatic masterpieces. Soon Clarksdale was being heralded as the Golden Buckle on the Cotton Belt and as Little New York. By 1921 it had been dubbed the Magic City, described by the *Wall Street Journal* as "thoroughly modern" and "in its joyful youth." One reporter could recall no other American town "so rich in architectural beauty, set in so pleasing [an] embrace of nature." Clarksdale was extolled as "the richest agricultural city of the United States in proportion to its population."[5] In fact, it boasted more millionaires per capita than any other city in the United States. Of course, that was on the white side of the tracks.

During the year of McKinley's arrival, 200 black Clarksdalians proudly set off for World War I, in the vain hope that by offering up their lives for their country, they would be treated as men. But Jim Crow retained his clawhold on the fabric of the Old South. Segregation and suppression remained the order of the day for the black populace.

Miss Della's ramshackle home on the Stovall Plantation was five miles northwest of town. Stovall's 5,000 flat, fertile acres extended southeast from the levees of the Old River (formerly a lazy loop of the Mississippi, now cut off from the main channel). It was a luxuriantly beautiful setting, where fields of cotton, corn and feed crops were punctuated by rich pastureland and frequent stands of pine, oak and sweetgum.

Long before the Chocktaw inhabited it, other tribes resided on what is now Stovall, leaving behind burial mounds that doubled as safe, high ground in times of flood. The Chocktaw cleared much of the wilderness for their settlement; traces of their pony racetrack can still be seen today. Upon signing the Treaty of Dancing Rabbit Creek in 1830, the Chocktaw ceded all their land east of the Mississippi River to the U.S. government.

Soon afterwards John Odum, a timber entrepreneur, ventured down from Memphis and bought the land from the federal government. From there the property was passed down the matrilineal line. Odum's daughter married John Fowler, and their daughter married William Howard Stovall, a lawyer who served as adjutant to General Beauregard during the Civil War. It wasn't until the turbulence of war had passed that Stovall began farming the land.

Stovall had two sons: the first was John, and then 35 years later when he was 61, his second, also named William Howard Stovall, was born. John lived on Stovall and farmed the nearby Praire Plantation. The younger Howard Stovall distinguished himself as a flying ace in World War I before taking over the Stovall Plantation. He would see action again in World War II.

The Stovall Plantation stood at the crossroads of the dissemination of the blues. In 1901, while on an archeological dig near Clarksdale, Charles Peabody heard a strange new music being sung by an old black man on Stovall. This resulted in the first documentation of Delta blues, in an article written by Peabody in the *Journal of American Folklore* in 1903.

With approximately 3,500 acres under cultivation, about 90 sharecropping families resided on Stovall when McKinley arrived and throughout the time he lived there. Miss Della was one of those croppers, a victim of a southern institution that continued to tie blacks to the land long after slavery had been abolished. Under this system the owner of the plantation — the planter — assigned a cropper family a house and 15 to 40 acres of farmland. In exchange for cultivating the fields, sharecroppers were given a small stipend of $15 to $50 per month and a percentage, or "share," of the profit at harvest.

What might sound good in theory, however, was devised to keep the black family down. The fact was that a sharecropper started out behind the game. With few funds to tide him over to harvest time and with most banks refusing to lend him money, the cropper had no alternative but to borrow from the planter and to buy his groceries and supplies from the plantation commissary at whatever price the planter decided to charge, often at 15 to 25 percent interest.

The cropper was in debt before he began, and generally stayed that way. Unscrupulous planters doctored their books to keep their laborers in economic bondage. To question their accounting could endanger one's life. When the cropper was paid, it was usually in plantation script, only valid in the plantation commissary. No opportunity for comparison shopping here. With very few legal or political rights, the cropper could never obtain the financial means to escape the cycle of bare subsistence. While there's no evidence to suggest that the Stovalls deceived their sharecroppers, nevertheless they were part of an insidious system that perpetuated poverty on black workers.

Della's home on Stovall was not a one-room shack, the oft-repeated myth that's become a standard of blues folklore. The existing one-room framework is all that's left from a tornado in 1983. That part of the dwelling was a pre-Civil War structure, sturdily crafted by an early settler as a cabin or farm building. Before McKinley called it home, three more rooms had been erected around this core, and the original structure had become the front bedroom. Two doors opened onto a front porch that extended across the front of the building. It would have looked much the same as all the other dilapidated sharecropper cabins that lined Stovall's main dirt road.

Inside it was likely similar to the majority of croppers' shacks, which were equipped with only the most rudimentary and essential furniture. Of course, there was no electricity or plumbing; even an inside washbasin was uncommon. Light was supplied by a bottle of coal oil; a plow line served as a wick. A wood-burning stove was the only heat source, as bitter winter winds penetrated fissures in the rough-hewn ceiling and walls, and torrential rains seeped through the roof. The walls were usually lined with newspaper for insulation, with magazine pictures providing the only artwork. Books were rare. The only floor coverings were rugs made from discarded stockings and clothing. Croppers generally slept on shuck mattresses, often three to a bed. Clothing and shoes were home-made. A typical meal consisted of salt pork, black-eyed peas, beans, greens, corn bread and black molasses.

Miss Della was strong and resilient. She had to be. As the sole breadwinner in the household, what she didn't earn as a share-cropper on her allotted 40 acres was done without. She had no alternatives; she had never been to school. And that meant body-breaking work that challenged the strongest man, plowing behind a mule, hoeing the fields and picking cotton. Her son Joe Brant, who was three years older than McKinley, lived with her as well, so as they got older, the two boys shared the tremendous labor necessary to put even the most meager meal on the table.

The great capacity that Della had for work was matched by the magnitude of love she had for her bereaved grandson. McKinley delighted her. His proclivity for playing in the mud prompted her to tease him as her "little muddy baby."[6] The appellation stuck.

Miss Della made it her duty to provide Muddy with the guidance that would serve as his foundation for the rest of his life. A firm disciplinarian, she set about instilling moral values and religious faith in the boy. He would have been very young when she first assigned him daily chores, necessary in such difficult straits, but also designed to inculcate him with a sense of responsibility and self-respect.

But there was time for fun, too. Muddy remembered trying to make music at about age three. He'd sing and drum on a washbasin, tin can or bucket — whatever was at hand — attempting to create different effects. "I'd take my stick and beat on the ground trying to get a new sound and be humming my little baby song along with it," Muddy recalled.[7]

It's no wonder. Music was in the very air of Stovall. The mournful cry and response of field hollers echoed from one horizon to the other: "Oh, Lawd, I'm tired, uuh / Oh, Lawd, I'm tired a dis mess."[8] The rhythmic shouts of the croppers slid down from falsetto yodels to sad strains of despair. Hollers were a means of expression and a way to pace work. Occasionally the haunting lament of a train whistle would resonate over the fields, turning the laborers from their melancholy cries to songs of escape and freedom.

Music permeated the rest of their lives as well. It was a form of expression for a people without a voice. It spoke of their frustration and sadness, their celebrations and their steadfast faith throughout it all. Music was as much the hub of a raucous Saturday-night fish fry as it was a benediction to uplift the pious on Sunday morning.

The Baptist Church was at the core of black society in the Delta. Only in church were black folks permitted to organize and gather in large numbers. It gave them a sense of self-worth denied them by the white world. Church was so basic to black culture that on most nights of the week there was either a prayer meeting, Bible study or choir practice, and meetings and services extended throughout the day and evening on Sundays.

Muddy maintained that as he grew up he attended church every Sunday. Stovall workers went to the plantation's Oak Ridge Baptist Church, where Muddy's uncle and his family were regular worshippers. In fact, his uncle Louis Matthews Morganfield became a preacher in 1929 and a pastor in southern Mississippi in 1936. Contrary to Muddy's assertion, however, his cousins Elve and Willie (who is also now a pastor) rarely saw Muddy in church. Yet because they were about 10 years younger, Muddy's churchgoing years were likely past him by the time Elve and Willie noticed his absence. Elve has the impression that Muddy went as a child, but that he stopped when the blues began to capture his full attention. It does seem probable that Miss Della, as a religious woman, saw to it that Muddy attended church long enough to absorb the fundamentals of the faith.

No matter what his actual attendance record, the Oak Ridge Baptist Church exerted a powerful influence over Muddy's future. Not only did it help imbue him with the faith that would sustain him for the rest of his life, but it also provided him with the best training a blues singer could have. He later declared that in order to sing deep, gutsy blues, "You got to go to church to get this particular thing in your soul."[9] For Muddy, Oak Ridge provided "all of my good moaning and trembling" that would enrich and deepen his brand of blues.[10]

A religion of West African origin also left its mark on black Delta culture. Vestiges of voodoo — or hoodoo, as it was called locally — survived in the form of conjurers, fortune-tellers and herbal healers. Mojo bags, or hands, which often contained such potentially powerful ingredients as John the Conquer root, lucky-hand root or a black-cat bone, were not uncommon as personal talismans. Such articles of faith provided some sense of control to a people whose lives had been severely limited by white society. Although Muddy was not a believer, he had seen too many unexplained phenomena related to hoodoo not to respect it. Some of his most colorful song lyrics would be drawn from hoodoo imagery.

When it came time to start school, Muddy attended the Oak Ridge School on Stovall. To his later regret, however, he didn't show much interest. From his vantage point, the young boy couldn't see the benefits of even a fundamental education. Looking back, Muddy admitted, "I didn't really know that you need schooling down through the years. It's one mistake I made."[11] He acquired only a third-grade education. Muddy remained illiterate throughout his life.

But even if he had pursued a decent education, Muddy was unlikely to have found it in the South. Widespread white views regarding the schooling of blacks varied from apathy to hostility. In the Delta much of the state funding earmarked for black schools was diverted to those for whites. As a result, education for blacks was substandard; they got the texts and desks discarded by white students. The school board in Clarksdale didn't consider it worthwhile to employ college graduates to teach black kids. In fact, most black teachers were suspected of being prostitutes. Eighth grade was as far as most black children could go; Clarksdale didn't have a black high school until the 1950s. Although the town had been designated as the site for a black college in the 1920s, local planters were alarmed at the prospect, fearing that the advances such an institution would bring would erode their pool of cheap labor. The site was subsequently shifted to Cleveland, 40 miles south and far enough away to exceed the reach of most black Clarksdalians.

If such an attitude prevailed just a few miles down the road, it's doubtful that the level of education offered on Stovall was much better. After all, schooling was counterproductive to sharecropping. Joe Brant, with whom Muddy was raised, received no education. Plantation schooling was typically very casual — all ages in one room. The four- to five-month school year was scheduled to accommodate the needs of the planter; classes were suspended when there was work to be done on the land. Muddy commented that "they didn't give you too much schoolin' because just as soon as you was big enough you get to workin' in the fields."[12]

Nevertheless, his cousin Willie Morganfield describes Muddy as having a "lot of mother-wit, a lot of good common sense."[13] He was a happy-go-lucky kid, one who rarely got angry, except, that is, with one of his earliest friends. That boy, who would also grow up to have a career in blues, was Edward Riley Boyd. He was related to Muddy's cousins; their mothers were cousins. Eddie was born on 25 November 1914 at a nearby farm belonging to Frank Moore, but from the time he was three months old, he was raised by his maternal grandfather on Stovall. Eddie and Muddy are said to have met on the first day of school, quickly becoming great pals, although their camaraderie often erupted into a brawl. Muddy's brawn was more than a match for Eddie. Eddie remembered, "He could whip me but I mean I never did accept that for real, you know. We'd still fight. But we couldn't stay away from each other, though. We loved each other."[14]

Clarksdalians were bitten by the baseball bug in the 1920s, and it quickly spread to Stovall, where ball games became an ideal way to socialize and relax on weekends. Muddy embraced the game with gusto. Third base was his position, and he was very adept until he injured a finger.

Young Muddy's unquenchable drive to create music persisted. He would spend hours banging on a five-gallon kerosene can and singing, "I don't want no woman to chollyham my bone," although he had no idea what it meant, either as a child or looking back as an adult.[15] An old man then gave him a beat-up accordion, and while Muddy must have felt fortunate to progress to a bona fide instrument, he just couldn't get the hang of it. He set it aside and took up the Jew's harp, a small, lyre-shaped percussion instrument that's held between the teeth and strummed with a finger. He played with that for a while, but as Christmas 1922 approached, what Muddy yearned for was a harmonica.

When Santa Claus delivered Muddy's harmonica — what they called a French harp — it was, as he later remembered, "the treat of my life."[16] The seven-year-old couldn't put it down. Miss Della tolerated the racket through the festive season, but finally in a bid for tranquility, she hid it. It took the budding musician a month or two to find his harmonica, and as soon as he did, he resumed his investigation of the instrument. He had no teacher; what he learned he discovered for himself.

By age nine Muddy was dedicated to mastering the harp. It's not known what tunes he played, but presumably he drew upon the sounds that filled the world around him — popular string-band music, field hollers, church songs and blues. Eddie Boyd also started on harmonica, so perhaps they traded licks and learned together.

But Muddy's drive to excel involved more than learning a popular tune. He was compelled to make something of himself, to achieve something better than life on Stovall had to offer. Without yet knowing how to accomplish this, he held an image of the future in his mind that he refused to relinquish, even if such dreams were foolish for a black kid mired in the muck of poverty, segregation and repression. "I had it in my mind, even then, to either play music or preach or do something that I would be known, that people would know me," Muddy maintained. "I kept that on my mind. I wanted to be a known person. All of my life that's what I worked for. I wanted to be internationally known. And I worked on it, from when I was a kid up."[17]

In the meantime, though, there was work to do on Stovall. As he was big for his age, at about 10 years old Muddy began laboring full time in the fields alongside the men. Gone was any chance of further education. Plowing, hoeing and chopping cotton filled his days. He was making between 50 and 75 cents per day working from dawn to dusk. And he was experiencing the blues firsthand.

"That's some of the hardest work you can get," Muddy recalled. "And that will *give* you the blues. If that don't give you the blues, *nothin'* will."[18] As the field hands hollered or sang their messages or feelings, young Muddy joined in. If a girl he was trying to impress or a pal was working nearby, he'd communicate through song. If his mule was stubborn or he was yearning to go home, Muddy would holler his sufferance. "I can't remember much of what I was singin' now 'ceptin' I do remember I was always singin', 'I can't be satisfied, I be all troubled in mind.' Seems to me like I was always singin' that, because I was always singin' jest the way I felt, and maybe I didn't exactly know it, but I jest didn't like the way things were down there — in Mississippi."[19]

It's not clear how strong an influence his father had on Muddy during his formative years. Although Muddy denied ever seeing Ollie when he lived on Stovall, Elve Morganfield remembers him visiting his son, so there was at least intermittent contact. Others say that Muddy was sometimes taken down to Rolling Fork to see his father. Muddy always maintained, however, that Ollie did not teach him to play blues.

Muddy's music was formulated from a mix of what he heard on Stovall and from the race records that disseminated blues music to black communities nationwide. There were no blues broadcast on Delta radio in those days. The blues programs on Helena's KFFA, Clarksdale's WROX and on WDIA out of Memphis were still in the future.

If he'd been raised in the city, young Muddy would have been excluded from hearing and learning from musicians playing in nightclub venues. Their doors were closed to underage patrons. But in the rural Delta, music was accessible to all. Blues entertainment was part of country suppers, picnics and fish fries, family events attended by all generations. The country taverns and dancehalls, called juke joints, placed no restrictions on who could enter. Here Muddy was free to soak up all the blues that flooded into his region of the Delta.

Anytime a celebrated blues act — such as Charley Patton, Big Joe Williams or the Mississippi Sheiks — were performing near Stovall, Muddy would get himself there somehow: "I just a young boy, but I loved it so well, anytime they in my vicinity I was there. Walk. Catch a ride on a wagon. Steal the mule out of the lot. I was there."[20] At one time the Mississippi Sheiks were the regular band for Stovall family functions, but of course, Muddy wouldn't have been permitted to hear them on those occasions. Instead, he listened to their records and walked 10 miles to see them play at a black venue.

Muddy heard a lot of music on Miss Della's phonograph. Her taste in records was almost exclusively religious, which reinforced Muddy's early appreciation of church music. But Muddy, ever eager for more blues, saved his nickels and bought his own discs from a general store in Clarksdale, borrowed others, walked miles across the fields to hear a friend's records and listened to jukeboxes in local roadhouses.

The first blues record Muddy remembered hearing was Leroy Carr's "How Long Blues," released in 1928 with Scrapper Blackwell on guitar. Soon he was studying the recordings of Charley Patton, Blind Arthur Blake, Blind Lemon Jefferson, Robert "Barbeque Bob" Hicks, Texas Alexander, Eurreal "Little Brother" Montgomery, Roosevelt Sykes and Tommy Johnson. He was particularly impressed by Blind Blake's "Detroit Bound," Jefferson's "Matchbox Blues," Sykes's "Forty-Four Blues," Montgomery's "Vicksburg

Blues" and Alexander's "Corn Bread Blues." Later Muddy recalled his initial reaction to this first generation of blues recording artists: "Goodgodalmighty, these cats goin' wild, ain't they."[21]

By at least age 13, the same year he first heard Leroy Carr on disc, Muddy had begun to concentrate on playing blues on his harmonica. He said it took a long time for him to get "a real good note out of it, before I started getting into the way of playing blues on harp."[22] This made Miss Della uneasy. She admonished her grandson out of concern for his soul: "Son, you're sinning. You're playing for the devil. Devil's gonna get you."[23] According to the southern Baptist Church, song and dance must only be used as a means for praising the Lord. Blues was called "devil music," and playing it, listening to it or dancing to it would earn one a sentence in hell.

But Della's dire warnings were drowned out by the blues. Muddy discovered that he could make money playing his harmonica. At 13 he began blowing his harp for Saturday-night fish fries, earning 50 cents, a catfish sandwich and a half-pint of moonshine for playing until sunrise. "A lot of mornings I get home and change my little ironed blue jeans and put on my cotton-picking clothes and go to the field and work," Muddy recollected. "Done picked cotton all day, play all night long, then pick cotton all day the next day before I could get a chance to sleep."[24]

Muddy thought he was a pretty good musician. The only thing he didn't like were the local kids shouting, "Hey Muddy Waters play us a piece."[25] He didn't mind his grandmother referring to him as Muddy, but objected to outsiders calling him that; furthermore, he wasn't happy with the additional moniker, "Waters." Eventually he got used to it; he had no choice. McKinley Morganfield would be known as Muddy Waters for the rest of his life.

By the next year, Muddy started singing in addition to blowing harmonica, and, accompanied by two older musicians, he fronted his first band. Guitarist Scott Bohanner — often called Bowhandle — was a good-looking man who also sharecropped on Stovall. Henry "Son" Simms played guitar, fiddle, bass viola, mandolin and piano; he was a tall, lean man with high cheekbones, a striking profile and a quiet temperament. Although it was Simms's band, Muddy always maintained that he was the de facto leader of the group: "[Son] was really what you call a pretty ancient man, but I did most of the singing."[26] Simms was 39 years old.

Henry Simms was born on 22 August 1890 and nicknamed "Son" by his sisters and mother. He grew up in Renova, Mississippi, an all-black community about 35 miles south of Clarksdale, not far from the Dockery Plantation where his friend Charley Patton lived. Simms began as a guitarist, then due to the influence of his grandfather, a former slave who played the fiddle, he took up that instrument when he was 20 years old. His sister Roberta Jamison described Son's sound on the violin: "He didn't put no resin [on his fiddle strings]. He'd come 'cross kinda like a saw."[27]

By 1924 Son was farming with 27-year-old Percy Thomas, a Clarksdale native, on the Wall Plantation near Farrell, close to Stovall. Simms formed a string band called the Mississippi Cornshuckers, modeled on the Mississippi Sheiks, and the combo performed throughout the Delta in the 1920s and 1930s. Son played fiddle and fingerpicked guitar while Thomas supplied lead chords and rhythm on a black Stella guitar with a kazoo. Louis Ford, a diminutive older musician also living in Farrell, played mandolin, while "a great big dude" from Greenville named Pitty Pat kept time on an upright bass and danced. The four-piece group performed most weekends. Percy recalled that Simms "really didn't sing much. He never did have a good voice."[28]

By 1930 Charley Patton had tracked Simms down and convinced him to travel with him to his second recording session for Paramount at its new studio in Grafton, Wisconsin. With Simms's accompaniment providing "the most blistering, crude tonal qualities ever heard on violin,"[29] Patton recorded over 28 songs, including preblues, ballads, spirituals and blues. At this session Simms was also persuaded to sing, and he recorded four tunes under his own name: "I'm Going Away To Get A Khaki Suit," "Tell Me Man Blues," "Farrell Blues" and "Come Back Corinna." These last two songs were issued on disc, but they sold poorly, and Simms never heard them. Regardless, he was more interested in the $300 he earned for the session than his crack at celebrity. Simms never saw Patton again.

It says something about Muddy's confidence and drive that as a boy in his mid-teens he could assume the dominant role in a band such as Simms's, taking the reins from a mature man with a strong musical background. Muddy's determination to succeed was palpable: "Ever since I can remember, this is what I wanted to be.

Something outstanding. If I couldn't make it in music, I'd be a big preacher, a great ball player. I didn't want to grow up with no-one knowin' me but the neighborhood people. I wanted the world to know a lot about me."[30]

NOTES

1 Alfred Duckett, "I Have a Right to Sing the Blues," *Louisville Defender*, 14 Apr. 1955.

2 Robert Morganfield, interview with author, 16 May 1995.

3 Nicholas Lemann, *The Promised Land: The Great Black Migration and How It Changed America* (New York: Alfred A. Knopf, 1991), 24.

4 John Ray Skates, *Mississippi: A Bicentennial History* (New York: W.W. Norton & Company, Inc., 1979), 129.

5 *Wall Street Journal*, 27 July 1921.

6 Charles Shaar Murray, "The Blues Had a Baby and They Called It Rock 'n' Roll," *New Musical Express* (30 Apr. 1977): 26.

7 Robert Palmer, "Muddy Waters Is Singing the Real Deep Blues," *New York Times*, 27 Mar. 1981, sec. C, 6.

8 LeRoi Jones, *Blues People* (New York: William Morrow and Company, 1963), 60.

9 *Sweet Home Chicago*, film, MCA Records – Initial Film and Television (Chicago) – Vanguard Films, 1993.

10 James Rooney, *Bossmen: Bill Monroe & Muddy Waters* (New York: The Dial Press, 1971), 107.

11 Pete Welding, "An Interview with Muddy Waters," *The American Folk Music Occasional* 2 (1970): 5.

12 Pete Welding, "Muddy Waters," *Bluesland*, eds. Welding and Toby Byron (New York: Dutton, 1991), 136.

13 Reverend Willie Morganfield, interview with author, 14 May 1995.

14 Jim O'Neal and Amy O'Neal, "Living Blues Interview: Eddie Boyd, Part One," *Living Blues* 35 (Nov.–Dec. 1977): 11.

15 Rooney, 104.

16 Vernon Gibbs, "The Entertainers: Muddy Waters," *Essence* (Dec. 1972): 23.

17 Rooney, 107.

18 Bruce Cook, *Listen to the Blues* (New York: Charles Scribner's Sons, 1973), 184, 186.

19 Paul Oliver, *Conversation with the Blues* (New York: Horizon Press, 1965), 30.

20 Margaret McKee and Fred Chisenhall, *Beale Black & Blue: Life and Music on Black America's Main Street* (Baton Rouge: Louisiana State University Press, 1981), 232.

21 McKee and Chisenhall, 235.

22 Welding, "Interview," 4.

23 Rooney, 105.

24 McKee and Chisenhall, 232.

25 Murray, 26.

26 Peter Guralnick, *Feel Like Going Home* (New York: Harper & Row, Publishers, 1989), 66.

27 Gayle Dean Wardlow, unpublished article for *78 Quarterly*, 1996.

28 Wardlow.

29 Wardlow.

30 Murray, 26.

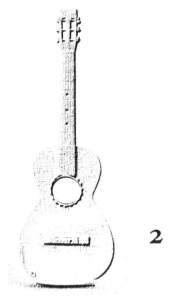

2

. . . the blues is for me. It's like a shoe.
You take a number seven shoe, you
sure can't wear a size four. You wear
the one that fits. The blues fit me.[1]

At juke joints, frolics and fish fries, even at white folks' functions, Muddy could pull in from two to three dollars a night blowing harmonica, significant money for a cropper who made 75 cents a day toiling in the fields. He sensed he was on the right track. He was gaining acclaim, the extra cash came in handy for a young man with a taste for smart clothes and pretty girls, and he was gaining exposure to other musicians and their styles of play. Muddy jammed with guitarist Robert Lee McCollum — later renowned as Robert

Nighthawk — who was also a very good harp player. It's likely he jammed with Eddie Boyd as well. Although he'd left Stovall by this time, Boyd had a steady gig playing piano at a juke joint on the edge of Clarksdale.

There's no doubt Muddy had an enterprising nature. As well as laboring on the land and playing on Saturday nights and Sundays, the young man went fishing most Friday nights, probably in the teeming waters of the Old River, and he would sell his catch for Saturday fish fries before he went out to play.

It was prophetic that most of Muddy's favorite recording artists were guitar players. Watching Son Simms on guitar also inspired him. It was only a matter of time before he took a stab at it himself, eagerly taking pointers from Scott Bohanner and Simms. Muddy recalled constructing his own guitar at the age of 17: "Made mine out of a box and bit of stick for a neck. Couldn't do much with it but you know, that's how you learn."[2]

Later that year, in 1932, Muddy bought his first commercially made guitar. One story goes that to raise the necessary funds he sold his horse; more likely it was a mule. Nevertheless, he made $2.50 on the transaction, enough to buy a secondhand Stella from a man named Ed Moore.

Muddy's appetite to master the guitar was voracious. Bohanner taught him to finger the basic chords, and Muddy tried to pick up what Scott was playing when they were out on gigs. "Those were great times," Muddy reminisced. "I didn't have no money in my pocket, but I had a ball."[3] He had an affinity for the instrument, and he practiced fingerpicking for one and a half to two hours every day. Among the first songs he learned were Leroy Carr's "How Long Blues" and a tune written and recorded by the celebrated Mississippi Sheiks, "Sitting On Top Of The World."

Another style of guitar playing was popular in the Delta as well. Instead of fingering chords or individual notes, the guitarist would hold a knife edge or wear a bottleneck, usually on his third or fourth finger, and slide it up and down the strings, making a slurring, swooping sound that mimicked and augmented the bluesman's voice. "Most of the guitarists could use that bottleneck or pocket-knife or something to get that winging sound," Muddy recalled. "I stone got crazy when I seen somebody run down them strings with a bottleneck, my eyes lit up like a Christmas tree and I said that I had to learn."[4] At first he wore the slide on his second finger, then realized it should be on his pinky.

The paramount source of inspiration for Muddy Waters — and for another rising luminary of the genre, Robert Johnson — was Son House, a seminal Delta bluesman. House was born on 21 March 1902 just outside Clarksdale, in a small community called Lyon. He'd only begun guitar in 1928, yet in three days he was playing a juke, and by 1930 he'd recorded his first sides for the Paramount Record Company, discs that Muddy admired. By the time Muddy first saw him, House had done time for murder and was trying to balance a vocation as a preacher with performing the music of the devil. After a night of serenading Satan, he was known to leap up on the bar to exhort the faith. Son's vocals were full and rich and his guitar style forceful with a pervasive beat. He played finger-style guitar as well as slide, but it was the moaning of House's bottleneck that fired Muddy's passion.

One Saturday night during the time Muddy was learning guitar, he went to a fish fry where House was performing and discovered an added dimension that was missing from Son's recordings. "When I heard Son House I should have broke my bottleneck," Muddy declared, "because this other cat [Scott Bohanner] hadn't learned me nothing!"[5] For him Son's blues revealed a new realm of musical possibilities, a higher artistry to strive towards. Muddy considered him to be the greatest guitar player in the world. House played at the same place about four weekends straight, and the young man would be there each night, studying House's technique and delivery as he made that guitar sing.

As Robert Johnson had done before him, Muddy learned from the master. Whenever House played in the vicinity, Muddy was there. House took an interest in his young disciple and helped him a great deal. He taught Muddy to fashion his own bottleneck by winding a kerosene-soaked string around the neck of a bottle, lighting it, then severing the neck and smoothing the jagged edge over an open flame. He demonstrated how to tune the guitar in open-G tuning, also called Spanish, as well as cross-note tunings. Muddy likely assimilated most of the older man's repertoire; one song he certainly learned from House was "My Black Mama," a tune he would later refashion into his own.

In the midst of his quest for guitar excellence, Muddy embarked on another kind of journey. On 20 November 1932, Reverend L.M. Field officiated at the marriage of Muddy Waters and Mabel Berry. The event took place on Stovall, perhaps at the Oak Ridge Baptist Church. Mabel was a church-going woman who appreciated the blues. She was supportive of Muddy's musical avocation, possibly because her brother Charles was a singer, whom Muddy later taught to play guitar.

Muddy's pal Robert Lee McCollum performed at the reception, accompanied by his brother Percy. When both Della and Mabel's father objected to guitar music at such a momentous event, Robert and Percy packed up their guitars and pulled out harmonicas instead. Muddy marveled at the way Percy could blow two or three keys on one harp, the first time he'd ever witnessed this phenomenon. Then, determined to celebrate his marriage with the kind of music *he* desired, Muddy organized another party at his place the following night.

Mabel moved into Muddy's house, where his grandmother still lived, and set about working the fields alongside her husband. But it's unlikely her life with Muddy was a fulfilling one; two years later he had a daughter outside their marriage.

As well as the pointers he'd received from Scott Bohanner, Son Simms and Son House, Muddy absorbed all he could from the myriad musicians who passed through the Clarksdale area. He studied the techniques of other skilled bottleneck players whose names are now forgotten and of a slide guitarist by the name of James Smith, whom Muddy considered to be on a par with Son House. Before long he had saved $11, enough to buy a Silvertone guitar from the Sears Roebuck catalog. "I had a beautiful box then," he declared.[6]

The great Charley Patton, considered to be the first important Delta blues musician, also performed in Muddy's locale. He was born in Edwards, Mississippi, in either 1887 or 1891. Soon after the turn of the century, his family moved to the Dockery Plantation in the heart of the Delta. He went on to live the life of an itinerant bluesman, traveling from gig to gig and from woman to woman, never far from violence, yet periodically singing spirituals to cleanse his soul. But his physical appearance was incongruous with what one would expect from one of the founding fathers of Delta blues. His skin was yellowish, reflecting his mix of European,

native American and African heritage, and his small thin frame
didn't suit a belligerent scrapper with the voice of a titan. Nevertheless, Patton's music was the wellspring from which succeeding
generations of bluesmen would draw.

It's interesting to note the link between Patton and Muddy,
provided by the man who played with them both: Son Simms.
Muddy was impressed with Patton's singing and his guitar work, in
which he employed string bending and a knife edge, as well as
percussive techniques. But it was his showmanship that seemed to
make the most vivid impression: "He was a real clown with the
guitar; he'd pat on the guitar, hit the guitar, he'd whirl it over his
head," Muddy recalled.[7] "I think he was the greatest in that field."[8]

After a year of practice, Muddy's guitar work surpassed that of
his band mate and teacher Scott Bohanner. Muddy became lead
guitarist — mostly on slide in open-G and open-E tunings — on
top of his existing duties as harp player and singer. Although he'd
tried blowing harmonica with a rack while playing the guitar,
Muddy couldn't get the hang of it. Bohanner was relegated to
rhythm guitar, especially important without bass or drums, and
switched to lead when Muddy was playing harmonica. An exception to this was when Scott "used to get him a little nip," and
Muddy was left to perform alone.[9] When Son Simms joined them
on a gig, he played both fiddle and guitar.

It was clear that Muddy's compulsion for blues was becoming a
career decision. In his mind there was no longer a choice. Blues was
the vehicle that would propel him to the level of acclaim he craved:
"From a kid up, I wanted to definitely be a musician or a good
preacher, or a heck of a baseball player. I just had to, I had three
choices. I couldn't play ball too good — like I hurt my finger and I
stopped that. I couldn't preach, and well, all I had left was getting
in to the music thing."[10]

His uncle Louis Matthews Morganfield, now a preacher, had
harbored hopes that Muddy would follow the same path. Although
Muddy had considered it, a career in the church would not jibe
with his taste in music. Matthews tried to set his nephew on the
righteous road, but it became a hopeless mission. Muddy was open
about his drive to succeed in music. "It's from the heart," he said
about his blues. "That's my religion."[11] Nevertheless, his uncle
respected him and the choice he had made. Muddy's cousin Elve

remembers his father counseling Muddy: "If that's what you're gonna do, then be the best."[12]

Muddy's ambition to be a great bluesman didn't carry with it any delusions of attaining riches or living a life of ease. His role models were itinerant musicians who led a hand-to-mouth existence. It wasn't so much a career as a way of life fated by destiny. Muddy *had* to be a bluesman; he had no choice. "I always thought of myself as a musician," he explained. "The jobs I had back in Clarksdale and so forth, they were just temporary things. . . . If I wasn't a good musician then, I felt that sooner or later I would be a good musician. I felt it in me."[13]

The attractions of that life were acclaim, more money than a cropper could earn and the hope that someday he wouldn't have to work the fields. For a man with Muddy's ambition, talent and drive, it was the only way he could escape the drudgery into which he was born. The portents were good: Muddy's popularity as a fine musician was spreading, and with it his reputation for being a good man.

But for the present, the fields of Stovall remained his primary living. Elve still remembers his older cousin in the midst of a wide, flat field, a solitary figure plowing behind a gray mule, his voice rising in song, adrift on the wind. Of those times Muddy said, "You just make things up when you're working out on the plantation. You get lonesome and tired and hot and you start to sing you something. . . . I can remember that a lot of the records I have made, I first made those songs up during my work days out on the farm."[14]

Back in the mid-1930s, Willie Morganfield was a young boy curious about the growing repute of his older cousin. Strictly against his parents' rules, the boy snuck a peek at Muddy performing in a honky-tonk where he often appeared on weekends. The crowded room was nearly devoid of furniture, except for a chair or two — not even a jukebox — and off somewhere catfish were being fried. Seated on a nail barrel, Muddy played guitar and sang while Scott Bohanner accompanied him on harmonica. Willie's brother Elve confirms that by this time Muddy was performing in juke joints all over the Clarksdale area and that he sometimes played alone. As his blues gigs began to carry him further afield, he'd give his young cousins a little money to do chores for him while he was gone.

Howard Stovall didn't object to the young cropper pursuing his musical ambitions on the side. In fact, he appreciated Muddy's talent and would hire his band to play at family parties and dances because, as Muddy recalled, "My boss really liked that kinda carrying on."[15] The general superintendents of Stovall — a Mr. Crombell and then William Holt — were also fans of Muddy's music. Of course, it doesn't follow that the whites at these entertainments were aficionados of blues. In order to get these choice gigs, Muddy's repertoire had to also span popular and country music. His performances included "Down By The Riverside," "I Ain't Got Nobody," "Dinah," "Home On The Range," "Deep In The Heart Of Texas," "Corinna," "Tennessee Waltz" and several Mississippi Sheiks songs, especially "Sitting On Top Of The World."

By the time Muddy's uncle and his family moved off Stovall in 1936, Muddy had already been to Memphis at least once to check out that city's music scene. Although it was only 73 miles north of Clarksdale, Memphis could be intimidating to a young man straight off the farm. Muddy joined the group of musicians playing for nickels and dimes in Handy Park on Beale Street, but as he put it, "they had some people down there that was runnin' rings around us."[16] He wasn't ready for the city yet, although his pal Robert McCollum — now using the name McCoy — was already living in St. Louis and would travel to Aurora, Illinois, in 1937 to record for Victor. When Robert suggested that Muddy go north with him, he responded, "Nah, I'd better not do this. I'll lay on down in here, you know."[17]

It wasn't that life was so grand on Stovall. "I know I got up one Christmas morning and we didn't have nothing to eat," Muddy recalled. "We didn't have a apple, we didn't have a orange, we didn't have a cake, we didn't have nothing. I came up hard."[18] As the Great Depression tightened its stranglehold on the Delta, plummeting cotton prices smashed the black economy, already laid so low it seemed it couldn't be squeezed any flatter. Tens of thousands of Delta families — black and white — were thrown off their land for failing to pay their mortgages or taxes. In order to stave off starvation in Coahoma County — where Clarksdale is situated — dairy products, fruits and vegetables were available at rock-bottom prices. The government sponsored vegetable plots in vacant county lots and the harvest was free. Plantations, such as

Stovall, were cash poor and couldn't make their payrolls, so the planters issued plantation script, a form of currency redeemable only at that farm's commissary.

As well, Muddy chaffed against the ingrained system of black suppression. He could never understand racial discrimination, blaming it on the insecurity of whites over their women and jobs. In Clarksdale there was a midnight curfew for blacks. Their segregation was further illuminated one dark night on 26 September 1937, when the renowned blues singer Bessie Smith bled to death after a car wreck outside Clarksdale. The medical facilities there were closed to blacks. The U.S. senator from Mississippi and its former governor, Theodore G. Bilbo, resolved to end the race issue permanently. By means of the *Greater Liberia Act*, which he introduced to Congress in 1939, he intended to deport all black Americans to Africa. It's not clear how he intended to replace them in the fields.

In 1937 Muddy was introduced to the recordings of an enigmatic bluesman by the name of Robert Johnson. Johnson's initial disc, by Vocalion Records, paired "Terraplane Blues" with "Kind Hearted Woman" on the flip. Like Muddy, Johnson had once sat at the knee of the great Son House for his inspiration, as evidenced by his reworking of House's "My Black Mama" to create "Walkin' Blues." At first House considered him a nuisance, a mediocre player at best. Then, as the legend goes, Johnson made a date with the devil. At a lonely crossroads shrouded in the blackness of a Delta night, he sold his soul to Satan in exchange for the brief flare of virtuosity that burned brightly for the remainder of his short life. When Johnson emerged from obscurity, he owned the blues; the strength of his songwriting and his command of the guitar, both as a finger-picker and a slide player, was extraordinary. His music had the rhythmic patterns of House, but the straight-ahead cleanness of House's guitar style was accelerated by a running bass line and embellished with shadings and texture.

Although Johnson spent some time at Friar's Point, only about eight miles from Muddy's shack, the two musicians never got to know each other. Muddy only saw him play once or twice, and then at a distance; he was too shy to approach Johnson. Once when Johnson was playing on a street corner in Friar's Point, a crowd of listeners dense around him, Muddy stopped to hear him, but as he said, "I got back into the car and left, because he was a *dangerous* man . . . he really was using the *git*-tar. . . . I crawled away and pulled out, because it was too heavy for me."[19]

The hellhounds continued to nip at Johnson's heels until one night at a gig outside Greenwood, Mississippi, they seized him by the throat in the form of a half-pint bottle of poisoned whiskey. He'd messed with the wrong man's woman, so the story goes. Johnson fought off the devil's final grip for several days, until Satan claimed his own on 16 August 1938. He died with his guitar across his heart. The 27-year-old had had only one successful 78 during the flash of his genius, but his legacy burns brightly still.

Despite being overwhelmed by Johnson's performance and declaring him one of the greatest bottleneck players he'd ever heard, Muddy maintained that Son House had equivalent guitar skills and that he ultimately had a greater effect on his musical development. Muddy analyzed his influences as follows: "I consider myself to be, what you might call a mixture of all three. I had part of my own, part of Son House, and a little part of Robert Johnson."[20]

As well as rocking the juke joints, Muddy took his talents to the street, where a man with a guitar could make a pretty good buck. In Clarksdale Muddy did his busking on Fourth Avenue, on the black side of the tracks, an area called the New World by the croppers who came from miles around to congregate there. The first time he tried it "it was a wonderful thing. I had my cigar box sitting out there, and I was sitting up on a Coca-Cola box, and I had such a crowd that the police moved me."[21] After working a succession of corners, Muddy found that he could make $20 to $30 a night, big money for a farmer making a small fraction of that in the fields.

Early Wright, who in 1942 became a DJ on radio station WROX in Clarksdale, remembers striking up a friendship with Muddy in the late 1930s. He'd go to hear Muddy play in Clarksdale and in the small surrounding communities, including Mattson, Dublin and Friar's Point. Wright saw Muddy perform by himself and with his band, and one thing was plain even then — Muddy's music had a distinctive sound that set him apart. He performed seated or standing, but either way he ruled the stage; the other band members played for him.

Muddy was charming, and his good nature was genuine; he never put on airs, despite his growing acclaim. Although he played the blues, he rarely felt sad. His relative success in music had allowed him to gratify his passion for smart clothes and to buy a car, status symbols that set him apart. He enjoyed chatting with Wright about baseball and spoke of the great influence his grandmother had had on his life. Blues was not an easy road — for example, Muddy complained to Early about the club owners who'd cheated him out of his pay — but his determination was rock solid. "He seemed like he was born for success," Wright recalls.[22] Muddy spoke to him about leaving Mississippi, that the kind of renown he was seeking lay elsewhere.

Willie Foster, a teenaged harmonica player at the time, would catch Muddy whenever he performed near Foster's home in Leland, Mississippi, 70 miles south of Clarksdale. As well, Muddy's half-brother remembers that he often played weekend gigs in Rolling Fork. The news that Muddy was coming to play a local juke would spread by word of mouth. For these more distant gigs, he left his band behind, as Foster only saw Muddy perform alone. It was clear to Foster, as it was to Early Wright, that Muddy was forging his own style of music, a style that made a lasting impression on those who came to listen. So did his personality: "He was a very nice fella," Foster recalls. "He seemed to love everybody, you know."[23]

Muddy especially had an eye for fine-dressed, pretty ladies, and the attraction was mutual. His appearance was striking; he was a tall, slim man with sculpted cheekbones angling off from slightly slanted, heavy-lidded eyes. But no matter what dalliances Muddy might enjoy, no woman was going to stand between him and his music. He told Early Wright that he believed a serious relationship with a woman would hamper his progress, an attitude that didn't bode well for his marriage to Mabel. Blues had claimed the upper hand.

To stay the course he'd chosen, Muddy had to get a record out. To his mind, the place to do that was St. Louis. Perhaps he was following the lead of his friend Robert McCoy — now calling himself Robert Nighthawk — who had gone there and forged the connections that led to a recording deal. In any case, one day in 1940 Muddy pulled out of his band, left Mabel to work the farm, and set off for St. Louis with his girlfriend.

His growing celebrity in the Delta couldn't help him here. It was the largest city he'd ever seen, and the most unfriendly. He soon realized that the record companies weren't based in St. Louis. He persevered for a couple of months, but this city was indifferent to Muddy's country blues. Work was scarce, and what there was paid only about three or four dollars a night, no more than he could pull in at home. The St. Louis experience soured him on big cities. He returned to Stovall, kicked Mabel out of the house and moved his girlfriend in.

By this time Scott Bohanner had had a daughter with one of Muddy's cousins and moved to Chicago. Muddy rejoined Son Simms's band, named the Son Simms Four following the departure of Pitty Pat. By about 1941, Simms had installed a pickup on his violin and was playing it through an amplifier. Percy Thomas, who continued to work as a plowman, was on second guitar. Louis Ford, who like Simms had played with Charley Patton, was on mandolin. With the full sound of a band supporting him, Muddy was learning the essentials of the music he later developed in Chicago. Although Muddy would recall that the combo had no drums — typical for string bands of that era — Early Wright is quite sure he was accompanied by a drummer at least part of the time.

As his work schedule on Stovall permitted, Muddy also played throughout the surrounding countryside with Big Joe Williams and his home-modified, nine-string guitar. Big Joe had a hit in 1941 with "Baby Please Don't Go," and it was from him that Muddy learned the song he would sing for the rest of his life.

During this period the Silas Green minstrel show, a traveling vaudeville entertainment, was performing in the community of Farrell, three miles south of the Stovall commissary. It was a big occasion for a small settlement. This tent show from New Orleans was the most popular touring act of its kind, featuring song-and-dance routines and comedy performances. They'd often draft locals to contribute to the entertainment, and so it was that Muddy joined the troupe in Farrell. Muddy reverted to harmonica for this gig and recalled that Scott Bohanner was on guitar; Louis Ford and Son Simms may well have performed with him, too. After playing with the show for a night or two, Muddy watched it leave town without him. He explained that the constant traveling would have been too much for him, "And I was crazy about my grandmother — I didn't want to leave her."[24]

About this time the ever-enterprising musician turned his hand to running his own juke joint out of his Stovall home. For a man with a taste for good corn whiskey, gambling, attractive women and lucrative ventures — and for a bluesman in need of a venue — a roadhouse offered numerous opportunities for Muddy to make his mark. It was an era of immobility, a time when towns imposed curfews on blacks, when most movie theaters closed their doors to them and before television had claimed its couch potatoes. The Baptist Church and the juke were two of the few places blacks could congregate outside working hours. Most plantations had their own juke joint, where every Saturday and Sunday night gambling, drinking, dancing and the blues would help deaden the despair from drudgery and deprivation.

Such an enterprise sat well with Howard Stovall. He believed that every plantation should have a juke and a still. He'd rather his croppers caroused on Stovall, where any trouble could be contained. If they went off the property in search of revelry and got arrested, they were on their own. Southern justice for blacks was a brutal incentive to stay home.

A typical juke squeezed most of the vices together in someone's small timber shack. On one side gamblers would slap down their meager savings on games of cooncan, pittypat, Georgia skin and the crank of the policy wheel. The clattering of dice, loud prayers for a seven or an eleven, shrieks of elation and despair were all part of a culture that had few other routes to a little easy money. Jars of smooth corn liquor, fresh from the still out back, lubricated the gamblers' confidence and loosened the limbs of the sweat-soaked dancers in the next room. There a single bluesman, a band or a jukebox would serve up those down-and-dirty gutbucket blues. Hands clapped, feet stomped, sexuality sizzled as the anthems of the Delta blared until sunrise. As Muddy said, his juke joint was open "from can to can't. . . . Oh, sometimes we'd ball all night and . . . way up in the next day."[25] Musicians would drop by his cabin to jam, but mainly the music was supplied by Muddy and his band, supplemented with nickel tunes from a Seeburg jukebox.

Mose "Brownie" Emerson was the moonshiner on Stovall. He brewed corn whiskey in 50-gallon oil drums he'd hidden in canal ditches deep in the woods. Although it's been said that Muddy made his own liquor, more likely he was in partnership with Emerson, retailing Brownie's white lightning in his roadhouse, the largest market share around. Emerson was a flamboyant rogue who'd served time in Atlanta for moonshining and actually enjoyed it. He'd give Muddy five dollars and all the moonshine he could drink to play at his parties until dawn.

As Muddy's celebrity burgeoned, it's not surprising that he eventually came to the attention of a folklorist named Alan Lomax. John Avery Lomax, Alan's father, had been one of the pioneers of the study of American folk songs. John launched his avocation in the early 1900s by collecting songs in the Southwest frontier, and by 1933 18-year-old Alan was traveling with him. That same year, at the Louisiana State Penitentiary, they recorded a murderer in jail for his third rap, a scarred brawler called Huddie Ledbetter, or "Leadbelly," who had an awesome repertoire of tunes and a reverberating 12-string guitar.

In the summer of 1941, Alan Lomax was on another quest to chronicle the music of the Deep South on disc. The Coahoma Study Project, a cultural examination of Coahoma County, Mississippi, and its county seat, Clarksdale, was jointly sponsored by the Library of Congress and Fisk University, a black college in Nashville. Lomax represented the Library of Congress for this project, and Charles S. Johnson, the renowned head of Fisk's social sciences department, was in charge at Fisk. Reporting to Johnson from the field was Lewis Jones, an assistant professor in Johnson's department. Professor John Work of the music department — a black composer, author and collector of black vernacular music — was assigned the task of transcribing the field recordings.

Alan Lomax set out to find Robert Johnson. He tracked down his mother Mary, but by that time her "little Robert" had been dead three years. On 28 August, Work left Nashville for Clarksdale to join Lomax, Lewis Jones and a Mr. Ross of Fisk's drama department. Acting on a tip, Lomax sought out Muddy at Stovall, accompanied by his wife Elizabeth and John Work. This was to be Work's only field trip of the project. Lomax puts the date between 24 and 31 August, and Muddy remembered it as a Saturday afternoon; therefore, 30 August 1941 is the probable date of their momentous meeting. Lomax's initial impression of the bluesman was that with his broad cheekbones and slanted eyes he resembled "a friendly dark Eskimo."[26]

At first Muddy was cautious, suspecting that this white stranger asking his whereabouts was a government revenue agent trying to ferret out the source of his moonshine. That Lomax offered Muddy a ride in his car, wanted to go to his house and drank water from the same cup Muddy used only aggravated Muddy's suspicions. These were boundaries white folks rarely crossed. "No, no, this was too much, he goin' too far, you know," Muddy recollected. "But my mind still thinkin', 'Oh, he'd do anything to see can he bust you.'"[27]

Although Muddy had never heard of the Library of Congress, the idea of recording was appealing, despite the fact it wasn't for commercial release. As well, $20 and two copies of the disc were promised as payment. Muddy brought the recording team to his house, and he recalled, "We set [Lomax's] stuff up, got it out of the trunk of his car, and all his long batteries and set 'em up on my front porch, and I was in my front room with my guitar, my little microphone, and he ground his wire down through the window and he went to work."[28] Considering that Muddy had gone as far afield as St. Louis in the hope of making a record, it was ironic that he was now cutting a disc in his own living room.

Lomax's new, improved recording machine — all 300 pounds of it — substituted the earlier aluminum discs for 16-inch acetate ones that could hold up to 15 minutes of sound per side. As Lomax remarked, "Soon the emerald needle of the recorder was cutting a blues track that literally made pop music history. Muddy called it 'Country Blues.'"[29] Accompanying himself on his Silvertone guitar, Muddy sings of one man's distress at the loss of his low-down woman. With his voice conveying all the torment of a jilted lover, Muddy swoops from the depths of melancholy up to falsetto summits of anguish, as his slide guitar accentuates the emotion of the lyrics.

In the subsequent interview with Lomax, Muddy said he composed this song while he was changing a flat tire around 8 October 1938, after being mistreated by a girlfriend. He admitted, however, that "Country Blues" didn't originate with him. Muddy traced its lineage to Robert Johnson's "Walkin' Blues," cut in 1936, then before that to Son House's "My Black Mama," recorded on 28 May 1930. The melody of Muddy's song comes from House's and is especially evident in the slide-guitar refrain at the end of each stanza. As well Muddy borrowed one verse from the second part of House's number. Johnson used that same verse, and Muddy took another from his version, but used them in a different sequence. Regardless of its esteemed provenance, however, Muddy stamped his own style on "Country Blues." His is the only one of these versions to feature a guitar solo, and in it he slams home the reality of his awesome talent.

"I Be's Troubled," the next tune Muddy cut this day, strays from the typical verse structure of 12-bar blues. He told Lomax that he made it up while walking along a road with the tune of a certain church song in his head. Muddy's creativity is masterful here, and he performs with complete authority. His slide guitar is an adjunct to his vocals, like another human voice; his rhythmic strumming adds unexpected texture.

"Burr Clover Farm Blues," the last recording that survives from this session, was written by Muddy and Son Simms at the request of Howard Stovall, who genuinely appreciated Muddy's blues. Of Stovall, Muddy later said, "I grew up hard. But I grew up with a good boss and that was Mr. Howard Stovall and I love him today."[30] Burr clover was planted as a cover crop to replenish the soil with nitrogen, and in 1935 Stovall invented the first burr-clover harvester. This is a fingerpicking tune, with Simms on second guitar; the first line of each verse is repeated in the standard blues format. The lyrics are too laudatory of life on Stovall to be credible, but then the song was written to please the boss. As indicated by later correspondence, Muddy also recorded a song called "Number One Highway Blues," although it has never been found.

"I was bowled over by his artistry," Lomax writes of his session with Muddy. "He sang and played with such finesse, with such a mercurial and sensitive bond between voice and guitar, and he expressed so much tenderness in the way he handled his lyrics."[31] In his interviews with Lomax and Work, Muddy revealed his creative process. Although he had a tune already in mind when he wrote "I Be's Troubled," his usual method was to write the lyrics first. Then he would try out two or three tunes until he found the one that fit.

Muddy never forgot the thrill when Lomax played his recordings back to him that day. "That was the great thing of my life," he declared; "never heard my voice on records, man, and to hear that, man, that was great, man."[32] Both Muddy and Lomax were impressed with what they heard. "When Mr. Lomax played me the record," Muddy recalled, "I thought, man, this boy can sing the blues. And I was surprised because I didn't know I sang like that."[33]

Lomax continued about 50 miles north to Lake Cormorant to record Son House with Willie Brown, Leroy Williams and Fiddlin' Joe Martin, while John Work returned to Fisk University. Although Work transcribed the music from all the sessions recorded by Lomax that summer — a total of 16 discs — all his work was subsequently lost.

Muddy must have been itching to possess copies of his own recordings. On 21 September 1941, three weeks after his session, he sent the following letter to Lomax (presumably written by someone else on Muddy's behalf):

> This is the boy that put out Burr Clover Blues and Number One Highway Blues and several more Blues. Want to know did they take? Please sir if they did, please send some to Clarksdale, Miss. Please sir answer soon to
> M.G. Morganfield
> and Son Sim[34]

Most likely Muddy gave up ever receiving his records, as Lomax waited four months to reply. Writing from the Library of Congress Archive of Folk Song on 27 January 1942, Lomax responded,

> Everyone here in the Library certainly liked your records, because they were very beautifully performed, and I am sending you under separate cover a copy of your two best blues.
> I think that you should keep in practice because I feel sure that sometime you will get the break you deserve.[35]

Muddy received two copies of his record, with "Country Blues" on one side and "I Be's Troubled" on the flip, plus the $20 Lomax had promised. "It would have taken me, well, how long to make twenty dollars if I worked [in the fields] five days for three dollars and seventy-five cents?" he later wondered. "That's good money, twenty dollars, and, boy, I really appreciated that."[36] Muddy must have been exultant as his disc took its place in his Seeburg jukebox alongside the established blues greats. He'd slip it on the turntable when no one was watching. The favorable comparison between his music and that of more celebrated bluesmen was not lost on Muddy.

In the meantime — in November 1941 — "King Biscuit Time" was born. Broadcast from radio station KFFA, located across the Mississippi River in Helena, Arkansas, the program saturated the Delta with live blues and a pitch to buy King Biscuit Flour. Every weekday from 12:15 to 12:30, while Muddy was enjoying his lunch break, he'd tune in to hear harmonica player Sonny Boy Williamson II (formerly Alex "Rice" Miller, who assumed the name after the original Sonny Boy scored some successful singles) and guitarist Robert "Junior" Lockwood, Robert Johnson's stepson. By the following year, the show's band was augmented by James "Peck" Curtis on drums and pianist Robert "Dudlow" Taylor. Joe Willie Wilkins, who'd learned guitar by watching Muddy at his Saturday-night gigs, also became a regular. It was on "King Biscuit Time" that Muddy first heard an amplified harmonica, played by Sonny Boy, and an electrified guitar, courtesy of Wilkins. These innovations would become an integral part of the sound he was to forge into his own in Chicago.

Muddy knew all the King Biscuit Boys; he and Son Simms had performed with them on their broadcast. "If we got a chance to set in and do a couple of songs," Muddy recollected, "man, when we got back on Stovall, that was the whole talk."[37] Once Muddy hired Sonny Boy and his band to play his juke for $50, which included a plug for Muddy's roadhouse on the hottest show in the Delta. It netted him the largest crowd for miles around, as well as a visit by a future pioneer of electric blues, Elmore James.

By this time Muddy's original blues repertoire included "Country Blues," "I Be's Troubled," "Burr Clover Farm Blues" and "Number One Highway Blues" — all of which he'd recorded for Lomax — as well as "Canary Bird Blues," "Rosalie" and "Ramblin' Kid." Other blues tunes his band played regularly were "Sugar Mama Blues," "Down South" and "Bluebird Blues" by John Lee "Sonny Boy" Williamson (the original Sonny Boy) and Walter Davis's "Thirteen Highway Blues," "Angel Blues" and "County Jail Blues." Of course, for dances and white gatherings, they also covered a range of popular tunes, such as "Down By The Riverside," "Chattanooga Choo-Choo," "Home On The Range," "Deep In The Heart Of Texas" and many more.

When the United States joined World War II in December 1941 in the wake of the Japanese attack on Pearl Harbor, Muddy became eligible for the draft. He was able to obtain an exemption, however, because he performed an essential service for an enterprise that produced the cotton required for military uniforms and bandages.

By the steamy summer of 1942, Alan Lomax, Lewis Jones and other members of the Coahoma Study Project were back in the Mississippi Delta collecting country blues for the Library of Congress in collaboration with Fisk. On 17 July the team recorded Son House, then on or about 20 to 24 July, they returned to Stovall for more sessions with Muddy. This time his band, the Son Simms Four, was included.

To an ear attuned to modern blues, the cuts with Son Simms on violin and Louis Ford on mandolin have a dissonant sound. The vocals are thinner, more high-pitched than on Muddy's solo tunes. And the fiddle work, especially, recalls the close kinship between some forms of early blues and hillbilly music. Of the songs he recorded with the band, "Ramblin' Kid Blues" and "Rosalie" were authored by Muddy. The origins of "Pearlie May Blues" are unknown, and "Joe Turner" dates back to the turn of the century.

Muddy also recorded more blues for Lomax without the backing of the full group. For these sessions, Muddy generally accompanies himself on guitar (both with and without the bottleneck), although Son Simms plays second guitar on "Take A Walk With Me" and "Burr Clover Blues," and his brother-in-law Charles Berry plays second guitar on both versions of "I Be Bound To Write To You" and on "32-20 Blues." (The latter was also the title of a Robert Johnson number, although that's the only similarity between the two.)

Muddy's choice of songs illustrates the fluidity of blues, its continual evolution as elements of earlier songs are melded with one's own creative touches to forge a new entity. "Take A Walk With Me" is similar to Robert Johnson's "Sweet Home Chicago" and was recorded by Robert "Junior" Lockwood in July 1941. The chorus of "You're Gonna Miss Me When I'm Gone" was taken from Buddy Moss's 1933 recording of "When I'm Dead and Gone," although the rest of the lyrics and the music were Muddy's own. The melody for "I Be Bound To Write To You" is the same as Muddy's "I Be's Troubled" from his 1941 cuts. These 1942 sessions also included "You Got To Take Sick And Die Some Of These Days" — which Muddy reprised in his 1956 recording of "Diamonds At Your Feet"

— and "Why Don't You Live So God Can Use You," the only religious song he ever committed to disc.

During the 1942 sessions, Muddy revised "Burr Clover Blues." The first two verses are essentially the same as they were in the 1941 recorded version, but the remainder of the lyrics are different. His reference to a soldier on a battlefield is a reminder that the burr clover man — Howard Stovall — had gone off to fight in World War II. Also this time Muddy plays with a bottleneck, whereas previously he'd fingerpicked this tune.

Muddy reprised his "Country Blues" with new lyrics for these sessions. In the 1941 version, the protagonist is victimized by a heartless woman. He hopes she'll change but leaves her anyway, ready to die of a broken heart. In the 1942 rendition, the singer is not interested in his heart; his sexual appetite is the motivating force. His unfaithful lover has been no more than a sexual convenience, so he sets off to the city to seek fulfillment, deliciously described through metaphors of food preparation.

In answering Lomax's questionnaire, Muddy indicated that his favorite radio star was Fats Waller, an unexpected response, as Waller's light, swinging jazz seems to have little in common with Muddy's music. Muddy singled out Walter Davis as his favorite recording artist, not surprising as he was regularly performing at least three of Davis's blues.

When asked about family matters, Muddy confirmed that his grandmother, now 64, was still residing with him, along with her son Joe Brant and Muddy's girlfriend (whom he referred to as his wife), Sally Ann Adams. His daughter Adeline, whom he had fathered outside his marriage to Mabel, was living elsewhere. He claimed that the family farmed eight acres, owned four pigs and seven chickens and earned a profit of between $100 to $300 per year.

Muddy owned a 1934 v-8 Ford, in which he drove to Clarksdale several times a week, took pleasure trips to outlying towns and traveled to Memphis once or twice a year. Muddy reminisced about the 73-mile journey that, back then, was the mark of a well-traveled man: "Couple of us what plays, like me and Son Simms, sometimes we'd go up to Memphis just to come back for the big word, 'We's in Memphis last night.'" They'd leave on a Saturday or Sunday and return for work at the beginning of the week. "Get back home, you'd catch that mule Monday morning," said Muddy. "Early. Get on that tractor, sharpen a hoe before you go so your wife could chop cotton."[38]

On 23 December 1942, Muddy married Sally Ann in a ceremony conducted by Reverend Cal Sanders. Muddy had neglected one thing, however — he was not divorced from Mabel. In the cropper world, this kind of omission was not unusual; after all, there was little communal property to divide. Sally Ann was probably the woman with whom Muddy had run off to St. Louis. She had a sixth-grade education, was 27 years old by the time of the nuptials and, like Mabel before her, attended church with Miss Della on a regular basis. She also enjoyed dancing every Saturday night, although presumably she wasn't stepping out with Muddy. "I don't dance — quit trying," Muddy stated. "Just wasn't no hand to dance. You be dancin' with a girl, and people snatch her and go."[39]

He may have been a newlywed, but Muddy was restless. On 23 January 1943, he'd received two copies of his 1942 recordings from Lomax, and this surely fueled his ambition to expand his horizons. Also the ravages of time were beginning to show on Stovall. Or maybe Muddy no longer belonged there. "If time don't get no better," Muddy would sing to himself, "Up the road I'm goin'."[40]

Howard Stovall was off in wartime Europe defending his way of life, and the general superintendent, a Mr. Fulton, was disliked by the croppers he managed. Muddy had always enjoyed a good relationship with Stovall and the previous superintendents, but Fulton was another matter. His condescending attitude ruffled the sensibilities of most of the workers, but Muddy felt that the general superintendent had singled him out for an additional dose of malevolence. As agricultural mechanization inched into the Delta, Muddy had been one of the first tractor drivers on the plantation. Why, then, was he was only earning 22 1/2 cents an hour when the other top hands got 27 1/2 cents? The unfairness irked him.

Another important contributor to Muddy's malaise had to be his dissatisfaction with the progress of his lifework. While his reputation flourished in the Delta, he seemed to be mired behind the next hurdle. A number of Muddy's colleagues had commercial recordings to validate their artistry and earn them an acclaim much wider than Muddy could hope to achieve with his live performances in Mississippi juke joints. Muddy knew he had what it took — he'd heard it on Lomax's discs. His reluctance to tackle another big city was fading fast. He had to grab the recognition he deserved.

The prospects of Mississippi's blacks had eroded steadily since emancipation. They were poorer now than they'd been a hundred years before. Solemn promises of equal rights withered into bitter fruit. Blacks remained a voiceless people, persecuted, exploited and entrapped in economic bondage. Northern cities bustling with wartime production beckoned southern blacks with well-paying jobs and opportunities denied them elsewhere. The call was heeded. In the first three and a half years of the 1940s, 50,000 blacks quit Mississippi for the North. Although Miss Della and others suspected that city life was overrated, Muddy was ready to try again. He knew if anyone could make it, he could.

"I wanted to get out of Mississippi in the worst way, man,"[41] Muddy later declared. The coup de grace came one Monday morning in May 1943. Muddy went to Fulton's office, hat in hand, and politely asked for a raise to 25 cents. The reaction was explosive. Fulton stalked around his office swearing and shouting. Muddy just stood there, an inscrutable expression masking his thoughts: "Ain't but one thing to do — he'd never like me no more and I'd never like him no more — kiss him goodbye." That quitting-time cornfield holler said it all: "Oh, I can't let this dark cloud catch me here / Oh, I can't stay here long."[42]

Fulton had done him a favor: he'd provided the final spark to detonate discontent into action. Even as a bluesman, Muddy was unlikely to break free from the oppressive limitations of being black in Mississippi. As long as he stayed down South, ol' Jim Crow would clip his wings.

Only one consideration tempered Muddy's decision to move on — the love and loyalty he felt for the grandmother he adored. Burdened by his dilemma, Muddy strode back to the run-down shack where she'd nurtured him as long as he could remember. With characteristic pluck and determination, Miss Della replied, "Well, if you think you're going to have some problem, you better go. I ain't going to let it whup me."[43] That clinched it. He worked the rest of Monday and through the week until Thursday. He told the Coahoma draft board that due to a death he had to go to Chicago for a few days and gave them his half-sister's address there. Friday was moving day.

That morning the air was heavy with moisture from the previous night's deluge. The fields were sodden as the morning sun shot its rays through a wall of cloud. It was not only the declaration of a new day, but also of a new life. He must have felt the tug of the majestic country scene and his link to those neighbors whose plaintive field hollers were signaling the start of another day of toil. But Muddy never wavered. He knew his ambition was leading him elsewhere. He also knew that he had the talent and drive to become a bluesman the world would remember: "I felt like I had it. I never doubted myself one time I didn't have it. I knowed that. Just knowed I had it."[44]

He sent a messenger to Fulton, claiming he was sick. Then he dressed in his only suit, jammed his possessions in a single suitcase and grabbed his Silvertone guitar, promising Sally Ann he'd send for her. Then came the most difficult separation of all; Muddy would not see his cherished Della Jones again.

Muddy had waited a lifetime for that four o'clock train out of Clarksdale. After changing over to the Illinois Central in Memphis, he was on the straight track to Chicago. The world of music would never be the same.

NOTES

1 Paul Oliver, *Blues Off the Record* (New York: Hippocrene Books Inc., 1984), 261.

2 Paul Oliver, *Conversation with the Blues* (New York: Horizon Press, 1965), 49.

3 Bruce Cook, *Listen to the Blues* (New York: Charles Scribner's Sons, 1973), 184.

4 Vernon Gibbs, "Muddy Waters," *Essence* (Dec. 1972): 23.

5 Pete Welding and Toby Byron (eds.), *Bluesland* (New York: Dutton, 1991), 139.

6 James Rooney, *Bossmen: Bill Monroe & Muddy Waters* (New York: The Dial Press, 1971), 105.

7 Pete Welding, "An Interview with Muddy Waters," *The American Folk Music Occasional* 2 (1970): 4.

8 Clas Ahlstrand, Peter Mahlin and Jan-Ake Pettersson, "Muddy Talkin' To," *Jefferson* 14: 15.

9 Jim O'Neal and Amy O'Neal, "Muddy," *Living Blues* 64 (Mar.–Apr. 1985): 33.

10 O'Neal and O'Neal, 16.

11 Lawrence Cohn, *Nothing But the Blues* (New York: Abbeville Publishing Group, 1993), 132.

12 Elve Morganfield, interview with author, 4 Aug. 1995.

13 Welding, 5.

14 A.X. Nicholas, ed., *Woke Up This Mornin': The Poetry of the Blues* (New York: Bantam Books, Inc., 1973), 99.

15 O'Neal and O'Neal, 19.

16 O'Neal and O'Neal, 23.

17 O'Neal and O'Neal, 17.

18 Margaret McKee and Fred Chisenhall, *Beale Black & Blue: Life and Music on Black America's Main Street* (Baton Rouge: Louisiana State University Press, 1981), 236.

19 Charles Shaar Murray, "The Blues Had a Baby and They Called It Rock 'n' Roll," *New Musical Express* (30 Apr. 1977): 26.

20 Peter Guralnick, *Feel Like Going Home* (New York: Harper & Row, Publishers, 1989), 67.

21 Rooney, 105.

22 Early Wright, interview with author, 18 May 1995.

23 Willie Foster, interview with author, 18 May 1995.

24 O'Neal and O'Neal, 23.

25 O'Neal and O'Neal, 19.

26 Alan Lomax, *The Land Where the Blues Began* (New York: Pantheon Books, 1993), 405.

27 McKee and Chisenhall, 234.

28 O'Neal and O'Neal, 21–22.

29 Lomax, 405.

30 McKee and Chisenhall, 230.

31 Lomax, 406.

32 O'Neal and O'Neal, 20.

33 Paul Oliver, *Blues Off the Record* (New York: Hippocrene Books Inc., 1984), 261.

34 John Cowley, "Really the Walkin' Blues: Son House, Muddy Waters, Robert Johnson and the Development of a Traditional Blues," *Popular Music 1: Folk or Popular? Distinctions, Influences, Continuities*, eds. Richard Middleton and David Horn (Cambridge: Cambridge University Press, 1981): 60.

35 Cowley, 61.

36 McKee and Chisenhall, 235.

37 McKee and Chisenhall, 233–234.

38 McKee and Chisenhall, 233.

39 Lomax, 413.

40 *Bluesland: A Portrait in American Music*, film, *Masters of American Music*, BMG Video–Taurus Film–VideoArts Music, 1991.

41 Guralnick, 67.

42 David Kingman, *American Music: A Panorama* (New York: Schirmer Books, 1979), 44.

43 Robert Palmer, *Deep Blues* (New York: Penguin, 1982), 7.

44 Rooney, 128–129.

3

. . . I changed my luck all the way around when I moved up there.[1]

The blacks-only coaches hitched to the back of the Illinois Central clattered through the night and into the soft light of the rising sun. On board the migrants chatted, dozed and dreamed, their life savings staked on the wager that in the North they could realize their full potential, that Jim Crow would wither in the northern climes.

At 9:30 that Saturday morning in May 1943, the train slid into the cavernous Illinois Central Station at 12th Street and Michigan Avenue, "the Ellis Island of the black migration to Chicago."[2] In 17 1/2 hours, Muddy had been transported into another galaxy. As the 28-year-old disembarked, Chicago embraced him in a dazzle of lights, a blur of speed and a clangorous din. "I got off that train,"

Muddy recollected, "and it looked like this was the fastest place in the world — cabs dropping fares, horns blowing, the peoples walking so fast."[3] But it was the clamor, the pulse, the braggadocio of this audacious metropolis that would define the development of Muddy's blues.

The cab that Muddy hailed shot up to the curb, then tore off, taking him to the South Side address of his half-sister, the unaccustomed velocity leaving him breathless. He craned his neck, marveling at the massive buildings to the north as they sped southward through the density of brick tenements and factories immersed in a thick industrial haze. Muddy made the cabbie wait for him at 3656 Calumet Avenue while he went up to the fourth floor to confirm that this was indeed the apartment where his half-sister and her husband Dan Jones lived.

Muddy must have known he was on the right track. That same evening he landed a job at the Joanna Western Mills container factory loading and unloading trucks on the 3:00 to 11:00 PM shift. The pay was $45 per week, with the opportunity to double that some weeks through overtime. At Stovall his entire family cleared $300 in a good year; here Muddy could earn that in seven weeks or less. "I have picked that cotton all the year, chop cotton all year, and I didn't draw a hundred dollars," Muddy recalled. "Goodgodalmighty, look at the money I got in my pocket."[4]

Muddy suspected that Fulton, Stovall's superintendent, had told the local draft board that he'd quit his job and moved to Chicago, for that Monday he received a notice to report to their office at 38th and South Park Boulevard to be drafted. Due to his illiteracy and weak eyesight, however, Muddy didn't make the grade. To his tremendous relief, he was rejected for military service.

Muddy was far from alone in Chicago; his pals Eddie Boyd and Scott Bohanner were living there, as well as other acquaintances and relatives, plus his uncle Joe Brant. After sleeping on his sister's couch for a week or two, he moved in with a cousin at 1857 West 13th Street. Within six months he was able to rent his own four-room apartment in a neighboring building at 1851 West 13th for only $12 a month, $23 less than his cousin paid. Muddy reveled in his good fortune: "Things was clicking for me, man."[5]

The South Side, where Muddy lived, was the nucleus of urban black America. Extending from its apex at the train and bus stations at 12th and Michigan, it sprawled southward for almost 15 miles in a widening wedge shape. It was a self-contained black enclave with its own shopping districts, clubs, hotels and industries. The local black newspaper, the *Chicago Defender*, disseminated its message of racial justice in Chicago and throughout the South. Home to William Dawson, the sole black member of Congress, and Joe Louis, the "Brown Bomber," heavyweight champion of the world, the South Side exuded the possibility that dreams could be fulfilled here.

During the 1940s the black population of the West and South sides expanded by 196 percent, as migrants from the southern states flooded North with the promise of the vote and the lure of a steady salary, away from the uncertain servitude of the sharecropping system. A surplus of employment existed in the defence and meat-packing industries, union jobs that finally gave the black man some power.

But whatever the new Chicagoans gained, they paid for at an exorbitant price. Government corruption, gambling and prostitution were rife; law enforcement was lax and easily swayed by the right amount of cash. With protection payments totaling almost $20 million per year, mob operations tarnished the entire city, but especially lucrative were its South Side numbers rackets.

White families had deserted the South Side with its proximity to the grit and noise from the railway lines and the stench of the stockyards. Where only a few of the affluent had resided, houses were chopped up into tiny ghetto apartments to house the onslaught of blacks in search of better lives. What they found was substandard housing, with heating and plumbing that was often out of order. One bed could be hired by three people on different shifts. Yet rents were jacked up to become the highest in the city. The black belt was fairly bursting, but there was nowhere to expand; the white communities formed an effective barrier.

The ways of the South may have been dressed up and urbanized here, but the repression had merely been transplanted. Higher rents and lower wages shackled black families to the slums. Blacks were largely confined to dead-end jobs; even work as bus or cab drivers was denied them. The roots of racial intolerance remained healthy. If black families dared to encroach on white neighborhoods, fire bombs were often a tool of dissuasion. Race riots erupted throughout the 1940s.

Black Chicago had engendered its own brand of blues back in the late 1930s. Known as the Bluebird beat — after the local label that spawned the majority of the talent — it emerged from the Depression as an overly processed elixir to soothe the senses after the cruel onslaught of hard times. Departing from its Delta roots, this style of swinging, buoyant blues had its rough edges polished and the angst diluted to appeal to more urbane sensibilities. Among the brightest stars of this genre were guitarists Lonnie Johnson, Big Bill Broonzy, Big Joe Williams and Hudson "Tampa Red" Woodbridge, pianists Major "Big Maceo" Merriweather and Peter "Memphis Slim" Chatman and harmonica player John Lee "Sonny Boy" Williamson. They were typically backed by bands comprising piano, guitar, bass, drums and occasionally horns.

Following on the heels of the Bluebird era, blues was infused with a shot of jazz to become the jump blues that was infatuating audiences at the time of Muddy's arrival. It, too, was scrubbed clean of Delta grit, but following Louis Jordan's lead, Buster Bennett, the Chicago All Stars, Jump Jackson and Roosevelt Sykes made the beat a crucial component of this new sound. As well, the jazzy songs of Nat "King" Cole, Billy Eckstine and Johnny Moore and the Three Blazers were national hits. In comparison, Muddy's country repertoire was considered old-fashioned.

The recording industry had sputtered to a stop by the time Muddy arrived in Chicago. In 1942, soon after the U.S. entered World War II, restrictions on the domestic use of shellac curtailed the output of blues recordings. Also that year the president of the American Federation of Musicians, James C. Petrillo, called for a national ban on recording to address his concern that live performances were being muffled in the face of competition from radio, phonographs and jukeboxes. The stricture hurt bluesmen such as Big Bill Broonzy, Big Maceo and Tampa Red. Many performers had to find alternative employment. Although the recording ban was lifted in 1944, shellac restrictions still limited the output of discs until World War II had ended.

In order to establish a toehold in the Chicago blues field, Muddy had to start again at the very bottom, playing guitar and singing in the homes of his sister and her friends. Although she had warned him that old-time blues wouldn't cut it here, Muddy stuck to what he knew and loved. Tunes by Leroy Carr, Robert Johnson and other blues greats, as well as his own compositions, made up his repertoire. He let himself in for a fair amount of derision. "They called it sharecropper music," Muddy recollected. "They said I was a square and would never get anywhere trying to sell the public that kind of stuff. They laughed at me when I wailed the blues."[6]

But he kept in mind his father's parting advice to pay no heed to ridicule. "Coming up through this life you've got to have some hassles," Muddy reflected. "You just don't walk in and say, 'Here I am. Take me.'"[7] He adopted a philosophical approach to the rejection, believing that audiences weren't ready for the honest emotions portrayed by his music. "They wanted to make believe trouble didn't exist." That wasn't Muddy's style. "The way to defeat trouble is to look it straight in the eye," Muddy declared. "That's what I was doing when I sang my blues."[8]

For a long time, Muddy had only his own determination to keep him going: "I was working [in music] but only because I wanted to work, not because anyone wanted me. People let me appear in their places because I would work for almost nothing."[9] Gradually his reputation strengthened. He got more and more gigs playing for rent parties in Chicago's black ghettos, where by charging a small admission, the host could earn his rent by inviting his friends for a generous helping of soul food, whiskey and blues. For Muddy these gigs meant added exposure, modest tips and all the liquor he could drink. A lot of these folks were from the South too, and a shot of down-home blues felt good after a bland diet of urban music.

One of the first well-known artists Muddy met in Chicago was Big Bill Broonzy, who'd been the nation's best-selling bluesman in the late 1930s. William Lee Conley Broonzy was born in Scott, Mississippi, on 26 June 1893, and his first instrument was a home-made fiddle. After a stint in World War I, he settled in Chicago, where he took up guitar and began recording in 1926. The tall, genial musician became the patriarch of the Bluebird sound. Muddy may have been a little surprised that the great man took time to be friendly and helpful towards him, never too busy to crack a few jokes with an obscure guitarist scrambling to make a name for himself. Thirty years later he still remembered Broonzy's advice: "'Do your thing, stay with it, man; if you stay with it, you goin' to make it.' That's what Big Bill told me. Mostly I try to be like him."[10] On another occasion Muddy remarked, "Big Bill, that's the nicest guy I ever met in my life."[11]

Big Bill introduced an intimidated Muddy to all the Chicago greats jamming at Tampa Red's apartment above a pawnshop at 35th and State streets. There Lester Melrose, the man behind the success of the Bluebird label, would preside over his stable of blues talent when he was in town. Muddy found himself in the company of legendary recording artists such as Big Bill, Tampa Red, Memphis Slim, Big Maceo Merriweather, Peter "Doctor" Clayton, John Lee "Sonny Boy" Williamson and J.T. Brown. He remembered being "a little shaky, because I . . . didn't want to say too much and I didn't want to get out of hand with 'em. . . . And they wasn't easy to meet as I am. . . . They looked at me like I was a little puppy dog or somethin'."[12]

The attitude of some established musicians was to keep the up-and-coming competition down. That wasn't the case with Big Bill Broonzy. He encouraged Muddy, helping him secure the necessary connections to get dates at house parties and introducing him as a promising new talent at Sylvio's, the hottest blues club on the West Side.

In 1945 Muddy's beloved grandmother died, and he returned to Stovall to settle her affairs. The Son Simms Four was still going strong in Clarksdale, with Pitty Pat back on bass, playing the first Friday of each month for black dances at the renowned Riverside Hotel. In the late 1940s, both Louis Ford and Pitty Pat died, marking the termination of the band. Simms underwent three operations for kidney stones in the late 1950s at the VA Hospital in Memphis and gave up blues for the church. Before his final surgery, he told his wife Lizzie, "Baby, you can keep my watch. I ain't comin' back this time."[13] Son Simms died on 23 December 1958 and was buried without a headstone at Bell Grove Baptist Church.

John Lee "Sonny Boy" Williamson was another well-known Chicago bluesman with whom Muddy struck up an early acquaintance. The harmonica player and singer had been recording since 1937 and was responsible for bringing the harp to the forefront as a lead instrument in blues, a concept that Muddy would later call upon in his own bands. Sonny Boy's innovations planted the seed for all the great harmonica players who followed. Sonny Boy hired Muddy and Eddie Boyd to back him at some gigs at 904 Avenue O in South Chicago, but it wasn't their prodigious talent that was the attraction. With his inheritance from Miss Della and the help of an uncle,

Muddy was one of the few bluesmen in Chicago with a car.

Sonny Boy's appetite for whiskey often meant the main attraction retired early from the stage. One night, with Sonny Boy slumped offstage too drunk to sing and Eddie's voice getting weak, Muddy finally had the opportunity to show the audience what he had to offer. He launched into Lowell Fulson's "Trouble, Trouble," and the crowd erupted in cheers. Roused from his stupor, Sonny Boy leapt to his feet and grabbed the microphone, but the patrons continued to yell for Muddy Waters. Eventually Sonny Boy's behavior got them all fired.

Soon after Muddy returned to Chicago from Stovall, his cousin Jesse Jones arranged for him to meet someone he thought had similar musical interests, a man who, as it turned out, would be instrumental in creating the Muddy Waters sound. He was born Jimmy Lane on 3 June 1924 in Ruleville, Mississippi, about 40 miles south of Clarksdale, and raised in Mississippi, Georgia, Missouri and Tennessee. When he was about seven, his mother remarried, and Jimmy assumed his stepfather's name — Rogers. Inspired by the recordings of John Lee "Sonny Boy" Williamson, Jimmy's first musical instrument was the harmonica. In Vance, Mississippi, at about age 13, Jimmy went to school for a time with Snooky Pryor, and the two played harp duets with the backing of a band. They would meet again later when Snooky became the progenitor of amplified blues harmonica in Chicago.

Since he was 10 or 11, Jimmy Rogers had also been learning guitar. He started, like so many other Delta guitarists, by playing on a length of broom wire stretched taut, often against the side of a house. Arthur Johnson, the uncle of one of Muddy's future band mates, Luther "Guitar Junior" Johnson, gave him a few pointers. Two of his strongest guitar influences were Big Bill Broonzy, whom he would get to know well in Chicago, and Joe Willie Wilkins, one of the King Biscuit Boys. So attracted was he to "King Biscuit Time," that Rogers went to Helena, where he sat in with Sonny Boy Williamson II (Rice Miller) using Joe Willie's instrument, the first time Jimmy had played an amplified guitar. Following stays in Memphis and St. Louis, he traveled to Chicago with his grandmother in 1939, but only remained a short while. Returning to Helena, Rogers occasionally got the opportunity to play second guitar behind Rice Miller's harp and Robert Nighthawk's masterful slide. He was gaining essential experience for his return to Chicago in about 1944.

After settling on the South Side, Rogers held a succession of jobs — at a chicken-packing plant, a shoe manufacturer, several meat-packing houses and in construction — while he pursued his musical ambitions during his off-hours. He still blew harmonica; the sweet, mellow tones he coaxed out of his harp were unique. He'd hang around clubs where John Lee "Sonny Boy" Williamson was playing, ready to take up the harp when the blues veteran was too inebriated to continue.

At this point, however, guitar was Rogers's primary instrument, an acoustic he'd electrified with a DeArmond pickup and a Gibson amplifier. He played with guitarist Claude "Blue Smitty" Smith, guitarist John Henry Barbee and harp player John Thomas Wrencher at the Maxwell Street market and at house parties. When the band did get the occasional club date, it wasn't paid by the house. The club would furnish the electricity and the musicians passed the hat. Blues pianist Albert "Sunnyland Slim" Luandrew got Jimmy his first Chicago gig, at the Club 21, where he accompanied Sunnyland on guitar and harp.

Around this time a blues aficionado by the name of Jesse Jones would stop by to hear Rogers play, buying him whiskey and hanging out with the musicians. Jones worked at the Sonora Radio Cabinet Company on Chicago's West Side and got Jimmy a job there. After they'd been friends for about a year, Jesse suggested he introduce Jimmy to someone with similar musical aspirations, his cousin Muddy Waters. Towards the end of 1945, when Muddy returned to Chicago from his trip to Stovall, Jesse arranged for the two to meet. They hit it off immediately and quickly decided to team up to see what they could accomplish together — Muddy supplied the vocals and guitar work, and Rogers concentrated primarily on harmonica.

Jimmy's first impression of Muddy's style was that it "wasn't too heavy," as Muddy was playing a lot by himself.[14] Accustomed to the backing of a complement of musicians, he preferred a fuller sound, as did Muddy. They were drawn together by their love of Robert Johnson's style of slide guitar; it was clear they were a good fit.

Jimmy remembers going with Muddy and pianist Little Johnny Jones to Tampa Red's jam sessions, but more often than not, Muddy would forego the camaraderie upstairs. Jimmy describes him as shy and never socializing much with musicians outside his immediate circle. Muddy admitted he was nervous around that coterie of recording artists, and their music didn't jibe with his, so he didn't try to fit in. Besides, Tampa's place was conveniently situated a short walk from Comiskey Park, so Muddy would often skip the jams and head over to see his favorite team play baseball instead. The fact it was floundering at the bottom of the league had no effect on his enthusiasm; he would remain devoted to the White Sox for the rest of his life.

Occasionally Muddy and Jimmy would play the Maxwell Street Market — also known as Jewtown — just a few blocks east of where Muddy was living on West 13th Street, close to Rogers's apartment as well. From late every Saturday afternoon to Sunday afternoon, this dilapidated slum, home to the poorest of Chicago's blacks, was transformed into a carnival atmosphere of joyful commerce. Street hustlers barked their wares, while gleeful, rambunctious children darted out of garbage-filled alleyways and vanished under shabby tables laden with gaudy trinkets. Amidst the decay and bustle of the ghetto, clouds of greasy smoke billowed from sausage and porkchop stands, and heady smells of alcohol, sweat and urine saturated the air.

Playing everything from bebop to blues, hopeful street musicians anticipated their big break or, failing that, an opportunity to earn a decent buck. The steadfast Tenner "Playboy" Venson made his harmonica wail, while further down the street Eddie "Porkchop" Hines danced a deft step while keeping time with his drum. Snooky Pryor and guitarist Floyd Jones collected shoeboxes full of money busking in Jewtown on weekends, much more than they could pull in at a small club.

Contrary to Muddy's assertion that Joe Brant bought him his first electric guitar in 1944, Rogers maintains that when he met Muddy the following year, he was still playing an unamplified acoustic. But attempting to cut through the raucous din of a Chicago tavern with an acoustic guitar was a futile exercise, even though Muddy had tried to articulate his sound by playing harder and by using a metal thumbpick. Amplification was essential, and the first way he achieved that was to attach an electrical pickup to the soundboard of his acoustic guitar, which fed the sound out through an amplifier. This technology had been available since the 1930s and was already being utilized by such bluesmen as Elmore James and T-Bone Walker. Jimmy remembers taking Muddy to "18th and Halsted there, and we bought him a DeArmond pickup [for] his first guitar that he brought to Chicago, and that started him on electric."[15]

Jesse Jones was responsible for bringing another musician into Muddy's life — Claude "Blue Smitty" Smith. Smitty was born in Marianna, Arkansas, on 6 November 1924. He was raised by an aunt in Chicago, where he learned to play piano, then returned to Arkansas at age 11. Like Jimmy Rogers, Smitty's first taste of playing guitar was strumming a couple of wires stretched up on a wall. His natural abilities were so pronounced that when he finally got the chance to borrow a real guitar at age 14, he could play it immediately. After a stint in the military, where he refined his guitar skills and learned to read music in the army band, Smitty lived in Memphis, then settled back in Chicago. Those artists who made an impact on Smitty's musical development were James "Yank" Rachell, Arthur "Big Boy" Crudup and jazz guitarist Charlie Christian.

One rainy day in Jewtown, Blue Smitty agreed to hold a fellow's guitar while he went into a music store to buy some strings. While he waited, Smitty played a few tunes on the remaining five strings, attracting the attention of Jesse, who was passing by. Convinced that this talented guitar player should meet his cousin, Jesse took him over to Muddy's nearby digs. There they found Muddy sprawled in the center of the floor, trying to repair his pickup. As soon as a wire was soldered in place, Smitty played a sample of his licks, and Muddy was impressed. Smitty's style incorporated country blues, the city blues of the 1930s and boogie-woogie. Muddy realized that Smitty's masterful fingerpicking and chording set him in the vanguard of blues guitarists.

Muddy hadn't advanced much as a guitar player since learning slide, so he seized the opportunity to pick up some of Smitty's techniques. As well, the added volume provided by his pickup meant total exposure for any errors. Muddy explained: "On acoustic you could mess up a lot of stuff and no one would know that you'd ever missed. So electric was really rough."[16] Smitty and Muddy would get together at Muddy's four or five times a week to work on Muddy's fingerpicking; he would practice bass lines while Smitty played lead. In that way Muddy was able to enrich his slide playing by combining it with finger-style solos or bass rhythms. In the meantime Smitty was saving his money to buy a pickup and amp for his Gibson guitar so they could play gigs together.

Anxious to keep improving, Muddy also took advantage of Jimmy Rogers's technical proficiency. Together they worked on Muddy's execution, turnarounds, turnovers and the different styles of play that Jimmy had mastered. Muddy had generally played in open G, but Rogers introduced him to some alternative tunings.

By the mid-1940s, Muddy had replaced his glass bottleneck slide with a piece of stainless-steel tubing, cut for him by a friend who worked in a Gary steel mill. It was one and a half inches long, covering only the top knuckle of his little finger. Muddy used it mainly for sliding on single strings, while the others were left open so he could fret bass lines or finger embellishments.

Yet despite his progress, Muddy's guitar technique was far from stellar, according to John Brim, a pioneer of postwar Chicago blues. He remembers playing a gig with John Lee "Sonny Boy" Williamson at the Purple Cat at 2113 West Madison Street when Muddy sat in. "I guess he was okay," is Brim's only comment on Muddy's ability then. "Everybody have their own style."[17]

Muddy and Jimmy played house parties together with the intermittent participation of Blue Smitty. Since Smitty couldn't be counted on to show up at every gig, Jimmy was always ready to set aside his harmonica and take up second guitar, tuning down his instrument to play bass lines. They performed several dates on the West Side, usually for five dollars each per night: a run at Mason & Dave's at Polk Street and Ogden Avenue, then at Dave's Tavern and Tom's Tavern, both on Roosevelt Road. But at this point Muddy's musical associations were still fluid; he was part of no set group. He'd gladly take a gig with anyone who asked — Jimmy Rogers, Eddie Boyd, Blue Smitty, James "Beale Street" Clarke or Sonny Boy Williamson. He often formed a trio with pianist Lee Brown and "Baby Face" Leroy Foster on guitar.

Still it wasn't enough. He ached to be heard on record. To achieve the level of renown he was after, Muddy had to reach a larger audience, those people who bought "race" records. With his fresh, innovative sound — the urban blues he was developing through the new medium of amplification — Muddy knew he had a product that would sell. He fantasized about the day he'd hear his tunes blaring out of a radio or ghetto jukebox. *Then* everyone would know the name Muddy Waters, and he'd reap the acclaim for which he hungered. His drive for vinyl never wavered, but circumstances had kept him from attaining his goal through the early and mid 1940s. While the 1941 and 1942 Library of Congress recordings had given him confidence and fired his ambition, they hadn't been made for commercial release.

Though Muddy himself forgot about it until he neared the end of his life, his first Chicago recording session took place in 1946. His memory lapse was probably attributable to the fact that he was unaware until years later that the track had been released on disc. He was a commercial recording artist and didn't know it!

When Muddy got the news that he was about to get this shot at recording, he must have wondered if this was finally the vehicle to propel him to celebrity. Muddy was included in the session thanks to Lee Brown, who had been recording for the session's producer, J. Mayo Williams, for some time. Memphis Slim, Othum Brown and Muddy's cohorts Sunnyland Slim, Jimmy Rogers and "Baby Face" Leroy joined him at Universal Studios at 204 North Wacker Drive to lay down their tunes for posterity. Trying to retrieve 30-year-old memories, Muddy said that accompanying him on guitar and vocals on his track "Mean Red Spider" were most likely Alex Atkins or J.T. Brown on alto sax and either Lee Brown, Sunnyland Slim, James "Beale Street" Clarke or Memphis Slim on piano. Big Ernest Crawford played upright bass.

Muddy remembered recording only one or two songs at that session. The lyrics of the sole surviving cut, "Mean Red Spider," were taken from Robert "Junior" Lockwood's "Black Spider Blues," recorded for the Bluebird label in 1941. Three verses are very similar, although Muddy added a new verse, altered the melody of Lockwood's original and made his spider red and male. Muddy's version is horn and piano driven; his finger-style guitar work remains in the background. Despite fronting at least one song, Muddy was paid only half the regular sideman rate of $41.25.

Paired with a previously recorded tune by vocalist James "Sweet Lucy" Carter — "Let Me Be Your Coal Man" — Muddy's track appeared on the B side of the obscure 78 released by the 20th Century label. Had Muddy known his "Mean Red Spider" was also credited to Carter, the injustice would have infuriated him. But, as it turned out, there was no harm done — the disc went nowhere. "I thought that was buried under the ground somewhere!" Muddy later remarked. "I never knew it was put out on records, man."[18] It was an inauspicious beginning to the dynamic recording career that followed.

At Columbia the next year, Muddy suffered another false start. Although his mentor Big Bill Broonzy had likely introduced him to Columbia's Lester Melrose over at Tampa Red's, it was pianist James "Beale Street" Clarke who talked Melrose into giving Muddy a shot at recording. Clarke already had a joint session booked with vocalist and guitar player Homer Harris at Columbia on 27 September 1946, and he convinced Melrose to include Muddy as a sideman. Harris recorded three sides, and Clarke did two. Then Muddy got the opportunity to cut three tracks of his own, backed by Clarke on piano and a rhythm section that probably comprised "Baby Face" Leroy Foster on second guitar, Ransom Knowling on bass and drummer Judge Riley. Performing under his given name, McKinley Morganfield, Muddy at least received the full sideman fee for this session.

In cutting "Jitterbug Blues," "Hard Day Blues" and "Burying Ground Blues," Muddy tried to transpose onto disc the innovative style of modern Chicago blues that he, Jimmy and Smitty were performing in South Side taverns, but Melrose was pushing for more traditional tunes. Muddy set aside his slide for this session, perhaps calculating that single-string leads would be his ticket to a record release. It was a good outing. His vocals are heartfelt in "Jitterbug Blues" as he implores Annie Mae — the name of his real-life girlfriend — not to fall prey to another man. "Burying Ground Blues," the most powerful of the three cuts, is a song of anguish at the death of his woman.

Melrose was blind to the gigantic potential of Chicago's next great blues artist. Columbia's lack of enthusiasm for his tracks prompted Muddy to explain, "They held 'em on the shelf, you know. . . . They're in the business for money. They didn't know. That country stuff might sound funny to 'em. I'd imagine, you know, they'd say, 'This stuff isn't gonna sell.'"[19] The cuts were not released until 1971, when they were included on a Testament album, *Chicago Blues: The Beginning* — far too late to boost the fortunes of a struggling bluesman. He was disheartened, although characteristic of Muddy, it was not enough to extinguish his fire of ambition. He *had* to get a record out.

In 1947 a feisty young harmonica wiz named Marion "Little Walter" Jacobs was blowing blues on Maxwell Street, playing his harp through a small Gibson amp. He was a good-looking teenager with a small build and a light brown complexion. Bristling with talent and creativity and beset by demons, Little Walter would revolutionize the status and sound of the harp, and along with Muddy and Jimmy Rogers, help create the legendary sound of Muddy Waters's blues.

Little Walter was born on 1 May (or 2 May, according to his sister) 1930 in Marksville, Louisiana. While not in the Delta, the town was located only about 30 miles from the lower Mississippi River. As a child Little Walter was drawn to the harmonica and, oblivious to the objections of his mother and the taunting of his friends, he taught himself to play at about age eight. Being pressured to give up the harp actually fired Little Walter's devotion to continue. The first harp player he remembered hearing was a white hillbilly musician and yodeler called Lonnie Glosson, but his primary influence was the recordings of John Lee "Sonny Boy" Williamson.

Always headstrong and impetuous, he left home that year and by age nine or 10 was scrambling to survive in St. Louis, blowing his harmonica for tips in pool halls and at shoe-shine stands, sleeping on pool tables at night. Walter pestered the local musicians in his bid to establish a blues career, and it was during this period that Jimmy Rogers recalls meeting the boy. Walter snagged his first professional gigs when he was 12; they were in small taverns in New Orleans, where he played polkas, waltzes and other popular tunes, as well as blues. By the early 1940s, he was in Helena, Arkansas, crossing Rogers's path once more.

Yet again Little Walter was reduced to using a pool table as his bed, scraping by with the benevolence of strangers. He persistently shadowed the King Biscuit Boys, undaunted by their disregard of the young nuisance. He'd always turn up at their gigs, awaiting the inevitable moment when their harp player, Sonny Boy Williamson II (Rice Miller), would step offstage to play craps, whereupon he'd occasionally be allowed to sit in. As Sonny Boy began to hear promise in Walter's style, he gave the eager teen some pointers on harmonica technique.

Little Walter was never far from trouble. Sonny Boy had to intervene one night at a West Helena roadhouse when a knife-wielding woman tried to stab the wayward youth. Walter went on to blow harp with guitarist Houston Stackhouse and pianist Henry Hill in Helena and its environs as he began to build a reputation as a budding bluesman. In 1945 he and pianist Robert "Dudlow" Taylor took over the "Mother's Best Flour Show" on radio station KFFA, playing jump blues and country blues. The show's popularity burgeoned until it eclipsed the ratings of the venerable "King Biscuit Time."

After returning to St. Louis for about eight months, Walter played harp with David "Honeyboy" Edwards and James DeShay before setting off for Chicago with Edwards in 1947. Little Walter's harmonica sound bore the imprint of several influential bluesmen: Rice Miller, John Lee "Sonny Boy" Williamson and jump-blues alto-saxophonist Louis Jordan. He'd also learned some guitar on his travels, first from Houston Stackhouse, then from Honeyboy, and in Chicago he would acquire pointers from Moody Jones. Too young to work the Chicago taverns, he plugged in his amplifier on Maxwell Street and blew his harmonica every Sunday from nine in the morning until four in the afternoon, often with Honeyboy.

One Sunday morning Jimmy Rogers went down to investigate an incredible harp sound emanating from Maxwell Street, just a half-block from where he was living, and discovered its source was the street kid from St. Louis and Helena. As they struck up a conversation, they got caught in a downpour and ran back to Jimmy's to get dry. Walter lived in the neighborhood, too — a couple of blocks away — so they began to see each other often.

Pianist Lazy Bill Lucas also befriended Walter, and soon the young harp player was joining Lucas and guitarists Johnny Williams and Johnny Young on their gigs. During one date with Williams at the Purple Cat, Young dropped by to jam and Walter's hot-blooded streak led to an onstage altercation and his subsequent dismissal. After retreating briefly to Helena, Walter returned to Chicago and plugged back in on Maxwell Street. He also hooked up with a few bluesmen, including Jimmy Rogers, as they traveled from club to club playing for the kitty. They'd hit up to six taverns a night, making from $15 to $20, substantial money for a musician.

By this time Jimmy had mentioned Little Walter's abilities to

Muddy and arranged an introduction. "When I met him he wasn't drinking nothing but Pepsi Cola," Muddy reminisced. "Just a kid."[20] As they jammed in Walter's living room, the 17-year-old so impressed his elders that they rated him second only to Rice Miller. "One thing I knew I wanted was that harp sound," Muddy later said, describing his concept for a band. "I guess I loved the harp 'cause that's the first thing I learned on."[21]

Walter already had a distinctive style, and his talent was clearly prodigious. Nevertheless, in the beginning it was apparent to Muddy and Jimmy that he still had a lot to learn, especially about timing. Muddy's singing style was to lag slightly behind the beat, forcing his backing musicians to drive the rhythm forward. Walter was anxious to learn. Other prospective mentors had been put off by Walter's irascible nature and bad timing, and so he was grateful to Muddy and Jimmy for taking him in hand. Jimmy recalls that Walter "was very interested in his harmonica and playing with us, because I think we were two guys that really accepted Little Walter for what he really was, and he appreciated that. He would listen to Muddy or myself more so than he would anybody else."[22]

Muddy and Jimmy — both harmonica players — worked with Walter for at least six months. He was a quick study; whatever was played for him, he could retain almost perfectly. "His mind was so fast," Muddy remarked, "he could think twice to your once; that's how he learned to harp so good."[23] Besides technique, Walter needed to temper his playing to complement and augment the music of a cohesive unit. Muddy said that they "taught him to settle down. He was *wild*, he had to play *fast!* He was always a jump boy, had that up'n-go power. *Lotta* energy!"[24]

Over and over as they played their guitars, they showed Little Walter how to merge the harmonica into the mix. He had to develop a rougher edge to his swing style in order to fit the sound of the two older bluesmen. What emerged from their tutelage was the preeminent master of postwar blues harmonica, a musical innovator who redefined the role of the harp and, following the lead of Sonny Boy, brought it into the spotlight. Of Walter Jacobs's astonishing artistry, Muddy reflected with deep affection, "He had a thing on the harp that nobody had. And today they're still trying for it, but they can't come up to it. . . . He is the greatest I've ever had."[25]

Walter teamed up with guitarist Othum Brown in 1947 for his first recording session, hired by the flamboyant, one-eyed Bernard Abrams of the Maxwell Radio Record Company. The result was a lackluster disc with Brown fronting "Ora-Nelle Blues (That's Alright)" on side A and Walters's "I Just Keep Loving Her" on the flip. The emerging, short-lived label assumed the name Ora Nelle Records after Brown's tune.

While Muddy enjoyed the Maxwell Street scene, playing there for change wasn't his style. "A lot of peoples was down there trying to make a quarter," he said, "but I didn't like to have to play outside in all the weathers, and I didn't like to pass the hat around and all that bullshit."[26] Although he'd busked there with Rogers, Muddy would only admit to having played there a couple of times with Walter, to help promote his debut disc. "I was down in front of the record shop," Muddy recalled. "Went down there and tried to push his record. We sold a good bit that Saturday afternoon."[27]

A fortuitous visit to the barbershop landed Muddy, Jimmy, Smitty and Little Walter one of their first club gigs together. Lugging his guitar and amp home from a guitar lesson at Muddy's, Smitty headed east, stopping off to get his hair cut at 12th Street and Ogden Boulevard. While he waited his turn, he was persuaded to play a few numbers. Another client, the manager of the Chicken Shack at Polk Street and Ogden, was so impressed he told Smitty that if he could get a band together, they could have a gig at his club that Friday, Saturday and Sunday. After his haircut, Smitty returned to Muddy's with the dilemma of what their fee should be. The group put Muddy in charge as he was the oldest. He determined that five dollars each per night would be fair, even though back then a band was expected to play as late as five o'clock in the morning.

Smitty took over lead guitar and vocals, Muddy played second guitar, Jimmy blew harp and an unidentified fellow played bass on a tub. They were such a hit at the Chicken Shack that they were kept on to perform Thursday nights and every weekend. Then Little Walter came aboard on harmonica, allowing Jimmy to join Muddy and Smitty on guitar. "Well, I was always the outstanding guitar player," was Blue Smitty's recollection. "When somebody walked in, right away they'd focus on me, you know. And I was singin', and then I'd do this till I'd get tired and then Muddy would sing some."[28]

Their repertoire was strictly blues. Two songs that Smitty remembered performing were "The Honeydripper" and Big Joe Williams's "Baby Please Don't Go," a number Muddy would sing for the rest of his career. When Muddy got the opportunity to front the band, he'd often perform his original compositions.

One night Eddie Boyd stopped by with a proposition. Doc Britton at the Flame Club wanted to hire a blues band, and Eddie knew that Muddy and Blue Smitty, with himself on piano, would fit the bill. The gig was only open to union musicians, so that Monday Eddie took his two pals down to join Local 208, then they went to see Doc and were hired. It was a definite advancement — $63 each for six nights' work per week.

Downstairs at the Flame, located at 31st Street and Indiana Avenue, blues lovers were packing the club to hear the trio play. They alternated sets with a Josephine Baker impersonator, described by Smitty as "a he/she what played piano while we was takin' intermission."[29] Once a week Doc would throw "Blue Monday" parties, where for a two-dollar cover, one could listen to the band and drink unlimited quantities of alcohol free of charge. Doc would always make sure there was plenty of whiskey for the musicians.

On one occasion Muddy overdid it with the drinks, and in an upset involving a woman, he smashed all the whiskey bottles on the table, then moved behind the bar and started tossing full bottles. "They put me in jail overnight," Muddy admitted. "But mostly, you know, I didn't do that. I wanted to be nationally known, and I worked on it."[30]

Eddie Boyd soon went his own way musically. Although he said he was looking for a guitar player with a jazzier, more uptown sound than Muddy could deliver — like recording artist Johnny Moore — he left to play with Sonny Boy Williamson in Gary, Indiana. Muddy said of Eddie, "He wanted it to be a kind of sweet blues."[31] That was not on Muddy's agenda.

Albert Luandrew, better known as Sunnyland Slim, took over on piano at the Flame. He'd been an acquaintance of Muddy's in the Delta, where in order to avoid his stepmother and plowing with mules, he found solace in teaching himself to play piano at the home of a neighbor and in honky-tonks. After playing throughout the South and living in Memphis for a stretch, he moved to Chicago in 1942. Of Muddy, Sunnyland commented, "He's a good person. Always was. He's the goodest person you could meet."[32]

With Sunnyland on board, the gig at the Flame stretched to four or five weeks. Then one night it ended abruptly. Smitty prolonged his break into a two-hour tryst with a young lady, abandoning Muddy and Sunnyland to carry the next set. Doc Britton, not amused at paying for three musicians and getting a duo, fired them all.

The band's next gig was at the Purple Cat on the West Side, where Little Walter joined them on harmonica. Blue Smitty claimed that Jimmy Rogers was having "girl trouble" at this point, so was taking a hiatus from the band. Sunnyland then got them a run at the Cotton Club, at Clybourn and Halsted streets. They had been there a week when Smitty's late arrival gave rise to a scuffle with Sunnyland, and another job was lost.

Perhaps it was because Smitty was more intent on jazz than on blues — or as Rogers maintains, because he wasn't very interested in any kind of music career — that he was an unreliable band mate to Muddy and Jimmy. Smitty didn't stay with their band long; he moved to the southern Chicago suburb of Harvey and started his own group. In 1952 he recorded for the Chess label, but poor sales effectively ended his recording career.

During this time Muddy took on other gigs as a sideman. Sunnyland Slim would call on him from time to time, as would Memphis Slim, Johnny Young and Big Bill Broonzy. With his eye on Muddy's car, Sonny Boy Williamson would still hire him, especially when he was booked at the Spot in Gary, Indiana. For these dates with Sonny Boy, Muddy would tune down his guitar and play bass.

Jimmy Rogers contends that club owners would bring in Sonny Boy knowing full well he'd get too drunk to finish off the night. His records had made him popular, so his name on the marquee was a drawing card. The band and most of the audience realized, however, that the rest of the musicians would have to take over once the lead attraction became too rowdy or passed out. Sonny Boy didn't care; he was being paid next to nothing. If Jimmy was playing that night, he'd switch from guitar to harmonica and fill Sonny Boy's spot singing his songs.

Not long afterwards Muddy, Jimmy and Little Walter stopped playing with other musicians and concentrated on working together — Muddy supplying vocals and slide guitar, Jimmy with his guitar tuned down to play bass and rhythm and Little Walter on

76

harmonica. According to Rogers, from its inception the band was meant to be an all-star unit; it was not intended that he and Walter be sidemen behind Muddy. Each band member possessed such extraordinary gifts that the purpose of the group was to showcase each one equally.

The three were in total accord in their driving ambition to achieve success. Jimmy says, "We never had any arguments or anything. Little Walter and Muddy and myself, we got along very good." Nevertheless, he does admit that "sometimes we had a little problem with Walter getting wild and trying to start humbugging with somebody."[33]

Their first gigs were house parties, then eventually the trio was hired at the Zanzibar, where they got their start. Then as other club managers dropped by to hear the band, they'd lure them to new venues with a few more bucks. As Muddy described it, he still played "deep-bottom" Delta blues. His was "a rustier sound, a grittier sound"[34] than was currently popular; it was music that evoked emotion, that tore at your heart and made your gut ache. By working with the meatier sound and the power of projection that electric amplification could deliver, as well as his more confident, aggressive vocals, Muddy contemporized the tone and tempo of his music while maintaining the soul of down-home blues. But despite his innovations, he remained a conservative performer, still lacking the confidence that was his hallmark in later years. He'd either stand in one place or sit to play.

As Little Walter struggled to perfect his timing, other musicians would sometimes laugh at him. Snooky Pryor remembers Walter's early harp work as sloppy and his singing poor. But his brilliant natural aptitude, his willingness to put in hours of solitary practice and his ability to absorb and mimic everything he heard combined to push him steadily towards a higher musical standard. His personality was his real impediment. When a more seasoned harpman would try to show him a few licks, Little Walter stalked off in a rage. Although he never admitted it, he'd practice the veteran's technique at home until he had it down. Then, typically, he'd reappear, claiming it as his own.

Outsiders may not have understood Walter, but Muddy and Jimmy did. "He had kind of a bad temper," Muddy confessed, "but he was a great guy, man . . . and if he wanted to love you he loved you."[35]

When Muddy's guitar and Jimmy's amp were stolen from Joe Rico's club on Lake Street, Walter was the main suspect. His band mates didn't believe it for a minute. They borrowed equipment to play the weekend gig, then used their credit account at the music store at 18th and Halsted to buy new gear, including a Gretsch guitar with a DeArmond pickup for Muddy.

The three musicians traveled in a pack; they were like brothers. "We always had laughing and talking and had our own little thing going to have fun whilst we were on the bandstand,"[36] Muddy recalled fondly. After playing a gig, they'd often appear at a jam session where they'd obliterate the other bands. Or they'd go somewhere to hear another musician's last set, and the audience would insist they get up and play. According to Muddy, if there was a battle of the bands, the trio would set out to burn the competition. It got to the point that they weren't allowed to compete. "Uh, uh, Muddy — you's *too heavy*," Muddy remembered a club manager admonishing him. "You can work for me if you wants, but you's too heavy to be in the contest."[37] People began to refer to them as the Headhunters and the Headcutters, although, according to Jimmy, those were never names they called themselves. When they performed in a club, the marquee would read Muddy Waters, Jimmy Rogers and Little Walter Jacobs.

Incongruous with its tough-guy image, the band was no rough-and-tumble outfit. No matter what ghetto tavern the three performed in, they adhered to the strict dress code dictated by union regulations. They always wore jackets and ties, and for years they sported matching uniforms.

Once they were getting regular club gigs, Muddy didn't want Walter busking on the streets anymore. Walter resisted; he was able to earn $35 to $40 a day on Maxwell Street, more than he'd get in a tavern. The memory made Muddy chuckle: "I had to chase him out of Jewtown regular. He'd see me coming, and grab his mike and *gone!*"[38] As for Muddy, he still maintained a day job. His half-sister's husband, Dan Jones, had gotten him a position driving a delivery truck for the Western Graves Venetian Blinds Company at 22nd and Canal streets.

Meanwhile, Leonard and Phil Chess were scouring the Chicago club scene, seeking out fresh talent for their fledgling record company. Leonard was born as Lazer Shmuel Chez on 12 March 1917 in the poor Jewish village of Motol, Poland, and Phil was born five years later. In the early 1920s, their father emigrated to Chicago, and in 1928 his wife and their three children joined him. At Ellis Island, New York, Leonard's mother hid the leg brace that Leonard wore as a result of his bout with polio, fearing it would prevent his admission to the United States. He never wore it again.

In their desire to break free from the persecution and poverty that oppressed many Jews in Europe, the Chez family was not unlike the black migrants who were trying to escape the same conditions in the South. They settled in a Jewish neighborhood on the western edge of the black South Side ghetto, and Leonard and Phil grew up speaking the black vernacular. After graduating from high school, Leonard moved through a succession of jobs — newspaper vendor, milkman, shoe salesman — and worked in his father's junkyard. Leonard and Phil Americanized their surname to Chess, and by the early 1940s they owned several liquor stores and bars on Chicago's South Side.

The last of their club acquisitions was the well-known Macomba Lounge at 39th Street and Cottage Grove Avenue. It was a raucous venue for emerging jazz performers — including Ella Fitzgerald, Billy Eckstine, Louis Armstrong, Lionel Hampton, Gene Ammons, Jump Jackson and Billie Holiday — as well as a hangout for dope dealers and prostitutes. Then in 1946, when various record companies expressed an interest in signing Andrew Tibbs, the singer of the Macomba'a house band, Leonard decided to do it himself. Together with Phil and partners Evelyn Aron and her husband, he set up a storefront office at 71st Street and Phillips Avenue . . . and the Aristocrat Record Corporation was born.

The company was launched to the accompaniment of outrage. Its first release by Tibbs paired "Union Man Blues" on side A with "Bilbo Is Dead" on the flip. Unionists, infuriated by the first song, refused to deliver the records, and many were smashed. "Bilbo Is Dead" — referring to the demise of the racist U.S. senator from Mississippi — so inflamed southern authorities that it was banned in the South. Still, enough copies were sold to keep the business afloat. This disc was followed by more recordings by Tibbs, as well as sides by the Five Blazes, Jump Jackson's Orchestra, the Dozier Boys, the Tom Archia All Stars, Jo Jo Adams and Lee Monti.

Muddy ran into Aristocrat's talent scout, Sammy Goldberg, down at the musicians' union hall. Although Aristocrat's initial discs were mostly jazz, Goldberg was betting that blues would be a hit with its black audience. Muddy, however, was in a terrible predicament — there was Goldberg asking for an impromptu audition and he didn't have his guitar! The great Lonnie Johnson, a guitarist, vocalist and composer who'd been winning acclaim for his prolific output of jazz and blues records since 1925, was also at the hall and, although they'd never met, Muddy asked if he could borrow his instrument. He was desperate not to let this golden opportunity slip away, but it seems Johnson had a rule never to lend his guitar. Looking back, Muddy believed that Johnson's motivation was to keep the field clear and not encourage new talent, in stark opposition to Muddy's own future actions. According to Muddy, Goldberg implored Johnson, saying, "Let the man play one piece on the guitar. What he gonna do to it? He can't *eat* it."[39] So Muddy did his thing, belting out a few numbers that left Goldberg with no doubt that here was a hot new property for Aristocrat to call upon.

Acting on his hunch that blues would be a big seller, Goldberg arranged a session with Sunnyland Slim at the tail end of an Andrew Tibbs recording date at Universal Studios, the facility where the Chess brothers made most of their recordings until 1954. Initially the session had been conceived as Sunnyland providing vocals and piano with only the bass player from Tibbs's session, Big Ernest Crawford, to back him. When it was later decided to add a guitar, Goldberg sent Sunnyland off on a streetcar in hot pursuit of Muddy. They needed him right away.

But Muddy wasn't home! His live-in girlfriend, Annie Mae, said he was off in the company truck, making deliveries for Western Graves Venetian Blinds. Muddy's pal Andrew "Bo" Bolden, who'd dropped by for a chat, knew how much this opportunity could mean to Muddy's career and managed to track him down. Muddy greeted the news with a whoop of excitement. He knew where his priorities lay, and they weren't with a truckload of blinds. He pulled up to the nearest phone booth and, as he later admitted, "I lied, a big old lie that time. I told him they found my cousin in the alley, dead, and I had to get off. But I had paid, I paid for it 'cause it was a big one."[40] Bo took over the wheel to complete his buddy's rounds, while Muddy rushed home, grabbed his guitar and tore off to the studios on North Wacker Drive in time for the two o'clock session.

Sunnyland fronted two recordings: "Johnson Machine Gun," in which Muddy's single-string guitar work remains strictly in the background, and "Fly Right, Little Girl," in which the guitar is more evident. Then Muddy piped up. "Let me do one by myself,"[41] he suggested, and gave them a sample of his full, rich vocals. Big Crawford joined in, bumping time on his upright bass. "It filled up the empty spots," Muddy explained. Big Crawford chuckled and had a good ol' time. "This is my type of stuff," he confessed.[42]

Hoping to hit upon what Aristocrat was after, Muddy was granted the opportunity to record two of his own compositions, "Gypsy Woman" and "Little Anna Mae." Stylistically this session is similar to his previous Columbia recordings; again Muddy lays aside his slide and plays finger-style guitar. The difference this time is that his picking is much improved, incorporating licks he'd worked hard to learn from Blue Smitty and Jimmy Rogers.

The lyrics of "Gypsy Woman" draw the listener into the mystic aura of the Delta, an ambience that Muddy would later call upon in numbers such as "Hoochie Coochie Man" and "Louisiana Blues." In "Little Anna Mae," he bemoans a breakup with his real-life lover, which he attributes to her outside escapades. Muddy and Sunnyland recorded their four numbers in less than an hour and a half. Once again Muddy was paid as a sideman.

Leonard Chess was uninspired. He wasn't convinced that Muddy's sound was what the black record-buying public really wanted. Even though Muddy would drop in at Aristocrat from time to time to try to instigate some movement on Leonard's part, the company held back release of "Gypsy Woman" for several months. As Muddy remembered it, Leonard "was believing in Tom Archia, and Andrew Tibbs, Gene Ammons, so everybody's record out two or three times before mine. I still was up on the shelf."[43]

When "Gypsy Woman" finally became available on disc in the spring of 1947, Leonard maintained his skepticism and barely promoted it. Public response was lukewarm. This, like Muddy's other false starts, left him frustrated. He knew he had what it took to record a hit. He was on the threshold of celebrity — he could taste it.

Muddy still spent his days driving a truck for Western Graves and, although it wasn't where his heart lay, he was able to make it rather enjoyable, later describing it as "the best job I ever had in my life."[44] After he learned his route, he adapted the day job to the demands of working every night with his band. Muddy would dash through his deliveries to finish by early afternoon, allowing him at least four hours' sleep before he had to make a final drop-off at the post office. Then he'd head out for a night of playing, taking aim at his dreams and almost doubling his income in the process.

At least one teenaged street-corner musician, amongst the band's burgeoning number of loyal fans, regarded Muddy as his hero. Because he was underage, Ellas McDaniel, better known as Bo Diddley, would sneak into clubs and hide behind the jukebox to hear Muddy play. He describes Muddy as being the "engine" in "a hell of a band."[45] Although he'd often get nabbed and tossed into the street, young Bo would soon be back. "I just had to hear me some more Muddy Waters," he explains.[46] He longed to emulate the source of his inspiration, "But I couldn't even begin to think about being the man he is in the blues bag," Bo concedes. "Muddy is the greatest."[47]

In April 1948 Muddy got a call from Aristocrat asking him to record again. It wasn't that Leonard had changed his mind about Muddy's music; one story goes that he simply wanted to amass recorded tracks in case the American Federation of Musicians enforced another recording ban, like it had done in 1942. It's also possible he was pressured into it by his partner Evelyn Aron or by Sammy Goldberg. Whatever the reason, Muddy agreed without hesitation. He was getting another kick at the can and that's all that mattered.

Before the recording began, Muddy ran through his tunes in the studio. Consistently dubious, Leonard grumbled that he couldn't understand the lyrics. But Evelyn was enthusiastic about Muddy's potential. She had a deeper understanding of blues than Leonard; furthermore, she'd picked up on the sexual undercurrent of Muddy's music, which could translate into big sales to the female market.

Backing Muddy again at this session were Sunnyland Slim and Big Crawford; the only new addition was Alex Atkins on alto sax. Muddy recorded all original material: "Good Lookin' Woman," "Mean Disposition," "I Can't Be Satisfied" and "I Feel Like Going Home." "Good Lookin' Woman" and "Mean Disposition" both feature Muddy's finger-style guitar work, which is suggestive of jump blues, particularly his solo in "Mean Disposition." Sunnyland is in fine form on the piano, especially in "Good Lookin' Woman"; Atkins's saxophone is mainly relegated to the background.

Sunnyland Slim then took over lead vocals on two of his own songs. Muddy grabs single-string guitar solos in Sunnyland's "She Ain't Nowhere," a jump-blues number propelled by a jazzy sax and thumping bass, and in the slow blues "My Baby, My Baby."

To balance Muddy's first two tunes, Leonard called for a more stripped-down, basic sound on "I Can't Be Satisfied" and "I Feel Like Going Home"; only Big Crawford's lively bass lines backed Muddy's amplified slide guitar. Leonard was looking for a down-home sound, an equivalent to Houston's hit maker, Sam "Lightnin'" Hopkins. Now that Muddy was recording on slide — for the first time since the Library of Congress cuts — the confidence and power of his musicianship were overwhelming. "I Can't Be Satisfied" was created from two songs Muddy recorded on Stovall: "I Be's Troubled" (1941) and "I Be Bound To Write To You" (1942). His slide work is similar to that of his earlier recordings, but the addition of amplification provides more volume and sustain for his guitar. As well, Muddy's voice has gained richness and expressiveness. In "I Can't Be Satisfied," his guitar not only mirrors his vocals, but his voice is like another swooping slide, enhanced by his unique phrasing. Big Crawford's snapping bass provides a sprightly rhythm.

"I Feel Like Going Home" was also rehabilitated from the 1941 and 1942 sessions, when Muddy recorded it as "Country Blues," but the lineage of the song ties it directly to Robert Johnson and Son House. In the Aristocrat cut, Muddy's masterful voice is again like an instrument, undulating throughout an impressive range, providing the lead for his echoing slide.

Because none of his other recording artists were selling well, Leonard reluctantly took a risk, and Aristocrat pressed 3,000 78s of "I Can't Be Satisfied" and "I Feel Like Going Home." Ironically those were the two tunes that, in their earlier versions, were paired on the disc that Alan Lomax sent Muddy back in January 1942. The Aristocrat sides hit the shops of South Side Chicago around noon one Saturday that April. There were few record stores then; discs were retailed primarily by little neighborhood businesses, ranging from corner stores to beauty salons. Muddy's record was a smash! Within 24 hours it was almost completely sold out.

Muddy was euphoric. Reality was finally catching up with his dreams. Puffed up with newfound glory, he ventured into the vibrant Maxwell Street Market the next morning to buy a couple of his own discs while they were still available. Weaving his way through the throngs of boisterous shoppers, Muddy headed for the Maxwell Radio Record Company. Crammed in amongst a hodge-podge of disorganized stock was the record Muddy was after. But the shrewd owner, Bernard Abrams, knew a hot piece of merchandise when he saw it. He'd already jacked up Muddy's 78 from the list price of 79 cents to $1.10 and was hoarding them, only allowing one per customer — even to Muddy! Annoyed and overcharged, Muddy left the store with a single copy of his disc tucked under his arm. He sent Annie Mae back later that day to buy another.

Leonard Chess hadn't bargained on this avalanche of sales. Aristocrat immediately began pressing more of Muddy's records, working around the clock to meet the huge demand. Thousands of copies were snapped up, mainly in Chicago's black neighborhoods and then throughout the South. It was that potent mix of traditional and contemporary blues, spiked with a heady dollop of sexuality, that satisfied the taste of the blues-buying public.

As the record mounted to number 11 on both the *Juke Box* and *Best Seller* R&B charts (at the same time Andrew Tibbs's sales were flat), Leonard became a converted man. He started calling his ol' pal Muddy, inviting him over to the studio for lunch. "Yeah, [Leonard] was my buddy," Muddy fondly reminisced, "but I was glad, though, man. Hey, I had worked all my life for that. I wasn't thinkin' about [the] money part of it that much because I had worked all my life to get my name up there, and that was the truth."[48]

From this first triumph, Leonard and Muddy formed a tight relationship that would play a key role in generating the string of successes that followed. Muddy believed that Leonard was the best producer in the business and recognized Aristocrat's contribution to his breakthrough as a recording artist. Without ever signing a contract, with only a handshake to seal the deal, Muddy stated flatly, "I belongs to the Chess family."[49]

At 33, Muddy's breakthrough was hard won — that track from Stovall had proven a long, rough road to tread. Suddenly celebrated recording artists were acknowledging his existence. As the toast of Chicago blues, he recalled his proclamation as a Delta field hand: "I wanted to be a known person. All of my life that's what I worked for."[50]

Still driving a truck by day, Muddy would drop in at the taverns along his route, checking their jukeboxes for his disc. He would swell with pride when a patron punched his tune. Now he was basking in the type of attention he'd always yearned for. The stamp of public approval was what Muddy craved, and by the steamy summer of 1948 he had it. "All of a sudden I became Muddy Waters," he reflected with amazement. "You know? Just overnight. People started to speakin', hollerin' across the streets at me."[51]

After a night of playing at a club, Muddy would cruise home in his convertible with the top down. He could hear his tunes wafting through the open windows of ghetto flats. Pulling up to the curb, he'd sit back and listen awhile. It was a profoundly satisfying experience, but also a little frightening. "One time I heard [my record] coming from way upstairs somewhere," Muddy recalled, "and it scared me. I thought I had died."[52]

NOTES

1 Robert Palmer, "Muddy Waters Is Singing the Real Deep Blues," *New York Times*, 27 Mar. 1981, sec. C6.

2 Nicholas Lemann, *The Promised Land: The Great Black Migration and How It Changed America* (New York: Alfred A. Knopf, 1991), 43.

3 Robert Palmer, *Deep Blues* (New York: Penguin, 1982), 14.

4 Margaret McKee and Fred Chisenhall, *Beale Black & Blue: Life and Music on Black America's Main Street* (Baton Rouge: Louisiana State University Press, 1981), 236.

5 Palmer, "Muddy Singing Deep Blues," 6.

6 Alfred Duckett, "I Have a Right to Sing the Blues," *Louisville Defender*, 14 Apr. 1955.

7 James Rooney, *Bossmen: Bill Munroe & Muddy Waters* (New York: The Dial Press, 1971), 109.

8 Duckett.

9 Duckett.

10 McKee and Chisenhall, 237.

11 Jim O'Neal and Amy O'Neal, "Muddy," *Living Blues* 64 (Mar.–Apr. 1985): 25.

12 O'Neal and O'Neal, 32.

13 Gayle Dean Wardlow, unpublished article for *78 Quarterly*, 1995.

14 Jimmy Rogers, interview with author, 26 Apr. 1995.

15 Jimmy Rogers, interview with author, 26 Apr. 1995. This assertion that Muddy

did not get an electric guitar in 1944 is substantiated by Blue Smitty's memory of Muddy trying to fix his pickup when they first met.

16 Tom Wheeler, "Muddy Waters & Johnny Winter," *Blues Guitar: The Men Who Made the Music: From the Pages of Guitar Player Magazine*, ed. Jas Obrecht (San Francisco: GPI, 1990), 73.

17 John Brim, interview with author, 28 May 1995.

18 O'Neal and O'Neal, 31.

19 O'Neal and O'Neal, 32.

20 Peter Guralnick, *Feel Like Going Home* (New York: Harper & Row, Publishers, 1989), 75.

21 Rooney, 112.

22 Jimmy Rogers, interview with author, 26 Apr. 1995.

23 Charles Shaar Murray, "The Blues Had a Baby and They Called It Rock 'n' Roll," *New Musical Express* (30 Apr. 1977): 27.

24 Murray, 27.

25 Guy "Doc" Lerner, "Muddy Harps," *Living Blues* 99 (Sept.–Oct.1991): 34.

26 Palmer, *Deep Blues*, 145.

27 Pete Welding, "An Interview with Muddy Waters," *The American Folk Music Occasional*, 2 (1970): 6.

28 Jim O'Neal, "Chicago Blues Yesterday and Today: Blue Smitty, Part Two," *Living Blues* 45/46 (Spring 1980): 55.

29 O'Neal, 55.

30 Palmer, *Deep Blues*, 156.

31 Mike Rowe, *Chicago Breakdown* (London: Eddison Press Ltd, 1973), 67.

32 Bruce Cook, *Listen to the Blues* (New York: Charles Scribner's Sons, 1973), 136.

33 Jimmy Rogers, interview with author, 26 Apr. 1995.

34 Wheeler, 73.

35 Murray, 27.

36 Guralnick, 77.

37 Jas Obrecht, "The Life and Times of the Hoochie Coochie Man," *Guitar Player* (Mar. 1994): 36.

38 O'Neal and O'Neal, 33.

39 O'Neal and O'Neal, 26.

40 O'Neal and O'Neal, 34.

41 O'Neal and O'Neal, 32.

42 O'Neal and O'Neal, 32.

43 O'Neal and O'Neal, 34.

44 Palmer, *Deep Blues*, 156.

45 Bo Diddley, interview with author, 26 July 1995.

46 Bo Diddley, interview with author, 26 July 1995.

47 Robert Neff and Anthony Conner, *Blues* (Boston: David R. Godine, 1975), 75.

48 O'Neal and O'Neal, 35.

49 Pete Golkin, "Blacks Whites and Blues: The Story of Chess Records, Part One," *Living Blues* 88 (Sept.–Oct. 1989): 25.

50 Rooney, 107.

51 O'Neal and O'Neal, 35.

52 Palmer, *Deep Blues*, 160.

4

I was hotter than a pepper pie.[1]

The birth of Chicago blues is said to originate with "I Can't Be Satisfied" and "I Feel Like Going Home." Not so. Without harmonica, piano, rhythm guitar or drums, these country tunes had only amplification to tie them to the future of blues. It was the sound Muddy Waters was creating in the clubs that hatched the revolution.

In those ghetto taverns, Muddy was spearheading an upheaval. He was infusing Delta blues with a shot of raw power that dislocated its focus from the languorous South to the raunchy vitality of postwar Chicago. This was not merely country blues dressed up for the big city. Muddy had no intention of simply transplanting his Delta blues to an urban setting.

It's obvious from his choice of instrumentation and band mates. A piano and harmonica replaced the fiddle and mandolin of the Son Simms Four. That alone transformed the sound of Muddy's music. As well, Muddy's trio represented a departure from the standard formula of one lead musician backed by a rhythm section that stayed strictly in the background. In this band all three members were featured performers. They interacted, playing off each other, ducking in and out of the lead.

By taking guitar lessons from Blue Smitty and Jimmy Rogers, Muddy proved he had no intention of standing still musically. He was stretching Delta blues from its rural roots to suit a city lifestyle, while retaining its primal soul. As he searched for his place and sound, Muddy tried both finger-style and slide guitar. And while he reverted to playing predominantly slide, he now combined it with finger-style techniques, setting it apart from the way he played in Mississippi.

The electric sound Muddy was originating updated traditional blues to express the realities of a mechanized, urban existence. As a tight, cohesive unit laying down a new brand of blues, Muddy's band was one of the first to work with amplification as more than a mere convenience to break through the background hubbub of ghetto bars. His brash, aggressive style mirrored the brutality of life in the slums. Black audiences heard their own struggle, their own emotions captured in his blues. By exploring electricity as a means of expression and as a way to create fresh sounds, Muddy predated the Jimi Hendrix Experience by 20 years.

But Muddy wasn't alone in his exploration of amplification. Charlie Christian and Aaron "T-Bone" Walker led the pack, with bluesmen Clarence "Gatemouth" Brown, Eddie "Guitar Slim" Jones, Willie Johnson, B.B. King and many others nipping at their heels. Large recording companies, such as Columbia and RCA Victor, and most independent labels didn't detect the lucrative market hungry for this conversion of country blues. By stepping into this void, Aristocrat made recording history.

Muddy's disc continued to sell in Chicago and Detroit and in the black belt down through St. Louis and into the South. He was in demand, although the stripped-down instrumentation of his 1948 hits contrasted sharply with the full palette of sound he was now producing with his band. The small tavern they were playing doubled its profits with the release of Muddy's record, and larger, more prestigious clubs were anxious to lure the trio their way. They packed them in at the Du Drop Lounge on the South Side and at the West Side's Boogie Woogie Inn and the Club Zanzibar.

Due to Muddy's successful record and the others that would follow, his popularity was gradually eclipsing that of Jimmy Rogers and Little Walter. The concept of the band as an all-star unit began to founder as Muddy's growing celebrity propelled him more and more into the role of frontman. "I made Chicago the blues town," Muddy asserted. "After I got out a few records, I was drawing so many people, I was overloading them houses every place I went. I was hotter than a pepper pie, you know."[2]

Nevertheless, Muddy was not yet confident enough in his burgeoning career to give up the security of his day job. "I was playing seven nights a week and working six days," he recollected, "making, I think I was getting on my job $38 or $40 a week. . . . I was making $35 a week from playing seven nights, $5 a night."[3] He'd keep delivering venetian blinds until he had a couple of hit records under his belt.

Amidst a ghetto percolating with violence, the clubs the band played were rough joints, especially the Zanzibar, where patrons ranged from hookers and rounders to factory workers looking to blow off some steam. Jimmy Rogers recalls the brawls that would often erupt: "Somebody'd look at somebody else's girl, and there you go."[4] Muddy confessed to packing a pistol for his own security, although he never had to fire it. Tragically, John Lee "Sonny Boy" Williamson fell victim to this rampant violence one night while walking a few blocks home from the Plantation, a South Side tavern located at 328 East 31st Street. A casualty of a savage robbery, he died of head injuries a few hours later on 1 June 1948. Cut down at only 34, the harmonica virtuoso had nevertheless blazed a trail along which subsequent masters, such as Little Walter, would tread.

By this time "Baby Face" Leroy Foster had become part of Muddy's group, playing some guitar and singing, but primarily laying down the beat as Muddy's first drummer. A cousin of pianist Little Johnny Jones, Foster was born in Mobile, Alabama, around 1920 and raised just east of the Delta, in Coffeeville, Mississippi. In about 1946 he moved to Chicago, where he performed with Sunnyland Slim, John Lee "Sonny Boy" Williamson and Lee Brown. He was a regular patron at Muddy's gigs, then started playing with the band, although Rogers maintains Foster was never committed to a career in music. Because Foster played Texas-style blues, Muddy admitted, "Baby Face on guitar never did fit very good."[5] Still, he was a jovial, likable fellow who loved to talk and crack jokes, notorious for his affinity for the bottle and his drunken escapades.

This then was the band that made music history: Muddy on slide, Jimmy on second guitar, Little Walter on harmonica and Leroy on drums. Muddy was the lead singer, although he did share vocals with Jimmy. (At this time, according to Rogers, Walter wasn't singing at all.) Now Muddy had all the components necessary to deliver the evolving sound of Chicago blues. "That's when we began hitting heavy," Muddy declared.[6]

With Foster's beat solidly backing the melody, Muddy considered his band the first to bring steady time to Chicago blues. He was modernizing that clocklike rhythm he'd heard from Rice Miller and Robert Johnson back in the Delta. He slowed down the beat and altered the rhythm of contemporary jazzy blues, transplanting it onto his own grittier sound. "The big drop afterbeat on the drum formed the foundation of my blues," Muddy explained. "Nothing fancy — just a straight, heavy beat with it."[7] While the backbeat — with the emphasis on the second and fourth beats of a bar — didn't originate with Muddy, he was the artist who popularized it. It was through Muddy's music that this rhythm would become the heartbeat of rock 'n' roll.

With amplification surging his music to new levels of intensity, propelled with a steady backbeat for added definition and drive, Muddy had developed his own signature sound: "I took the old-time music and brought it up to date. You've got to stay alive with it. . . . I am still an old-time singer, but I brought it out more."[8]

Jimmy Rogers was an essential ingredient in the mix, laying down bass and rhythm riffs with an impeccable sense of timing, providing the bedrock on which Muddy and Walter could build. Because he'd been a harmonica player, Rogers knew how to make his guitar support and complement the harp. "I guess that's why we could team together so good," Jimmy reflects. "We fit in real good together . . . because we had worked together a long time, and I knew which way [Muddy] was going and how to cover him, and Walter was the same way."[9] Describing his contribution to the band, Jimmy says, "I put some gravy to what we was doing."[10]

And Muddy knew his harmonica player was the best in the business. "He had a thing on the harp that nobody had," he said of Little Walter. "He could really understand the blues and he knew what to put in there and when to put it in there. So all I can say is that he is the greatest I've ever heard."[11] James Cotton, a future member of Muddy's band and a harmonica titan in his own right, declares that Walter was a genius with the instrument. "He changed the times, you know, like the Beatles or the Rolling Stones. Not only changed the songs . . . he changed the times along with it."[12] Harp bluesman Shakey Jake Harris said that "Walter could take one harmonica — an A harmonica — and play pretty near every key that's possible on harmonica." Of the emotion he exuded, Harris stated simply, "Walter could make you cry."[13]

It was Walter's acute imagination, combined with his masterful technique and the unerring finesse of what to play and when, that ensconced him at the forefront of blues harmonica giants. With his towering talent, the previously humble harp could wail like a saxophone, swell like an organ into a mountain of sound or lay down the percussive framework of a rhythm guitar. Roaring like a tornado, Walter's harmonica could burst forth with pyrotechnical bedazzlement, then break your heart with a moan.

Muddy's biting slide guitar can be heard behind "St. Louis" Jimmy Oden on Oden's 1948 Aristocrat recording of "Florida Hurricane" and "So Nice And Kind." Backed also by Oliver Alcorn on tenor saxophone, Sunnyland Slim and Big Crawford, Oden's numbers are lightweight in comparison with Muddy's. Only when Muddy slides in with his solos does Oden's music drop down deep into soulful blues.

A momentous recording session, also in 1948, brought Muddy and Little Walter together on vinyl for the first time, although not under the auspices of Aristocrat. Again it was thanks to Sunnyland Slim, who'd booked studio time with a club manager named Big Earl, owner of Tempo Tone Records, a small and ultimately unsuccessful Chicago label. In addition to Muddy, Walter and Sunnyland, Floyd Jones played guitar and Leroy Foster manned the drums. The first cut on the Tempo Tone session, "Blue Baby," features Walter on vocals and harmonica, with Muddy finger-picking the guitar behind him. The second track, "I Want My

Baby," is a jump-blues number more reminiscent of the past than the future; here again Muddy supplies finger-style guitar backing. Sunnyland takes lead vocals, and Muddy and Walter sing the refrain. While the session was less than impressive, it was the closest thing to Muddy's full band that had so far been recorded.

In the fall of 1948, Muddy was back at Aristocrat, cutting a session with only Big Crawford behind him on bass. In contrast to the Tempo Tone outing, Leonard Chess compelled Muddy to take a backward step and leave his band in the South Side taverns. Muddy's originality was lacking this day. He recycles the tune of his 1946 "Mean Red Spider" in "Train Fare Home" and "Sittin' Here And Drinkin'." Vestiges of that melody are also detectable in his cover of "Kind Hearted Woman," a Robert Johnson composition. The roots of Muddy's 1951 hit "Honey Bee" may also be traced to these songs. The other cut from this session, "Down South Blues," borrows heavily from the tune of "Hambone" Willie Newbern's "Roll And Tumble Blues."

On 30 November 1948, Muddy returned to Aristocrat, again with Big Crawford, but also with Leroy Foster on guitar. "You're Gonna Miss Me" was the title of a song Muddy had recorded twice for Alan Lomax in 1942. This time out, however, the verses are different, the tempo is accelerated and the tune resembles that of "I Can't Be Satisfied." Accompanied by Big Crawford's slapping bass, Muddy's slide solo is a savory feast.

The other numbers recorded during this session — "Mean Red Spider," "Streamline Woman" and "Hard Days" — share similarities in melody. "Mean Red Spider," of course, predated the other two, as it was the song that Muddy recorded for the 20th Century label in 1946. Here, however, Muddy adds a verse from Robert "Junior" Lockwood's "Mean Black Spider," drops two previous verses and makes the spider female. The stripped-down instrumentation of this 1948 version is in favorable contrast to the busy horns of the 1946 cut.

"Streamline Woman" was the number with the most longevity; in live performances throughout Muddy's life, he would whip audiences into delirium with the song's raw, vicious slide solo. The 1948 Aristocrat session also included a rare instrumental, "Muddy Jumps One," a country-influenced, upbeat number, anchored by Big Crawford's memorable bass. After Muddy's cuts, Foster took over lead vocals and guitar, backed by Muddy on second guitar and Crawford on bass, to record a jump blues called "Locked Out Boogie" and "Shady Grove Blues."

Also that month Muddy repaid an old friend who'd taught him some guitar licks on Stovall. He took Robert Nighthawk to Aristocrat for an audition. Leonard liked what he heard, and Nighthawk recorded his first cut for the label — "My Sweet Lovin' Woman" — on 10 November 1948. Although Muddy also recommended Robert "Junior" Lockwood, Leonard declined to sign him on.

About this time Muddy met and married Geneva Wade, a woman one year younger than himself from Lexington, Mississippi. "I'd come across many, many women," Muddy reflected, "but it seems like you know immediately when you find the one who's exactly right for you.... [She] encouraged me to ... fight for what I wanted to accomplish. I'll never be able to put into words the way I feel about her, her love and support."[14] Geneva and Muddy raised Geneva's young sons Charles and Dennis, and Muddy's teenaged daughter Isoline, born out of wedlock in Mississippi, also lived with them from time to time.

According to Muddy's half-brother Robert Morganfield, "[Geneva] was a very nice and devoted wife. She was always kind and helpful," and because she was more educated than Muddy, she took charge of his business affairs.[15] "I got along with Geneva real good," Jimmy Rogers recalls. "She called me her brother. She would come to our sets sometimes, not too much because she had to stick around and try to watch her son, and Muddy had a daughter who was older than her son Charles was. Muddy would try to keep her sometimes, but he couldn't do very much with her because she was kind of wild."[16]

Muddy paid tribute to his new love in "Little Geneva," which he cut on his next Aristocrat session in or about July 1949, backed again by Big Crawford's bass. As well, he recorded "Canary Bird," a tune with roots in "Mean Red Spider"; "Burying Ground," which he'd cut for Columbia in 1946 and would record with Little Walter in 1950 as "Sad Letter Blues"; and an unissued cut, "You Gonna Need My Help." Also that summer Muddy shared a session with pianist Johnny Jones and Leroy Foster on guitar and drums. After backing Jones on guitar for his two numbers, Muddy took the lead on the powerful "Screamin' And Cryin'," a wail of desolation lamenting happier times. In addition he recorded "Where's My Woman Been" and the up-tempo "Last Time I Fool Around With You." That same year Muddy, Little Walter, Big Crawford, either Sunnyland Slim or Johnny Jones on piano and an unknown drummer backed Jimmy Rogers on his unissued Regal cut of "Ludella." Once again Muddy and his fellow band members had to venture away from Aristocrat in order to record together.

"Chess wouldn't upset things," remarked Muddy, explaining Leonard's refusal to record him with his group.[17] That winning combination of Muddy backed by Big Crawford was not to be tampered with. Muddy and his band mates were frustrated. Every night they'd crank out their innovative blues as a tight, cohesive unit, yet each time Aristocrat called, only Muddy was welcome.

Aristocrat had sent Muddy on a few solo tours, but he wasn't keen to abandon his group. Finally he resolved to deliver his full band sound to southern audiences by combining radio performances with a tour of the area. Inspired by the blues programming on radio station KFFA in Helena, Arkansas, he phoned a Mr. Anderson there, who assured him that, if they came down, the band could play on its own show. What Anderson failed to mention until they arrived in October 1949, was that their spot was from six to seven o'clock each morning.

The show was sponsored by Katz Clothing in Helena. Although it only earned the band $5 a week, it proved the perfect vehicle for acquiring gigs and advertising those they already had. For about six weeks, the band rocked juke joints and dance halls in towns throughout the Delta, such as Cleveland, Boyle, Shelby and Clarksdale. Then in the wee hours of the morning, the exhausted crew would hop a ferry back across the Mississippi to Helena for a scant few hours' sleep before their six o'clock broadcast. One morning Little Walter and Jimmy awoke to the voice of their KFFA announcer on air: "Well, Jimmy Rogers and Little Walter is somewhere sleepin' off. If they hear us, come on in."[18]

The radio show and his successful recording career raised Muddy to a new level of prestige back on Stovall. Howard Stovall was entertaining a group of congressmen when Muddy dropped by, and the plantation owner proudly introduced his distinguished guests to the local celebrity. He insisted Muddy play. "He gives us, like seven dollars or eight dollars apiece and a whole good fifth of whisky," Muddy recalled. "Well when I was there living, you know, I couldn't make but a dollar and fifty cents there, you know."[19]

The stellar B.B. King, a fervent admirer of Muddy's recordings, met his icon for the first time in 1949, at a Chicago club where Muddy was appearing. "To me Muddy Waters was . . . the godfather of the blues, especially Chicago [blues],"[20] King remembers fondly. The fledgling performer held Muddy in such awe that he wouldn't consider joining him onstage. "I'd be afraid to. . . . Oh, God, no! To me he was like royalty," B.B. reminisces. "We later became good friends, but to see him *then* and jam, oh, no!"[21]

The flames of Muddy's passion could singe a crowd. While King and Muddy possessed divergent guitar styles, King would come to demonstrate a similar ability to stir an audience with the sincerity of his emotions. Early on, Muddy's spirit was the primary influence he exerted on B.B. "He had a lot of soul in what he did," King reflects. "He made you believe it. And that I like so much. He didn't do like a lot of entertainers do, just sing, just say it or just do it. . . . To me it seemed like each word he spoke in a song, his lyric, meant something to me, like a teacher or someone telling a story, and make sure you get the punchline and make sure you understood it. That's what he was to me."[22]

Freddie King was another future blues master who was inspired by Muddy and his band. As a teenager living with his parents right behind the Club Zanzibar at 13th and Ashland, Freddie would sneak in the side door and sit up front, even though the manager knew he was underage. As he intently studied the guitar techniques of Muddy and especially Jimmy, he kept an eye on the front door; if his father appeared, he'd have to make a speedy getaway. During the band's breaks, young Freddie would pester Jimmy with questions. It was Jimmy and Muddy who first taught Freddie to play with a thumbpick and a pick on his index finger. Later he'd occasionally sit in with the group.

Unhindered by Leonard Chess's ongoing refusal to record Muddy with his full band, the musicians (minus Jimmy Rogers) went to Parkway to cut a session in January 1950. The Parkway label had only recently been launched by Monroe Passis and brothers George and Ernie Leaner of Hit Record Distributors. Their first artists were Muddy, Little Walter and Leroy Foster, recording under the names of the Little Walter Trio and the Baby Face Trio. Here, at last, on disc was a taste of what Muddy and the band were dishing out each night in Chicago's clubs.

Still under contract to Aristocrat, Muddy attempted to remain incognito by foregoing lead vocals; of course, his ferocious slide blew his cover. Walter sings and plays harp on the rocking "I Just Keep Loving Her" and sets aside his harmonica for guitar and vocals in "Bad Acting Woman," "Muskadine Blues" and "Moonshine Blues." Foster's three numbers — "Boll Weevil," "Rollin' And Tumblin'" and "Red Headed Woman" — are unbridled free-for-alls. Especially raucous is his two-part version of "Rollin' And Tumblin'." A longstanding Delta standard, "Rollin' And Tumblin'" was first recorded by Gus Cannon's Jug Stompers in 1928 as "Minglewood Blues," then covered the following year by Charley Patton under the title "It Won't Be Long" and by "Hambone" Willie Newbern as "Roll And Tumble Blues." Muddy learned it from a recording he'd heard back on Stovall. "Ah, I think I played it better than anybody else I know and I was a 'Johnny-come-lately,'" he commented. "I met Son House, James Smith and all of them people, but I played it better than either one of them — except the one who made it on the record."[23]

Part one of Parkway's "Rollin' And Tumblin'" is an instrumental; Foster leads Walter and Muddy through a series of moans and wails, backed by Walter's harmonica, Muddy's vicious slide and the insistent beat of Foster's bass drum. The theme persists through part two, which includes some of Newbern's lyrics. Muddy and Walter battle to outdo each other here; their slide-guitar and harp duel still ranks among the most inspirational Chicago blues ever recorded. "To me that track's an example of somebody who transcends anything we think we know about the guitar,"[24] proclaims an awestruck Ry Cooder.

"Muddy got himself in pretty big trouble with Chess," chuckles Rogers, recalling the immediate fallout from the Parkway session. "Yeah, yeah they had a lot of fun! I laughed myself sick about it. Leonard didn't want Muddy to use that slide on any other label."[25] As a result Muddy was compelled to record his own version of "Rollin' And Tumblin'" for Aristocrat a few weeks later, in February 1950. This was to be the last Muddy Waters cut released on the Aristocrat label. Yet even Parkway's show of confidence in Muddy's band hadn't convinced Leonard to record Muddy with the other musicians. Again Muddy was relegated to the country format with only Big Crawford to lend a hand, forgoing the full-throttle, innovative sound he could achieve with the rest of his band.

In the two Aristocrat cuts of "Rollin' And Tumblin'," Muddy's slide resonates with his vocals in front of the snapping, percussive bass of Big Crawford. Although Muddy was given composer credit, this version, too, is clearly a knockoff of Newbern's "Roll And Tumble Blues"; it includes two verses from the 1929 disc. Robert Johnson had recorded much the same song in his mid-1930s number "If I Had Possession Over Judgment Day," and the melody of his "Traveling Riverside Blues" also resembles that of Newbern's song.

In the wake of his strong outing with Parkway, Leroy Foster left Muddy to embark upon his own career as a frontman. Meanwhile, Leonard put no stops on his headlong rush to release Aristocrat's version of "Rollin' And Tumblin'" in an attempt to steamroll the competition. It worked. Foster's rendition on the smaller, newly established and less influential Parkway label was effectively muffled. Foster went on to make further recordings, including another version of "Red Headed Woman" for Savoy in 1954. Unable to sustain a successful career as a recording artist, he later played with Snooky Pryor and Homesick James. Foster died of tuberculosis in 1961.

During his February 1950 Aristocrat session, Muddy also recorded "Rollin' Stone," a song that had been a hit for Robert Petway in 1941 as "Catfish Blues." Muddy's rendition was to become the progenitor of a mighty rock legacy: a shaggy group of young English blues rockers took the song title as the name of their band; the world's premier rock periodical claimed the title as well; and it inspired Bob Dylan to compose his anthem "Like A Rolling Stone." Better known for what it engendered than for itself, "Rollin' Stone" was more a peek back at Muddy's Delta days than a glimpse into the future of Chicago blues. Nevertheless, the power of Muddy's delivery can make one forget he was unaccompanied for both takes of this cut. He put down his slide and kept the rhythm driving with bass patterns on the bottom strings of his guitar, embellishing the end of each phrase with finger-style riffs. The recording so affected the young Jimi Hendrix that he later recorded it under its original title.

The last song recorded on that February day — "Walkin' Blues" — also had a well-established pedigree. Muddy first learned the tune from Son House, then was influenced by Robert Johnson's cut of it in the mid-1930s. In 1941 and 1942, Muddy had recorded his reworked version of the number for Lomax under the title "Country Blues." But the song Muddy delivered in 1950 was closer to Johnson's, except the verses were rearranged and one was omitted.

The year 1950 also marked the dissolution of Aristocrat Records. Unhappy in his partnership with the Arons, Leonard Chess had bought them out and was looking for a way to boost the company's growth when a record presser in Memphis suggested that he change the company's name from Aristocrat to Chess. Leonard liked the idea, and Aristocrat folded its tent as Chess Records assumed its position at the vanguard of popular-music history. Muddy's first disc for Chess paired two songs from his February session, "Rollin' Stone" and "Walkin' Blues." It was a hit in the black record-buying market, selling 80,000 copies in Chicago, Gary, Detroit and in the St. Louis-Memphis corridor into the South. While it was strictly a black phenomenon and limited to specific areas, the success of this 78 propelled Muddy to a new level of celebrity.

Muddy and his band were a smash at Ada's Lounge, the Ebony Lounge and the Du Drop Lounge, at 3609 Wentworth Avenue, where they waged blues battles against Memphis Minnie and Big Bill Broonzy and took no prisoners. Leonard Chess could no longer ignore the impact of Muddy's group. He finally relented and opened the door wide enough to permit Little Walter to join Muddy in the studio in the summer of 1950. Even without the rest of the group, the inclusion of Walter's wailing harmonica on Muddy's sides would mark the inception of a new era of Chicago blues.

In his long-awaited premiere on a Muddy Waters recording, Little Walter is anything but subtle. In "You're Gonna Need My Help I Said," his harp seizes center stage, backed by Muddy on slide and Big Crawford on percussive bass. His blowing is more restrained on "Sad Letter Blues," previously recorded in 1946 and 1949 as "Burying Ground Blues." In these cuts, however, Walter's playing lacks the effortless quality so evident in his later recordings. Perhaps Leonard had tried to curtail him, for this session, like all previous Aristocrat and Chess outings, has its stylistic feet planted resolutely in the Delta. Chess was still not willing to risk a sure thing for Muddy's urban blues.

And in Leonard's view, that risk included Jimmy Rogers. Although he was not permitted to play as part of Muddy's session, the band finished early and Muddy suggested that Jimmy cut "That's All Right," a number that Walter had recorded for Bernard Abrams in 1947. Backed by Little Walter, Big Crawford and what sounds like Muddy on guitar, Rogers ventures no closer to the urban sound the band was kicking out nightly — Leonard still resisted the inclusion of drums. But "That's All Right," with an August 1950 recording of "Ludella" on the flip, quickly became a hit for Rogers. Walter was so enthused by its success that he pushed Jimmy to leave the band with him and go off on their own. Although Jimmy did form another group with Eddie Ware on piano and a drummer named Willie, he maintained his commitment to Muddy's band while continuing to record as a frontman. Nevertheless, Walter's intention to quit Muddy was evident even now.

Then finally, on Muddy's session of 23 October 1950, Leonard allowed a drummer, Elgin Evans, to participate. At last Chess was ready to present the true sound of Chicago blues. With Evans's drums and Big Crawford on upright bass, "Louisiana Blues" is supported by a backbone of rhythm that would come to be a defining characteristic of Muddy's subsequent recordings. Little Walter breaks out in full force here with Muddy accompanying on slide. While lyrically it harkens back to the Delta, "Louisiana Blues" transcends its rural roots and identifies Muddy's blues as part of the urban landscape. It would earn Muddy the number-10 spot on the *Best Seller* R&B chart in January 1951, extending his reach to both coasts, far beyond his previous range.

Muddy also recorded "Evans Shuffle" at this session, as a tribute to Sam Evans, a club owner and disc jockey who'd promoted Muddy's blues on radio station WGES. Later Muddy attributed a large part of his success to the help of DJs all over the U.S., but Evans was the instigator, the one DJ who'd been right behind him from the beginning. This instrumental number is a departure from traditional blues, incorporating a touch of jazz set to a boogie beat. Walter is allowed full rein here. The track showcases his extraordinary ability, punctuated by Muddy's shouts of encouragement.

Muddy's all-time favorite song, "Long Distance Call," was recorded on 23 January 1951 along with "Too Young To Know," "Honey Bee" and "Howling Wolf." With Muddy on slide, Little Walter blowing harp and Big Crawford snapping behind them on bass, "Long Distance Call" presents the sound of a tight, seamless ensemble at work. It earned Muddy another berth on the top-10 *Best Seller* R&B chart in April 1951; at number eight, it was his strongest outing yet. And the victory was twofold; in July of that year, "Honey Bee" climbed to tenth position on the *Juke Box* R&B chart.

"Honey Bee" — a refashioning of Memphis Minnie's 1929 cut "Bumble Bee" — is an exceptional example of Muddy's artistry on slide, as his guitar stings and flutters behind his forceful, implicitly sexual vocals. For this song Little Walter switches to second guitar and plants down a bass line alongside Crawford. In "Howling Wolf" Muddy's lyrics are predatory, spiked with danger and echoed by Walter's plaintive harmonica.

With Muddy's session of 11 July 1951, the revolution continued apace. Little Walter used an amplified harp in the studio for the first time, although he'd been using one in live performances for years. From this point on, Walter's recorded output was unshackled, freed by the possibilities of technology. His playing became smoother, more hornlike as he forged ahead into unexplored musical territory. He was defining the harmonica as a lead instrument in Chicago blues.

This session also marked Leonard Chess's musical debut. The drummer they'd hired kept inserting a turnaround where there should only have been a straight-ahead beat, and according to Muddy, "Leonard knew where it was. So Leonard told him, 'Get the fuck out of the way. I'll do that,' " and took over on bass drum.[26] His sometimes faltering, plodding effort detracts from "She Moves Me," yet Leonard's drumming complements "Still A Fool" to perfection, a dark song — another descendant of "Catfish Blues" — fairly bursting with pent-up emotion and sexual tension. Here Little Walter sets aside his harmonica and backs Muddy on guitar. "[Walter] would get to the studio before time and play around — he did love to fool around with somebody's guitar," Jimmy recalls.[27]

This outing produced a double win for Muddy and Chess. "Still A Fool" held the number-nine position on the *Juke Box* R&B chart for three weeks straight beginning in November 1951. The following February *Best Seller* ranked "She Moves Me" number 10 on its R&B list.

Most of the songs Muddy recorded up to this point and for the next two and a half years were either his own compositions or reworked standards credited to him. They constitute a powerful library of tunes. In creating and recreating them, he conjured up the mystic essence of the Delta, set it to an urban pulse and probed the essence of universal human emotions. Muddy was able to tap his subconscious for much of his inspiration. "I used to dream a song when I was really deep into it," he recalled. "I'd dream and get up and wake my wife up and say, 'Hey, baby, put this down *now!*'"[28] Once he'd hit upon a concept, it took Muddy only about two hours to write a song. Looking back as an older performer, he described songwriting as a young man's game, a creative process that required a very sharp mind. Before a recording date, Muddy said he'd isolate himself for about a day in order to compose the four songs required for the session. "I didn't write down the tune either," he insisted. "I'd be thinking, singing the song in my mind and playing my guitar right along with it."[29]

Yet Jimmy Rogers doesn't share in the accolades over Muddy's songwriting skills. "You see Muddy wasn't a very good writer for himself," he states. "He was a nice guy and he was sincere in what he was doing, but he never was a very good writer."[30] Jimmy maintains that Muddy's songs were often a group effort — the entire band would develop the lyrics and the music together. "He'd come up with an idea, and we'd build from that," declares Rogers.[31]

For a while Muddy's handshake deal with Leonard Chess was close to collapse. Jimmy's rhythm guitar was a key component of the Muddy Waters sound, yet he continued to be excluded from Muddy's sessions. Rogers was frank in his assessment of Muddy's recordings to date, saying, "We have a good sound onstage, and the record don't sound as good."[32] Muddy was in full agreement.

"Well, I'm not going to record any more of this," Muddy told Jimmy. "If [Leonard] can't accept you with the group, I'll just go and find another company."[33] Sunnyland Slim was recruiting talent for some fledgling record labels and suggested Muddy ditch Chess for a company owned by fellow Mississippian Narvel Eatmon, popularly known as Cadillac Baby. Muddy seriously considered it. His departure from Chess Records was narrowly averted when Leonard finally agreed to try Rogers out at a session scheduled for 29 December 1951. "After [Leonard] decided to use me, we felt like that it was going to mean something if we could stick with it," Rogers explains. "Wasn't too much money, but [Leonard] had a good spread. He had good connections for promoting records and stuff."[34]

At last the Muddy Waters band could detonate the fuse of modern music. All the components of their unique sound were now assembled at Chess, backed by Big Crawford on bass and Elgin Evans on drums. On "Lonesome Day" and especially "Stuff You Gotta Watch" (which was based on a jump-blues hit by Buddy Johnson), the cohesive mix of instruments, led by Little Walter's harmonica, provides a full bed of sound to complement Muddy's rich vocals. Two versions of "All Night Long" were cut, one with the full band, the other — minus Rogers and Evans — an eerie cry for sexual satisfaction backed by echoing guitar and harmonica.

By this time the Muddy Waters band had developed an untitled instrumental it played at gigs several times a night. Reportedly a combination of Snooky Pryor's "Snooky And Moody's Boogie" and Sunnyland Slim's "Get Up Those Stairs Mademoiselle," the number was reworked by Muddy, Jimmy and Walter into a signature piece. Junior Wells, then the harmonica player for the Three Deuces, disagrees, claiming that it was originally the Deuces' theme song. Regardless of its lineage, audience reaction to the tune was so enthusiastic that Muddy resolved to record it.

In a May 1952 studio session, Muddy cut "Please Have Mercy," a scoundrel's plea for a second chance, and Little Walter assumed lead vocals on "Can't Hold Out Much Longer." At the end of the session, the band ran through its popular instrumental, and Leonard liked it immediately. They recorded the number, and then tried to give it a name. "We kept tossing it around," Jimmy says, "and eventually came up with the name 'Juke.'"[35] Because Muddy and Jimmy already had hits of their own, they agreed to give Little Walter's career a push by releasing "Juke" under his name.

Shortly afterwards the band embarked upon a southern tour. By the end of the summer, "Juke" had become the first release on Chess's new subsidiary label, Checker. It shot up the R&B charts that September, holding steady at number one for eight weeks. Following a gig in Louisiana, while the band was relaxing in a club, Walter was elated to hear his tune being punched on the jukebox time after time. The next day, when the rest of the group went to pick up new uniforms, Walter sneaked back to Chicago, heady with the exhilaration of his success. To replace him Muddy hired a horn player, who unfortunately could never get the hang of Muddy's music. At the end of the tour, Walter came back to the band.

It's likely that Walter had made his decision to leave Muddy permanently when the excuse he was looking for cropped up one night at the Club Zanzibar. A patron requested the band play "Juke," and tipped Muddy and Jimmy much more than Walter, who received only a dime. Insulted at the slight — it was his hit, and it was soaring up to number one — Walter's volatile temper flared and he quit the band outright.

Muddy realized that his sidemen were searching for a vehicle that could launch their own solo careers, and he accepted and generously encouraged their ambitions. "I know it when you make 'em a star they're gonna leave — I know that, you know," he mused. "But I can't hold the whole world by myself — they should get out there and do something."[36] He remembered his own hunger for success and understood that craving in others. Instead of trying to quash the ambitions of his musicians, as other less confident frontmen have done, one of Muddy's outstanding qualities as a bandleader was his willingness to foster emerging talent. "I always have believed, if somebody can shine put the light on him, let him shine," Muddy proudly proclaimed. "I think that's about the right thing to do, don't try to do it all yourself."[37] In this way he not only created some of the tightest ensembles in blues history but also expanded his legacy as former band mates went on to forge significant careers of their own.

Yet the consequence of his generosity was the sorrow he felt at their departure. "Oh, it went hard when they left," Muddy admitted. "It goes hard, man, when you get used to one sound and you got to go out and get another one."[38] Almost 30 years after Walter's resignation, Muddy could still recall the trauma it caused. "When Little Walter quit me in '52, it was like someone cutting off my oxygen. I didn't know how I was going to play without him. But soon I realized I had to put the slide back on my finger and go out and be Muddy Waters."[39]

Already a pioneer of blues harmonica and a veteran musician at 22 years of age, Little Walter Jacobs went on to record such songs as "Sad Hours," "Blues With A Feeling," "You're So Fine" and "My Babe." He often outranked his former bandleader on the R&B charts, achieving two number-one and three number-two hits, a level of commercial success Muddy never attained. The Muddy Waters band backed Walter during a session he did early in October 1952, and Walter continued to play the occasional club gig and tour with the band; he also lived from time to time in Muddy's basement. But more significantly, until June 1959, Chess insisted on hiring Little Walter for the majority of Muddy's recording sessions. Leonard had a winning formula. He wasn't about to dilute the mix.

After leaving Muddy, Little Walter had his sights set on joining the Four Aces. But the band already had a harmonica player, a teenager named Junior Wells. Walter suggested that Wells remain in the Aces and they play together. Since Wells and Muddy had been close for years, Junior was Walter's logical replacement in Muddy's band; it seems Walter was trying to make things difficult for Muddy by preventing an easy succession. But Muddy had already advised his young friend, "Junior, no sooner'n they make a move, you come to me."[40] Consequently, the two bands simply switched harmonica players: Walter went over to the Aces, and Wells joined Muddy.

Muddy's new harp player was born Amos Wells Blakemore in Memphis on 9 December 1934. His parents lived in Marion, Arkansas, about eight miles north of West Memphis, where his father farmed on a plantation and his mother Lena bootlegged corn whiskey with Sunnyland Slim. By 1942 Junior's parents had parted. He moved to Chicago with his mother so he could acquire a better education and more opportunities than the South could offer.

One day he found himself drawn into what he thought was a blues club, enticed by the music that was spilling through its doors and onto the street. It was, in fact, St. Paul's Church, and as a bonus Wells was unwittingly baptised. He soon discovered the real blues, however, via radio station WLAC from Nashville. When John Lee "Sonny Boy" Williamson's tunes hit the airwaves, Wells was hooked. The sound seized hold of his imagination, and from nine years of age, he devoted himself to learning to sing and play the harmonica. He was resolved to a career in blues.

Even if the schooling was better in Chicago, Junior wasn't the most attentive student. He played hooky one week so he could work on a soda truck, determined to earn enough money to buy a Marine Band harp he'd seen in a pawnshop. Since he'd been told the price of the prized instrument was $1.75, Wells spent the rest of his earnings on 12-cent movies. When he handed over his money, he was given a regular Hohner, but Wells insisted that it was the Marine Band harmonica he wanted. That one, he was informed, would cost 50 cents more.

Junior pleaded with the shopkeeper, but to no avail. Finally in desperation, he snatched the Marine Band and ran off, leaving only $1.75 on the counter. Wells was arrested, and at his trial the judge asked him to explain himself. "I told him I *had* to have that harp," Wells recalls. "The judge asked me to play it and when I did he gave the man the 50 cents and hollered 'Case dismissed.' "[41]

On a Saturday afternoon when Junior was 12, he went with his sister's boyfriend, a police officer, to hear Muddy's band play at the Ebony Lounge at 44 West Chicago Avenue on the North Side. The club owner, disc jockey Sam Evans, wouldn't let Wells in, until the cop flashed his badge and said he'd be responsible for the boy. During the intermission, the policeman asked Muddy if Junior could sit in with the band. Junior recalls the conversation:

> So Muddy asked me, "Young man, do you know your timing?" I said, "I think so." He said, "Well, if you think you can do it, I'll let you do it, but we got to talk to Walter because this is Walter's amplifier and his microphone, and I can't give you permission to go up there and do it."
>
> So he went and was talking to Walter, and Walter said, "What? . . . That little ol' peepsqueak over there? . . . Well, if he thinks he can do it, he can do it. Let him."
>
> So he played a couple more tunes out there . . . then he called me up. I . . . went up there and started singing the blues and dancing around and stuff like that, and people started standing up. Muddy got up, and he started telling everybody, "That's my son."[42]

Even Little Walter seemed impressed. Afterwards Walter managed to con the boy out of enough of his tip money to buy a bottle of gin. He led Junior out to the back alley to take his first drink, but Wells resisted until his cop friend convinced him it would show he was a man. "And I taken a swig of that stuff and, Lord have mercy, it cut my wind off," Junior laughs.[43]

Wells became the leader of a street gang, a group he'd organized to defend his friends from a rival group of teens who'd been attacking them on their way to the Drake School at 26th Street and Calumet. After hitting someone with an iron pipe, Junior was again brought up before a judge. When the judge threatened to send the teenager to a juvenile facility, Junior's distraught mother asked if she could bring in some character witnesses to speak on his behalf. Lena rounded up Muddy, Tampa Red, Sunnyland Slim and Big Maceo Merriweather. Wells remembers that "Muddy and all them came over there, and . . . they told the judge that they thought it would be an unjust thing to incarcerate me 'because he might turn out to be a worser person than he is now.' They said, 'We got a lot of respect for him, and he's a good musician, and I think he has a future.'"[44]

To show their confidence in Junior, all the bluesmen signed documents making them Wells's court-appointed guardians. Wells remembers the judge admonishing them, saying, "And whatever Junior does, you *all* did it. Now you all got to keep him straight."[45]

Like the others, Muddy took his new role seriously. As Junior was leaving court, Muddy caught up with him and ordered the boy to get in his car. Junior refused and started heading for the bus stop. "Oh, you'll get in this car," Muddy declared. "I just went and signed my name on that thing. Do you know what that said?"[46] Junior knew, but he still had no intention of obeying Muddy. He'll never forget Muddy's response: "He said, 'Oh, you're getting in there.' And he grabbed me, and I snatched away from him. . . . And he went *bang*, and he hit me right there [points to his forehead] and knocked me down. He pulled out his gun. He had an old .25 automatic. . . . 'You know I'll shoot you, boy. Now get in that car.' I got in that car."[47]

That display of tough love finally got through to Junior. "It made me feel that [Muddy] really was concerned and that he cared about me," he recalls. "'Cause I never had anybody to do anything like that for me before, you know what I mean? And that's when I really realized that these older musicians that signed their name on the thing, they had a lot of love for me."[48] It turned Wells around. "Muddy not only helped me out," Wells maintains, "he straightened me out."[49]

In 1949, when he was only 15, Junior met the Myers brothers, Dave and Louis, at a house party, and they subsequently formed the Three Deuces (the trio was later renamed the Four Aces when drummer Fred Below was recruited). During this period Junior developed his saxophone-like harmonica style, which bore the influence of the horn players he'd listened to practicing at guitarist Reginald Boyd's place.

Before he joined Muddy's band, while still with the Myers brothers, Junior was called in to substitute for Little Walter, who was too ill to travel with the others to a gig at New York's prestigious Apollo Theatre. Wells ventured onto the stage while the curtain was down to set out his harmonicas. His back was to the audience, so he had no idea the curtain had risen until he heard the applause. Flustered, Junior spun around, was confronted with the largest crowd he'd ever faced in his life and promptly toppled over his amplifier.

Trembling with stage fright, Wells needed a boost of self-confidence. Muddy gave the teenager a couple of shots of gin, then introduced him to the audience: "I got this young kid with me now — my son — and I'm gonna get him out here because when you all saw him fall . . . it scared him because he never played to an audience like this before, and I want you all to know that when you really hear him that you know why I care so much about him."[50] Bolstered by Muddy's support, Junior joined the rest of the band in bringing the house to its feet that night. Muddy beamed at his young protégé and declared, "Hey, you're mine for life."[51]

Muddy continued to be a father figure to Wells even after Junior became a member of his band, passing on lessons the older bluesman had himself lived by. "I always want you to remember one thing," he told Junior: "Don't nobody owe you nothin'. You owe your own self somethin'." Yet even when you achieve success, Muddy advised, "Always remember, whatever you do, do not disrespect the public . . . because these are the people that can make you and they are the people that can break you."[52]

But Muddy wasn't always serious. "He did a lot of crazy things," Junior recalls. "He liked to have a lot of fun, you know. He was always pulling some jokes on some of the band fellows. He was a nice person to get along with."[53]

While Muddy claimed it was his original intention to incorporate a piano into the band, Jimmy Rogers maintains the idea was his. In his after-hours rambling on the West Side, Jimmy came to know a musician who was playing with his friend, guitarist and vocalist Morris Pejoe, and who "kinda caught my ear there on the piano, and I could see we could use him."[54] Rogers took him to meet Muddy, and the incomparable Otis Spann was hired to bring his deep-down blues piano to the mix.

While the notion of combining guitar and piano wasn't a new one — it had been popular in the late 1920s and early 1930s — it hadn't produced that full, deep sound that Muddy envisioned for his own. He'd never had a piano player in his band and hadn't recorded with one since Little Johnny Jones backed him on the 1949 Aristocrat recordings of "Screamin' And Cryin'," "Where's My Woman Been" and "Last Time I Fool Around With You." Now with Spann, Muddy had the robust support for which he'd hankered. "I kept that backbeat on the drums plus full action on the guitar and harmonica and the piano in the back," he explained. "Then you've got a big sound."[55]

With the addition of Spann to the group in 1952, the Muddy Waters sound was complete. From this point on, the combination of two guitars, harmonica, drums, bass and piano would be the norm for Chicago blues bands. But Otis was more than just a sideman: he was eventually proclaimed one of the preeminent blues pianists of all time. As Muddy said, "Otis has got that rollin' left hand, he's got the blues in his fingers. And he's the ace card in my hand. Man, when he plays, he works!"[56]

Spann was born in Belzoni, Mississippi, on 21 March 1930. His parents were both musicians — his father, Frank, was a preacher who played piano, and Josephine Erby, his mother, was a guitarist and singer who'd performed with Bessie Smith and Memphis Minnie. Otis denied, however, that his parents inspired his choice of vocation. It was a local barrelhouse pianist named Friday Ford who set him on the road to becoming a blues piano player.

Spann claimed that Ford was a piano genius. He'd sit young Otis on his knee and try to teach him to play, but Otis's fingers weren't yet developed enough, and he was unable to copy his mentor. By the time Spann was eight and ready to learn, Ford was dead. Still, he'd made an indelible impression on the boy. Spann remembered his lessons well and learned them after the maestro was gone.

Frank Spann appreciated his son's blues aspirations and bought him a piano of his own. Josephine objected to Otis playing the devil's music, but she was overruled by Frank, who was so pleased with his son's musicianship that he once kept him up for three nights playing blues classics.

While still only eight years old, Otis won first prize and $25 in a blues competition held in nearby Jackson, Mississippi. By age 14 he was playing in a band at juke joints and house parties around Jackson. Along the way he also took lessons from local pianist Coot Davis and from Little Brother Montgomery. The recordings of Big Maceo Merriweather exerted a significant influence on Spann's stylistic development as well. He also became proficient on the guitar and harmonica. As a student of Campbell Junior College in Jackson, he played semi-professional football and was a Golden Gloves boxer.

When Otis was 17, his mother died, and he moved north to Chicago, where he worked as a plasterer and pursued his musical ambitions at night. Following a stint in the army — he served in Japan and Germany — Spann formed his own group and occasionally played with Louis Myers and Morris Pejoe.

During this time Spann had the privilege of receiving instruction from a man whose recordings he'd emulated as a child back home in Mississippi: piano master Big Maceo. He assimilated the assertive touch and vibrancy of Maceo's playing and some of the melancholy quality that characterized the elder man's vocals. Maceo's health had deteriorated following a stroke in 1946, and he would sometimes ask Otis to fill in for him at engagements. Young Spann even helped Maceo out at his recording sessions by playing one hand for him.

Yet the protégé was not a mere clone of his mentor. Otis's creativity was dazzling. He elevated the piano from a percussion instrument to a centerpiece of Chicago blues. While his left hand discharged a barrage of solid bass lines, his right hand exhilarated with elegant cascades of sparkling runs. Ranging from a riffle to a rumble, Otis's piano would unobtrusively lay down the foundation of Muddy's sound then roll to the forefront with a stunning burst of virtuosity.

Initially Otis had to work hard to mesh his style with Muddy's delay timing. Muddy remembered the two of them driving around the city until dawn, discussing how Otis's piano should be amalgamated into Muddy's blues: "He used to come to my house and park in front of the door with a bottle of whiskey, and I'd sit there and teach this man, tell him exactly what to do with the piano when I was singing the blues."[57] The two men grew so close, both musically and personally, that they referred to each other as brothers. For a long time they were referred to in the press as half-brothers, but they were not related. "Otis Spann, that was my mainline man," Muddy lovingly proclaimed.[58]

For Leonard Chess's son Marshall who grew up in the Chess studios, the success of the Waters-Spann pairing was grounded in their shared sensibility to the music: "Otis Spann *felt* the blues, boy. He locked in with Muddy Waters. They both felt the blues in the same way . . . and I think together they were greater than each one was as an individual, musically."[59]

Despite the strength of this bond, Otis continued to accept outside session work throughout his tenure with Muddy's band. Willie Dixon at Chess hired him regularly to back other artists — with his prodigious talent, Spann had the knack of making everyone else sound better. As the years went by, his impeccable piano accompaniment would be heard on the discs of such luminaries as Little Walter, Howlin' Wolf, Sonny Boy Williamson, Buddy Guy, Bo Diddley and Chuck Berry.

Junior Wells claims harmonica credit on the band's session of 17 September 1952, one of the few occasions before the late 1950s that Chess allowed anyone but Little Walter to assume harp duty. Elgin Evans makes heavy use of his hi-hat cymbals in "Standing Around Crying" and "Iodine In My Coffee," while Junior wrings wails of pain and lamentation from his harp. Muddy's vocal phrasing is especially effective in "Standing Around Crying"; he draws out his lyrics in similitude with the moans of Wells's harp.

On or about 9 January 1953, Muddy was back in the studio; this time Big Walter Horton, soon to be a member of Muddy's band, was the harmonica player. The first cut, "Flood," evokes images of a stormy Delta landscape amid Evans's overbearing use of the hi-hat cymbals; the tune would be reworked and recorded in 1955 as "Clouds In My Heart." As well, Muddy sings of his desolation in "My Life Is Ruined," and the woeful cry of the harp is a perfect companion to Muddy's melancholy vocals in "Sad, Sad Day."

Muddy recorded two songs during a 4 May 1953 session: "Turn The Lamp Down Low (Baby Please Don't Go)" and "Loving Man." He was erroneously identified as the composer of the first number. It had, in fact, been recorded by Papa Harvey Hull and Long Cleve Reed in 1927 as "Don't You Leave Me Here," and then scored a hit for Big Joe Williams in 1941 as "Baby Please Don't Go." Williams

had been the one who taught Muddy the song back on Stovall.
Muddy uses all but one verse of Williams's lyrics and rearranges
them in his own order. Little Walter is in magnificent form here;
his harp work is varied and seamless as it flows around Muddy's
robust vocals.

Around this time guitarist Eddie Taylor joined Muddy's band for
a few months. He'd previously played with Big Walter Horton,
Jimmy Reed and Earl Hooker and had recorded with Reed and John
Lee Hooker. Muddy also hired Rudy Pernell as a weeknight drummer, as Elgin Evans had a day job.

As the summer of 1953 drew to a close, Junior Wells was drafted
into the army, and was compelled to leave Muddy for Fort Sheridan,
just north of Chicago. But Junior and the military didn't get along.
He was sent to boot camp at Camp Robertson in California, but as
soon as he got a pass, Wells jumped a bus back to Chicago and
Muddy's band. Although he was apprehended and ordered to return
to California, Wells disobeyed and evaded the authorities for as
long as he could. Under the circumstances he was not a very reliable
band member. As Muddy said, "I had to get another harp blower,
'cause [Junior would] go there and run off and come back and they'd
be looking for him and he'd be scared to come out of the club.' "[60]

Junior's replacement was Walter Horton, a man with several
monikers: Mumbles, Tangle Eye, Shakey and Big Walter. Born on
6 April 1918 in Horn Lake, Mississippi, a town hugging the Tennessee border less than 10 miles south of Memphis, Horton took up
the harmonica at the age of five. When he was 12 years old, he
moved to Memphis, where his father worked for the city. Shortly
afterwards his father died, and Horton helped supplement the
family income by taking odd jobs and blowing his harp on Beale
Street (on those occasions when his mother hadn't tracked him
down and dragged him home).

By age 13 he was playing with the Memphis Jug Band and reportedly recorded "Kansas City Blues" with the group. He also worked
and recorded with a dwarf named Little Buddy Doyle, a guitarist
and vocalist. Horton's day jobs were chef at the prestigious Peabody
Hotel and later cabbie. By the late 1930s, he was blowing with
guitarists Jack Kelly, Dan Sane and Frank Stokes. He also toured
Louisiana and Mississippi with Big Joe Williams, Floyd Jones and
David "Honeyboy" Edwards.

Horton said that he first played amplified harmonica in 1940 in Jackson, Mississippi. Although his subsequent travels with Floyd Jones took him to Chicago, he returned to Memphis, where he blew harp with guitarist Eddie Taylor and recorded for Sun Records in the early 1950s. It is a testament to Big Walter's stature as a harpman that along the way he taught such harmonica greats as Rice Miller, Little Walter, Carey Bell Harrington and James Cotton. Soon after Horton recorded "Easy" with Jimmy DeBerry in 1953, Eddie Taylor came down to Memphis to conscript him as the new harmonica player in Muddy's band. Taylor himself only lasted two more weeks with the group before he left to tour with John Lee Hooker, then joined Elmore James in 1955.

Big Walter was tall and lean and burdened with poor health. He was a slow-moving man who never saw the need to hurry. His personality was a complex of opposites that was likely augmented by the magnitude of his drinking. To those who knew him well, he was "a real kitten inside."[61] He could be exuberant and playful, gentle and shy, but to outsiders he was dour, his problems locked away behind a steely exterior.

When he played, however, Horton's demons took flight. His harmonica soared to heights of triumph; his ethereal tone caressed the heavens. Willie Dixon lauded him as one of the best harp blowers in the business: "They underestimated Big Walter because he'd stay loaded most of the time but once you'd get him in good condition, he could run rings around all of them." Dixon remembered, "He would cup the harmonica with a glass to make it sound like a horn. He'd take a beer can, cut the top out of it, cup the harmonica in there and make that sonuvagun sound like a trombone and no one could tell the difference."[62] With the best of intentions, Horton tried to impart some of his expertise to Little Walter, who, true to form, responded with outbursts of fury. But in the end, despite his assertions that his style was all his own, Little Walter was a prime beneficiary of Horton's techniques.

The illustrious Spann-Waters recording partnership was inaugurated at the Chess session of 24 September 1953. Here Otis's piano surges to the forefront to assume its rightful position; his solo on "Blow Wind Blow" is a but a sample of the stunning musicianship to follow. "Mad Love (I Want You To Love Me)," another number recorded this day, uses spare instrumentation to full effect with a stop-time rhythm that anticipates the distinctive style of the following year's "Hoochie Coochie Man." These riffs — which originated with the Muddy Waters band — would serve as starting blocks for many future rock 'n' roll tunes. "Mad Love" was a smash by November, ascending to Muddy's highest ranking yet at number six on the *Juke Box* R&B chart and number 10 on the *Best Seller* R&B list.

"Once he got up in the world, he didn't forgot those people that was around him and those folk that he had known prior to his reaching stardom," Muddy's cousin Reverend Willie Morganfield reflects.[63] Muddy's welcome mat was always out. From time to time, Willie would travel to Chicago to stay with his cousin. Muddy enjoyed and valued his relationships with family and old friends, and he made a special effort to maintain them. Man Morganfield, one of Muddy's half-brothers, lived with him; another half-brother, Robert, would come up from Rolling Fork to visit. And Muddy always stopped by to see his kinfolk when he was in Mississippi. "He was just plain Muddy Waters," Willie remembers. "When he'd come to Memphis, he would call my dad, talk with my mother. When he come to Cleveland, Ohio, he'd call me, and we would get together, you know. He liked good country food, and we would fix it for him."[64]

Willie Morganfield, an extraordinarily talented gospel singer in his own right, enjoyed ribbing his cousin about the devil's music: "I used to kid him that that stuff he was singin' wasn't any good, but he said, 'Must be some good. You see what I'm riding in?'" and Muddy would shoot an appreciative glance at his gleaming new Cadillac.[65]

It wasn't until 1954 that Muddy plugged in his first solid-body, built-in electric guitar, a Les Paul Custom which had just been introduced that year. Jimmy Rogers, who was playing a hollow-body Silvertone at the time, remembers Muddy showing off his new instrument at a gig the night he acquired it. "We tried to learn how to play it, to figure out stuff on it," Jimmy recalls. "It was a Les Paul, gold front, solid body. . . . He didn't like it 'cause it was thin and real heavy. But we were sitting down playing during the time, and it could rest on his leg; he didn't have to carry it. Later on he got used to it, and then he started standing up with it."[66]

Muddy wanted to preserve the style he'd developed on acoustic guitar with a pickup, but capturing that on an electric instrument took some work. Although he always preferred the warmer sound of the acoustic, it was impractical. He remarked that the electric guitar "was a very different sound, not just louder. I thought that I'd come to like it — if I could ever learn to play it."[67] The solid-body guitar would come to define Muddy's sound. It was the ax he would use to hew a new musical landscape.

NOTES

1 Peter Guralnick, *Feel Like Going Home* (New York: Harper & Row, Publishers, 1989), 69.

2 Vernon Gibbs, "Muddy Waters," *Essence* (Dec. 1972): 85.

3 Guralnick, 69.

4 Dan Forte, "Jimmy Rogers," *Blues Guitar: The Men Who Made the Music: From the Pages of Guitar Player Magazine*, ed. Jas Obrecht (San Francisco: GPI Books, 1990), 89.

5 James Rooney, *Bossmen: Bill Munroe & Muddy Waters* (New York: The Dial Press, 1971), 114.

6 Jas Obrecht, "The Life and Times of the Hoochie Coochie Man," *Guitar Player* (Mar. 1994): 36.

7 Rooney, 120.

8 Rooney, 120.

9 Jimmy Rogers, interview with author, 26 Apr. 1995.

10 Jimmy Rogers, interview with author, 26 Apr. 1995.

11 Rooney, 113.

12 *Sweet Home Chicago*, film, MCA Records – Initial Film and Television (Chicago) – Vanguard Films, 1993.

13 Neil Slaven, "Confessin' the Blues, Part 2," *Blues Unlimited* 113 (May–June 1975): 9.

14 Alfred Duckett, "I Have a Right to Sing the Blues," *Louisville Defender*, 14 Apr. 1955.

15 Robert Morganfield, interview with author, 16 May 1995.

16 Jimmy Rogers, interview with author, 26 Apr. 1995.

17 Pete Welding, "Muddy Waters," *Rolling Stone* 21 (9 Nov. 1968): 11.

18 Jim O'Neal and Bill Greensmith, "Living Blues Interview: Jimmy Rogers," *Living Blues* 14 (Autumn 1973): 12.

19 Margaret McKee and Fred Chisenhall, *Beale Black & Blue: Life and Music on Black America's Main Street* (Baton Rouge: Louisiana State University Press, 1981), 238.

20 B.B. King, interview with author, 24 Aug. 1995.

21 B.B. King, interview with author, 24 Aug. 1995.

22 B.B. King, interview with author, 24 Aug. 1995.

23 Clas Ahlstrand, Peter Mahlin and Jan-Ake Pettersson, "Muddy Talkin' To," *Jefferson* 14: 14.

24 Jas Obrecht, "Muddy Waters: The Life & Times of the Hoochie Coochie Man," *Blues Revue* 20 (Dec.1995–Jan. 1996): 31.

25 Mike Rowe, *Chicago Breakdown* (London: Eddison Press Ltd., 1973), 75.

26 Robert Palmer, *Deep Blues* (New York: Penguin, 1982), 165.

27 David Walters, Lawrence Garman and John Matthews, "Jimmy Rogers," *Blues Unlimited* 105 (Dec. 1973–Jan. 1974): 18.

28 Robert Neff and Anthony Conner, *Blues* (Boston: David R. Godine, 1975), 104.

29 Neff and Conner, 104.

30 Jimmy Rogers, interview with author, 26 Apr. 1995.

31 Jimmy Rogers, interview with author, 3 May 1996.

32 Forte, 87.

33 Jimmy Rogers, interview with author, 26 Apr. 1995.

34 Jimmy Rogers, interview with author, 26 Apr. 1995.

35 Willie Leiser, "Down in the Alley," *Blues Unlimited* 101 (May 1973): 16–17.

36 Jim O'Neal and Amy O'Neal, "Muddy," *Living Blues* 64 (Mar.–Apr. 1985): 36.

37 Peter Guralnick, "Muddy Waters: A Man of the Blues," *Rolling Stone* 91 (16 Sept. 1971): 37.

38 Guralnick, "Muddy Waters," 37.

39 Bob Margolin, "I Can't Be Satisfied," *Blues Revue* 20 (Dec.1995–Jan. 1996): 15.

40 O'Neal and O'Neal, 36.

41 Rowe, 117.

42 Junior Wells, interview with author, 9 Dec. 1995.

43 Jim O'Neal, "Junior Wells," *Living Blues* 119 (Feb. 1995): 18.

44 Junior Wells, interview with author, 9 Dec. 1995.

45 Junior Wells, interview with author, 9 Dec. 1995.

46 Junior Wells, interview with author, 9 Dec. 1995.

47 Junior Wells, interview with author, 9 Dec. 1995.

48 Junior Wells, interview with author, 9 Dec. 1995.

49 Paul Oliver, "Muddy Waters," *Nothing But the Blues*, ed. Mike Leadbitter (London: Hanover Books Ltd., 1971), 28.

50 Junior Wells, interview with author, 9 Dec. 1995.

51 Junior Wells, interview with author, 9 Dec. 1995.

52 O'Neal, 17.

53 Junior Wells, interview with author, 9 Dec. 1995.

54 Jimmy Rogers, interview with author, 3 May 1996.

55 Rooney, 124.

56 Paul Oliver, *Blues off the Record* (New York: Hippocrene Books Inc., 1984), 265.

57 Guralnick, "Muddy Waters," 37.

58 O'Neal and O'Neal, 36.

59 *Sweet Home Chicago.*

60 Rooney, 128.

61 Jerry Portnoy, interview with author, 13 Nov. 1995.

62 Willie Dixon and Don Snowden, *I Am the Blues: The Willie Dixon Story* (London: Quartet Books, 1989), 97.

63 Willie Morganfield, interview with author, 14 May 1995.

64 Willie Morganfield, interview with author, 14 May 1995.

65 Willie Morganfield, interview with author, 14 May 1995.

66 Jimmy Rogers, interview with author, 3 May 1996.

67 Tom Wheeler, "Muddy Waters & Johnny Winter," *Blues Guitar: The Men Who Made the Music: From the Pages of Guitar Player Magazine*, ed. Jas Obrecht (San Francisco: GPI Books, 1990), 73.

5

When I sing the blues
it come from the heart.
From right here in your soul.[1]

The way Muddy chose to define his music reveals a lot about the inner man: "The blues are an expression of trouble in mind, trouble in body, trouble in soul. And when a man has trouble, it helps him to express it, to let it be known."[2] To do otherwise, Muddy believed, would give the devil a victory.

One of the strengths of blues, as Muddy saw it, was its unfaltering capacity to uplift its audience through the expression of shared emotions. "When a person thinks he's the only one in hot water, he's miserable," he professed. "But when he gets to realize that others have the same kind of trouble — or even worse — he understands that life isn't just picking on him alone."[3]

The material rewards and the accolades garnered by his music pleased Muddy profoundly, but they were ultimately of secondary importance to him. He admitted that the joy of creating music would have been an integral part of his life, regardless of his success. "Even if I couldn't make a great deal of money at it," confessed Muddy, "I'd be playing the blues in somebody's place where somebody could hear me play them."[4]

Throughout 1954 (and possibly before and after) Fred Below was Muddy's session drummer, although he was never a member of the band. A native Chicagoan, Below was born on 6 September 1926. After a two-week tryout on the trombone, he switched to playing drums in the Du Sable High School Band, which also included budding musician Gene Ammons. At the age of 18, he was drafted into the infantry and served two years in the South Pacific, completing his tour of duty in late 1946. Back in Chicago, Below took an advanced course in drumming at the Roy C. Knapp School of Percussion, where his classmates included Elgin Evans and Odie Payne, Jr. His musical focus was bebop, but gigs were hard to come by when he graduated in 1948, so Below reenlisted. This time he was stationed in Germany and served as drummer in the prestigious 427 Army Band.

When Below finished his second tour of duty in 1951, he returned to Chicago to discover that blues had eclipsed bebop. He sought out Elgin Evans, then playing with Muddy, who'd heard of an opening with the Three Deuces blues band, which comprised Dave and Louis Myers and Junior Wells. The trio took him on, but after just one gig Fred was ready to call it quits; he couldn't get the hang of blues drumming. But the Myers brothers and Junior knew he possessed the necessary ability and worked with him until he developed a feel for blues. With Below on the skins, the band was renamed the Four Aces.

After the Four Aces and Muddy traded harp players in 1952 and Fred began backing Little Walter, he came into his own as a blues drummer and was in great demand as a session musician at Chess. Muddy reportedly asked Below to join his band during the time Elgin Evans was his drummer, but Fred declined due to his friendship with Evans.

Below's collaboration with Muddy was confined to the recording studio. Fred remarked that Muddy came to his sessions knowing exactly what he wanted to hear. If that's what his sidemen delivered, Muddy was satisfied. Fred especially enjoyed these sessions. He marveled at Muddy's unerring sense of rhythm: "Muddy has one of the best sense[s] of timing [—] more than any other musician I've ever come across. His timing is perfect man, I mean perfect. . . . It seems like he's singing like a drummer should be able to play."[5] With the introduction of Fred Below as Muddy's session drummer, the drums were elevated from merely marking time to embellishing and enhancing the tunes they were backing.

Muddy's collaboration with Willie Dixon — launched on disc in 1954 — detonated the development of Chicago blues, its fallout igniting the evolution of the popular music to come. Like Below, Dixon was never a member of Muddy's band, but was a key component of Muddy's studio sound and a prolific source of his material. An outgoing, personable man with a massive build, the upright-bass player and baritone first met Muddy and his band mates back in the late 1940s when he was playing with the Big Three Trio. Occasionally at the end of their own gigs, Dixon and piano player Leonard "Baby Doo" Caston would venture over to Muddy's venue for a jam.

The seventh of Daisy and Charlie Dixon's 14 offspring, Willie was born on 1 July 1915, in Vicksburg, Mississippi, at the southernmost tip of the Delta. Under the guidance of his mother, young Willie learned to read and compose poetry. His musical education started in church, where he first began singing at the age of five, and like Muddy, he enjoyed beating out rhythms on a can. Dixon soon fell under the spell of the great bluesmen — among them Charley Patton and Little Brother Montgomery — who performed at the tavern next door to his mother's restaurant.

Dixon first left home at 11, and at age 12 he was serving time at a county correctional farm for stealing plumbing fixtures from an abandoned house. It was here that the youngster became immersed in blues. Two years later he was incarcerated in another county facility after being arrested outside Clarksdale for vagrancy. When he wasn't released after his 30-day sentence, Willie jumped a freight train and escaped to Chicago, then to New York and other destinations. Returning to Vicksburg he sang bass with the Union Jubilee Singers. By this time he was enjoying some initial success at songwriting; his compositions were being recorded by white country-and-western groups.

After working his way to Hawaii on a freighter and nearly starving in New Orleans, Dixon was back in Chicago with a new career as a boxer. The strapping young man was the victor in the novice heavyweight division at the Illinois Golden Gloves championship and even sparred with Joe Louis. He fought four pro matches, but was suspended for brawling in the commissioner's office over his contention that he was being cheated out of his full winnings.

Fortunately Dixon had already met Baby Doo Caston. The pianist constructed an upright bass for Willie from an oil can and a single string, and as a duo they gigged on Maxwell Street and in clubs and recorded for Mayo Williams in the late 1930s. Along with Bernardo Dennis, Gene Gilmore and Ellis Hunter, the pair formed the Five Breezes and cut eight sides for the Bluebird label in 1940. The following year Willie was arrested onstage for ignoring his draft notice; he was making a deliberate protest against what he considered to be the U.S. government's subjugation of its black citizens. After serving time in prison, he recorded for Mercury with the Four Jumps of Jive.

The Big Three Trio was formed in 1946, comprising Willie Dixon on vocals and bass, pianist Baby Doo Caston and guitarist Bernardo Dennis (later replaced by Ollie Crawl). They concentrated on pop tunes and light blues, a startling contrast to Willie's future recordings with Muddy and other Chess artists. That same year the Big Three cut "Lonely Roamin'" and "Signifying Monkey" for Lester Melrose on the Bullet label, and it became a hit. In 1947 the trio released another successful disc — "Wee Wee Baby, You Sure Look Good To Me" — on Columbia. As well, Dixon was a busy session man, working with such artists as John Lee "Sonny Boy" Williamson, Big Bill Broonzy, Roosevelt Sykes and his childhood idol, Little Brother Montgomery.

It was through this session work and his initial producing efforts that Dixon hooked up with the Chess brothers and began working for them full time in 1951. As producer, arranger, leader of the studio band and bass player, Dixon became so indispensable to the Chess operation that Leonard later described him as his right arm. At first, however, Leonard was blind to Willie's most formidable talent — his astonishing songwriting skill.

Willie had long found inspiration in Muddy's blues, and the kick and vitality of Muddy's compositions began to influence Dixon's own writing. While Willie was still with the Big Three Trio, he told Muddy about a song he'd written and then sang it at one of their jams. Muddy was impressed. After Dixon had been working at Chess for a while, he told Leonard about the number, describing it as tailor-made for Muddy. Leonard said Muddy was playing at the Club Zanzibar, and if Muddy agreed, the song was his.

That night at the Zanzibar, Willie waited offstage for the band to take its break. Muddy was anxious to learn the piece, so he grabbed his guitar and the two found refuge in the washroom, away from the tumult of the club. It took about 20 minutes for Muddy to run through the lyrics and the intonation and get the riff down. Dixon suggested, "Well, just get a little rhythm pattern, y' know. . . . Do the same thing over again, y' know, and keep the words in your mind."[6] Muddy was eager to perform the song while it was still fresh in his memory. He strode onstage, briefed the band on the rhythm pattern and launched into the number, leaving the audience shrieking for more. It was "I'm Your Hoochie Coochie Man," a piece that was to become a trademark of Muddy's career, one of the most renowned songs of his lifelong repertoire.

It may have been cold outside, but Muddy's Chess session of 7 January 1954 sizzled with the recording of "I'm Your Hoochie Coochie Man." Its stop-time rhythm, with Fred Below on drums and Willie Dixon on bass, is the perfect backdrop for Muddy's bombastic vocals, proclaiming in no uncertain terms that he's arrived, in case anyone could ever doubt it. In lyrical content Dixon's pervasive use of hoodoo imagery draws the listener back to the mysticism of the Delta, but stylistically the song's bearing was pointed straight to the future. Later the number would be covered by such diverse artists as the Allman Brothers, Dion, Chuck Berry, Steppenwolf, Manfred Mann, Lou Rawls and Jimi Hendrix. Also recorded that day was "She's So Pretty," an up-tempo tune driven by piano and harp; then Jimmy Rogers took over the lead for "Blues All Day Long" and "Chicago Bound."

"I'm Your Hoochie Coochie Man" hit the charts with sales of 4,000 in the first week. It remained in the top 10 for 13 weeks starting in mid-March and sold over 75,000 copies. It climbed the *Best Seller* R&B chart to number eight, and brought Muddy his highest ranking ever: third place on the *Juke Box* R&B chart. Leonard Chess realized that Dixon's instincts and songwriting abilities were pure gold. His songs were an irresistible amalgamation of rural images with the brawn and bravado of the city, and they expedited Muddy's progress towards the national spotlight. For the next decade, Muddy would draw heavily on Dixon's material for his recordings; for the rest of his life he'd perform them.

Now Leonard wanted everything that Willie wrote. He'd sift through Dixon's tunes looking for the perfect vehicle for Muddy. If someone ran short of songs on a session, Chess would look to Willie. This did not, however, prevent Dixon from moonlighting as a writer for other labels. Having proven his knack for spotting rising hit makers, he also became a talent scout for Chess.

It's been claimed that Dixon's songs injected an overt sexuality into Muddy's image and repertoire and that his performing persona changed as a result. This is true only in degree, not in essence. Country blues is rife with sexual themes and innuendo; Muddy had been performing this music since his juke-joint days on Stovall. And even though his performing style had been more restrained initially, Muddy had always been a sex symbol.

While Dixon's songs did demand a more exclamatory style of singing than he'd been delivering previously, Muddy would still have been compelled to adopt more forceful vocals to front the full band playing behind him. His growing onstage boldness was likely an upshot of the combination of Dixon's cocky lyrics and the confidence engendered by his own success. But in Junior Wells's opinion, "Muddy was Muddy regardless of what he was doing, a Willie Dixon song or not. That didn't change Muddy, because Muddy had a style of his own, a unique voice."[7]

On 13 April 1954, the band recorded two Dixon tunes: "I Just Want To Make Love To You" and "Oh Yeah." Both were infused with a haunting quality by Little Walter's chromatic harp. Muddy had never heard this type of harmonica before Walter brought it to the studio that day, provoking him to warn Walter, "Don't rehearse on my session, motherfucker."[8] But when he heard the tape played back, Muddy was won over. "The big ones [chromatic harps] have a sound more like an organ," Walter said, explaining the difference, "an' the small one [the Hohner Marine Band harp] is rather loud unless you know how to blow it."[9]

Overall, Muddy didn't resist Walter's innovations — he welcomed them. Recalling his sessions with Walter, Muddy fondly reminisced, "While you're recording, [Walter] be dashin' all around you everywhere, changing harps, you know, running all around the studio, but he never get in your way. He put a lot of trick things in there, getting all different sounds, aww he was the greatest. He always had ideas."[10]

"I Just Want To Make Love To You," with its heavy emphasis on the first beat of each bar, cuts through the niceties of social conventions to proclaim a hunger for unencumbered sexual indulgence. There are no holds barred here; Muddy's vocals are wrenched from the pit of his belly. It was another hit. Beginning that June and for 13 weeks running, it held fourth place on both the *Juke Box* and *Best Seller* R&B charts. The tune would go on to exert an enormous influence in the realm of popular music; versions of it were recorded by Chuck Berry, Lou Rawls and the Rolling Stones, among others.

A new harmonica player had been performing with the group since the previous year. In late 1953, while the band was playing the Zanzibar, Big Walter Horton called in sick and arranged for Henry "Pot" Strong to replace him. Suspicious, Muddy sent out a scout who reported back that Big Walter had found a gig of his own in a Madison Street tavern. To Muddy, who always insisted that his band members be punctual and reliable, Horton's actions were intolerable. Despite Horton's vehement denials and his claim that he'd been stricken with pneumonia, he was fired, and Strong was hired to take his place.

Henry "Pot" Strong was born in Arkansas on 1 September 1928, and moved from West Memphis to Chicago in 1947. He was short in stature, but as Little Walter said, "He was the best harp-blower in Chicago next to me because I taught him all I knew."[11] It was through Strong's close friendship with Little Walter that he got to know Muddy.

Typical of so many musicians who would join the band, Pot was still a developing player, but Muddy saw great promise in him. "He was very good," Jimmy Rogers asserts. "The way he was improving, he would have been a great harmonica player."[12] Willie Smith, who later became a drummer in Muddy's band, comments, "In my opinion he was just as good a harmonica player as Little Walter was."[13] Because Chess was still insisting that Little Walter be used for Muddy's sessions, Strong never did get to record with Muddy.

In the early morning of 3 June 1954, Jimmy dropped Pot and a girlfriend off at Strong's place at 4554 South Greenwood Street. The couple had quarreled in the car, but afterwards as their confrontation escalated, she plunged a knife into Pot's chest, penetrating a lung. "After I'd left, a fellow who lived there in the building, he called Muddy 'cause Muddy was real close to where [Pot] was living at," Rogers reports. "And Muddy shot right over there and . . . grabbed him and carried him to the hospital."[14]

It was too late. The promise of Henry Strong's unfulfilled blues career was over. The 25-year-old harmonica player bled to death on the back seat of Muddy's car. His body was taken to Memphis for burial. Little Walter later paid tribute to his friend with his recording of "Last Night" for the Checker label.

Muddy was shaken by the tragedy and could not easily find a replacement. He finally decided on Little George Smith, an accomplished amplified-harp and chromatic-harp player who was gigging around town with guitarist and singer Otis Rush. Analyzing George's harmonica skills, Otis Spann called him "a real deep player," and compared him to Little Walter. "They have the same sound, use the same patterns."[15]

Belying his moniker, Little George was tall and lanky. Though he was born in Cairo, Illinois, on 7 April 1924, his parents were both natives of Mississippi. George's mother, Jesse, played guitar and harp, and from the time George was four, she set about molding him into a musician by coaching him to mimic what she played on the harmonica. "She would also have a switch," George recalled, "and if . . . I wasn't able to catch what she played on my harp, then I'd be sure to catch something from that switch!"[16]

It was a method that produced results. At age 12, Smith was already on the road with his harp touring the South, and in 1941 he joined a swing band in Rock Island, Illinois, with another future Muddy Waters alumnus, drummer Francis Clay. Smith then became a gospel singer in Mississippi as a member of the Jackson Jubilee Singers. By 1944, however, he was focusing on blues, amplifying his harmonica through the audio component of a motion-picture projector. He played on the streets of various Mississippi towns, and because his sound was so innovative, he lined his pockets with generous tips. When he decided to settle down in 1949, George moved to Chicago where he found employment as a janitor and played several nights per week with Otis Rush.

Willie Foster, a harmonica player who'd been a fan of Muddy's back in Mississippi, was living in St. Louis in 1953 when he caught a Muddy Waters performance on a trip to Chicago. He sat in with the band, and Muddy liked what he heard. Muddy asked Willie if he would fill in on the occasional out-of-town gig while he left his band behind to play an engagement in Chicago. Beginning in late 1953 in Detroit, Willie sporadically played for Muddy on the road while maintaining his own group in St. Louis.

The money was good; Muddy paid above the union scale of $16 per night. They'd travel in Muddy's red Chevrolet station wagon and take turns driving. Before a gig Muddy would typically sit out front socializing with the audience and having a few drinks. Always the center of attention, Muddy enjoyed his fans gathering around him.

Onstage Muddy would often perform seated, especially if he had a long show to do. But according to Foster, he'd be on his feet during a band mate's solo, "dancing 'round the microphone, and people'd just scream, you know . . . kind of like the James Brown thing."[17] Muddy's suave, mustachioed good looks and unabashed sexuality provoked the unrestrained appreciation of the ladies in the audience. "They went crazy," Foster admits, "and he'd see one and *he'd* go crazy. A maniac I'd call it."[18] After a gig Muddy and Foster would often return to their motel to talk and enjoy a drink. Muddy was a bourbon drinker in those days. "He could drink, too," Willie recalls.[19]

Like so many who associated with Muddy, Willie Foster was profoundly affected by the example of the older musician. "He taught me to be true to myself," Willie declares.[20] Throughout his life it was a lesson Muddy would impress upon those he cared about, one of the guiding principles of his own existence. Willie remembers Muddy's advice: " 'When you're doing your show [with your own band], if you do my songs, do 'em with your own style'. . . . He said, 'You're welcome to do my songs. Don't try to sound just like me. Put your own voice in it, and do your own thing.' "[21]

Muddy's character was a great influence on Willie. "Everybody say he was a good man, good-hearted person," Foster says. "Never did try to hurt somebody. . . . He wanted to try to keep the whole world happy. He was just a good ol' black man. I never met a person no better. I tried to be just like him."[22]

One Friday night in 1954, Willie Foster traveled up from St. Louis to join Muddy; they were scheduled to leave for a tour to Canada the next day. Willie Dixon answered the door at Muddy's residence while Muddy was busy shaving. Foster recounts the conversation as Muddy stuck his head out the bathroom door to greet him, asking, " 'Are you ready?' and I said, 'Ready as anybody can be.' Muddy went back in the bathroom to wipe the shaving cream off his face. Then he came back out and said [to Dixon], 'Willie, are you thinking about what I'm thinking about? Let's make a song out of it.' We sat up there, I don't know how long, trying to figure out what to put on it, you know. It took [Dixon] three days, I think, to finish it out."[23] The completed product, "I'm Ready," became a Muddy Waters classic. He recorded it later that year and performed it throughout his career.

Sometime before Muddy's Chess session of 1 September 1954, he came to the conclusion that he no longer needed to play guitar. "The band sounded so good to me," he recalled, "I didn't think I had to play."[24] Perhaps it was Muddy's way of signaling his arrival, that at his level of success he'd earned a break. This studio outing marked the beginning of Muddy's hiatus from the instrument. Nevertheless, it was a strong session, comprising "I'm Ready," "Smokestack Lightning" and "I Don't Know Why." The haunting reverberations of Walter's chromatic harp soar throughout each number.

In "I'm Ready" — the battle cry of a hard-drinking, street-fighting dude with carnal pleasures on his mind — Muddy belts out Dixon's lyrics with a swagger, while Little Walter's harmonica speaks of desolation when the braggadocio is stripped bare. The next month "I'm Ready" hit number five on the *Best Seller* R&B chart and fourth place on the *Juke Box* R&B listing.

Fred Below's contribution is evident on both "I'm Ready" and "I Don't Know Why," an up-tempo piece propelled by a dynamic rhythm section, above which Walter's harmonica work floats. And when Muddy sings about riding a train on "Smokestack Lightning," the listener can hear, through his voice and the instrumentation, a lonely train steaming across a Delta landscape. At this session it's also likely that Muddy recorded "I'm A Natural Born Lover," a declaration of unrivaled sexual superiority, and "Ooh Wee."

"Smokestack Lightning" was written by Chester Burnett, better known as the bestial bluesman, Howlin' Wolf. Five years older than Muddy, Wolf was born in West Point, Mississippi, on the eastern edge of the state, and grew up in the Delta near Ruleville. He had the good fortune to learn guitar from Charley Patton and then harmonica from Rice Miller. Wolf cultivated his trademark howl by trying to yodel like country singer Jimmie Rodgers. "I couldn't do no yodelin'," he said, "so I turned to growlin', then howlin', and it's done me fine."[25]

After combining farming with music, then serving in the army, Wolf settled in West Memphis, Arkansas. There he played with, among others, James Cotton and guitarist Pat Hare, both future band mates of Muddy's. The immensely talented, irrepressible, six-foot, 250-pounder was known to prowl the stage on all fours, baring his teeth and growling. It's no wonder he captured the attention of Sam Phillips, then operating the Memphis Recording Service. In 1951 Wolf cut his first record for Phillips, who in turn leased it to Chess. Straight away his recording career was launched as he ascended the charts with "Moanin' At Midnight" and "How Many More Years." The Chess brothers persuaded Wolf to move north, and towards the end of 1953, he stepped off the bus in Chicago to be greeted by Willie Dixon.

Although they'd never met, Wolf and Muddy had certainly heard of each other. Wolf planned to stay in a motel, but Muddy intervened and invited the newcomer to stay at his house, saying, "I'll make room for you until you get yourself together, and get you a job."[26] Wolf lived at the Morganfield residence for about two months. Each night and for every matinee, Muddy took him to the club he was playing to introduce him around, trying to help him get his own gigs. Thanks to Muddy, the Club Zanzibar was the first to hire Wolf, for a small tavern it owned on Paulina Street. By the time Muddy left town on his next tour, Wolf had been engaged to stand in for him at the Zanzibar, Sylvio's and at the 708 Club.

The existence, or not, of a rivalry that simmered between Muddy and Wolf is a contentious issue in blues lore — some observers swear they were antagonistic adversaries, others are as resolute that it's baseless hype. The fact is they were both Chess artists, competing on the same turf. Willie Dixon often found himself squeezed in the middle and maintained that "both of them wanted what they called 'the top spot in the blues.' "[27] He supplied both Muddy and Wolf with songs, but each one was vigilant as to what Willie gave the other, in case he detected favoritism or lost out on a hit. Dixon remembered, "A lot of times you have to use backwards psychology on these guys. I'd say this is a song for Muddy if I wanted Wolf to do it. He would be glad to get in on it by him thinking it was somebody else's, especially Muddy's."[28]

However, their songs were not interchangeable. "Muddy is the kind of person you can give any kind of lyric," Dixon said, "he's what you call a quick study." Wolf, according to Dixon, had trouble remembering the words, "And if he gets 'em right, he still ain't gonna get the right meaning," so his songs had to be more basic.[29]

"They cut heads," Wolf said, referring to Muddy's band, "but when they got to me they'd back up, 'cause I was too heavy for them."[30] Wolf bragged that Muddy had steered clear of West Memphis because it was Wolf's territory and that even in Chicago the band was wary of him. When he and Muddy did gigs together at Silvio's, Wolf maintained there was a discernible lack of applause for the other musician. Then assuming the role of the slighted party, Wolf complained, "Seems like [Muddy and his band] always had a cold side towards me. But I never did quit trying to be friends."[31]

Muddy contended that Wolf was jealous, that despite their friendship, he couldn't accept that anyone was equal or better than he: "I know the peoples thought we hated one another, but we didn't, but Wolf wanted to be the best and I wasn't gonna let him come up here and take over the best."[32] When Wolf would announce that his band was superior to Muddy's, Muddy always refuted the allegation. A very ambitious man himself, Muddy could appreciate Wolf's drive to excel, but he believed it was a passion better kept to oneself.

Wolf's guitar player Hubert Sumlin — who would also play for Muddy in 1956 and 1966 — saw the rivalry up close and describes it less diplomatically. "Those two were just like the McCoys, man!" he exclaims.[33] Sumlin insists that "they were enemies: 'You stole my shit.' 'You did this.' 'You did that.' It was endless, because they were the two biggest dudes in Chicago, and they were always arguing and competing about who was number one."[34]

In 1954 Muddy hired a booking agent and set out on a nationwide tour designed to capitalize on the popularity of "I Just Want To Make Love To You" and "I'm Ready." Despite his recording success, he was still, for the most part, relegated to ghetto taverns for his performances, earning from $300 to $500 a night for the entire band. Touring was an exhausting grind of one-night stands strung across the country, and the designated driver was always cautioned by Muddy to obey the rules of the road conscientiously and beware of inclement weather. Despite the fatigue of travel, Muddy strove to maintain his professionalism at each gig along the way. "Every time you go on stage somebody's looking for you to do your best. Do top-notch entertainment," Muddy remarked. "Sometimes you go up there, you're half sick."[35]

Muddy was part of the spiritual and rhythm-and-blues lineup at the annual Goodwill Revue for Handicapped Negro Children, sponsored by Memphis radio station WDIA, on 4 December 1953 and 3 December 1954. Each year over 6,000 fans would cram the Ellis Auditorium to enjoy such artists as Muddy, Little Walter, B.B. King and Eddie Boyd, all of whom had donated their time for the cause. According to one account, Muddy cut a rather colorful figure: "Wearing an iridescent aquamarine sapphire silk suit, huge green-and-white jewelled cuff links, and matching pinky diamonds, Muddy walked onstage, sang the opening bars of one of his earliest recordings, and was greeted by a roar of welcoming applause."[36]

WDIA radio personality Rufus Thomas, who was embarking on a recording career of his own, recalls Muddy's performances at the Goodwill Revues. He describes Muddy as "a gracious, fine man [and] blues singer, and they came no better. . . . And I don't mean just music; I mean the person himself. He was a nice, warm individual that you could talk to and you could laugh with. . . . He liked what he was doing, and it helped to make his living. . . . That's what you call givin' it to you in twos."[37]

During this period harp player George Smith departed to concentrate on his own career. He performed and recorded in Kansas City, then toured the United States as part of a traveling revue that included Champion Jack Dupree. Eventually Smith moved to Los Angeles, where he cut some sides for Sotoplay under the name of Little Walter, Jr. By this time Junior Wells had earned a dishonorable discharge from the army, so he rejoined Muddy's band to take over on harmonica.

On 3 February 1955, the band assembled in the studio to record "This Pain," "Young Fashioned Ways," "I Want To Be Loved" and "My Eyes Keep Me In Trouble." In "Young Fashioned Ways," Muddy may be anticipating his 40th birthday when he expresses confidence in his sexual prowess despite the advancing years. The band is on fire — the tight ensemble showcases the superb talent of each musician, especially Otis Spann's superlative piano. "I Want To Be Loved" finds Muddy in a more romantic mood, complemented by some inspiring harmonica and piano interplay between verses. But Muddy's libido gets the better of him in "My Eyes Keep Me In Trouble," where he claims his desire can only be quelled by prodigious numbers of women.

The distinct and celebrated studio sound that emerged from this and other Chess sessions was not the result of an acoustic engineer's scientific plan, but rather a product of trial and error with a dollop of ingenuity and a measure of luck thrown in. In May 1954 Leonard and Phil Chess had built their first studio at 4750 Cottage Grove Avenue, and in the process discovered that a five- or six-foot clay sewer pipe provided the means to achieve the reverberation they were seeking. "They would put a speaker on one end and a microphone at the other," Marshall Chess reveals. "They would feed the sound from up in the studio . . . and it would come out of the speaker, travel the length of pipe, be picked up by the microphone with the echo from the pipe and then fed back onto the tape."[38]

> They were constantly working on the mike placement, drum sounds . . . doing experiments [Marshall continues]. I remember my father even took back these German microphones from Germany, these little thin ones. . . . They were always trying different sounds, echoes, taped echoes, all kinds of things. We were a very creative company. We were always striving for a different, newer sound. Black people at that time were very attracted to those new kinds of sounds. . . . We were one of the first, you know, with Muddy's amplified slide guitar, then we had Little Walter with the amplified harmonica, which was very special with all that echo, that Chess echo.[39]

Stylistically, as well, Chess discs were recognizable. A Chess blues artist was typically backed by a drum-driven rhythm section. Marshall recounts, "My father wanted drum, drum, and more drum.

I think he was responsible for doing that to blues, to bring out a heavy beat."[40] Willie Dixon credited a great deal of Muddy's innovative sound to its rhythm: "You know when you go to changin' beats in music, you change the whole style. The difference in blues or rock and roll or jazz is the beat."[41] It was the propulsive beat of Muddy's blues that provided the structure for rock 'n' roll, as well as for all subsequent popular music.

Muddy's 24 May 1955 recording of "Mannish Boy" delivers that beat and then some. Inspired by Muddy's 1951 cut "She Moves Me," Bo Diddley had scored a hit earlier that month with "I'm a Man" on Chess's Checker label. Muddy's "Mannish Boy," largely copied from Diddley's number, intensifies the rhythm and jacks up the sexual tension. Using stop-time rhythm — executed by Junior Wells, Jimmy Rogers, Willie Dixon and Fred Below in unison — he melds the beat with the tune, making it one. (Ironically Spann played piano on Diddley's number, but was omitted from "Mannish Boy.") Muddy borrows heavily from Diddley's lyrics, but presents them with an unabashed braggadocio not found in the original. On this track he leaves out several of Diddley's verses, although they were restored in subsequent performances.

"Mannish Boy" became a staple of Muddy's repertoire for the rest of his life. Considered by some to be a proclamation that black men are not boys, that notion is belied by the sexual manner in which he consistently delivered it. Here Muddy serves up a sizzling treat of raw rhythm and steamy lyrics, roaring out exclamations of his manhood amid screams of confirmation. By July 1955 the song had climbed to number nine on the *Best Seller* R&B chart, six on the *Jockey* R&B chart and five on the *Juke Box* R&B chart. It would eventually galvanize a generation of young British musicians, and one band led by David Jones — later reinvented as David Bowie — named itself the Manish Boys. The tune was recorded by the Yardbirds, the Who and Jimi Hendrix, and along with Bo Diddley's original, it spawned many answer songs; as a tribute to Muddy, Koko Taylor wrote and recorded "I'm A Woman."

Muddy's success at Chess was one of the primary factors in that company's growth, and as it garnered more hits with Jimmy Rogers, Little Walter and others, Chess gained a reputation as being the premier label for blues. Muddy had provided the kick start; now every artist wanted to record there. Looking back on a childhood spent largely in the Chess studio, Marshall Chess recalls the great affection the Chesses felt for Muddy: "We were like a family. With Muddy it was more like a father-son or a brother-brother thing than a business relationship."[42]

Marshall's first clear recollection of Muddy dates from about 1950, when Muddy had come by the Chess residence to speak to Leonard: "He was wearing an electric bright green suit with shoes that had Pinto pony inserts. His hair was very high, done in a shiny process. Muddy radiated a regal aura. You just knew he was special and you treated him with respect."[43] Marshall venerated Muddy beyond his talent as a great bluesman: "Muddy Waters was like a king. He had tremendous presence. You never treated Muddy Waters with disrespect. He was a leader, always in control, always a gentleman. He liked women and Cadillacs."[44]

Marshall describes Muddy's personality as

extremely dominant, regal and soft, at least with me. . . . He used to call me Grandson. . . . He once wrote me lines to send to a girl when I was like 14. We used to talk about girls all the time. . . . I had a good close relationship with him because it was mainly because I was my father's son, and he had that thing with my father, and I knew him from being really small. Numerous times Geneva, which was his wife then, would send me down fried chicken — she made unbelievable fried chicken — wrapped in foil.

I remember him with deep respect, as a man, as an artist, as a surrogate grandfather who told me about women. I had a really good thing with him. I liked him a lot. I loved him. My family loved him. My father loved him, and my uncle loved him, and I did, too, no matter what people say.[45]

Marshall recalls the intensity — and equality — of the special relationship between his father and Muddy. As for Muddy, he considered one of the most positive results of his recording career to have been his friendship with Leonard Chess, "for which I wouldn't take a million dollars. Here was a guy who had blind faith. He didn't believe in my blues but believed in me as a person when we started out. I got a big kick out of proving myself to him as a performer. I got more of a kick out of the fact that we became

more than business associates — real intimate friends. I tell everyone who asks that the one person responsible for my success is
Leonard."[46]

Leonard had a domineering personality and "an extraordinarily
coarse outer manner," according to Chess engineer Malcolm Chisholm.[47] He would come to a session doggedly determined to achieve
a certain sound, and he would stubbornly push his musicians, with
obscenities soaring, until he got what he envisioned, no matter how
long it took. With Muddy, however, Chisholm noted a divergence:
"With some of the blues players, the whole session would be Leonard and whoever it was calling each other stacks of motherfuckers.
But in the case of Muddy Waters, who was intelligent, perceptive,
and all that good stuff, Leonard dealt with him in a very gentle-
manly manner, on the basis of absolute mutual respect."[48]

Prior to recording, Muddy and the band would usually rehearse
the numbers they intended to cut. New songs couldn't be worked
out at gigs or they'd be stolen by some eager rival before Muddy had
a chance to record them. If they were playing a Dixon arrangement,
Jimmy Rogers says, "We would stop playing and listen to the way
[Willie] would phrase the lyrics and changes, we'd get that down
and practice on it until we got it straightened out."[49] Sometimes
Muddy needed some coaching to express a particular emotion in a
song. "Our job was to try to bring out points in his mind that he
might have forgotten," Phil Chess explains, "to give him ideas, to
get him to think about some things that were happening down in
Rolling Fork, Mississippi, or wherever. It's actually like psychiatry[;]
you try to talk to him to bring out the things himself."[50]

When the recording process was underway, Muddy would either
cut his tracks first and then have the rest of the musicians lay down
their parts, or he would record with the band while sitting separate
from them in a booth. Occasionally Muddy would invite a friend,
such as John Lee Hooker, to watch the procedure. After B.B. King
got to know Muddy well, he also enjoyed the privilege of observing
a couple of recording sessions. "You stand and look," recalls King
at the honor of being present in the studio. "That's what I did, look
and listen and try to learn something from him, because he was a
real professional. What he did, he did well. Nobody, I don't think,
has been able to do what he did as he did it. He was a professional
at what he did."[51]

However, Little Walter's approach to recording was more laissez-faire. He would often explode at what he interpreted to be Leonard's interference and abruptly stalk out of a session. As his alcoholism reeled out of control, he'd show up drunk, deny his condition in the face of Leonard's accusations, then leave. He sometimes kept the band waiting for two or three days.

At first it took Muddy about four hours to record four or five songs. As his popularity increased, so did the stakes, and Leonard would keep the band at it for two or three days, working and reworking songs. Because Chess paid the musicians by the session, not by the hour, it mattered little to Leonard how long it took to achieve what he was after, but prolonged sessions naturally sparked bad feelings amongst the sidemen. As leader, Muddy earned double fees, and if band members owed him money, their checks would also go straight to him.

While Leonard Chess has often been credited with prescient insight into the development of blues and how it should be recorded, it was admittedly frustrating to cut a session with a stubborn perfectionist. Occasionally the camaraderie between Leonard and Muddy would crack. After working incessantly on a Charles Brown number, "Merry Christmas Baby," Muddy lost his patience with Leonard's continuing dissatisfaction and exclaimed, "God damn it! If it's this hard, I'm taking my God damn contract and go on back to Mississippi! Got to work this damn hard."[52] They never did reach an accord. Chess had Chuck Berry record the song in November 1958. Sometimes Jimmy Rogers would kick back, enjoy a drink and be entertained by the battle of wills: "Whoo, they'd be fightin' mad. One would be thinkin' the other one would knock him on the head, man."[53]

Yet Rogers also felt hindered by Leonard's demands, particularly when he tampered with the timing of a song after it had been thoroughly rehearsed. Such intervention could change the feeling of a number, causing Muddy to forget his lyrics and the band to get confused. Jimmy believes that a few tunes were overproduced, that the soul of a song dies with too much analysis and revision.

Although Muddy's music had earned him a nationwide black audience, sales of Chicago blues discs had been ebbing since the spring of 1954. The adult market was shrinking and teenagers were becoming mindful of a new sound rumbling into a groundswell.

Elvis Presley and Bill Haley & His Comets ignited the initial explosion in 1954, and rock 'n' roll erupted out of the core of urban blues. The new music accelerated the beat of blues and sanitized its lyrics, keeping it just sassy enough to titillate teenage tastes. The fallout would almost bury the blues market.

In May 1955 Ralph Burris, a young man from St. Louis, traveled up to Chicago with a friend to visit Ralph's mother. The two went barhopping on the South Side, taking in performances by Elmore James and Howlin' Wolf. Ralph was anxious to move on since he'd seen these bluesmen before. His companion left with reluctance and accompanied him to the Palladium on Wabash Avenue. When he caught sight of the club's marquee — "Muddy Waters Tonight" — Ralph's pal became ecstatic. He charged up the stairs in rapture. He was about to see his hero.

The history of music would soon change forever. That friend's name was Chuck Berry.

NOTES

1 Paul Oliver, "Muddy Waters," *Blues Unlimited Collector's Classics: Muddy Waters*, B1 (Mar. 1964): 3.

2 Alfred Duckett, "I Have a Right to Sing the Blues," *Louisville Defender*, 14 Apr. 1955.

3 Duckett.

4 Duckett.

5 Bill Greensmith, "Below's the Name, Drummin's the Game," *Blues Unlimited* 131 (Sept.–Dec. 1978): 17.

6 Bob Corritone, Bill Ferris and Jim O'Neal, "Willie Dixon, Part II," *Living Blues* 82 (Sept.–Oct. 1988): 21.

7 Junior Wells, interview with author, 9 Dec. 1995.

8 Bob Margolin, "I Can't Be Satisfied," *Blues Revue* 20 (Dec. 1995–Jan. 1996): 13.

9 Valerie Wilmer, "Little Walter Blows In," *Jazzbeat* 10 (Oct. 1964): 15.

10 Peter Guralnick, *Feel Like Going Home* (New York: Harper & Row, Publishers, 1989), 75.

11 Mike Rowe, *Chicago Breakdown* (London: Eddison Press Ltd., 1973), 147.

12 David Walters, Laurence Garman and John Matthews, "Jimmy Rogers," *Blues Unlimited* 105 (Dec. 1973–Jan. 1974): 18.

13 Willie Smith, interview with author, 10 Dec. 1995.

14 Jimmy Rogers, interview with author, 26 Apr. 1995.

15 Pete Welding, "Little George Smith," *Nothing But the Blues*, ed. Mike Leadbitter (London: Hanover Books Ltd., 1971), 99.

16 Welding, 99.

17 Willie Foster, interview with author, 18 May 1995.

18 Willie Foster, interview with author, 18 May 1995.

19 Willie Foster, interview with author, 18 May 1995.

20 Willie Foster, interview with author, 18 May 1995.

21 Willie Foster, interview with author, 18 May 1995.

22 Willie Foster, interview with author, 18 May 1995.

23 Willie Foster, interview with author, 18 May 1995.

24 Jas Obrecht, "The Life and Times of the Hoochie Coochie Man," *Guitar Player* (Mar. 1994): 31.

25 Arnold Shaw, *Honkers and Shouters: The Golden Years of Rhythm and Blues* (New York: Collier Books, 1978), 302.

26 Jim O'Neal and Amy O'Neal, "Muddy," *Living Blues* 64 (Mar.–Apr. 1985): 39.

27 Anthony DeCurtis, "Living Legends," *Rolling Stone* 561 (21 Sept. 1989): 128.

28 Willie Dixon and Don Snowden, *I Am the Blues: The Willie Dixon Story* (London: Quartet Books, 1989), 149.

29 Guralnick, 162.

30 Guralnick, 156.

31 Guralnick, 157.

32 O'Neal and O'Neal, 39.

33 Paul Trynka, "Deep Blue," *Mojo* 27 (Feb. 1996): 47.

34 Alan Paul, "Of Wolf & Man," *Guitar Legends*, vol. 3, no. 1 (1994): 17.

35 James Rooney, *Bossmen: Bill Monroe & Muddy Waters* (New York: The Dial Press, 1971), 133.

36 Stanley Booth, *Rythm (sic) Oil: A Journey through the Music of the American South* (New York: Pantheon Books, 1991), 86.

37 Rufus Thomas, interview with author, 5 May 1995.

38 Marshall Chess, interview with author, 4 Nov. 1996.

39 Marshall Chess, interview with author, 4 Nov. 1996.

40 Guralnick, 227.

41 Robert Palmer, *Deep Blues* (New York: Penguin, 1982), 168.

42 Guralnick, 216.

43 Mary Katherine Aldin, liner notes, *Chess Blues*, MCA Records, 1992, 13.

44 Joe Smith, *Off the Record: An Oral History of Popular Music* (New York: Warner Books, 1988), 114.

45 Marshall Chess, interview with author, 4 Nov. 1996.

46 Duckett.

47 Palmer, 162.

48 Palmer, 162.

49 Dixon and Snowden, 97.

50 Guralnick, 227

51 B.B. King, interview with author, 24 Aug. 1995.

52 Jim O'Neal and Bill Greensmith, "Living Blues Interview: Jimmy Rogers," *Living Blues* 14 (Autumn 1973): 15.

53 O'Neal and Greensmith, 15.

6

*I do my thing. Count does his
thing. Duke does his thing. And
we do it good. We are creators.*[1]

"Muddy Waters was the godfather of the blues," Chuck Berry
proclaims. "He was perhaps the greatest inspiration in the launching of my career. I was a disciple in worship of a lord."[2] Berry and
pianist Johnnie Johnson had gained a devoted following at the
Cosmopolitan Club in St. Louis by primarily performing numbers
by Nat King Cole and Muddy Waters. "Definitely Muddy," exclaims
Berry, when asked to identify his primary influence. "His sound!
That's what I played before 'Maybellene' — before I turned pro,
I guess you call it."[3]

Following Muddy's show at the Palladium, Chuck was granted the opportunity to speak with his idol, a momentous event he likened to an audience with a pope or a president. Caught up in a swarm of jostling fans, Berry had only a minute to express his esteem for Muddy's music, then quickly inquired whom he should see about cutting a record of his own. Chuck was impressed that, in the midst of the uproar, Muddy made the effort to respond. "Yeah, see Leonard Chess," Muddy answered. "Yeah, Chess Records over on 47th and Cottage."[4]

Leonard's advice that Monday morning was for Berry to return with an audition tape. During the intervening period, Chuck sat in with Muddy's band. He learned a lot from his mentor. Muddy's respect for his audience and the way he communicated with them were valuable examples that Berry has tried to emulate in his own career.

Muddy immediately recognized that Berry's innovative style signaled the onset of a musical upheaval. Yet Leonard almost overlooked Chuck's potential, specifically in regard to a hillbilly tune called "Ida Mae." "You better record that," Muddy advised Leonard, "that's something new here."[5] The title was changed, the record was cut, and "Maybellene" exploded to number one.

Although it was typical of Muddy's generosity towards other musicians, his influence in igniting the Chuck Berry phenomenon and all that followed cast blues even deeper in the shadow of rock 'n' roll throughout the latter half of the 1950s. As Muddy remembered, "Rock 'n' roll, it hurt the blues pretty bad. People wanted to 'bug all the time and we couldn't play slow blues anymore. But we still hustled around and kept going."[6]

Ironically it was urban blues — especially Muddy's blues — from which rock 'n' roll borrowed its beat, then quickened the pace to leave the older music biting the dust. And while black artists such as Chuck Berry, Bo Diddley, Little Richard and Chubby Checker were drawing ever-increasing black and white audiences, Muddy's market was exclusively black and dwindling.

As Berry's popularity eclipsed Muddy's, it was a logical move for Chess to channel most of its resources into flogging its biggest star. Jimmy Rogers recalls that Leonard Chess "was right on Chuck. Every time you'd turn on your radio, he was pushin' him on out there, see. And the stuff [blues] that really started him, he kind of pushed it aside a little."[7]

Like Berry, Junior Wells was another impassioned young artist who craved his shot at recording as a frontman; he was not content to stay in the background for the rest of his career. When he approached Leonard Chess about leading his own session, he was advised, "I'll let you know when you're ready to record. All you do is just stay back there and play harmonica behind Muddy."[8] With that response, Junior made his decision to leave Muddy's band. "I didn't have anything against Muddy," Junior says. "It's just that I thought it was time to go and build a future for Junior Wells. . . . [Muddy] realized that you just don't stay there and make somebody else and don't try to do nothing for yourself. This is the challenge of being a musician."[9]

Junior called it quits in Tampa, Florida, while the band was on a southern tour in 1955. Muddy arrived in Memphis on a Friday for a gig the next night without a harmonica player. His driver, James Triblett, recommended a young harp blower named James Cotton, and offered to take Muddy to check him out. Meanwhile Cotton had finished his shift as a truck driver on a construction site and headed off to his weekend gig at an Eighth Street restaurant in West Memphis, where he played with guitarist L.D. McGhee. Cotton was already well lubricated with a half-pint of Echo Springs whiskey when Muddy approached him. "And he said, 'I'm Muddy Waters,' and I told him, 'I'm Jesus Christ,'" Cotton relates. "I didn't believe he was Muddy Waters."[10]

After listening to Cotton play for about an hour, Muddy offered him the job playing with his band the next night. Cotton was still cautious, however. Despite Triblett's assurances, he was still not entirely convinced that this was the mighty Muddy Waters. Muddy told him to be at 500 Beale Street in Memphis the following night at nine o'clock, and just to hedge his bet, Cotton showed up. Still skeptical, he went onstage with Muddy's band and performed a few songs with them before Muddy appeared. Then as Jimmy announced the star of the show, Muddy walked out and launched into "I'm Ready," finally leaving no doubt in Cotton's mind that this was, indeed, the great bluesman. The following day he left for Chicago as a member of the Muddy Waters band.

James Cotton was born in Tunica, Mississippi, located about halfway between Clarksdale and Memphis, on 1 July 1935, the youngest of nine children. The family did farm work, and James's father, Mose, was also a Baptist preacher. Cotton's first exposure to the harmonica was through his mother, Hattie, although all she could play were train and hen imitations. When James was about five or six, she gave him his first harp as a Christmas gift. Once the boy had mastered what his mother knew, he lost interest — that is, until he heard the harmonica of Rice Miller on KFFA's "King Biscuit Time."

James was Wiley Green's favorite nephew, and he expanded the boy's blues horizons through the records of John Lee "Sonny Boy" Williamson, Lightnin' Hopkins, Big Bill Broonzy, Blind Lemon Jefferson, Arthur "Big Boy" Crudup and Leadbelly. Pretty soon Cotton was learning to play these tunes and those he heard in the fields. Mose Cotton, however, was far from pleased with his son's taste in music.

Under the tutelage of his Uncle Wiley, James grew up fast. When other children were in primary school, he was carousing in juke joints with Wiley, shooting dice and knocking back corn liquor; he even sold moonshine for his uncle. Wiley taught James to drive a tractor at age six, when he began plowing fields alongside his adult counterparts. He made $36 a day, more than any of the manual field laborers, including his father. But when his uncle saw Cotton earn $45 in tips playing his harp for a half-hour outside a juke, he knew his nephew belonged elsewhere.

Cotton was nine years old when Wiley took him to Helena, Arkansas, and convinced Rice Miller (Sonny Boy Williamson II) to take him on as his student. James already knew Sonny Boy's repertoire, so the six-foot-four legend began performing with the child, an odd couple to be sure, but a definite crowd pleaser. A prodigious drinker and gambler, Sonny Boy seldom gave James lessons, but the youngster was eager to learn and rapidly assimilated whatever his mentor played.

"He'd get that knife open he'd sure cut cha," is how Cotton describes Sonny Boy's quick temper. "Crazy guy. But other than that he was a good man you know."[11] When James was 15, Sonny Boy left for Wisconsin, leaving the teenager as leader of his band — which comprised James "Peck" Curtis, Robert "Dudlow" Taylor and Joe Willie Wilkins — although it soon broke up. At various times James played for Howlin' Wolf and Willie Nix, and he also formed a group with guitarists Hubert Sumlin and future Muddy Waters band mate Pat Hare. Performing on his own radio show broadcast from station KWEM outside Memphis, Cotton attracted the notice of Sam Phillips of Sun Records. His first recording for the label was with Howlin' Wolf and then Willie Nix. As frontman of his own sessions in 1953 and 1954, he cut "Straighten Up Baby" and "Hold Me In Your Arms."

Returning to Chicago after their 1955 southern tour, the Hoochie Coochie Boys — as Muddy's band was now called — resumed their long-standing gig at the 708 Club, and Cotton settled in on the second floor of Muddy's brick house at 4339 South Lake Park on Chicago's South Side. It was a big adjustment for the 21-year-old; he had giant shoes to fill. Cotton recalls Muddy's expectations: "Well, he was kinda fussy about his music, and I can understand that now. Then I didn't. But he wanted it just like it was on record, and Little Walter . . . was making records with him . . . so I had a big job there on my hands. I played like him for a while, then I finally had to tell him. I said, 'Hey, Muddy, I'll never be Little Walter, so you'll have to accept me for what I can do and what I am.'"[12] And Cotton was a powerhouse in his own right. With his accomplished technique, unerring sense of rhythm and intuitive feel for when to hold back, Cotton provided an essential textural counterpoint to the rest of the band.

One time Little Walter left his chromatic harp behind, and Cotton began to experiment on it. Muddy made no comment. The next evening as Muddy walked in the club where he was playing, he slipped on some wet snow that had been tracked in from outside. As his feet skidded out from under him and he landed on his backside, a new chromatic harmonica shot out of his hand. He pointed to it lying in a puddle and snapped at Cotton, "That's your God damn harmonica right there! . . . You get it."[13]

Cotton remembers seeing Muddy play the harp a couple of times offstage. "You couldn't fool him because he could play it hisself," James relates. "He wasn't as good as me playing harmonica, but he could play it. And he could play it just enough to know when you wasn't playing it."[14]

Muddy was an exacting bandleader. He expected his musicians to behave well, be on time, dress appropriately, "and he wanted his music played properly," Cotton adds. "Every time he was on-stage it was for business. . . . He was Muddy Waters and he was up there, and he wanted his music played. He didn't come down on me onstage, but every night when we got off, if he thought I'd messed up, he truly told me about it. . . . At first I thought it was kind of hard, but after a while I realized that he was a star, people were buying his music; he wanted it right. And I really respected that."[15]

"We got along good as friends, even though he was kind of fussy about his music," Cotton reminisces. "He was a beautiful guy, very easy to get along with. . . . He was a gentleman."[16] For Cotton the only negative aspect of working with Muddy was the dress code. "Every time you went to work, you had to have on whatever uniform there was for you to wear that night," says James. Muddy would tell his band members what to wear ahead of time, "and if you didn't have it on, you had to pay for it."[17] The uniform was always some type of tuxedo. Cotton found it hot and the tie especially restrictive for a wind player.

For a time the Hoochie Coochie Boys included tenor-sax player Bob Hadley, although he didn't record with the band. "We was playing them black dances," Muddy explained, "and it's kind of hard just to play a dance with a harmonica and guitars."[18] However, Hadley left Muddy by late 1956 or 1957 to pursue a career with the Chicago Police Department, eventually becoming a detective.

Despite his recording success, Muddy was not always appreciated when he ventured beyond the Chicago area or his regular Deep South circuit. The band was roundly booed at both the Highland Theater in Washington, D.C., and at the Apollo Theatre in New York. Muddy "felt really bad," says Cotton, "but you got to do the work, you know. What can you do? It's just part of being a musician, you know. You try to get better for the next show, because you don't want to face that same thing again."[19]

As a result, when Muddy and the band joined the Sarah Vaughan tour — which also included Nappy Brown, Al Hibbler, the Moonglows, Chuck Willis and Red Prysock — they performed more popular tunes. On that excursion the headliners traveled in a separate bus from the supporting musicians. Muddy maintained, however, that it was more fun riding with the sidemen, drinking and playing poker. "I don't feel like no star anyway," he acknowledged. "Forget the star, just plain Muddy Waters."[20]

Yet when he hit the road for his own tours, Muddy would typically ride separate from the band in his Cadillac with a girlfriend — often Mary Jo from Cleveland or Mary from Hallandale, Florida — and a chauffeur, usually his dear old friend Andrew "Bo" Bolden. "He was a big, dark-skinned guy that had this mean countenance," Paul Oscher, a future member of Muddy's band, says of Bolden. "He'd try to be mean. Like when someone talked shit, he had this little case knife he'd pull out of his pocket at the slightest provocation. 'I'm gonna cut you, motherfucker.' He never really cut anybody."[21] Cotton would drive the Chevrolet station wagon, crammed with the rest of the band, their instruments and three amps. Their contracts stipulated that a piano would be provided at every gig.

Life on the highway was dangerous, and Muddy knew it. "I keep 'em down with that speed. And be sure you obey signs and obey that weather. Ice on the ground, come out of there — starts a'raining, cut that speed . . . the highway is wet, just try to live."[22] Fatigue and alcohol compounded treacherous road conditions. In Tuscaloosa, Alabama, Muddy and Cotton were thrown in jail for drinking corn whiskey and then attempting to drive to their next gig. Muddy's one phone call was to Leonard Chess, who arranged for Muddy to be released after a couple of hours, then Muddy got Cotton out.

The further south they traveled, the more responsive the crowds were to their music, yet racial hatred intensified as well. "It was really bad. People didn't know no better, you know," Cotton recalls.[23] "We had to go around to the back door to get food or use the bathroom and we couldn't go in the same door as the paying folks."[24] Cotton remembers an incident at a Florida gas station where several truckers, suspicious of a black man in a brand-new Cadillac, accused the band of stealing it. High on corn whiskey, the guys just laughed, paid for their gas and left, narrowly escaping a violent confrontation.

But touring the South had its benefits as well. Whenever he was in Mississippi, Muddy would call friends and family in Clarksdale and Rolling Fork. Cotton accompanied Muddy on one visit to Rolling Fork to visit his half-brother, half-sister and father. Muddy's relationship with Ollie appeared to be good. "I think his father was glad to see him," Cotton says. "He said, 'This is my son!'"[25] James believes that by this time Ollie had forsaken blues for the church, so father and son did not play together.

As a connoisseur of fine young women — and with ample opportunity to indulge his roving eye and satisfy his appetite away from
Geneva — Muddy usually toured in the company of a girlfriend.
One of these was Mary Brown, a girl in her late teens whom Muddy
had met at a Hallandale, Florida, gig in about 1955. Just being on
the road together soon wasn't enough, however. Muddy moved her
to Chicago and ensconced her in an apartment on the West Side,
which she shared with Muddy's adult daughter Isoline. In 1956
Mary gave birth to Muddy's son, Williams Morganfield, although
he didn't assume Muddy's last name until after Geneva's death.
Williams was raised by his grandmother in Fort Lauderdale, Florida,
and had very little contact with his father during those years.

Muddy's recording session of 3 November 1955 produced "I Got
To Find My Baby," a Willie Dixon number, and two up-tempo songs,
"Sugar Sweet" and the harmonica- and bass-driven "Trouble No
More." Erroneously credited to Muddy, "Trouble No More" actually
originated with "Sleepy" John Estes's "Someday Baby" and a vari-
ation of that tune entitled "Worried Life Blues," recorded by Big
Maceo Merriweather in 1941. As well, Muddy recycled "Flood,"
his 1953 composition, fashioning it into "Clouds In My Heart."
It has the same melody as "Flood," they share several lyrics, they
both concern a wayward woman and they feature the same climatic
imagery. The stormy scene is further evoked by simulating a thun-
derstorm with cymbals and drums.

Little Walter is identified as the harmonica player on these cuts.
Cotton contends, however, that although he was scheduled to do
the session, Walter got drunk and never showed up. Muddy suggested to Leonard that Cotton fill in, even though "he ain't no
Little Walter."[26] Leonard liked what he heard, so apparently it was
Cotton who played harp that day. "Sugar Sweet" would earn Muddy
a number-14 spot on the *Jockey* R&B chart and climb as high as
11th place on the *Best Seller* list. "Trouble No More" would outdo
it by reaching seventh position in the *Jockey* R&B standings.

Yet despite the success of his recorded output, Muddy believed his
music was better heard live than on disc. After all, the stage was
his turf. When Muddy performed he owned the crowd. He wasn't a
dancer; he didn't have a stage routine. In fact he often performed
seated. But onstage Muddy personified the emotion of his music.
Whether he was singing about the cruelty of a callous lover or

bragging about his sexual prowess, he made the audience feel it. There was no doubt he'd been there. It exuded through his voice and gestures — an all-knowing glance, a wag of his finger, his body jolting in time with the beat.

"I like to think I could really master a stage," Muddy declared. "I think I was a pretty good stage personality. . . . I just had a natural feel for it."[27] He'd delve down deep to deliver the soul of a song, wringing every emotion from his blues, often keeping it up until three, four or five o'clock in the morning. "It was sex," states Marshall Chess, explaining Muddy's charisma. "If you had ever seen Muddy then, the effect he had on women. Because blues, you know, has always been a women's market. On Saturday night they'd be lined up ten deep."[28]

Setting aside his guitar didn't subdue Muddy's onstage presence. Unbeknownst to the audience, he'd stash a Coke bottle in his pants during Cotton's solo in "Mannish Boy," then back at the microphone he'd work it in a risqué fashion as he declared his manhood. While the men egged him on and the ladies shrieked with lust, Muddy would tease the crowd as he suggestively loosened his belt. Then, as Charlie Musselwhite, who witnessed the routine in the early 1960s, recalls, "He would shake the bottle and release the cap spraying the audience and the stage. The people would go crazy. There would be women screaming and swinging their purses in the air. The audience just loved it."[29]

With such heightened emotions, it wasn't uncommon for violence to erupt at a gig, provoked by the potent combination of liquor and sex. The band was always able to avoid the melee, however, even when jealous tough guys tried to avenge their girlfriends' flirtatious advances to members of the group.

Requiring a guitarist for his next tour in 1956, Muddy dispatched his chauffeur to the Zanzibar to lure Hubert Sumlin, Howlin' Wolf's guitar player, into taking the gig. Wolf's association with Sumlin had been turbulent, resulting in knocked-out teeth on both sides. While such flare-ups were soon forgotten, Sumlin was still rankled by Wolf's refusal to respect his musicianship. So when Muddy's driver appeared at intermission, bedecked in diamonds, offering him the thickest wad of cash he'd ever seen, Hubert was hooked. "Muddy done sent him over there to bribe me, man!" Sumlin declares. "He's telling me, 'Muddy say he'll triple the money that

Wolf paying you, what do you want to do?' "[30] Hubert succumbed and sought sanctuary in the washroom to count Muddy's down payment. As soon as he heard the news, Wolf stalked in with a murderous look on his face. "Man, he was changing colors," Sumlin says of Wolf. "I knew he was mad."[31]

Because Muddy was no longer playing his instrument onstage, Sumlin had to take over lead guitar. Every day at noon, he'd be in Muddy's basement going over the band's repertoire and working on his timing with Otis Spann. Muddy would venture down from time to time to supervise his progress. Hubert was with Muddy for about a year, and of his tenure he declares, "Lord, I learned a lot from that man. I also learned a lot from Jimmy Rogers."[32]

Those times were grueling. Muddy's schedule was brutal, and the 25-year-old Sumlin had to struggle to keep up with the older man. "Sometimes we'd drive a thousand miles to make it to the next gig," Hubert recalls. "Get off at three, four o'clock in the morning. Get right in the car and start to driving."[33] He maintains that "we did so much driving, I got the haemorrhoids so bad I couldn't sit down! They brought me feather pillows that I had to sit on!"[34]

On one trip home from Florida, Spann decided to purchase a Saturday night special, and in a capricious moment, the rest of the band followed suit. The two-car contingent arrived back in Chicago with everyone packing heat. Muddy and his chauffeur were ahead of the band vehicle when the Chicago police pulled the second car over. Upon discovering Spann's pistol, the rest of the group was hauled from the car at gunpoint while the officers called for reinforcements. "They thought they had captured the black mafia or something," Sumlin remembers. "We all got thrown away in jail; we'd be there today without Muddy. He came down as soon as he found out and made them let us go. But they kept the guns."[35]

Though Sumlin insists that he enjoyed working with Muddy, their disagreements sometimes got physical. Still their relationship was never as stormy as Sumlin and Wolf's. Cotton witnessed a couple of brawls between them. "They'd get full of whiskey," he says of Muddy and Hubert, "and anything might happen."[36]

Sumlin's engagement with the Hoochie Coochie Boys ended badly. Exhausted after 40 one-nighters on the road, he expected some time off to recuperate. Instead, the band was booked at the

708 Club as soon as it hit town. Sumlin was incensed as he watched Muddy sitting in the audience, drinking Old Grand Dad and flirting with a young woman, only rising to sing two numbers while the rest of the musicians carried the gig.

Just before intermission Sumlin suffered a severe shock from a cooling fan and told Muddy he was finished for the night. According to Hubert, Muddy exploded with a tirade of abuse and was about to kick him when, "Here come Spann with a trace chain, gonna whip me about Muddy. I had ahold of Muddy, and every time Spann tried to get me with that chain, I put Muddy next to him. Every time he hit Muddy."[37]

Although Sumlin completed the show that night, he called Wolf from the club and said, "Hey, man, that's it. Whoever you got in there, they got to go. I'm coming back."[38] When Wolf heard about the incident, he stormed over to Muddy's house in a fury. "Next time you do that, man," he threatened Muddy, "I'll kill you over him."[39]

Muddy's only comment about Sumlin's departure was, "me and Hubert didn't get along."[40] Sumlin contends that Muddy ignored him for a year, then reinitiated their friendship. "Things were never right between him and Wolf, though," Sumlin maintains. "A kind of rivalry started up between them about who was the boss of the blues. After I went with Muddy, Wolf didn't speak to him no more."[41]

While Cotton admits, "There was something there," he remains convinced that the relationship between Chicago's two senior bluesmen was less acrimonious than Sumlin alleges. "I think they liked one another, but they didn't get along musically," he says. "Wolf had his way of doing things, and Muddy had his way of doing things, so they accepted that for what it was."[42] S.P. Leary and Calvin Jones — two musicians who'd later play for both Wolf and Muddy — concur. "They were two businessmen," explains Leary. "It was all work and no play. They never had no problems, not to my knowledge, and I worked with both of them a long time. . . . They didn't have no argument, no. Muddy did his thing, and Wolf did his thing. I enjoyed working with both of them."[43]

During a 1956 Chess session, Muddy cut "Forty Days And Forty Nights," along with "All Aboard" and four unissued tracks: "Tears Of Joy," "Three Time Loser," "Is This Goodbye" and "Get Off

My Wagon." Although attributed to Muddy, "All Aboard" is, in fact, a derivation of Arthur "Big Boy" Crudup's "Mean Old Frisco Blues," recorded in 1942. In "Forty Days And Forty Nights" Muddy's ferocious delivery portrays the anguish of heartbreak, accentuated by Little Walter's superb harmonica artistry. In May the song reached number 12 on the R&B *Best Seller* chart, and *Juke Box* tracked it at number seven.

Little Walter played with the band for this session, although Muddy had a very capable harmonica player in James Cotton. Cotton's only contribution was to provide the eerie sound of a whistle behind Walter's solos as "All Aboard" simulated a train chugging across a lonely Delta landscape. "In some kinda way I felt I wasn't good enough, and I always felt I had to get better," comments Cotton when asked about his reaction to being sidelined in the studio. "So it made me work harder at what I was doing because I wanted to be better. . . . It kept me under pressure there for a while. And the only way out was to play my way out."[44]

Every time Little Walter backed Muddy at a session, Cotton was there; he was determined to learn all he could about recording. As well, he kept busy replenishing the band's glasses from a quart bottle of whiskey, a requisite lubricant for all Muddy's sessions. Also observing the proceedings was Muddy's current girlfriend Mildred.

Although Walter would never teach Cotton any harmonica techniques, Cotton learned a lot from simply watching. Along with Rice Miller, Walter was one of the greatest influences on his harp style. "He was the best harmonica player I ever heard in my life," Cotton recalls, "but he had his ways, you know. He didn't like harmonica players . . . but me and him got along all right because I respected him. . . . He had a quick temper."[45]

Muddy returned to Chess later that year to record "Just To Be With You," Willie Dixon's "Don't Go No Farther" and "Diamonds At Your Feet" with Little Walter, Otis Spann, Willie Dixon, drummer Odie Payne and either Jimmy Rogers or his eventual replacement, Pat Hare. For the last number, Muddy reprised a song he'd recorded for Alan Lomax on Stovall — "You Got To Take Sick And Die Some Of These Days" — repeating the lyrics for verses one and three and inserting two new verses. "Don't Go No Farther" reached number 12 on the R&B *Best Seller* chart and was listed by *Juke Box* at number nine.

Marshall Chess vividly recalls Muddy's recording sessions. As a teenager he was fascinated by what he refers to as "blues women," hefty black ladies whom Muddy brought in to observe the proceedings: "And these guys would be sitting there in this very funky-smelling recording studio, wearing real old-time, sleeveless T-shirts and drinking bourbon whiskey right out of paper cups, and three or four of these heavy blues women sitting on folding chairs, you know? I guess that having the women right in the studio stimulated them."[46]

According to James Cotton, when Willie Dixon wrote a song for Muddy all he provided were the lyrics. It was then up to Otis and Cotton to create the melody and arrangement for Muddy. "Spann would read the words, sit down at the piano and start playing, and I'd get my harmonica and start playing," reveals Cotton. "And when we got it together right, then Muddy would come in and sing the words, and that was it." Furthermore, Cotton contends that, during this period, songs credited to Muddy were actually composed by Otis and him. "[Muddy] had musicians putting things together for him," Cotton says. Except for the frontmen, "Chess didn't give nobody credit for nothing."[47]

On 1 December 1956, Muddy was back at the studio laying down some memorable sides. Although Willie Dixon had left his job at Chess earlier that year over a financial dispute and gone to Cobra Records, he continued to do some session work for Muddy. The first cut this day was a Dixon-penned song, "I Live The Life I Love (I Love The Life I Live)," followed by "Rock Me," a sexy number attributed to Muddy but actually taken from Melvin "Li'l Son" Jackson's "Rockin' And Rollin'," released on the Imperial label in 1951. As "Rock Me Baby," the same number would be a hit for B.B. King in 1964, as well as a staple for black and white blues-based bands in the future. For these first two numbers, James Cotton had finally earned the privilege of taking Little Walter's place on harmonica.

In addition to the heavyweight impact of "Rock Me," this session was noteworthy for producing "Got My Mojo Working," a vibrant crowd pleaser that would become a mainstay of Muddy's repertoire. Repeatedly identified as Muddy's own composition, the song was, in fact, written by Preston Foster. Immediately preceding this session, Muddy and the band had toured Florida, Georgia, Alabama and Mississippi for close to a month backing a singer named Ann

Cole, who'd made a name for herself with a best-seller on the Baton label. "Got My Mojo Working" was part of her repertoire. "The first time we heard 'Mojo,' she was doing it," confirms Cotton. "We were playing the music behind her, so we had to learn the song to play it. And me, I was good at learning words."[48]

Muddy knew this was his kind of song. Cotton taught him the lyrics, then Muddy headed into the studio and recorded it with Little Walter. Although it's a clear copy of Foster's number, in words and melody, Muddy adds his own verse and cuts many of the original hoodoo lyrics, repeating the first line of each verse in the typical blues format, unlike Foster's version. Ann Cole finally recorded the song for Baton on 27 January 1957, complete with background singers and saxophone, but Muddy's cut was already pressed and credited to him. The two versions were released the same week, and while neither climbed onto the charts, Cole's disc edged out Muddy's in popularity. A lawsuit ensued over the composer credit on Muddy's "Mojo." It was settled out of court with the stipulation that all subsequent pressings would list Foster as the songwriter, an agreement that Chess did not fulfill.

By 1957 Jimmy Rogers had established himself as a recording artist in his own right, so it was inevitable that he leave Muddy to pursue his own career. His departure was also precipitated by his growing disappointment that the original concept of the band — that of an all-star unit — had been derailed by Muddy's fame. Financial considerations were yet another factor. As blues audiences dwindled and the rock 'n' roll market boomed, Jimmy explains, Muddy "wasn't gettin' gigs too good durin' that time. . . . He'd get a gig once in a while that was small and he couldn't afford to pay me, see."[49] But Otis Spann maintained that Jimmy's decision wasn't entirely voluntary, that he was forced out due to smoking and drinking onstage in violation of Muddy's standards and those of the union. "Different little things caused us to break up," Rogers states, "but we were still friends until he died."[50]

Jimmy fronted his own band for a while, then joined Howlin' Wolf for a couple of years, but the financial demands of his growing family forced him to retire from music in 1960. He and a partner bought into a cab company; after that Jimmy purchased a clothing store. Occasionally he would sit in with Muddy or Magic Sam, but it wasn't until 1971 that he resumed his blues career.

With the departure of Jimmy Rogers, the band had a yawning gap to fill. Cotton suggested a guitarist he'd played with back in West Memphis and Memphis, and Muddy concurred. Auburn "Pat" Hare was an Arkansas native, born in Cherry Valley, northwest of West Memphis, on 20 December 1930. By the time his family moved to Parkin, Arkansas, in 1940, Hare was practicing on an old guitar he'd discovered under a bed, and he soon began taking lessons from Joe Willie Wilkins. In his late teens he played part time for Howlin' Wolf and drove a tractor by day. His pugnacious streak was evident even then; one time the diminutive Hare climbed onto a chair to punch Wolf in the mouth and, on another occasion, fired shots at him. Undeterred by this behavior, Wolf hired Hare on a full-time basis in 1951. The following year Pat began recording for Sam Phillips in Memphis and played with harmonica player and vocalist Herman "Little Junior" Parker, as well as James Cotton.

Acclaimed as the originator of power chording — a key element of rock 'n' roll — Hare became one of Sam Phillips's favorite guitar players. In 1954 he recorded at Phillips's Sun studio with James Cotton, his vicious guitar style and amp distortion evident on Cotton's "Cotton Crop Blues." James was slated to play harp on Pat's two cuts, but a fistfight erupted, and Cotton bowed out. Hare then recorded his own singles, "Ain't Gonna Be That Way" and a menacing blues entitled "I'm Gonna Murder My Baby," a prescient statement as events transpired.

Pat was short of stature, rowdy and mean. "He's a real tough baby," Muddy commented, "and when he's liquored up, man he can really play!"[51] Still, some maintain that Jimmy had been so in sync with Muddy that he was irreplaceable. Cotton disagrees. According to him, Pat didn't have to worry about emulating Jimmy Rogers's style: "[Pat] played so much better that it didn't make no difference."[52]

During this period the Muddy Waters band received several infusions of new blood. Eddie Shaw, a saxophone player from Greenville, Mississippi, played with Muddy for a short time in 1957, then Marcus Johnson signed on with the band about the same time as Hare. Sometimes jokingly referred to as Marcus Garvey, the black political leader of earlier in the century, Johnson was a master of many instruments. He backed Muddy on clarinet, saxophone and bass; but for small-club dates, Johnson would stick mainly to bass.

When Elgin Evans departed, also in 1957, both Cotton and Johnson recommended a dynamic jazz drummer as a replacement. There was only one snag — Francis Clay had never played blues.

Born on 16 November 1923 in Rock Island, Illinois, Francis Clay was nurtured by a family of musicians. His father played country music on most instruments, and his mother played piano, organ and violin. About the only instrument not found in their house as Francis was growing up was drums, which was precisely what had fascinated the child since before he was two. At that early age, Clay had gone to stay with his Aunt Katie and Uncle Will while his mother was ill, and his uncle's drum kit made a fateful impression on the toddler. Clay's parents resisted his desire to take up drumming, and instead the boy learned guitar at age five. As a child he received musical inspiration from the Duke Ellington and Cab Calloway orchestras, but when, at age 10, he went to see the Chick Webb ensemble play in Davenport, Iowa, he knew that drumming had to be his life.

Soon afterwards Francis began drum lessons, some classical, but mostly jazz. By age 15 he was playing professionally in Rock Island, and in between weekend gigs, he'd catch the train for Chicago to learn from the musicians he saw there. At 16 Clay temporarily replaced the regular drummer in the Jay McShann Band, who was recuperating from an accident, and a few years later he moved to Chicago, where he formed his own jazz band. Along the way he drummed briefly with Gene Ammons, who later recorded for Aristocrat, and was a member of Reginald Page's band. In 1945 he recorded with pianist R.J. Allen for the Rhumboogie label.

In 1957 Clay was living in New York City, but was on tour with an eight-piece jazz band playing for six nights at the Heat Wave, a South Side Chicago club. The owner suggested Francis come by on his night off to see the Tuesday-night sensation: Muddy Waters and the Hoochie Coochie Boys. Clay was flabbergasted; Muddy had amassed a huge audience, larger than Clay's band attracted the rest of the week combined. Francis was puzzled; what he heard did not impress him.

In fact before he was hired to join Muddy, Clay had listened to only a couple of Muddy's discs. "I did hear his first recording of 'Got My Mojo Working,'" he recalls. "Boy, what lousy playing, and I was thinking what it *could* be."[53] When Marcus Johnson told him that Muddy needed a drummer for a trip to Cincinnati, Clay accepted only because it would get him part way home to New York.

"We opened up with no rehearsal," Clay recounts, "and I had no idea how to play. I told [Muddy] I hadn't played down-home blues before, and so he said, 'Just go out and keep time.' Anyway, they opened up on the theme song — it sounded like they went that-a-way and I went this way! It was quite a surprise. I had no idea how to play. It was so simple, I couldn't get it. It was crazy."[54]

For Muddy the importance of the backbeat was primary. "I had to find me a drummer that would *drive*," Muddy declared. "My drummer [Elgin Evans] was straight right down — bop bop bop bop. I had to part from him 'cause he just couldn't hit the backbeat."[55] This style of drumming was unfamiliar to Francis. "I wasn't used to playing the backbeat unless it was really swinging," he says. "In the modern jazz you didn't play much of a backbeat. But I altered that when I joined Muddy, of course."[56]

Clay was critical of the state of blues drumming and set out to make some changes. "The blues drummers didn't really play with coordination," he states. "They just slapped straight forward — you know, straight ahead — no embellishments . . . no coloring or shading, just slap the beat behind whatever was played, you know."[57] But Francis's musicianship adorned and enriched the sound he was backing. "Clay was always a much freer player than the average blues drummer," says Elvin Bishop, one of the original members of the Paul Butterfield Blues Band and a fan of Francis's since the early 1960s. "Most guys just lay on the two and four, you know. He always had a lot of melodic stuff going on."[58]

"Blues at that time sounded like it was about four or five or six one-man bands going separate directions," Clay laughs. "What I was trying to do was to bring them together and make them sound like a more formal style of music, so it would be appreciated by more people and more musicians would be attracted to it." He adds, "I suppose what I was really trying to accomplish was helping the blues to grow up a little bit."[59] In his quest to achieve this goal, Clay worked with his band mates to tighten up their harmonies and work on dynamics.

Francis often bucked Muddy's directives to play a certain way. "I had to," he chuckles. "You do whatever's necessary to accomplish what you have to do. . . . I started adding things and changing things a little, but not just for the drums, but for the other instruments, too. And we had to do it so slight, that [Muddy] don't even notice too much, but sometimes he'd detect it, and he'd start getting all crazy. But he saw the response, the way the people reacted to it, then he was all right, see. He worried too much about what others thought."[60]

"After I was with him for five or six months, we went to Smitty's Corner on 35th and Indiana, and that's where it all began," Clay notes. "I had played there a few times with different jazz groups, and the place was empty all the time. And so [O'Brien Smith, the owner] said he thought he'd try the blues, and since Muddy was the favorite in Chicago, he called him. And so he went in there, and we had the place crowded every night, six nights a week."[61]

There installed on a low bandstand behind a wooden barrier, a string of White Sox pennants festooned from the rafters, the band dished out its banquet of blues. "We had the place full, and it accommodated about 350 people," Francis comments. "They were lined up outside on Indiana two blocks and two blocks on 35th Street. That's what attracted writers from Europe — *Jazz Hot* from Paris and *Blues Unlimited* in London — coming over and doing stories on us."[62]

Clay tried to help Muddy overcome some of his insecurities about being thrust into increasing celebrity. He attempted to teach Muddy how to read and write, but was largely unsuccessful. As well, Muddy was finding it difficult to converse with the white European journalists who were beginning to seek him out. "Muddy couldn't even go out to meet them, to talk to them," Clay reports. "He would send me out. . . . He said they would make fun of the way he talked. And he was quite backwards, and so I would meet them. So I started training him how to greet them and everything. . . . I said, 'Look, Muddy, this is getting bigger than we had anticipated.' I said, 'I'll go and meet them, then I'll bring them up to meet you' . . . so he got on pretty good that way. Within three months, he would go down to the table after coming off the stand from the set [and say], 'Good evening, I'm Muddy Waters,' "[63] Francis laughs as he mimics Muddy's newly refined speech.

Yet despite Clay's willingness to help and the new wave of acclaim the band was riding, Clay's relationship with Muddy was tempestuous. "Muddy hated my guts, don't you know that?" he asserts.[64]

He'd get on the stage and brag about me and my playing, but offstage he hated me. Crazy. I did everything to try to get along with him, everything possible to try to get along with him. I figured why throw all this away, as hard as we had worked, you know. . . . When I first joined Muddy, not only Muddy but a number of the bluesmen resented me because I wasn't from Mississippi or whatever. Muddy said, "I don't like the way you act, I don't like the way you dress, I don't like the way you eat. Givin' all my money to that white woman" — I was married to a Swedish woman. He resented everything about me.[65]

"The band was often described as a well-oiled machine," Clay continues. "That happened after I went to work with the band and made it possible. It was a tough task. That's why I stayed with the band, because I couldn't throw all that out, all that work, plus fighting with [Muddy] all the time. He used to draw blackjacks on me and everything, talking to me, getting angry and putting his hand on his gun. All that crazy stuff. I couldn't get used to that kind of life."[66]

Clay believes Muddy's attitude towards him was rooted in jealousy and insecurity, two characteristics most people insist Muddy did not possess. "There were times when he, if he dug a girl and she dug me, he would offer her a hundred dollars *not* to go with me," Clay claims. "Now that was *money* then; that's like a thousand dollars today. Silly things like that. He wouldn't allow his girlfriends to even speak to me."[67] At one point Francis lived with a school-teacher, and she'd often be waiting for him when the band came off the road: "When we'd pull in, she'd be sitting in the car waiting for me and help to put the instruments in her car. Muddy'd sit there, and he'd get so mad, you could see him frown, and one night he started charging after me with this blackjack. He couldn't stand that. The women he had were nothing like that, you know," says Clay, referring to the fact that his girlfriend was educated and had a respectable career.[68]

According to Francis, another source of Muddy's jealousy was Clay's songwriting and arranging abilities. He maintains that he wrote over 20 songs for the band — including "Close To You," "She's Nineteen Years Old," "Walkin' Thru The Park," "She's Into Something" and "Tiger In Your Tank" — none of which were copyrighted in his name. Francis claims, "A lot of times Leonard

Chess would say, 'I know, Francis, it's your music. We'll copyright it in your name. We'd go back on the road, it'd come out 'McKinley Morganfield.' That's not right." Clay insists that this was no oversight. "It was a conspiracy with Muddy and Leonard Chess," he contends.[69]

Francis describes the songwriting process this way: "Most of the time [Muddy] was laying upstairs [in his house] while we were doing all the work downstairs in the basement — Otis Spann, James Cotton, Pat Hare and myself. We rehearsed in the basement. He'd come down, 'Well, what've you got for me?' It was mostly Willie Dixon, St. Louis Jimmy — Jimmy Oden — and sometimes it'd be some other person. They'd come in with lyrics, and somebody had to come up with some ideas about music."[70]

Despite the fact that a studio session was thoroughly rehearsed ahead of time, or maybe even because of it, Francis was largely dissatisfied with the results. "I hear all these glorious things about Muddy and Leonard Chess," he remarks. "They even called Leonard Chess a genius. He messed up most of our music. If we could've played them, recorded them, as we wrote them and arranged them, it would have been much better. He thought he knew what made people respond in the manner that they did, but he didn't know."[71] Once Leonard found a winning formula, Francis declares, he resisted innovations and messed around with the rhythm and effects of the music until it all came out sounding the same.

On Muddy's relationship with Leonard, Francis is characteristically blunt, maintaining that Muddy sustained a plantation mentality: whatever the bossman — in this case Leonard — said had to be right. "He was a yes-man, so was Willie Dixon," Clay contends. "Little Walter was not his yes-man, nor was Zeb Hooker or myself. I guess we were the rebels in the camp. Leonard didn't know what he was talkin' about. . . . I mean why should we play wrong to satisfy him? I mean, music don't work that way. You have a lot of pride about your music, as hard as you worked and studied and practiced."[72]

"In some ways an outsider looking at the relationship could say, 'Yeah, [Muddy] treated Leonard as the plantation owner,'" says Marshall Chess. "The buzz of it was that Muddy probably never could have talked that way to a plantation owner. He respected my father tremendously, and the relationship was definitely a mutual respecting relationship. . . . Yes, Muddy may have looked that way, but that's how a black person who looked up to a white person they respected acted. That's the way I've always viewed it."[73]

"Muddy definitely had influence," Marshall continues, maintaining that Muddy enjoyed a great deal of input at his recording sessions. "He was a leader. If he felt something, he would express it. He would *try* things, that's why he was great. He would try a lot of different things."[74]

Marcus Johnson and another unknown musician played tenor sax for Muddy's session of May or June 1957, the first time since 1948 that Muddy had used a saxophone on a recording. He was in a celebratory mood for his composition, "Good News," an expression of fatherly pride at the birth of a baby girl. It's likely his infant son Williams was on his mind. In abrupt contrast, Muddy growls out a proclamation from the devil incarnate in "Evil," another of his own tunes; its imagery conjures up the dark mysticism of the Delta. At this session Muddy also recorded "Come Home Baby, I Wish You Would" and "Let Me Hang Around" with Robert "Junior" Lockwood on rhythm guitar.

"The Muddy Waters Blues Show," from two to four in the afternoon, made its debut on Chicago radio station WOPA in the late 1950s. Of his gig as a disc jockey, Muddy said, "I'd come in on 'em *rough*, boy. I'd come in there with the blues."[75] "He was pretty good," remembers Willie Smith, a future drummer with the band.[76] He touted the sponsors, Al Abrams, Lydia Pinkham and "all that little different medicine jive. . . . I never will forget the sausage, pork sausage, you know, them boys talkin' 'bout 'more sausage, mama,' " Muddy laughed.[77]

"He'd say a few words, you know," Smith recollects, "and he'd be doing it high pitched like he was excited or something, and put on a record."[78] Muddy recalled his rejoinder to an irate caller who suggested he stop talking so much or get off the air: " 'He ain't got brains enough to get *on* the air! And I'm sitting here looking at my pretty white Cadillac.' Oh, I come on strong. Man, I was scared to go home that night."[79]

Muddy could pack a club by announcing his local gigs on the show. Other perks of being a radio personality also proved lucrative. One record producer paid him $50 to mention his name on the show. "Boy, I hollered *some*, then!" Muddy said. "He sent me all his new releases after that."[80] Yet Muddy's career as a DJ was short-lived. It took too much out of his voice for his evening performances, so after six or eight months he gave it up. "I can't wear but one shoe," he maintained. "I tried, I couldn't make no disc jockey. At night I'd be hoarse."[81]

In August 1958 Muddy was saddened by the death of his dear friend and mentor, Big Bill Broonzy. "Big Bill was my mainline man," Muddy reflected. "He was one of the greatest in the business. He was just *great* [to me] comin' up."[82] Muddy served as lead pallbearer at Broonzy's funeral, assisted by Tampa Red, Brother John Sellars, Otis Spann, Sunnyland Slim, Francis Clay and others.

Little Walter continued to maintain the harmonica spot on most of Muddy's studio outings of 1958, and a temporary member of the band, guitarist Luther Tucker, may have traded licks with Pat Hare on the second session. Although he only stayed about a month, Tucker came to Muddy with some impressive credentials — he'd previously played with Little Walter, Junior Wells and Sunnyland Slim.

The most notable releases from Muddy's first two sessions of 1958 were "She's Nineteen Years Old" and "Close To You"; the second of these tunes reached number nine on the *Billboard* R&B chart that October, Muddy's final appearance on the best-seller charts. "Born Lover" was a reconstructed version of his 1954 disc "I'm A Natural Born Lover," with a smattering of Delta imagery in the form of a gypsy fortune teller, and the stop-time riffs of "Mannish Boy" were resurrected in "She's Got It." Its melody is similar to "Close To You," a rousing blues that finds Muddy chuckling, perhaps at his own insincerity, as he belts out his hankering for another conquest.

Muddy growls and hollers his appreciation for young ladies in "She's Nineteen Years Old," a song credited to Muddy and apparently inspired by his latest girlfriend, Lois. While Francis Clay maintains that he penned the song, British bandleader Chris Barber was told that it was composed by "St. Louis" Jimmy Oden. "Jimmy used to live on South Calumet, and he roomed in this house with this lady, and the lady in question was . . . not very bright, shall we say, mentally," Barber recounts. "And he wrote this song about her, which was '40 years old, ways like a natural child,' but it meant that she was a bit childish, you see. Muddy just changed one word in it to '19 years old, ways like a natural child,' with a quite different connotation."[83]

About this time Muddy replaced his Les Paul Gibson guitar with a red Telecaster, the instrument that would become his trademark. He had a heavier rosewood neck custom made for it, in order to support his thick strings and to help create that big sound. On Muddy's Telecaster the nut — the crosspiece at the top of the neck — protruded much higher than most. This lifted the strings well off the fretboard of the neck — in musicians' parlance it created high "action" — necessary for playing slide. Muddy's action was notoriously high, and since he concentrated on slide work more than bending strings, he played with heavy strings to achieve a meatier tone.

Muddy's first album, *The Best Of Muddy Waters*, came out in 1958, one of the first LPs released by a blues musician. A compilation of Muddy's most popular tunes, the record spanned his output from the 1948 hit "I Can't Be Satisfied" to 1954's "I'm Ready" and included such favorites as "Hoochie Coochie Man," "I Just Want To Make Love To You" and "Honey Bee." In the liner notes, Big Bill Broonzy interpreted Muddy's style this way: "Muddy's real. See the way he plays guitar? Mississippi style, not the city way. He don't play chords, he don't follow what's written down in the book. He plays notes, all blue notes."[84]

While this album would eventually achieve classic status and influence legions of budding rock stars, the black audience of the late 1950s was focused on soul, rhythm and blues and rock 'n' roll. But unbeknownst to Muddy, a small but lively interest in American blues was effervescing elsewhere. His music was about to hit the worldwide stage.

NOTES

1 James Rooney, *Bossmen: Bill Munroe & Muddy Waters* (New York: The Dial Press, 1971), 149.

2 Chuck Berry, *Chuck Berry: The Autobiography* (New York: Harmony Books, 1987), 98.

3 Tom Wheeler, "Chuck Berry: The Interview," *Guitar Player*, vol. 33, no. 3, issue 219 (Mar. 1988): 58.

4 Berry, 98.

5 Jim O'Neal and Amy O'Neal, "Muddy," *Living Blues* 64 (Mar.–Apr. 1985): 33.

6 Robert Palmer, "Muddy Waters: The Delta Son Never Sets," *Rolling Stone* (5 Oct. 1978): 56.

7 Jim O'Neal and Bill Greensmith, "Living Blues Interview: Jimmy Rogers," *Living Blues* 14 (Autumn 1973): 16.

8 Junior Wells, interview with author, 9 Dec. 1995.

9 Junior Wells, interview with author, 9 Dec. 1995.

10 James Cotton, interview with author, 26 Sept. 1995.

11 Bill Greensmith, "Cotton in Your Ears," *Blues Unlimited* 120 (July–Aug. 1976): 6.

12 James Cotton, interview with author, 26 Sept. 1995.

13 Helen Doob Lazar, "Living Blues Interview: James Cotton," *Living Blues* 76 (1987): 25

14 James Cotton, interview with author, 26 Sept. 1995.

15 James Cotton, interview with author, 26 Sept. 1995.

16 James Cotton, interview with author, 26 Sept. 1995.

17 James Cotton, interview with author, 26 Sept. 1995.

18 O'Neal and O'Neal, 38.

19 James Cotton, interview with author, 26 Sept. 1995.

20 Rooney, 133.

21 Tom Townsley, "Paul Oscher: Long Overdue," *Blues Connection*, vol. 3, issue 7 (May 1996): 8–9.

22 Rooney, 133.

23 James Cotton, interview with author, 26 Sept. 1995.

24 Lazar, 26.

25 James Cotton, interview with author, 26 Sept. 1995.

26 Lazar, 27.

27 Peter Guralnick, *Feel Like Going Home* (New York: Harper & Row, Publishers, 1989), 71.

28 Guralnick, 71.

29 Andrew M. Robble, "Charlie Musselwhite: Blues From the Heart," *Blues Revue Quarterly* 13 (Summer 1994): 23.

30 Paul Trynka, "Deep Blue," *Mojo* 27 (Feb. 1996): 47.

31 Hubert Sumlin, "My Years with Wolf," *Living Blues* 88 (Sept.–Oct. 1989):15.

32 Alan Paul, "Of Wolf & Man," *Guitar Legends*, vol. 3, no. 1 (1994): 15.

33 Sumlin, 15.

34 Trynka, 48.

35 Sumlin, 15.

36 James Cotton, interview with author, 26 Sept. 1995.

37 Sumlin, 15.

38 Sumlin, 15.

39 Sumlin, 15.

40 O'Neal and O'Neal, 39.

41 O'Neal and O'Neal, 39.

42 James Cotton, interview with author, 26 Sept. 1995.

43 S.P. Leary, interview with author, 11 June 1996.

44 James Cotton, interview with author, 26 Sept. 1995.

45 James Cotton, interview with author, 26 Sept. 1995.

46 Robert Palmer, "Muddy Waters: 1915–1983," *Rolling Stone* 398 (23 June 1983): 40.

47 James Cotton, interview with author, 26 Sept. 1995.

48 James Cotton, interview with author, 26 Sept. 1995.

49 O'Neal and Greensmith, 17.

50 Jimmy Rogers, interview with author, 3 May 1996.

51 Paul Oliver, *Blues Off the Record* (New York: Hippocrene Books Inc., 1984), 266.

52 James Cotton, interview with author, 26 Sept. 1995.

53 Francis Clay, interview with author, 23 Mar. 1996.

54 Francis Clay, interview with author, 23 Mar. 1996.

55 Palmer, 168.

56 Francis Clay, interview with author, 23 Mar. 1996.

57 Francis Clay, interview with author, 23 Mar. 1996.

58 Elvin Bishop, interview with author, 30 Nov. 1995.

59 Francis Clay, interview with author, 22 Mar. 1996.

60 Francis Clay, interview with author, 23 Mar. 1996.

61 Francis Clay, interview with author, 23 Mar. 1996.

62 Francis Clay, interview with author, 23 Mar. 1996.

63 Francis Clay, interview with author, 23 Mar. 1996.

64 Francis Clay, interview with author, 22 Mar. 1996.

65 Francis Clay, interview with author, 23 Mar. 1996.

66 Francis Clay, interview with author, 23 Mar. 1996.

67 Francis Clay, interview with author, 23 Mar. 1996.

68 Francis Clay, interview with author, 23 Mar. 1996.

69 Francis Clay, interview with author, 23 Mar. 1996.

70 Francis Clay, interview with author, 23 Mar. 1996.

71 Francis Clay, interview with author, 22 Mar. 1996.

72 Francis Clay, interview with author, 23 Mar. 1996.

73 Marshall Chess, interview with author, 4 Nov. 1996.

74 Marshall Chess, interview with author, 4 Nov. 1996.

75 O'Neal and O'Neal, 39.

76 Willie Smith, interview with author, 10 Dec. 1995.

77 O'Neal and O'Neal, 39.

78 Willie Smith, interview with author, 10 Dec. 1995.

79 Robert Neff and Anthony Conner, *Blues* (Boston: David R. Godine, 1975), 76.

80 Neff and Conner, 76.

81 O'Neal and O'Neal, 39.

82 O'Neal and O'Neal, 25.

83 Chris Barber, interview with author, 4 June 1996.

84 Studs Terkel, liner notes, *The Best Of Muddy Waters*, Chess, 1958.

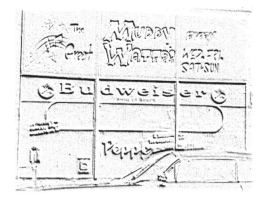

7

I believe whitey's pickin' up on things that I'm doin'[1]

As the boisterous rebelliousness of rock 'n' roll was supplanted by the sugary pap of teenaged heartthrobs such as Ricky Nelson, Fabian, Pat Boone and Paul Anka, another genre of music was bubbling up across the Atlantic in Britain. Combining turn-of-the-century New Orleans jazz with the black jug-band music of the 1930s, British skiffle lay claim to a generation of that nation's youth. A Leadbelly song, "Rock Island Line," scored Lonnie Donegan his first skiffle hit, inevitably drawing attention to the source of the material. As well, traditional jazz enthusiasts were searching for the fount of its origins. Both paths led to the same place: the spring that fed the well was Delta blues.

For white audiences in Britain, the race issue was not the stumbling block to music appreciation that it had proven to be for their American counterparts. English journalist Val Wilmer addressed this issue to James Baldwin, the esteemed black writer and civil-rights advocate:

> He said . . . "You never saw your slaves 'til lately." We, the British colonial power, had slaves worldwide, but only in small numbers living in our midst. So the blues was an interesting folk music, you know, authentic overseas sound and not something played by the people who we'd abused on our own doorsteps for centuries. . . . Anything created by black people was bound to be accepted more in this country because of that distance between us and the people we enslaved. And in America people couldn't get away from that, so how many white people were going to listen to black music? Very few. Certainly not the blues.[2]

The blues that British jazz and folk fans were concentrating their attention on was the style they considered to be authentic — acoustic country blues. When Big Bill Broonzy made his first foray into England in 1951, he cast aside the electric accoutrements and repertoire for which he was acclaimed in the U.S. and sagely delivered the Delta standards the Brits craved. And although Alexis Korner was bucking convention by playing amplified blues in jazz clubs, such music was generally frowned upon as a corrupt departure from the "real" thing.

As a few more acts crossed the ocean and blues records began to trickle into the British Isles, blues remained tied to the wider genres of folk and jazz. By the late 1950s, a limited number of Muddy Waters's records were available in Britain, although Muddy was still known to only a very narrow segment of the listening public. On the other hand, most young music aficionados were followers of the most popular group in Britain at the time — the Chris Barber Jazz Band. And bandleader Chris Barber was on a mission to broaden the musical experience of his British fans:

> We had worked with Bill Broonzy, and in late '57 we brought Sister Rosetta Tharpe over, the gospel singer, which was a wonderful success. At that time my business partner and I

and another guy, we used to run an organization called the National Jazz Federation, and their aims were to make sure to keep doing things in the jazz line, because the major promoters don't usually do it because there's not enough profit in it to be worth their while bothering. We had the idea of presenting one or two American small bands, modern-jazz attractions.[3]

But there was a snag. A dispute between the British and American musicians' unions had prevented members from one country playing in the other, supposedly to preclude jobs from being lost by local musicians. Barber continues:

My band started out in '54, very popular and also very keen and enthusiastic and wanted to play the music better. We knew the way to learn better is to play with the better guys — the "real" guys — which you couldn't do because they weren't allowed to play in Britain. But we realized that singers didn't come under that ruling. . . . So that's how we came to work with Big Bill Broonzy and then Rosetta Tharpe, and then not long after Sister Rosetta Tharpe, we had Sonny Terry and Brownie McGhee — that was in May '58.[4]

As Muddy weathered the chill in blues popularity stateside, he was unaware that sparks of interest in the music were igniting overseas, fanned by a very small but passionate following. While he always believed it was Big Bill Broonzy's personal recommendation that prompted Chris Barber to invite him to perform in Britain in October 1958, Barber says otherwise:

That's not my recollection. In fact, the last time I saw Big Bill was in February '57, along with Brother John Sellars — the two of them toured with my band — and we didn't get Muddy Waters booked until the beginning of '58, and he appeared in October '58. . . . We were always trying to talk about things to Big Bill and ask him questions and what was going on and what do you think and so on, but I don't recollect him saying much about Muddy. I mean, if you asked about him, he would say, "Yeah, he's very good," but he didn't really, to my knowledge, ever recommend us to get him. I think 'cause if he had, we might have got Muddy sooner.[5]

Rather, Muddy's first tour of Britain came about through Barber's association with the National Jazz Federation, which worked with the Modern Jazz Quartet from the U.S. Chris became acquainted with the band's director, pianist John Lewis. "John, who was a very enthusiastic music lover of all kinds . . . was saying to us, 'You get Rosetta Tharpe and Big Bill, why don't you get Muddy Waters?' " Chris reveals. "We said, 'Well, how can you get a guy like that?'. . . He said, 'Well, I'm sure I can find out where to find him.'"[6] Lewis subsequently tracked down an agent who booked Muddy and put Barber in touch with him.

In order to circumvent the ban on hiring American musicians, "[Muddy] came over with a permit based upon being an entertainer, and he brought Otis along as his accompanist," says Barber. "That was allowed."[7] But Muddy had to leave the rest of his group behind. He put Cotton in charge, and the Hoochie Coochie Boys kept working their Chicago gigs. "First of all we couldn't afford his whole band," Chris explains. "Secondly, the whole idea — not to be selfish about it — our idea was that we wanted to play with these people. We wanted to have a chance to learn from these people." Besides, Barber admits, they didn't actually know that Muddy had a band. After all, on many of his early recordings, he was backed by only Big Crawford on bass.[8]

Chris booked Muddy and Otis for a 10-day tour — which included concerts in Newcastle, London, Bournemouth, Bristol, Manchester and Glasgow — and Muddy's agent tacked on another gig at the front end of the trip and sent his clients over one day early. That first appearance was at the prestigious Leeds Jazz Festival, run by Lord Harewood, a cousin of Queen Elizabeth, prompting Muddy to bid farewell to his band with the promise that he'd serenade the Queen with "Close To You."

"[Muddy's] agent put [Muddy and Otis] on with a band who were kind of a semi middle-period modern kind of jazz outfit who didn't really know blues from Chilean music," laughs Barber as he describes Muddy's first taste of performing in Britain.[9] The next evening was the opening night of Muddy's tour with the Chris Barber Jazz Band at the City Hall in Newcastle. By this time the Chicagoans must have been wondering what they'd gotten themselves into.

Muddy and Otis, they had no idea what to expect [Barber continues] — we didn't have a rehearsal. . . . My band played the first half of the concert, then there'd be an intermission, and then the second half we'd play about one tune, then we'd call on the guest artist, if we had one.

They had heard my band playing our regular first half of the concert, which was basically New Orleans jazz orientated really, certainly nothing in the sort of Chicago blues idiom, although there was some blues that we were doing, like Big Bill type things, but that's not the same thing that Muddy plays. There was a door [on the side of the stage] with a glass in this door, and I could see Muddy and Otis peering through this, looking out. I thought, I bet they're wondering how we're gonna play.[10]

When it was time to bring on his guests, Chris led his band through the introduction of "Hoochie Coochie Man": "The doors were swung open, Muddy and Otis came in with these enormous grins on their faces, because they didn't know what to expect, and here they're getting someone who actually knew their music. So they joined in and we played that, and then we left it to them — they had our bass player and drummer play with them all the way through — and then we joined in with them at the end of the concert."[11]

Muddy and Otis thrilled concertgoers throughout Britain, yet horrified critics. "Screaming Guitar and Howling Piano" trumpeted the lead to one review, an expression of one journalist's outrage at the electrification of acoustic blues. Muddy was stunned. "Although his singing is authentic and he uses his voice as an instrument for conveying melancholy and dissatisfaction, I cannot class him as a true blues artist," wrote a Manchester critic. "Apart from the beautiful 'Blues Before Sunrise,' most of his songs seemed to me to owe too much to the rhythm and blues style."[12] Confusing the progenitor with his heir was, according to Barber, indicative of the poor standard of jazz and blues critique that existed in Britain at the time.

"They oughta tol' me they didn't want electric guitar," exclaimed Muddy, referring to his critics. "I didn't know they want that ord'nary box, what they call 'coustic guitar. And I only *half*-done my songs then."[13] Yet later, after he had seen Muddy in action at his home club, Smitty's Corner, Barber maintains that Muddy's British performances were just as potent and forceful as those he dished out in Chicago.

Even so, Muddy wasn't the first amplified blues performer to play in Britain. Barber had brought over Sister Rosetta Tharpe a year earlier, and she'd played electric guitar; Brownie McGhee, who'd toured there in May 1958, used an electric pickup on his acoustic. Although Muddy later claimed that he'd turned down his amplifier out of respect for British tastes and at Barber's request, Barber denies this was so. "He didn't play too loud," he maintains. "We were playing with him — I know it wasn't too loud." Barber continues, "The point is this. We had no sound system. There were about two mikes on the stage in Manchester, that's all, maybe three. . . . Now, we put one of them on the piano to make sure it was heard, one for Muddy singing and one somewhere else. Muddy's amplifier was nowhere near any of them."[14]

Chris states that "some of the traditional jazz enthusiasts — who we were basically playing [for] and whose minds we were trying to broaden and improve by bringing people like Muddy over to play to them and for us to play with them — some of those traditional jazz fans didn't understand or didn't like it particularly. But by and large, the fans who came to see him with us, you know, liked him very, very much."[15] It was a stark divergence from white America's neglect of Muddy's blues.

Muddy's 26 October concert at Manchester's Free Trade Hall is preserved on *Muddy Waters And Otis Spann In Concert 1958*, the surreptitiously taped album that was subsequently released on the Krazy Kat label. That night the capacity crowd was clearly enthused by Muddy's program, which included a number of his biggest hits, plus a mix of his vintage blues — "Can't Be Satisfied" and "I Feel Like Going Home" — and his most current material — "Close To You" and "Walkin' Thru The Park."

Without Muddy's regular lineup of harmonica and second guitar, the backing is spare, but it serves to highlight Muddy's vocal mastery and brings Spann's stunning piano work to the fore. Muddy's slide slices through "Long Distance Call" and "I Feel Like Going Home," and he performs "Rollin' Stone" without accompaniment, presenting it in a country-blues style, perhaps in an attempt to mollify the critics. For "Walkin' Thru The Park" and the encore, Muddy and Spann are joined by the dixieland backing of the Chris Barber Jazz Band, a unique combination that delights the exuberant audience.

"He didn't jump around; he didn't move very much — a little bit here and there, just pointing his finger at people more or less," says Barber, describing Muddy's onstage persona. "He wasn't a kind of an active performer like a Little Richard or somebody. He never was. He got up and sang his songs properly and well."[16]

When Val Wilmer met Muddy and Otis backstage at St. Pancras Town Hall after their 20 October London concert, she was struck by how nervous they were at being surrounded by swarms of appreciative white fans. It stands to reason; they were in a foreign country, and such adulation was a totally alien experience. Chris Barber was also surprised by Muddy's demeanor, but in a different respect:

> He was very nice. It was quite funny because we'd been expecting him to be difficult in the sense of being really stuck up. . . . We had toured in '57 with Big Bill Broonzy and Brother John Sellars. Now Brother John Sellars, who was a gospel singer and kind of a blues singer . . . was very affected, you see. If anything didn't go to his liking, he would say, "Muddy Waters wouldn't stand for this!" So we had this image of this guy who wouldn't stand for no nonsense, wouldn't stand for not having his own dressing room, wouldn't stand for not having this or not having that or not having a supply of whatever it was he wanted, a drink or whatever. When Muddy arrived we found a very good, professional, down-to-earth musician who knew what he did, did it properly, made no fuss and was very practical to work with, so there was no problem and no difficulty.[17]

Apart from the minority who had voiced their objection to Muddy's so-called debasement of the "real" blues, crowds of inspired young concertgoers were discovering a sound they wanted to hear more of. From Newcastle to London, from Bristol to Glasgow, Muddy was shaping a generation of musicians and music fans, arming them for the upcoming British invasion. Barber elaborates:

> For example, you had Eric Burdon, who was in Newcastle. He was in [the Newcastle College of Art], and he told me it was his first day in the college and he, in September '58 in the new class of people, he got up and said, "Who's going to the Chris

Barber concert?" And the guy at the back named John Steel, who was the first drummer of the Animals, got up and said, "Yes, me." So the two of them came to the concerts and saw Muddy Waters, and Eric became a blues singer. I think that applied to many other people, too. That's great. We hoped we would turn people on to that music. That was the idea.[18]

"I thought we got across pretty good on our first trip," Muddy commented. "As for Otis, I think they preferred him to me. Otis is the greatest blues player in the world today, on piano. He's my ace."[19] As a parting promise, Muddy said, "Back home they want to hear the guitar ring out — over here they listen to what you sing. Next time I come, I'll learn some old songs first."[20]

In the United States, Muddy's audiences continued to be almost exclusively black and diminishing. Those listeners he hadn't lost to the onslaught of rock 'n' roll were now turning in increasing numbers to the smoother, more sophisticated sound of soul. To an upwardly mobile generation of blacks, the gut-bucket blues that harkened back to the Delta was an uncomfortable reminder of a heritage they were struggling to leave behind. With deep sadness Muddy noted, "Young Negro kids now . . . they just turn away from the old blues. It's not the music of today; it's the music of yesterday."[21]

James Cotton was a regular participant at the Playhouse Club jams, just down the street from Muddy's house. Andrew "A.W." Stephenson, an electric bass player, would often join him there, and they'd run through Muddy's repertoire. Although Fender had been making electric bass guitars since 1953, Muddy didn't have a full-time electric-bass player until 1958, when he heard A.W. jamming with Cotton and hired him. Consequently, Marcus Johnson gave up his role as intermittent bass player and concentrated on clarinet, or sometimes sax, for Muddy's larger gigs. "We were more fortunate than most blues bands," Francis Clay acknowledges. "As a matter of fact, we were the only blues band out there playing jazz sessions and big shows, big stage productions where they had modern jazz, blues and big jazz bands. . . . That was before B.B. [King] and Bobby [Bland] and them came along."[22]

Late in 1958 Muddy cut "Walkin' Thru The Park," which he'd performed on his tour of Britain. He set aside his guitar once again and roared out the lyrics to this up-tempo tune punctuated by rousing harmonica and guitar solos, courtesy of Cotton and Pat Hare.

Muddy, Luther Tucker and Spann had backed Little Walter for his August 1958 Chess session, where he laid down the memorable "Key To The Highway," a cut that climbed to number six on the charts. Walter returned the favor in January 1959 when he joined Muddy and the Hoochie Coochie Boys to record "Blues Before Sunrise," "Mean Mistreater" and "Crawlin' Kingsnake," in which he blows both regular and chromatic harp. In concert with Muddy's vocal dynamics, Walter's harmonica wrings all the emotion from his soul, particularly on "Blues Before Sunrise," which although credited to John Lee Hooker, was in fact written and first recorded by Leroy Carr. Previous versions of "Mean Mistreater" had also been performed by Leroy Carr and Scrapper Blackwell, as well as Tampa Red.

"I think that at this time it was the biggest thing that he ever did," Cotton says of Muddy's first performance at Carnegie Hall on 3 April 1959.[23] Entitled "Folksong: '59," the program, presented by Alan Lomax and Louis Gordon, sought to chronicle the evolution of American music from work songs, gospel, blues and country and western to its popular culmination in rock 'n' roll. In addition to Muddy, the roster of participants included Jimmy Driftwood, Memphis Slim, the Stoney Mountain Boys, Isaac Washington, Mike and Pete Seeger and the Selah Jubilee Singers. Bobby Darin, the representative of the rock 'n' roll genre, failed to appear.

The concert was recorded by United Artists Record Company. Accompanied by Otis Spann, Isaac Washington on harmonica, Al Hall on bass and drummer Shep Sheppard, Muddy cut four tracks that evening. His "Hoochie Coochie Man" is less exuberant than usual, and "Walkin' Thru The Park," retitled "Goin' Down," also pales in comparison to the original recording. But Muddy and Spann steam full throttle ahead on "Rock Me" and "Sunrise Blues," previously recorded as "Blow Wind Blow." Muddy then provided guitar backing for Memphis Slim's portion of the concert.

In a heartfelt tribute to his Chicago mentor, the late Big Bill Broonzy, most of Muddy's June and July/August 1959 sessions were devoted to rerecording selections from Broonzy's repertoire. No doubt the Chess marketing department was hoping the resultant album, *Muddy Waters Sings Big Bill Broonzy*, which was issued in

June 1960, would find an entrée into the lucrative white market to which Broonzy appealed.

The musicians Muddy assembled for these sessions were Cotton, Hare, Spann, Andrew Stephenson and two drummers. Francis Clay played on one session and Willie Smith — whom Muddy first heard at his Sunday jam at Smitty's and who would later join his band — was the drummer for the other. "We did it in about two hours," Clay says of the June session. "What we did was go in one studio and listen to the [Broonzy] record, go across the hall to another studio and cut it. It takes a good caliber musician to do it, of course."[24]

Willie Smith remembers his session as an exhausting experience: "At the time it was kind of hard for what they made you do, you know. They just make you play tunes 'til you just go to sleep with your eyes closed."[25] Leonard was a stickler to please. Muddy may have raised a little hell over a few points of contention, Willie recalls, but inevitably he'd toe the line. "If [Leonard] told you he didn't like that," Willie continues, "there was no argument. It was his way. It was a one-way street. . . . I didn't like it. Now I do, because it brought out mainly the best in me."[26]

Broonzy had said of Muddy, "Muddy, he can really sing the blues. I mean the country, wide open blues. He ain't like those pretty boy singers who dress up the blues so you don't know what it is."[27] On his tribute album, Muddy verifies that statement and then some. Broonzy's originals are generally slicker, more polished, whereas Muddy's versions aim right for the gut. In numbers such as "Tell Me Baby," "Southbound Train," "When I Get To Thinking" and "Double Trouble," Muddy's vocals are masterful; the dynamics of his presentation range from a murmur to a gravelly roar. When he sings he's got trouble, there's no iota of doubt. Also notable here is the superlative backing of Cotton and Spann.

Whether it was due to Cotton's proven excellence on the harmonica or Little Walter's increasingly erratic behavior, from this point on, Walter's talents were enlisted only sporadically for Muddy's sessions. Muddy and Walter's 11-year musical partnership had been a peerless pairing that defined the heyday of Chicago blues. But despite his success as a frontman, since the mid-1950s Walter's inner demons had gained hold; the harmonica virtuoso was foundering amid accusations of unreliability, an uncontrolled temper and alcohol abuse.

Jimmy Rogers was back with the band for Muddy's session of 23 April 1960, and at last Muddy reverted to slide guitar in "Woman Wanted" and "Deep Down In My Heart." Also recorded that day were "I'm Your Doctor," which finds Muddy so enthused he fairly bellows the lyrics, and "Read Way Back," a departure from Muddy's usual blues format, a song he co-wrote with "St. Louis" Jimmy Oden. Willie Dixon's vocals on the latter number may have been added later.

On 7 June, Muddy returned to the studio, accompanied by Cotton, Hare, Spann, Stephenson and Clay. The first song recorded that day was "Tiger In Your Tank," a number credited to Willie Dixon, although Francis Clay insists that he composed it. It's a fun, up-tempo double entendre of automotive mechanics, rhythm driven and featuring Muddy on slide. Dixon's rollicking blues, "Got My Brand On You," which portrays a particularly proprietary notion of love, is a strong song that showcases the great musicianship of Spann and Cotton. "Soon Forgotten" and "Meanest Woman" were also cut in this session.

A milestone of Muddy's career, and the kickoff of his subsequent success, was his triumph at the Newport Jazz Festival in Newport, Rhode Island, on 3 July 1960. The wheels had been set in motion early that year when the vice president of Atlantic Records, Nesuhi Ertegun, visited Chicago and dropped in at Smitty's Corner to hear his favorite singer. The power of Muddy's performance left Ertegun in a fevered pitch of enthusiasm, declaring this band was the best in the country. He convinced Newport producer George Wein to include Muddy in the special blues program Wein was booking to demonstrate the roots of jazz.

Muddy didn't want to do the Newport Festival [says Francis Clay]. We almost didn't get there because the offer was made, and Muddy kept turning it down. And I had to talk myself blue in the face over and over and over and over. He kept rejecting the offer. Well, for one thing [it was] for the same reason that Howlin' Wolf turned down the "Dick Clark Show" — it wasn't enough money. [Although] Howlin' Wolf said it was only $150 — "That's no money" — it would have made him millions for the exposure. Muddy never heard of the Newport Jazz Festival, and Muddy . . . couldn't imagine even taking this gig. I had to convince him what it would do for him and his career and the band. . . . That's the one that really exposed the blues to the whole world.[28]

Even when Muddy was finally persuaded, the event came dangerously close to being scuttled. A mob of ten thousand gate-crashers touched off a riot so serious that Saturday in Newport that the rest of the festival was canceled, with the fortuitous exception of the Sunday afternoon blues program. Joining Muddy for the show were John Lee Hooker, pianist Sammy Price and the duo of fiddler James "Butch" Cage and guitarist Willie B. Thomas. The master of ceremonies was Langston Hughes, the celebrated black poet and writer.

It was John Lee's first big concert, and backstage he was quaking with fear. Muddy, always unflappable, advised his old friend, "Do your thing. You're the pro. Go on up there." Fortified by Muddy's encouragement, John Lee proudly proclaims, "And I got on up there, and I knocked them dead."[29]

Muddy and his band took the stage at the end of the show. "To us it was just another gig," says Cotton. "We knew that we had to play once we went on the stage with Muddy regardless if it was three thousand people there or if it was two."[30] Here at Newport, however, Muddy was about to confront a new phenomenon for him in the United States — an almost exclusively young, white audience.

Muddy strode onstage dapper and elegant in a dark gray suit and white shirt, tie and shoes; the band wore white jackets and dark bow ties and trousers. Launching into the recently recorded "I Got My Brand On You," Muddy kicked off the set, then gave the crowd a taste of some earlier material with "I'm Your Hoochie Coochie Man" and "Baby Please Don't Go," followed by "Soon Forgotten." He played his guitar for part of this performance, something he still was not doing for his regular club dates.

Even though Muddy had recorded "Tiger In Your Tank" earlier that year, he forgot the lyrics onstage at Newport. Nevertheless, he bluffed his way through with bravado, singing the chorus repeatedly when he couldn't come up with the verses, leaving spaces for the band to fill and inserting an extra instrumental break. It left Cotton bewildered and Muddy blaming him for messing up his part. "I knew the words," Cotton asserts. "I didn't know what to play because I didn't know what he was saying, right? And I got fired that same day." The rupture was, fortunately, short-lived. When Cotton insisted it was Muddy who'd erred, Muddy listened to the tape and admitted Cotton was right. "And from that point on, he respected me for it, you know," Cotton says.[31] After that incident Muddy often huddled backstage with Cotton to review his lyrics before a gig.

On that momentous day at Newport, Muddy followed his somewhat scrambled rendition of "Tiger In Your Tank" with "I Feel So Good," a Big Bill Broonzy song he'd recorded the previous year. Then, for what he planned to be the last number, he announced, "I got my mojo working, woman. You hear me?" and plunged into a vigorous, animated version of "Got My Mojo Working." Francis Clay defied Muddy here by embellishing his drumming with vibrant intricacies that injected even more potency into the brew. This crowd may not have known what a mojo was, but Muddy's song intoxicated them nevertheless. Claps, cheers and whistles accompanied the performance, and ecstatic fans sang out the chorus in unison. They exploded into applause at the close, refusing to let the Hoochie Coochie Boys leave so soon.

For the encore the crowd demanded a second helping of "Mojo," which Muddy served up with equal gusto. He proclaimed his message with all the force of an evangelizing preacher, erect and proud, shaking his finger at the audience for emphasis. As Cotton was ending his solo, Muddy suddenly lunged over to him, grabbed him in a dancer's embrace and led him in a two-step as the crowd screamed out in rapture. (The dance wasn't as impromptu as it appeared, however; it was a part of Muddy's regular routine.) Then Muddy kicked up his heels, hiked up his trouser legs and flapped his knees in a solo dance before he made his way back to center stage. He belted out the final chorus, tilting back on his heels, jabbing his elbows backwards and clapping. As he sang the closing line, "But it just don't work on you," he rose up on his toes and shot the crowd a knowing look that implied the exact opposite.

In the midst of the onstage victory, Langston Hughes received word — erroneously, as it turned out — that, due to the previous day's riots, the Newport Jazz Festival would not be held again. Anxious to commemorate the death of a beloved institution, he quickly jotted down a poem expressing his sorrow and handed it to Otis during the band's set. When Spann closed that day's program with "Goodbye Newport Blues," no one in the band had had a chance to hear the lyrics or arrange the music. Otis began the number, creating the tune as he went along, and the rest of the band gradually joined in, singing it as a slow, plaintive blues.

It was a somber note on which to end Muddy's conquest, but that day's recording of "Got My Mojo Working" became a successful single. It earned him his first Grammy nomination in the category of Best Rhythm and Blues Performance, although the award ultimately went to Ray Charles for "Let The Good Times Roll." As well, the band's entire Newport set was released by Chess as the album *Muddy Waters At Newport, 1960.* The lyrics Muddy ad-libbed in "I'm Your Hoochie Coochie Man" that July day were prescient. "We're the Hoochie Coochie Boys," he had sung. "The whole United States know we here." It was about time.

Even so, for the time being, at least, Muddy was still relegated to playing mainly at black Chicago clubs — such as Sylvio's, the 708 Club and Pepper's Lounge — performing one night a week at the F&L Lounge in Gary, Indiana, and touring the black venues of the South.

As his black audience continued to wane, a small flicker of interest had been ignited amongst some unconventional white kids. Back in 1957, an 18-year-old harmonica player named Paul Butterfield began haunting the South Side, seeking out the source of his musical inspiration: Muddy Waters. At the same time an unorthodox 14-year-old guitarist was on the same mission, even though he was too young to enter a tavern. "From two blocks away," Michael Bloomfield remembered, "you'd hear that harmonica, and then you'd hear Muddy's slide, and I'd be like a dog in heat."[32] Shaking with excitement, he'd stand on the sidewalk outside Pepper's, staring through the window at the master. Muddy would come out between sets to shake hands and say hello. "Muddy and Otis Spann were very fatherly about it in an amused fashion, you know," Bloomfield recalled. "They'd figure what's with this little white boy down here."[33]

Another aspiring guitar player, Elvin Bishop — who, like Butterfield and Bloomfield, would achieve a successful music career — chose to leave Tulsa, Oklahoma, in 1960 so he could be closer to the blues, his primary passion. A recipient of a National Merit Scholarship, Bishop could attend any university he wished, but he selected the University of Chicago for its location in the midst of the South Side ghetto. Soon after his arrival, Bishop was sitting on a university staircase playing blues guitar when some black cafeteria workers expressed their admiration for his music. They befriended Elvin and started escorting him to all the city's hottest blues clubs.

"They would take me down to Pepper's Lounge on 43rd and Vincennes," Bishop remembers, "which was a happening South Side club, and see Muddy Waters. . . . There were . . . less than a dozen white people who even expressed any interest in blues at the time. It was a totally black phenomenon. People originally from the South mostly were in the audience."[34]

Gradually folk-music aficionados from the University of Chicago came to realize that they could experience firsthand some of the greatest examples of indigenous American music by merely traveling a few blocks. Muddy began to notice a very slight whitening of his audience: "Then the college kids started comin' to see me in places where I was afraid for 'em even to be there, maybe twelve or fourteen of them a night."[35] Elvin recalls how rough some of those clubs could be: "I've seen knives pulled at Pepper's when Muddy was there. I've seen the whole place empty out."[36]

"Boy, it was a strong thing happening," Elvin stresses, recalling Muddy's South Side performances. "Muddy was a sex symbol. He was . . . right in the middle of his glory, and they treated him like the Beatles were later treated. It was that kind of mania."[37] Looking imposing and debonair, Muddy would preside over the audience, always impeccably dressed in a suit and tie, his hair processed in a conk style. Band members continued to wear uniforms, which consisted of a suit jacket and white shirt.

Muddy would still only rarely play guitar for his Chicago audiences. Although he stood for all his performances, lead guitarist Pat Hare was seated. "But that was because he couldn't stand," Bishop comments. "He was a wine drinker."[38] Elvin describes Muddy's performing style with relish:

Muddy would stand up there, and he was sharp, sharp as a tack. He was just beautifully dressed, stood up ramrod straight and always had that natural dignity, you know. And he would get going on a song, and he would sing 'em a long time, it wasn't those three-minute songs. He would do that tune ["Mannish

Boy"], you know, and sometimes before the show, he'd go back in the bench room and stick a Coke bottle down his pants. . . .

He would be up there, and he would be sweating profusely, and Spann was playing that great piano and Pat Hare played guitar, and they would just get it worked up to a pitch, and people would be crowded around the front . . . it was mostly women, and they would be just going nuts. He would just work them up to a lather. . . .

He'd stand there and he'd be kind of dignified at first, and then he'd get to moving a little, and then when it came to a certain point and he wanted to emphasize a word, he'd almost make a violent movement. . . . They'd be waving their checks in the air, begging him to take them, and the whole place was just sweating and rocking back and forth. It was amazing.[39]

Reflecting on Muddy's personality, Bishop remarks, "He was a nice guy. He was friendly, and yet he maintained a kind of reserve. He was always like that. He was a regular guy, one of the fellows, but even with his band people, he kept a certain little distance, you know."[40] Elvin got closer to Otis, who'd invite him to his house where they'd jam, eat pork-chop sandwiches and drink whiskey.

Cotton remembers nights at Smitty's Corner when the only white faces in the room belonged to Michael Bloomfield, Elvin Bishop, Paul Butterfield and another aspiring blues musician, vocalist and harmonica player Nick Gravenites. Muddy would encourage them to sit in for a couple of numbers, declaring, "That's the way kids learn, you know, settin' in and getting the feeling and getting the smoke of it."[41] Further explaining his generosity in sharing his stage with these young hopefuls, he commented, "I like to take kids tryin' to get across and give 'em a helpin' hand, you know. I didn't get so many helpin' hands, and that's why I'm so nice to people."[42]

In assessing the vocal abilities of both Butterfield and Bloomfield, Muddy was candid. "You're not man enough to sing it yet," he advised them. "And he was right, too," Bloomfield admitted.[43] Muddy's initial reaction to Paul Butterfield's harp playing was similarly unenthusiastic: "He wasn't too good when I first noticed him, but he got good."[44] James Cotton claims some of the credit for steering Butterfield in a more bluesy direction. However, Bloomfield's guitar talent was an entirely different story. "When I first heard Michael, I knew he was gonna be a great guitar player," Muddy maintained.[45] As a guitarist for the Paul Butterfield Blues Band, Bloomfield would soon achieve eminence as a founding father of psychedelic rock. Although he was influenced by a potpourri of musical styles, he received great inspiration from playing with and observing Muddy.

"Overwhelming" is how John Hammond describes his first taste of Muddy live in a Chicago club in 1960, where he was brought by Bloomfield to meet the great bluesman.[46] Although he had yet to launch his career as a country-blues singer and guitarist, Hammond credits Muddy with exerting a powerful influence over the style he'd later cultivate.

Chris Barber embarked on his first American tour in 1959. After completing a concert near Chicago, he defied dire warnings that he'd be shot if he ventured into the South Side, and went to hear Muddy play at Smitty's Corner. Pleased to see his British friend again, Muddy made Barber promise to stay at his house the next time he came to town, and Barber took him up on the offer the following year. "Muddy's appeal was quite largely to older people," notes Chris, as he recalls the times he and his band jammed at Smitty's. "As Muddy said, 'I do well on the South Side here . . . because my audience are older people; they drink whiskey. Now you get the bands who play the Key Show Lounge down on Cottage Grove, their audiences drink beer. There's no money in that.' So Muddy said, 'I get good money for playing because my public will drink whiskey.'" Barber also observed that Muddy attracted people who worked in downtown clubs and would stop by Smitty's after work: "They were people who were experienced in music, but to them Muddy was the real thing, and it was home. So it wasn't like the young people's raving music, it was kind of older people's nostalgia."[47]

Although his commitment to deliver the blues never lessened, Muddy had now shortened his onstage appearances, leaving his band to open each set for him. He was in his mid-forties and felt he'd earned the right to take it a little easier. "I do three, four songs and that's it," he admitted. "And I put everything I got in it. But you can't do that all night."[48] Chris Barber recollects Muddy's time management at a typical gig:

Muddy only used to play a couple of songs every now and then anyway, you know, his general routine. At Smitty's the band played about five sets of about 40 minutes, from about 10 to about four. Muddy would come on for the last song of each set. He'd socialize with the audience during the sets. You see he'd sit down and have drinks with them, no doubt encouraging them to spend money on drinks, which O'Brien Smith, the owner of the club, liked. And then the band would do all these songs, Otis singing and Cotton singing, for example, and playing instrumentals even. And then for the last song, Muddy would get up and sing. So one set would finish with "Mojo," and one set would finish with "Five Long Years," his best numbers . . . and that would just bring the house down, and that was the end of the set, and then there'd be a break for 20 minutes, then it'd start again.

Muddy used to ask [the Chris Barber Jazz Band] to get up and play with him, which we did. We played with the whole band at Smitty's Corner in '61 and were very well received, in spite of the fact that most of the black people in that neighborhood probably wouldn't have considered going to see a band play our kind of jazz really, but they enjoyed it.[49]

Muddy's influence on both established musicians and on developing styles of popular music continued. Not only Chris Barber, but another denizen of the jazz world, John Coltrane, was alarming the sophisticates by withdrawing to Smitty's Corner with a recorder in hand to study the superb tone of Muddy's voice. Dizzy Gillespie and Cannonball Adderley would make the same pilgrimage to examine the roots of their genre. Rockabilly composer and guitarist Carl Perkins also cited Muddy as an influence. And Muddy's effect on rock 'n' roll endured. In 1958 he'd heard the stop-time riff from his 1954 recording of "I'm Your Hoochie Coochie Man" duplicated in Elvis Presley's "Trouble." "I better watch out," he mused. "I believe whitey's pickin' up on the things that I'm doin'."[50]

While remaining a key member of Muddy's band and a popular session pianist, Otis Spann began his solo career in 1960 with the release of his first album, *Otis Spann Is The Blues*, on which he was accompanied by Robert "Junior" Lockwood. Although he would never reach Muddy's level of acclaim, Spann's future output of solo work would include *Good Morning Blues*, recorded in Copenhagen in 1963; *The Blues Of Otis Spann, The Blues Never Die!* and *Half Ain't Been Told*, cut in 1964; two 1966 sessions which produced *The Blues Is Where It's At* and *Take Me Back Home*, and *The Bottom Of The Blues*, recorded in November 1967. At many of his recording sessions, Spann was backed by the musicians in Muddy's band, often including Muddy himself. When he supported his band members on rival labels, Muddy would sometimes be identified only as "Dirty Rivers" in a feeble attempt to hide his participation from Chess.

Sometime in 1960 a crazed would-be musician set out to annihilate the top bands in Chicago, issuing threats to kill everyone in Muddy's, Guitar Red's and Lucky Charmichael's bands. He'd brandished a gun at Smitty's Corner, but Muddy and his band were playing out of town that weekend. As a parting statement, he fired a couple of bullets into the ceiling, then dropped out of sight for about a year.

Then in 1961, just before catching a city bus to a gig, Cotton lingered over a drink in a South Side tavern at Lake Park and 43rd Street. He saw the gunman cross the street and enter the bar. "I knew I hadn't done anything to him," says Cotton, "but he walked up to the door and said, 'Why did you treat me like you did?' He pulled back his coat and I could see the gun and he started shooting."[51] Cotton was hit five times by a .38-caliber pistol. He still carries a bullet in his head. The perpetrator was convicted, but as Cotton puts it, "He got off kind of light."[52]

On the evening of 13 May 1961, a program entitled "Blues at Carnegie Hall" was presented at New York's premier concert venue. On this, Muddy's second Carnegie Hall appearance, he shared the bill with Jimmy Reed, Big Maybelle, Jimmy Witherspoon and Oscar Brown, Jr. Chris Barber, who happened to be in town, caught the show:

> They had the penthouse suite in the Theresa Hotel in Harlem. The one that Castro stayed in, you know, when he went to the U.N. We went to the concert at Carnegie Hall and Muddy played very well . . . and then there were some other guests on the concert, and they had Muddy's band to accompany them, you see. That was okay with Big Maybelle — that was fine because she sang straight blues — but Witherspoon

was another one. Now Witherspoon, he sang tunes . . . bluesy ballad singing. The point was that Muddy had no conception of playing those kind of chord sequences, so when Spoon sang, as he had to sing, "Ain't Nobody's Business," because it was one of his big numbers, which is not a 12-bar blues, the chords behind it were not exactly what he was used to. [laughs] There was some eyebrow raising.[53]

Eyebrows were not the only ascending objects that evening. "I was sitting back on my riser," says Francis Clay, who was conducting the band, "and in order to see me to get the cues, they'd have to turn around, and their pride wouldn't allow them to do that, so . . . every couple of numbers they'd move my drums further downstage, see. And so at intermission they said, 'We'll fix this,' and so they set me right on the curtain. And when the curtain went up after intermission, it caught on my bass drum. . . . . Jimmy Witherspoon was standing there — we were vamping to bring him in, waiting for the curtain to go up. When the curtain went up, so did my drums!"[54]

In the meantime Muddy was planning an injection of new blood into the band. "In spite of the fact that I was coming up with ideas for music," Clay contends, "Howlin' Wolf and Little Walter kept telling him . . . that I didn't like the blues, that I was a jazz musician. Why didn't he get rid of me? And they kept it up until he finally told me — and A.W. Stephenson after — that he wanted to make some changes. And he give a two-week notice . . . and the owner of the club [where the Hoochie Coochie Boys were playing regularly] found out and gave *him* [Muddy] a two-week notice and asked me if I'd stay there and get a band together, so I did."[55] That night, as soon as he heard of the firings, Cotton quit. The three sidemen formed a group without their former boss, then Cotton went to Britain to tour with Chris Barber. When Wolf and Little Walter heard that their ploy had worked and Francis was free of Muddy, they both tried to hire him for their own bands. Muddy knew then that he'd been duped.

Except for Otis Spann and Marcus Johnson, Muddy used all new personnel for his session in July or August 1961, most likely because his band was in transition. For these cuts Muddy dispenses with the harmonica and features horns instead. Marcus Johnson and Boyd Atkins blow tenor sax, Matt "Guitar" Murphy is on guitar, Milton

Rector plays bass and drummer Al Duncan lays down the beat. "Real Love" and "Messin' With The Man" boast tasty sax solos, a sound that veers from Muddy's usual fare. Also recorded this day were "Lonesome Room Blues" and an untitled, unissued number.

As Cotton's replacement, Muddy chose George Buford, Jr., a harmonica player who was to become a recurrent member of the band for the remainder of Muddy's career. Buford was born in Hernando, Mississippi, on 10 November 1929. By age nine he was plowing behind mules and singing with the M&O Gospel Singers. When he was about 12 years old, George followed in his father's footsteps by learning to blow blues harmonica, which he played at local box suppers and house parties.

At 15 he went to live in Memphis, where he became increasingly attracted to blues. When Muddy's first discs were released, Buford fell in love with his music, and when he heard Little Walter's recording of "Juke," he discovered his calling: "That set my soul on fire, you know, for harmonica."[56] As a singer Buford's chief influences were Muddy and B.B. King.

In 1953 George moved north to pursue a blues career in Chicago under the name Little Junior B. His first band there was the Savage Boys, with Dave Members on guitar and drummer "Cadillac" Sam Burton. Buford became acquainted with several of the Hoochie Coochie Boys, and they took him over to the 708 Club to meet Muddy. "I was nervous, shaking," says Buford, recalling his introduction to one of his blues heroes. Muddy asked the young harp player to join him at his table. "He was a great guy. He treated me real nice," Buford remembers, but he was so intimidated he soon made his excuses and left.[57]

Otis Spann took Muddy to hear the Savage Boys play in 1957. "We was pretty good," Buford claims. "There wasn't but three of us, but we was putting the sounds out, and he liked it enough, and he liked the music we was playing, because we was mostly playing *his* music really and Jimmy Reed's."[58] Muddy was sufficiently impressed that he hired the band to fill in for the Hoochie Coochie Boys at Smitty's Corner when they were on the road.

Although it wasn't Muddy's idea, the Savage Boys became known as the Muddy Waters Junior Band, and as he was trying to sing like Muddy, Buford gained the moniker Muddy Waters Junior. Muddy showed his support by advertising their gigs on his radio show.

While Buford held down a job at the University of Chicago and played with the trio at night, a variety of sidemen passed through its ranks: Jo Jo Williams, Big Smokey Smothers, Elgin Evans, Johnny Young, Dave Myers, Lazy Bill Lucas and Willie Smith.

Muddy expressed his admiration for Buford's harmonica skills: "He done told me, 'One of these days I'm gonna get you in my band,' but I just took it for a joke, you know. So I was working one day and he sent his chauffeur out there to get me because James Cotton had done quit. . . . He told me Muddy Waters wanted me to join his band and go on the road with him the next night."[59] Buford was shocked, but overjoyed.

Nevertheless, he needed some convincing. "My wife didn't want me to leave town," Buford says. "I had little childrens, you know."[60] It took a couple of hours for Muddy and Otis to win him over. Before they set off on tour the next day, Muddy bought George several harmonicas, paid his union dues and arranged for him to borrow Cotton's amps and mikes. "We went to St. Louis in his 1960 Fleetwood Cadillac," Buford remembers, "and I'm sitting in the back, quiet as a mouse, scared to death."[61]

Buford was well used to playing before live audiences, but the sheer size of the crowds that came out to hear Muddy on that initial tour terrified him. "I used to turn my back to the audience," Buford admits, chuckling. "Muddy Waters grabbed me by the coat, 'Turn around! Turn around!' I was ashamed, you know. . . . I didn't want them looking at me, not then."[62]

At first Muddy went easy on Buford, but as he recognized George's latent potential, he got tough and pushed him hard. One aspect of Muddy's brilliance as a bandleader was his ability to recognize and nurture raw talent, polishing it under his tutelage. With his guidance Otis coached Buford every day in Muddy's basement, and he steadily improved. "Him and Spann taught me the notes and all that kind of stuff," Buford recalls. "I was blowing them wrong, and then they straightened me out."[63] Although Buford didn't record with the band during this period, Muddy often insisted he attend the sessions as a learning experience. "He taught me the dynamics of the blues," Buford says of Muddy, "the beginning and the ending and how to make solos and things like that, when to come in and when not to do something."[64] In the end Muddy got more out of Buford than Buford himself knew he possessed.

To fill Clay's spot, Muddy chose Willie "Big Eyes" Smith, the drummer who'd worked with him on *Muddy Waters Sings Big Bill Broonzy*. Willie hails from Helena, Arkansas, where he was born on 19 January 1936. Raised by his grandparents, who were sharecroppers just outside town on the Wooton Epps Plantation, Willie had no inkling until he was nearly grown that his life's path would lead to the blues. Still, there were connections to Muddy even when he was a child. Muddy's friend Robert Nighthawk farmed next to Willie's grandparents, and Pinetop Perkins, who would later join Muddy as well, lived nearby. James Triblett, who became Muddy's valet and driver, baby-sat young Willie. And as an avid listener of blues radio shows, Willie remembers hearing Muddy's early morning broadcasts on KFFA in 1949.

Late in 1953 when he was 17, Willie traveled to Chicago to visit his mother for a couple of weeks and ended up staying a lifetime. She smuggled him into a tavern where Muddy was playing with Otis, Jimmy, Elgin Evans and Henry Strong. Willie's life was forever changed. While he'd yearned for a saxophone in the past, he could never afford one. He left Muddy's show determined to play blues in some capacity: "It was something I always wanted to do, but seeing it, I knew I *had* to do it."[65] Those farm and construction jobs he'd held in Helena weren't for him. Willie stayed on in Chicago and learned to play harmonica and drums.

The following year Willie and his friend Clifton James formed a trio: Willie blew harp, Clifton was on drums and Bobby Lee Burns played guitar. In 1955 Willie got married and gave up music, although he did play harmonica that year on Bo Diddley's recording of "Diddy Wah Diddy." He'd jammed with Bo when they were both learning music together.

Willie's retirement from blues was short-lived, however, and he passed through a series of bands in quick succession. By 1956 he was blowing harp with a group that included singer and guitar player Arthur "Big Boy" Spires. Leaving after only three months, Willie fronted his own band on harmonica, but soon joined Little Hudson Shower's Red Devil Trio, where he began his career as a professional drummer. The two most significant influences on the development of his drumming style were Muddy's drummers Fred Below and Francis Clay.

From there Willie played drums for the Muddy Waters Junior

Band, which comprised harmonica player George Buford, Dave Myers and Jo Jo Williams. Another brief stint followed with singer and guitar player Willie Johnson, then while he was with Jo Jo Williams's new band, Smith was hired to back Muddy on *Muddy Waters Sings Big Bill Broonzy*. Although Willie had considered pawning his drum kit a year or so earlier, he was still playing with Jo Jo when he was summoned to meet with Muddy in 1961 at a club on 63rd Street where Muddy was appearing. It was a Sunday night, and Muddy asked Willie if he would start work for him on Thursday.

"It couldn't get no closer," is how he describes his relationship with his new boss. "I was by him and he was by me, just like father and son. That's the way we were. Even though we'd have our little arguments — he'd always win — it was like father and son."[66]

Muddy's session of January 1962 was the first of many subsequent Chess experiments that sought to market him to a new young, white audience, when in fact they seriously marred much of Muddy's recorded output of the 1960s. Separated from his band, he was backed by A.C. Reed on tenor sax, John "Big Moose" Walker on organ, bass player Earnest Johnson — who would join Muddy's band in 1980 — drummer Casey Jones, an unknown guitar player and several unidentified female background singers. Although Muddy's voice would always soar above whatever craze Chess was trying to cash in on, this session, like many following, failed to present Muddy at his finest. "Record companies try to push you up there," Muddy later said. "They want you to sell all the records you can, but they forget what you're cut out for, what you've lived for."[67] The January 1962 session produced "Muddy Waters Twist," a blatant attempt to endear Muddy to the teenaged record buyer. "Going Home" and "Down By The Deep Blue Sea," also cut this day, are defaced by out-of-tune background vocals. The best track of the session is "Tough Times"; Muddy's voice undulates with despair as he appeals to President Kennedy to solve the unemployment problem.

On 27 June 1962, Muddy's vocals for "You Shook Me" were dubbed onto an instrumental track laid down by guitarist Earl Hooker, Willie Dixon, A.C. Reed, "Big Moose" Walker, pianist Lafayette Leake and drummer Bobby Little. This number would later be covered by Led Zeppelin and Jeff Beck with Rod Stewart, but the deep, full richness of Muddy's voice on this track would never be approached.

Having been struck by the warm response blues artists were eliciting on their overseas tours and having concluded that blues promotion could be a profitable venture, German promoter Horst Lippmann — with the assistance of Willie Dixon — staged the first American Folk Blues Festival, which toured Europe in 1962. The package show included John Lee Hooker, Memphis Slim and Shakey Jake; Muddy joined them for the final leg of the road trip.

Returning home, Muddy and his band took a gig at a Boston club called the Jazz Workshop. Here Muddy acquired his first manager, a young drummer named Bob Messinger who'd been so knocked out by Muddy's appearance at the Newport Jazz Festival that he was convinced the bluesman could break into the white market. Based only on a handshake deal, Messinger set out to book Muddy into as many white venues as possible. The pay didn't matter; if the crowd was white, Muddy was there. The majority of his gigs, however, were still for black audiences. During 1962 bass player Jo Jo Williams and harp blower Otis "Smokey" Smothers joined Muddy's band, but each lasted only a short time.

Meanwhile, Muddy's house on South Lake Park continued to serve as a gathering place for visiting musicians and a home to several others. There was a small living room at the front of the Morganfield residence, and on the mantelpiece above the fireplace was a framed photograph of Little Walter and others of Muddy at the Apollo Theatre. On the walls were a reproduction of *The Last Supper* and a portrait of Jesus. But the kitchen was the true nerve center of the home: here Geneva cooked for a house full of family (including, for a while, her mother) and boarders. Muddy — whom Geneva called Old Man — was known to pitch in occasionally to concoct his specialty, short ribs.

Cotton was still living on the second floor; Muddy's uncle Joe Brant, George Buford and "St. Louis" Jimmy Oden were ensconced in the basement. Otis Spann and his family also took up residence at Muddy's place for a time. Now and then when his luck would falter, Little Walter would live there as well. One earlier boarder had fallen from grace and was forced to move on. According to Buddy Guy, Junior Wells pulled a knife on Muddy when he heard another member of the band was living in the house rent free. Sometime later Muddy cornered an unarmed Junior, grabbed him by the collar and smacked him in the face, declaring, "I'll whoop your ass!"[68] Junior accepted the punishment with his head bowed. Buddy asked if he was going to fight back, but Junior had learned his lesson. "No, I ain't going to fool with that old man," he concluded.[69]

Muddy's daughter Isoline was a regular visitor to her father's house, sometimes dropping in to watch the band rehearse. By this time, however, she was a troubled woman with a serious drug problem. "She was very nice," Buford remembers, "she just got strung out on the wrong thing."[70] Cotton recalls that "she respected Muddy quite a bit, and she had to be nice around Pops, you know."[71]

Muddy knew his daughter was losing the battle with her habit. "He was worrying pretty bad," says Buford. "Tore him up pretty bad, really did."[72] Drugs eventually engulfed her, and Isoline died from an overdose, leaving behind a young daughter Amelia, nicknamed Cookie, for Geneva and Muddy to raise. Later in life Muddy said that he sang of Isoline when he performed "Sad Letter Blues," although he'd written the song long before her death.

"Sweet lady, very sweet lady," is how Cotton describes Geneva, whom Muddy and the band affectionately called Grandma.[73] Buford concurs: "Oh, she was a great lady!"[74] Although their relationship was strong, her husband's compulsion for extramarital conquests brought considerable pain to Geneva's life. "Young womens was his thing," Buford comments,[75] and although he endeavored to keep that part of his life secret from Geneva, she inevitably discovered a portion of it. "That hurt her tremendously," says Francis Clay sadly. "She knew, of course. They used to call the house."[76]

Most likely it was the fact that Muddy had children by these women that caused Geneva the deepest anguish. She and Muddy had had no offspring together. Buford recalls one girlfriend — the inspiration for the song "She's Nineteen Years Old" — who gave birth to a boy and a girl fathered by Muddy and refused to stay quietly in the background. "The gal was named Lois," he remembers. "She brought the kids over there one day and set 'em on Muddy Waters's front porch . . . sure did, and went off and left 'em there."[77] Muddy quickly hustled them away, but the heartache of this and other incidents took their toll on Geneva.

Over the years Muddy had maintained his relationship with his father, Ollie, and visited him and his other siblings in Rolling Fork, Mississippi, whenever he was touring in the vicinity. In 1962 Ollie died, and Muddy immediately traveled to Rolling Fork to be with his family and to serve as a pallbearer at the funeral. "It affected everyone very deeply," Muddy's half-brother Robert Morganfield reports sadly, "because he was such a good father. His death had a great impact on the entire family."[78]

Muddy was back in the studio on 12 October 1962, dubbing vocals on instrumental tracks laid down by Earl Hooker, A.C. Reed, Jackie Brenston on baritone sax, "Big Moose" Walker, Earnest Johnson and drummer Casey Jones. This session was most notable for "You Need Love," a Willie Dixon composition, later recorded by Led Zeppelin then Tina Turner as "Whole Lotta Love." "Little Brown Bird," buried amidst a cacophony of imitation birdcalls, was later covered by Elvin Bishop. The other number recorded that day, "Black Angel," was never issued.

As a driver for an exterminator company, Charlie Musselwhite often passed through Chicago's ghettoes and was dazzled by the marquees advertising all the blues performers whose records he'd listened to growing up in Memphis. "Man, I was like a kid in a candy store," he remembers fondly. "Every night I was in a different club. Every night it was a decision who did I want to hear, Muddy or Wolf or Sonny Boy. I wish I had that decision to make again."[79]

It was 1962, and Charlie's favorite hangout was Pepper's Lounge at 403 East 43rd Street, Muddy's home club since the closing of Smitty's Corner the year before. "He worked in this club every night," Musselwhite recalls, "and you could go in there and they'd be in there until four in the morning. Different musicians would hang out there and sit in. It was such a scene. . . . They were such wonderful times, and at the time I was so young I didn't think it would ever end."[80]

At the time Musselwhite had no notion that he'd become the renowned blues harmonica player and singer he is today. Unbeknownst to Charlie, a waitress at Pepper's told Muddy that he played harp and suggested that he sit in. When Muddy called him onstage, Charlie was reluctant; nevertheless, he did his best, and stemming from that initial exposure with Muddy, Musselwhite's talent began to be recognized. Soon he was being offered gigs, and he realized that a career in music could be an escape from the drudgery of a dead-end job.

"He was real friendly to people, real outgoing," Musselwhite says of Muddy, who'd later nickname him "Good Time" Charlie, after a song by Bobby Bland. Yet he also possessed the unshakable confidence of a man in total control. "He was . . . kind of like regal, like he was royalty or something, but not in a way like he was bigheaded or anything. He treated everybody respectfully, and he was very humble, but at the same time, he was this real proud man, too. . . . He was the kind of guy who could walk into a room, and even if you didn't know who he was, you knew he was somebody. He wasn't no average person."[81]

Pat Hare left Muddy's band in 1963 with the law in hot pursuit. In a jealous rage fueled by alcohol, he'd fired a rifle through his girlfriend's front window. Muddy hid him briefly, but Hare soon fled Chicago to stay with Joe Willie Wilkins in Memphis, then to his parents' place in Parkin, Arkansas. Not long afterwards George Buford quit as well. He'd received an offer to lead the house band at a club in Minneapolis for more money than Muddy could afford to pay him. Today Buford still admits his debt to Muddy: "I learned how to be a good bandleader, I learned how to play good blues, and I picked up all my style from him — personality and how to treat people and how to talk to people and stuff like that. He taught me the ropes."[82]

With Hare in mind as the guitar player for his new group, Buford says, "I went back down to Arkansas, picked him up and brought him up here [to Minneapolis]. That was the wrongest thing I ever did in my life."[83] Hare's chronic alcoholism and volcanic temperament were way out of control. After a two-day suspension for dozing onstage, Pat became infuriated at not getting paid. "He threatened to kill me," Buford claims. "He was very treacherous."[84]

Then one day Hare's violent streak effectively extinguished his promising music career. He'd had a stormy relationship with live-in girlfriend Agnes Winje, an older white woman who'd left her husband for him, and had threatened her at gunpoint. On 15 December 1963, upset that Agnes was contemplating a reconciliation with her husband, Hare spent the afternoon drinking wine with S.P. Leary, a drummer who'd later become a member of Muddy's band. Returning home, Pat fired several shots at Agnes, prompting the neighbors to call the police. Two officers responded, and as the first entered the apartment, Hare gunned him down with three bullets. The second policeman disabled Hare with two shots, then discovered Agnes, who was suffering from two bullet wounds inflicted by Pat. The wounded officer died en route to hospital, and Agnes succumbed to her injuries on 22 January. In a one-day trial on 19 February 1964, Hare was found guilty of the first-degree murder of the police officer and of the third-degree murder of Agnes Winje. He was sentenced to life and incarcerated in Stillwater State Prison.

Filling the vacancy created by Buford's resignation, James Cotton returned to Muddy's band. Although he possessed the talent to make it on his own, Cotton knew that his earlier departure from the Hoochie Coochie Boys had been premature. "I was into the music," he says, "not watching the business end of it. When I left in '61 I knew how to play the music, but I didn't know nothing about the business end of it. So I went back [to Muddy] and stayed until '66 while I could learn the business end of it."[85]

After two recording sessions where his vocals were dubbed on instrumental tracks, Muddy finally returned to the studio with a band on 2 May 1963. Joining Cotton and Muddy were Otis Spann, guitarist Luther Tucker, Willie Dixon and Willie Smith. With the startling exception of "Coming Round The Mountain," Muddy performs the style of blues he did best, presenting a strong lineup of numbers: "Brown Skin Woman," "Twenty Four Hours," "Let Me Hang Around" and "Five Long Years," written by Eddie Boyd, Muddy's childhood pal on Stovall. Muddy's 6 June session was a solid outing as well. Out of it came such cuts as Sonny Boy Williamson's naughty "Elevate Me Mama" and Jimmy Reed's "You Don't Have To Go." Muddy croons over his latest teenaged conquest in "Early In The Morning" and delivers an introspective, emotional blues with "One More Mile."

On the simmering summer evening of 26 July 1963, a coterie of blues musicians gathered at the Copa Cabana, a West Side Chicago club on West Roosevelt Road. The lineup was a blues-lover's dream: Little Walter, Sonny Boy Williamson, Buddy Guy, Willie Dixon, Howlin' Wolf and, of course, Muddy Waters.

The recordings of these performances were later released as *Blues From "Big Bill's" Copa Cabana*. For the first time ever, Muddy was captured live on disc in a raucous club atmosphere, with a boisterous audience whooping its approval. For his numbers Muddy was backed by Otis Spann, Buddy Guy on lead guitar, Jack Myers on bass, Fred Below on drums and a horn section. The album features Muddy performing "Wee, Wee Baby" with Willie Dixon and Buddy Guy assisting on vocals, "Sitting And Thinking," "Clouds In My Heart," "Got My Mojo Working" and "19 Years Old."

As the folk-music craze swept through coffeehouses from coast to coast, Chess seized upon the opportunity to transform its aging bluesmen into marketable commodities. By repackaging blues as folk music — which it surely was in any case — the record company could tap into the lucrative Caucasian market to revive the sagging careers of its blues artists. White North America — burdened with the yoke of racism — was late in recognizing the store of riches buried in its own coffers. On the other hand, American blues performers had been a popular draw in white European venues since Leadbelly began performing there in 1949.

Muddy wasn't always a willing participant in his redefinition. Chess was urging him to develop a 40-minute program containing a central theme exhorting a particular cause. As Chess lawyer John Burton explained, they wanted Muddy to "become identified with a movement — with something. You know, like Joan Baez."[86] While Muddy didn't buy that strategy, he was recast as a folkie and booked at folk-music venues and festivals.

"Somewhere along the line, record companies discovered they could sell more records by appealing to a broader buying public and labeling country and blues [as] folk music," commented Ralph Bass in the liner notes for Muddy's next LP, *Muddy Waters: Folk Singer*.[87] Although Bass also maintained that the purpose of the album was to present "the blues without any stigma of commercialism attached to it,"[88] this, of course, belies the financial realities of the Chess Producing Corporation, which was endeavoring to market Muddy's music to a new niche of consumers.

Muddy's "folk" album was recorded in September 1963 for release on 30 January 1964. Comprising mainly his own compositions, it includes encore performances of several previously recorded tunes: "Long Distance," "You Gonna Need My Help," "Country Boy" and "Feel Like Going Home." Attempting to strip Muddy's music down to its bare essentials, Chess had him leave his band at home. Backing him instead were Willie Dixon on upright bass, drummer Clifton James and a young session guitarist Muddy had had his eye on for several years — Buddy Guy.

Back in September 1958, a 22-year-old guitar player from Letts-worth, Louisiana, stepped off a train in Chicago. Lonely and broke, George "Buddy" Guy hadn't eaten for three days when he got a gig at the 708 Club. Muddy had heard this newcomer had talent. He drove to the club in his red Chevrolet station wagon and summoned Buddy outside. "A guy just grabbed me on the collar and went to slappin' me and tellin' me, 'I'm the Mud,' " Guy recounts. "And all I was hearin' was 'I'm gettin' mugged.' "[89]

Ordered to get in the front seat, Buddy hesitated, overwhelmed at the realization that this heavy-handed stranger was, in fact, the king of Chicago blues. "He called me a motherfucker or somethin'," says Buddy, "so I got in the car."[90] "Muddy was sittin' there, looking sharp, and had him a loaf of bread and some salami and he was eating a sandwich. He looked at me and said, 'You hongry?' I said, 'No.' He said, 'That's a damn lie, boy — go ahead, fix you a sandwich!' "[91] Guy was starving, but he was so embarrassed about his situation and so overjoyed to be in the company of his hero, that his hunger vanished. "My stomach was empty," Buddy recalls, "but my soul was *full*."[92] Muddy persisted, however, swatting at Buddy until he finally relented and ate something.

On another occasion Muddy called out for Buddy to play. Para-lyzed by shyness, the guitarist shrank into a corner. "And he just turned around and slapped me, man! . . . He said, 'I don't want to hear that from you. You gonna play.' After that he just took over like a daddy to me, man."[93]

Except for his live recordings in Manchester, at Carnegie Hall and at Newport, Muddy had played guitar on only a scant few studio cuts since April 1954, nearly 10 years before. *Folk Singer* marked the welcome return of Muddy's stinging slide, which, thanks to Spann's encouragement, he was now playing at club gigs as well. The LP bears witness to the fact that the long hiatus had done nothing to diminish Muddy's guitar mastery.

The album also underscores Muddy's complete command of the music, even without the backing of a full band or electric instru-ments to empower his delivery. He presents the songs with an unaccustomed intimacy; it's a one-on-one experience. He delivers his blues at a leisurely pace and with a haunting quality that suggests vast Delta vistas of solitude and lonely hours of intro-spection.

Folk Singer is a feast of unadorned acoustic guitar and vocals. Muddy's slide is clearly audible as it works the strings, occasionally knocking the fretboard; the listener can hear him quivering his slide to coax the maximum sustain and vibrato from his notes. His vocals are stunning. Without the usual body of sound behind him, one can more easily appreciate the range and dynamic of Muddy's voice, grown warmer and richer with the years. The power behind his delivery pervades even his quietest whisper. Emotion oozes from every phrase.

If Chess's objective was to portray Muddy as he was in former times, or present a sampling of his roots, this was not the result. *Folk Singer* was not a step backward, no matter what the marketing strategy. It has a contemporary feel — due in large part to Buddy Guy's guitar fill-ins and solos, as well as to the recording technique. There's an accrued sophistication that separates this sound from the country blues Muddy once performed on Stovall.

That year the German promotion team of Lippmann and Rau, with help from pianist Memphis Slim, organized the 1963 American Folk Blues Festival. The performance roster boasted some big names: Muddy, Otis Spann, Big Joe Williams, Sonny Boy Williamson, Lonnie Johnson, Victoria Spivey, Willie Dixon, guitarist Matt "Guitar" Murphy and drummer Billy Stepney. From the end of September to October, the festival toured 17 European cities, including Brussels, Strasbourg, Frankfurt, Bremen, Baden-Baden, Paris and Copenhagen.

Four of the German concerts Muddy did on the tour that October — in Frankfurt, Bremen, Baden-Baden and possibly in Heilbronn — were recorded and released on disc. On it Muddy was backed by Spann, Matt Murphy, Willie Dixon, Billy Stepney and, on the Baden-Baden release, Sonny Boy Williamson. Muddy's impassioned version of Eddie Boyd's "Five Long Years" from Bremen is enhanced by Spann's and Murphy's fine solos. Also that month in Copenhagen, Spann recorded an album entitled *Good Morning Blues*.

The National Jazz Federation then arranged to bring the American Folk Blues Festival to Britain. The touring stars did three concerts in Croydon, just south of London, which were emceed by Chris Barber. By the time of these performances, Muddy had seen his overseas reputation become more solidly established. Since the

Muddy (right) accompanied by Henry "Son" Simms, outside
Clarksdale, Mississippi, 20 June 1942. (John W. Work III Field Collection,
Center for Popular Music, Middle Tennessee State University)

Above. Muddy's cabin on the Stovall Plantation as it appeared in 1995
Left, above. The Old River as it borders the Stovall Plantation, 1995
Left, below. The cotton field behind Muddy's cabin, 1995 (Sandra B. Tooze)

(Courtesy Bill Greensmith)

A 1950 publicity shot
(courtesy Showtime
Archives [Toronto])

Little Walter, 1950s (courtesy Showtime Archives [Toronto])

Jimmy Rogers, 1950s (photo by Jim Marshall/courtesy Showtime Archives [Toronto])

Early Chess publicity photo (Michael Ochs Archives)

Early Chess publicity photo (Michael Ochs Archives)

From the left: Big Walter Horton, Willie Nix, Patty Nix, J.T. Brown, Katie, Muddy and Jimmy Rogers in Chicago, 1954 (courtesy Patty Nix/© 1974 Delta Haze Corporation)

From the left: Muddy, Jerome Green, Otis Spann, Henry Strong, Elgin Evans and Jimmy Rogers, 1953 or 1954 (Bill Greensmith Collection)

Thirteen-year-old Marshall Chess with Leonard
in Florida on his first road trip with his father, 1955
(courtesy Marshall Chess)

(Courtesy Showtime Archives [Toronto])

Big Bill Broonzy's funeral, 15 August 1958. *From the left:* unknown,
Muddy, Francis Clay, unknown, unknown, Brother John Sellars,
Tampa Red, Sunnyland Slim and Otis Spann (Mickie Pallas)

Muddy, c. 1957 (Michael Ochs Archives)

St. Louis Jimmy, George Adins (photographer), Robert "Junior" Lockwood
and Muddy, 1959 (Blues Unlimited Collection/courtesy Bill Greensmith)

Muddy's home club, Pepper's Lounge (Raeburn Flerlage)

George Buford (left) and Muddy at Pepper's, 28 June 1961 (Raeburn Flerlage)

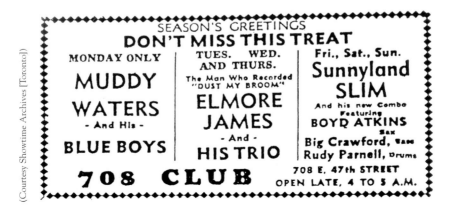

SEASON'S GREETINGS
DON'T MISS THIS TREAT

MONDAY ONLY

MUDDY WATERS
- And His -
BLUE BOYS

TUES. WED. AND THURS.
The Man Who Recorded "DUST MY BROOM"
ELMORE JAMES
- And -
HIS TRIO

Fri., Sat., Sun.
Sunnyland SLIM
And his new Combo
Featuring
BOYD ATKINS Sax
Big Crawford, Bass
Rudy Parnell, Drums

708 CLUB

708 E. 47th STREET
OPEN LATE, 4 TO 5 A.M.

James Cotton (left) and Muddy at a jazz concert at the Opera House, Chicago, early 1963 (Raeburn Flerlage)

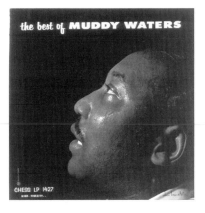

Muddy performing at the Opera House, Chicago, early 1963 (Raeburn Flerlage)

John Lee Hooker invited Muddy to join him at an interview at
Chicago's Sutherland Hotel, 3 February 1963 (Raeburn Flerlage)

At the reception for the artists of the Lippmann and Rau American Folk Blues
Festival, Marquee Club, Oxford Street, London, October 1963 (Val Wilmer)

Muddy and Geneva's South Side
Chicago home, 4339 South Lake Park,
9 January 1964 (Raeburn Flerlage)

Muddy and Geneva's living room, 9 January 1964 (Raeburn Flerlage)

Michael Bloomfield with Muddy and his granddaughter
Cookie, 9 January 1964. Bloomfield was at Muddy's home
interviewing him for a magazine article. (Raeburn Flerlage)

Ransom Knowling (bass), Willie Smith (drums) and Muddy onstage at Fairfield Hall,
Croydon, England, as part of the American Folk Blues Caravan, 3 May 1964 (Val Wilmer)

Passing time backstage, Fairfield Hall, Croydon, 3 May 1964 (Val Wilmer)

The staff at Chess Records (from the left): "Peaches" from the shipping department, Esmond Edwards, Marshall Chess, Leonard Chess, Phil Chess, Max Cooperstein and Dick LaPalm, c. 1964 (courtesy Marshall Chess)

Leonard (left), Marshall and Phil Chess, c. 1965 (courtesy Marshall Chess)

Otis Spann (left) and James Cotton rehearsing in Muddy's basement, 24 February 1965 (Raeburn Flerlage)

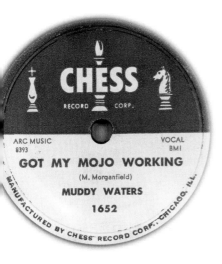

Muddy performing at the Down Beat Jazz Fest, accompanied by (from the left)
Dizzy Gillespie and James Moodie, 14 August 1965 (Raeburn Flerlage)

From the left: Otis Spann, Luther "Georgia Boy Snake" Johnson, Sammy Lawhorn, Big Mama Thornton, Francis Clay, Muddy and James Cotton, 1966 (courtesy Showtime Archives [Toronto])

(Courtesy Showtime Archives [Toronto])

The boss Muddy Waters

McKinley Morganfield

Luther Johnson on piano 1975 with Muddy Waters

Pine Top Perkins " " on drums 1975

W. Smith Big Eyes on bass 1975

Calvin Jones

JAMES COTTON

Homesick James

Sunny Land Slim

Lord Willie Dixon

The taping of "The Blues" at the CBC studio, Toronto, 27–29 January 1966. *From the left:* Jimmy Lee Morris, Bukka White, Big Joe Williams, Willie Dixon, Muddy, Otis Spann, Peewee Madison, Sunnyland Slim, James Cotton, Mabel Hillary, Sonny Terry, Jesse Fuller and Brownie McGhee (Bill Smith/courtesy Showtime Archives [Toronto])

Muddy (courtesy MCA/Chess files)

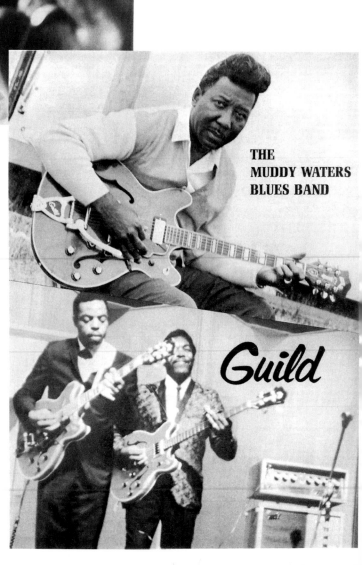

Muddy with Sammy Lawhorn (left) and probably Luther "Georgia Boy Snake" Johnson (right) advertising Guild musical instruments and equipment, c.1968 (courtesy Showtime Archives [Toronto])

From the left: Muddy, Luther "Georgia Boy Snake" Johnson and Paul Oscher onstage
at the Odeon, Hammersmith, London, during "Jazz Expo '68" (Val Wilmer)

(Courtesy Showtime Archives [Toronto])

Muddy looking skeptical during the taping of *Electric Mud*, May 1968.
From the left: Muddy, Marshall Chess and Otis Spann (courtesy Marshall Chess)

Publicity shot for *Electric Mud*, 1968 (Michael Ochs Archives)

Otis Spann (left) with Muddy in St. Louis, February 1969 (Bill Greensmith Collection)

Howlin' Wolf (left) and Muddy relaxing before their gigs at
the Ann Arbor Blues and Jazz Festival, 1969 (Tom Copi)

John Sinclair (left), Lucille Spann and Muddy dedicating the Otis Spann Memorial
Field at the Ann Arbor Blues and Jazz Festival, 9 September 1972 (Leni Sinclair)

Muddy and Mojo Buford playing at the Ann Arbor Blues
and Jazz Festival, 9 September 1972 (Bill Greensmith)

From the left: Louis Myers, Marcus Johnson, Willie Smith, Muddy, Mojo Buford and Peewee Madison at the Ann Arbor Blues and Jazz Festival, 9 September 1972 (Bill Greensmith)

From the left: Bill Wyman, Muddy, Dallas Taylor, Junior Wells, Terry Taylor and Buddy Guy at the Montreux Jazz Festival, 1974 (Gianfranco Skala)

Muddy (James Fraher)

Pinetop Perkins and Muddy, London, 30 October 1976 (Bill Greensmith)

Muddy (John Gibbs Rockwood)

Muddy and Jerry Portnoy at Mandel Hall,
The University of Chicago, October 1977 (D. Shigley)

At The Hague, Holland, 1977 (Val Wilmer)

From the left: Ron Wood, Muddy, Mick Jagger and Keith Richards (D. Shigley)

Johnny Winter and Muddy (© Jon Sievert, Michael Ochs Archives)

President Jimmy Carter looks on as Bob Margolin and Muddy perform at
the White House, 9 August 1978 (courtesy of the Jimmy Carter Library)

At the Capital Radio Jazz Festival, Alexandra Palace, London, 1979 (Val Wilmer)

With Chuck Berry and a fan at the Capital Radio Jazz Festival,
Alexandra Palace, London, 21 July 1979 (Paul Harris)

Muddy, *above and facing* (© Jon Sievert, Michael Ochs Archives)

With his wife Marva (© Jon Sievert, Michael Ochs Archives)

In Memory
of

McKinley Morganfield
(MUDDY "MISSISSIPPI" WATERS)

WEDNESDAY, MAY 4, 1983
VISITATION: 7:00 P.M.   FUNERAL: 7:30 P.M.

METROPOLITAN FUNERAL PARLORS, INC.
4445 South King Drive ● Chicago, Illinois

REV. C. W. HOPSON, Officiating

The program from Muddy's funeral, 4 May 1983, *and overleaf.*
(courtesy of the Blues Archives, University of Mississippi)

Obituary

In Memory
of

McKINLEY MORGANFIELD
(Muddy "Mississippi" Waters)

McKINLEY MORGANFIELD was born April 4, 1915 to Mr. and Mrs. Ollie Morganfield in Rolling Fork, Mississippi.

He accepted Christ as his Savior and was baptised at an early age.

Della, his beloved grandmother, raised him from a baby to the fine man he grew up to be. She also gave him the name he became internationally known as, Muddy Waters.

In 1943, he moved to Chicago, and through hard work and determination, became the Godfather of the blues.

In 1973, he made his home in West Suburban, Westmont, where he resided until he departed this life, April 30, 1983.

He leaves to cherish his memory his loving wife, Marva; seven children, Joseph, Mercy, Renee, Roslind, Charles, Deltwaine and Larry, four grandchildren, Amelia, Lawrence, Kathleen and Tony; a dedicated manager and friend, Scott Cameron; seven great-grandchildren and a host of brothers, sisters, other relatives, friends and fans.

Order of Service

PRELUDE	
PROCESSIONAL	The Family
SCRIPTURE	Minister
PRAYER	Minister
SELECTION - *"Glory, Glory"*	Pop Staples
ACKNOWLEDGEMENT OF CONDOLENCES	
SELECTION	
OBITUARY (Read Silently)	
SELECTION	
EULOGY	Rev. C. W. Hopson
REVIEWAL	
BENEDICTION	
RECESSIONAL	

— INTERMENT —

RESTVALE CEMETERY
THURSDAY, MAY 5, 1983 — 10:00 A.M.

Mayor Harold Washington (bottom left) and Marva Morganfield (bottom right)
helping to erect the Muddy Waters Drive sign, Chicago, 2 August 1985
(Jack Lenahan, reprinted with permission, *The Chicago Sun-Times* © 1996)

The plaque honoring Muddy in the town of his
birth, Rolling Fork, Mississippi (Sandra B. Tooze)

The Muddy Waters U.S. stamp, part of the American
Music series, 1994 (Sandra B. Tooze)

previous year, Chess recordings had been available in the United Kingdom and throughout Europe on the Pye International and London-American labels. To fervent, young British music buffs, Muddy Waters, Bo Diddley and Chuck Berry were now icons of American popular music. Muddy's discs were being scrutinized by a generation of young musicians keen on emulating his sound. Everyone was primed to revel in Muddy's loud, raunchy electric blues. What they got, however, was something different.

Still smarting from the painful memory of the bad reviews of his 1958 British appearances, Muddy had polished up a program of country blues, which he delivered to Croydon audiences on an acoustic Gibson guitar amplified with only a mike. "The first thing they wanted to know," Muddy said of the English musicians who'd flocked to these 1963 performances, "was why I didn't bring the amplifier. Those boys were playing louder than we ever played."[94] As Val Wilmer reports, Muddy was puzzled: "Back at his London hotel after the concert, sharing a bottle of Johnny Walker with Memphis Slim, Matt 'Guitar' Murphy and me, he sat shaking his head in disbelief. . . . Just what did they want, these white folks?"[95]

"I was disappointed. I felt the same way as everybody else," declares Clive Blewchamp, one of Muddy's avid admirers.

I wanted to hear him play an electric, and I wanted to hear him play really loud, like all the stuff that we'd heard about, you know, Chicago blues clubs being really small and everything cranked to the max, distortion plus. And it was all so very tasteful. Nothing was really amplified, you know. It was all kept down to a very tasteful level of sound.

It was more like *Muddy Waters: Folk Singer* than we were expecting. Everyone wanted to hear the wonderful stuff that we'd heard on *The Best Of Muddy Waters* that every kid had in their record collection, you know. And he just didn't do it. . . . He was playing an acoustic guitar throughout a lot of that, and people [were saying], "What the hell? Turn it up!"[96]

"Muddy was, as everyone says, ever so regal," continues Blewchamp, who spent some time with the bluesman during his stay in London. "He wasn't snotty, but he just had a regal presence, you know, that demanded reverence. And everybody did give him reverence, all his peers that were on the show."[97]

Although Muddy's concerts fell short of many people's expectations, his British fans still displayed enough veneration to stun a musician who continued to entertain primarily all-black audiences. "He was really bewildered, I remember that," says Blewchamp. "He just couldn't get over the people that came to see him. Just didn't get it. 'Why do they want to come to see me?'. . . . I think he was scared a lot of the time, because he just didn't know what was going on. A lot of them didn't."[98]

A young bass guitarist named Nigel Paul, who'd later play with Manfred Mann and Donovan, was just starting out when he caught Muddy headlining at a small north London club. By now Muddy had learned his lesson; at this venue he played both acoustic and electric guitar. "You could tell he was really into what he was doing," Paul remarks. "He was just really into the music. I think he was kinda pleased to have such a reaction that he got, you know. He was happy; he was having a good time up there. . . . [Paul and his musician friends] just thought it was unbelievable and just loved every second of it. . . . I think just about the whole of England was [influenced by Muddy's blues] at that time."[99] Paul elaborates, stressing how crucial to his own professional development this first encounter with Muddy was:

> I can still remember the performance, and it just made me go out and search out for more blues and really get into the music. And I've never looked back since, really, so I think it was a big turning point in my life. . . . I think he was like one of the biggest factors in my continuing [in music]. I just thought his performance was so powerful. . . . I'd been sort of looking for blues, you know, a lot. Back in those days, blues records weren't that available in England, so I guess, really, he inspired me to keep on looking and keep on listening and keep on learning.
>
> We were all so knocked out about it, then afterwards we were doing anything we could to get hold of Muddy Waters's records, you know. And through that we learned about Willie Dixon and so much more, which we probably would never even have bothered to find out about if we hadn't seen that performance.[100]

The Muddy Waters effect now seemed to be at work everywhere. An obscure young American guitar player who'd modeled his technique on Muddy's finally got to meet the master face to face. Jimi Hendrix, a former paratrooper who'd performed on bills with Little Richard, Solomon Burke, B.B. King, Ike Turner and the Supremes, made his pilgrimage to Chess Records in 1963. When Muddy walked into the room, Hendrix was awestruck; he had taught himself to play to Muddy Waters records.

"The first guitarist I was aware of was Muddy Waters," Jimi said. "I heard one of his old records when I was a little boy and it scared me to death. . . . It was great."[101] Hendrix's inspiration came from raw, unadulterated blues. "I liked Muddy Waters when he had only two guitars, harmonica and bass drum," he declared. "Things like 'Rollin' and Tumblin' ' were what I liked, that real primitive guitar sound."[102]

That day at Chess, Hendrix listened with rapt attention as Muddy and Willie Dixon reminisced about their lives in the Delta over shots of Chivas Regal. When Jimi demonstrated some of his supersonic interpretations of down-home blues, Muddy responded by expounding the importance of remaining within the parameters of tradition. Apparently Hendrix hit him up for a job that day. "Oh, yeah, he tried to get into my band once," Muddy later remarked, "but I already had somebody."[103]

Throughout the brief blaze of luminosity that was Jimi Hendrix, he used the blues as his launching pad from which to blast past the confines of popular music. Muddy's licks provided a portion of that fuel. Hendrix's "Catfish Blues," which he often introduced as "Muddy's blues," incorporated the melody and guitar licks of Muddy's "Rollin' Stone" and "Still A Fool." As well he recorded Muddy's anthems, "Hoochie Coochie Man" and "Mannish Boy." Jimi's "Voodoo Chile Blues" is the lyrical beneficiary of "Hoochie Coochie Man."

Muddy won *Down Beat* magazine's 1964 critics' poll award for "talent deserving of wider recognition — male singer" and appeared again that year at the Newport Jazz Festival. Nevertheless, the blues scene continued to falter. "You know, at that time things was kinda rough, especially for blues musicians," Willie Smith explains. "To be honest, Muddy was struggling, you know, so we actually wasn't making no money."[104] To help make ends meet,

Willie took a job driving a cab and could therefore only play with Muddy for in-town gigs.

For part of that year, drummer S.P. Leary — known to other musicians as Kelly — worked with Muddy. Born on 6 June 1930 in Carthage, a small town in east Texas not far from the Louisiana border, S.P. began drumming as a young teenager growing up in Dallas. At age 14 he juggled schoolwork with drumming gigs for the legendary vocalist, guitarist and pianist Aaron "T-Bone" Walker and T-Bone's father, Maurice Rocco. Leary's dad, however, wouldn't permit his boy to travel any farther than Oklahoma City. Of T-Bone's impact on his formative years, S.P. declares, "He was just like a godfather to me. He helped raise me — showed me the way, he did."[105]

Leary joined the Third Armored Division of the U.S. Army in 1948 and served with it and the Second Armored Division in Korea. Upon his discharge in 1952, he attended business college, then moved to Chicago in 1954 to find an accounting job. His new neighbor Rice Miller (Sonny Boy Williamson II) heard Leary practicing and recruited him for his band. S.P. later drummed for Morris Pejoe, Jimmy Rogers, Magic Sam, Howlin' Wolf and for George Buford in Minneapolis. He met Muddy through his friendship with Cotton and Spann, and when he returned from Minneapolis, he joined Muddy's band. On his nights off, he provided the backbeat for James Cotton.

"Muddy was a nice man to work for, yes indeed," says Leary. "All he wanted you to do was do your job, and that's it. That's all he wanted. After you did the job, he just wanted you to be a gentleman at all times. He wanted you to respect everybody as you would like to be respected."[106]

Muddy presented two impressive blues at his recording session of 9 April 1964: "The Same Thing," penned by Willie Dixon, and his own "You Can't Lose What You Never Had." These tracks feature Muddy at his best; his indomitable slide guitar and vocals are embellished by Spann's impeccable piano. In "The Same Thing," Muddy's voluptuous voice expresses unabashed sensuality. Howlin' Wolf was reportedly rankled at the resemblance the song bears to his own hit, "Spoonful," also written by Dixon.

In late April and early May of the same year, Muddy again crossed the Atlantic to take part in the American Folk Blues Caravan tour of Europe and Britain. His fellow travelers included Sonny Terry and Brownie McGhee, Sister Rosetta Tharpe, Ransom Knowling and Cousin Joe. Muddy brought along Otis Spann and Willie Smith, while James Cotton kept the rest of the band working in Chicago. This time out, Muddy resolved not to second-guess his British fans; he pulled out the throttle and rammed them with the full impact of his electrified, electrifying Chicago blues. It was exactly what they craved.

While in Europe that May, Muddy recut several of his most popular recordings — including "Country Boy," "Baby Please Don't Go," "Hoochie Coochie Man" and "19 Years Old" — backed by Spann, Willie Smith and Ransom Knowling on bass. Then on 4 May in London, Muddy stepped back into the role of sideman for a recording session for Otis Spann. Muddy supplied vocals on "You're Gonna Need My Help" and served as the guitarist on every cut. For "Pretty Girls Everywhere" and "Stir's Me Up," Muddy was joined on guitar by a young devotee who still cites Muddy as the foremost influence on his musical career. As Muddy's music percolated the creative juices of a generation of fledgling British musicians, Eric Clapton was far from alone in succumbing to the potent spell of Muddy's blues.

NOTES

[1] Charles Shaar Murray, "The Blues Had a Baby and They Called It Rock 'n' Roll," *New Musical Express* (30 Apr. 1977): 30.

[2] Val Wilmer, interview with author, 14 May 1996.

[3] Chris Barber, interview with author, 4 June 1996.

[4] Chris Barber, interview with author, 4 June 1996.

[5] Chris Barber, interview with author, 4 June 1996.

[6] Chris Barber, interview with author, 4 June 1996.

[7] Chris Barber, interview with author, 4 June 1996.

[8] Chris Barber, interview with author, 4 June 1996.

[9] Chris Barber, interview with author, 4 June 1996.

[10] Chris Barber, interview with author, 4 June 1996.

[11] Chris Barber, interview with author, 4 June 1996.

[12] Jack Florin, "Muddy Water Blues," *Manchester Evening News*, Monday, 27 Oct. 1958, 2.

[13] Paul Oliver, *Conversation with the Blues* (New York: Horizon Press, 1965), 6.

[14] Chris Barber, interview with author, 4 June 1996.

[15] Chris Barber, interview with author, 4 June 1996.

[16] Chris Barber, interview with author, 4 June 1996.

[17] Chris Barber, interview with author, 4 June 1996.

[18] Chris Barber, interview with author, 4 June 1996.

[19] Max Jones, "This World of Jazz," *Melody Maker* (8 Nov. 1958): 11.

[20] Jones, 11.

[21] Jas Obrecht, "The Life and Times of the Hoochie Coochie Man," *Guitar Player* (Mar. 1994): 42.

[22] Francis Clay, interview with author, 23 Mar. 1996.

[23] James Cotton, interview with author, 26 Sept. 1995.

[24] Francis Clay, interview with author, 22 Mar. 1996.

[25] Willie Smith, interview with author, 10 Dec. 1995.

[26] Willie Smith, interview with author, 10 Dec. 1995.

[27] Liner notes *Muddy Waters Sings Big Bill Broonzy*, Chess, 1960.

[28] Francis Clay, interview with author, 22 Mar. 1996.

[29] John Lee Hooker, interview with author, 9 Aug. 1995.

[30] James Cotton, interview with author, 26 Sept. 1995.

[31] James Cotton, interview with author, 26 Sept. 1995.

[32] Ed Ward, *Michael Bloomfield: The Rise and Fall of an American Guitar Hero* (New York: Cherry Lane Books, 1983), 21.

[33] Don DeMichael, "Up with the Blues: Mike Bloomfield," *Downbeat*, vol. 36, no. 13 (26 June 1969): 16.

[34] Elvin Bishop, interview with author, 30 Nov. 1995.

[35] Murray, 30.

[36] Elvin Bishop, interview with author, 30 Nov. 1995.

[37] Elvin Bishop, interview with author, 30 Nov. 1995.

[38] Elvin Bishop, interview with author, 30 Nov. 1995.

[39] Elvin Bishop, interview with author, 30 Nov. 1995.

[40] Elvin Bishop, interview with author, 30 Nov. 1995.

[41] Ward, 113.

[42] Ward, 113.

[43] Michael Brooks, "Michael Bloomfield," *Blues Guitarists from the Pages of Guitar Player Magazine* (Saratoga, CA: Guitar Player Productions, 1975): 15.

[44] Ward, 24.

[45] Ward, 113.

[46] John Hammond, interview with author, 17 Oct. 1991.

[47] Chris Barber, interview with author, 4 June 1996.

[48] Peter Guralnick, *Feel Like Going Home* (New York: Harper & Row, Publishers, 1989), 82.

[49] Chris Barber, interview with author, 4 June 1996.

[50] Murray, 30.

[51] Helen Doob Lazar, "Living Blues Interview: James Cotton," *Living Blues* 76 (1987): 26.

[52] Lazar, 26.

[53] Chris Barber, interview with author, 4 June 1996.

[54] Francis Clay, interview with author, 22 Mar. 1996.

[55] Francis Clay, interview with author, 22 Mar. 1996.

[56] Steve Wisner, "Chicago Blues, Yesterday & Today: Mojo Buford," *Living Blues* 42 (Jan.–Feb. 1979): 22.

57 Mojo Buford, interview with author, 7 Mar. 1996.

58 Mojo Buford, interview with author, 7 Mar. 1996.

59 Mojo Buford, interview with author, 7 Mar. 1996.

60 Mojo Buford, interview with author, 7 Mar. 1996.

61 Jeff Titon, "Mojo Buford, Part 2," *Blues Unlimited* 77 (Nov. 1970): 10.

62 Mojo Buford, interview with author, 7 Mar. 1996.

63 Mojo Buford, interview with author, 7 Mar. 1996.

64 Guy "Doc" Lerner, "Muddy Harps," *Living Blues* 99 (Sept.–Oct. 1991): 36.

65 Emily Tidwell, "Going Back to Where I Had Been," *Living Blues* 99 (Sept.–Oct. 1991): 19.

66 Willie Smith, interview with author, 10 Dec. 1995.

67 Cliff Radel, "Muddy Waters Is the Blues," *Cincinnati Enquirer*, 6 July 1976.

68 Jas Obrecht, "Buddy Guy," *Blues Guitar: The Men Who Made the Music: From the Pages of Guitar Player Magazine*, ed. Obrecht (San Francisco: GPI Books, 1990), 143.

69 Obrecht, "Buddy Guy," 143.

70 Mojo Buford, interview with author, 7 Mar. 1996.

71 James Cotton, interview with author, 26 Sept. 1995.

72 Mojo Buford, interview with author, 7 Mar. 1996.

73 James Cotton, interview with author, 26 Sept. 1995.

74 Mojo Buford, interview with author, 7 Mar. 1996.

75 Mojo Buford, interview with author, 7 Mar. 1996.

76 Francis Clay, interview with author, 23 Mar. 1996.

77 Mojo Buford, interview with author, 7 Mar. 1996.

78 Robert Morganfield, interview with author, 16 May 1995.

79 Charlie Musselwhite, interview with author, 13 Aug. 1995.

80 Charlie Musselwhite, interview with author, 13 Aug. 1995.

81 Charlie Musselwhite, interview with author, 13 Aug. 1995.

82 Mojo Buford, interview with author, 7 Mar. 1996.

83 Mojo Buford, interview with author, 7 Mar. 1996.

84 Mojo Buford, interview with author, 7 Mar. 1996.

85 James Cotton, interview with author, 26 Sept. 1995.

86 Lawrence Cohn, *Nothing But the Blues* (New York: Abbeville Publishing Group, 1993), 358.

87 Ralph Bass, liner notes, *Muddy Waters: Folk Singer*, Chess, 1964.

88 Bass.

89 *Sweet Home Chicago*, film, MCA Records – Initial Film and Television (Chicago) – Vanguard Films, 1993.

90 Paul Trynka, "Chicago Stories," *The Guitar Magazine*, vol. 1, no. 4 (Sept. 1991): 15.

91 Bob Claypool, "Claypool's Column," *Houston Post*, 24 Mar. 1988.

92 Claypool.

93 Obrecht, "Buddy Guy," 143.

94 Robert Palmer, *Deep Blues* (New York: Penguin, 1982), 259.

95 Val Wilmer, "The First Time I Met the Blues," *Mojo* 22 (Sept. 1995): 84.

96 Clive Blewchamp, interview with author, 5 July 1996.

97 Clive Blewchamp, interview with author, 5 July 1996.

98 Clive Blewchamp, interview with author, 5 July 1996.

99 Nigel Paul, interview with author, 24 June 1996.

100 Nigel Paul, interview with author, 24 June 1996.

101 Charles Shaar Murray, *Crosstown Traffic: Jimi Hendrix and Post-War Pop* (London: Faber and Faber Limited, 1989), 132.

102 Michael J. Fairchild, liner notes, *Jimi Hendrix: Blues*, MCA Records, 1994, 7–8.

103 Bob Margolin, "The Home of the Blues," *Blues Revue* 18 (July–Aug. 1995): 12.

104 Willie Smith, interview with author, 10 Dec. 1995.

105 S.P. Leary, interview with author, 11 June 1996.

106 S.P. Leary, interview with author, 11 June 1996.

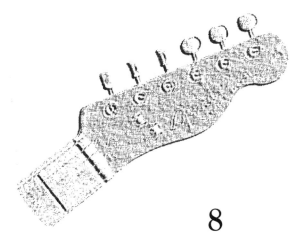

8

It took the people from England to
hip my people — my white people —
to what they had in their own backyard.[1]

When John Lennon and Paul McCartney were asked what they'd most like to see or do on their first tour of the U.S. in February 1964, they replied, "Muddy Waters and Bo Diddley." A perplexed reporter inquired, "Muddy Waters? Where's that?" An incredulous McCartney laughed, "Don't you know who your own famous people are here?"[2]

Leading the first bombardment of the British invasion, the Beatles assailed white American youth with armaments from their own arsenal. Heavily influenced by American music — particularly

black American music — the English upstarts reworked the indigenous music of the U.S. and peddled it back to America's youngsters,
who had no inkling of its source.

"When we started the Rolling Stones," guitarist Keith Richards
reveals, "our aim was to turn other people on to Muddy Waters."[3]
Blues was the bedrock upon which the Stones was founded. One
day in 1960, Keith's attention was drawn to three LPs tucked under
Mick Jagger's arm — *Chuck Berry Is On Top*, one by Little Walter
and *The Best Of Muddy Waters* — which reignited a friendship that
had lapsed since childhood. Richards knew then he'd found a
kindred spirit. When they formed a band, they named it after
Muddy's 1950 hit, "Rollin' Stone." The sexual intensity of the
Stones's lyrics and performing style, the composition of their instrumentation — originally including piano and harmonica — and the
black drawl of Jagger's vocals bespoke the weighty influence of
Chicago blues bands and, especially, of one of the founders and
greatest practitioners of the genre, Muddy Waters.

The scandalous Stones first stormed the shores of the United
States in May 1964, leaving in their wake a hit song that testified
to their origins as a blues band. Willie Dixon's "I Just Want To Make
Love To You," originally popularized by Muddy Waters, introduced
a generation of white American teens to a brand of music that had
been largely imprisoned on the other side of the color barrier.

During this initial onslaught, the Stones made a pilgrimage to
Chicago's Chess studios for a recording session in an attempt to further emulate the unmistakable Chess sound. For them the site was
hallowed ground. As they entered, they passed a figure in white
overalls holding a dripping paintbrush. When someone remarked
in passing, "Oh, by the way, this is Muddy Waters," Richards was
stunned. "I get to meet *The Man* — he's my fucking god, right? —
and he's painting the ceiling!"[4]

With sales to black consumers plummeting and inroads yet to be
made in the white record-buying market, Chess put Muddy to
work at whatever needed doing. Richards learned a poignant lesson
that day. In their brief, polite conversation, Muddy's expression
conveyed to Richards that, regardless of his talent or achievements,
he, too, could one day find himself in similar straits.

Of the Stones's Chess recording session, Muddy commented, "I
thinks to myself how these white kids was sitting down and thinking

and playing the blues that my black kids was bypassing. That was a hell of a thing, man, to think about."[5] That blacks were turning their backs on their blues heritage broke Muddy's heart. But if whites were eager to pick up the baton, then so be it. Instead of resenting the Stones for attaining superstardom on the back of *his* blues while he was reduced to menial labor, Muddy encouraged them, suggesting how they could do it better. For Muddy it was the music that was of paramount importance.

The Stones, in turn, always acknowledged the source of their inspiration. "They told the truth about it," Muddy said, "and that really put a shot in my arm with the whites. I tip my hat to 'em."[6] The Stones and the rest of the blues-based British invasion alerted white America to the formidable cache of black talent within in its own borders. As Muddy remarked, it took the Rolling Stones and the Beatles "to wake up the people in my own country . . . that a black man's music is not a crime to bring into the house."[7]

In addition to the Rolling Stones and the Beatles, Muddy's blues fueled the formation of such British bands as Long John Baldry and the Hoochie Coochie Men, the Mojos and David Bowie's Manish Boys. He also influenced a stellar list of young British musicians, including Alexis Korner, Eric Clapton, Peter Green, John Mayall, Eric Burdon, Jack Bruce, Jimmy Page, Robert Plant, Alvin Lee, Steve Winwood, Rod Stewart and Jeff Beck. For them Muddy was the umbilical cord extending from the birth of the blues to the development of the popular music it enriched.

For Muddy it wasn't the race of the musicians, it was how well they could play. "He never saw the color thing as being a threat to him or anything," confirms American bluesman John Hammond. "He thought that anyone who loved the music enough should absolutely go ahead and play it."[8] While Muddy maintained that the musicianship of white blues artists was often superb, he always insisted that no one could sing blues like a black vocalist. "We're expressing our lives, the hard times and different things we been through," he said, comparing white singers with artists such as he and Wolf. "I don't think you can feel the blues until you've been through some hard times."[9]

Hammond is grateful for the interest Muddy showed in his developing blues career: "He encouraged me a lot and would call me up on the stage with him. . . . As I remember he was just extremely intense on the stage and very generous with his spotlight. He was a very together guy."[10]

In about 1964 aspiring blues singer Cora "Koko" Taylor first got the opportunity to sit in with Muddy Waters. "He was real thrilled when he learned that he was my idol," Koko remembers fondly. "That just thrilled him to death. He said, 'Girl, if you really want to be a singer and make a career out of it, you got to put your whole heart into it . . . you can do it. Don't look at nobody in the audience, just close your eyes and do it.' He was really helpful and was always inspirational. He was always a person that I admired and just loved so much. Muddy Waters was one of my biggest influences."[11]

Over the years Muddy remained a special friend to Koko. "He was a wonderful guy," she reminisces with deep affection. "He always wore a smile and always had something nice to say. And always had something to say to make you laugh."[12] When Koko recorded "Spoonful" and "Let Me Love You," Muddy dropped by the session to offer his support.

Despite the good wishes he extended to those starting out, these were lean times for Muddy. As he watched white blues-based bands reaping huge financial rewards, he questioned where his own slice of the pie had gone. According to Willie Dixon, Chess told him that Muddy was getting the royalties, while claiming to Muddy that Dixon was the beneficiary. Muddy approached Dixon, saying, "You oughta give me some of that money you're making off these songs I caused them boys to have."[13] Of course, the money trail hadn't made it as far as Dixon either.

While launching a new generation of musicians towards the future, Muddy never forgot to look back over his shoulder. He remained acutely aware of his debt to the great bluesmen — such as Son House, Robert Johnson and Big Bill Broonzy — who'd hewn the way for his own success. Charlie Musselwhite, who was living with Bluebird recording star Big Joe Williams, recollects Muddy's reaction whenever the venerable Williams appeared in a venue where Muddy was performing: "Joe was a much older man than Muddy, and Muddy remembered Joe from when he was young. And when Joe would come in, he'd make a fuss, get a table, you know, and send over a setup, which is a bowl with some ice in it, some glasses and a half-pint or something, and he would introduce him to the audience. He would be like a little kid around Joe. He'd say,

'This is the man that wrote "Baby Please Don't Go,'" and he respected him and looked up to him."[14]

As well, Muddy always remembered his family and old friends back in Mississippi. "Even though he was a big-time blues singer, and he went on tours throughout the United States then all overseas, you know, but he never did forget," says his half-brother Robert Morganfield. "He was just a common person. He was always ready to talk to anybody, regardless of who they were. That's the way he was, just a common person. He was nice and always jolly."[15]

A son, Joseph, was born to Muddy and his girlfriend Lucille in 1964, and the next year they had a daughter, Renee. The children lived with their mother near Muddy in the 38th Street projects, and their father maintained steady contact with them as they grew. Joseph remembers, "He used to come and visit us usually when he was in town, maybe twice a month, depending on how his schedule was. He would come and take us shopping and buy us clothes and give us money. We saw him as much as we could, considering his schedule."[16] Sometimes Muddy would take Lucille and the children out for a picnic, grocery shopping, to a lake or for a ride in his Cadillac; however, there were no family outings to places where Muddy's cover could be blown.

By the end of 1964, Willie Smith, still tied to Chicago by his day job, had to stop drumming part time with Muddy because the band was preparing for a 90-day tour. Paul Butterfield tried to recruit him for his new group, but Willie declined; he could make more money driving his taxi than he could playing blues.

That year guitarist Sammy Lawhorn became a new addition to Muddy's band. Lawhorn was born in Little Rock, Arkansas, in 1935. At age 18 he began a four-and-a-half-year stint in the navy, then played with the King Biscuit Boys and worked as a session musician in Memphis. In Chicago Lawhorn backed Otis Rush, Elmore James, Junior Wells and others before he joined Muddy.

Lawhorn's first recording session as Muddy's guitarist was held in October 1964. In "My John The Conquer Root," a song with a sexual double entendre, Muddy sings about the hoodoo root that is said to impart power to believers. The upbeat "Short Dress Woman," backed by a jazzy clarinet, and "Put Me In Your Lay Away" were also recorded that day. On 18 May 1965, Muddy returned to the studio to record four more songs: "Come Back Baby

(Let's Talk It Over)," "I Got A Rich Man's Woman," the risqué "Roll Me Over Baby" and "My Dog Can't Bark," a rhythm-driven tune reminiscent of "Tiger In Your Tank."

Carnegie Hall welcomed Muddy back on 17 and 19 June 1965, this time under the umbrella of the New York Folk Festival. He shared the billing for the opening-night program, entitled "The Evolution of Funk," with Mose Allison, Chuck Berry, Son House, Manse Lipscomb, Dave Van Ronk, Eric Von Schmidt and narrator Sam Charters. Two evenings later Muddy was joined by Johnny Cash, Jimmy Driftwood, Buffy Sainte-Marie, Chuck Berry and the Staple Singers for a concert called "The Contemporary Singer-Composers, Part 11," then returned with the opening-night lineup at midnight. Also in New York that summer, Muddy did a turn at the Apollo Theatre and debuted at "Jazz in the Garden," a series of performances presented on the patio of the Museum of Modern Art.

Ever since Muddy had been conned by Wolf and Little Walter into firing Francis Clay in 1961, he'd been determined to get his former drummer back. "He'd asked me a number of times to come back, but I wouldn't come back," says Clay, who'd gone on to drum for Buddy Guy, Otis Rush, Magic Sam and others. "I was too angry from how he treated me before."[17] Finally after the departure of S.P. Leary, Muddy tried again. "He said, 'Well, are you ready to come back home?'" Francis remembers. "I said, 'Yeah, let's try it again.' Things were looking pretty good then."[18]

Meanwhile, Cotton had been jamming with his friend Michael Bloomfield who had a steady gig at Big John's, a white club on Chicago's North Side. Manager Bob Witlaufer asked Cotton to bring Muddy in, but Cotton claims it took two years of persuasion to get Muddy to perform at a white bar. When Muddy at last relented, Witlaufer booked the band for two weeks, but held them on for 12. If Muddy had been concerned about delivering his blues across the racial line, his anxieties were assuaged. "Everyone treated him so nice," remarks Cotton. "He could do no wrong."[19]

As blues audiences gradually whitened, Muddy was able to make the transition with remarkable ease. On the other hand, B.B. King was concerned about the racial shift, and one night in Denver, he approached Muddy for advice. When King asked, "How do you play to a white audience?" Muddy replied, "The same way I played a black one."[20]

"When he was doing clubs where it was primarily white," King recounts, "he would say to me, 'Don't change what you do, because the people come to see you and hear you do what you do. So don't try to do what you think they want. You do what *you* do, and this will help you.'"[21] Not that Muddy was always convinced he was getting his music across. "He said there were many times that he played when he wasn't sure if the people enjoyed it," King recalls, "but he was having a good time, so he did what he did."[22]

Muddy's philosophy was to stick to his strengths, not tailor his output to what he thought his audience wanted, although a few of his discs from the 1960s would belie his own doctrine. "To me today," King explains, "I hope people enjoy what I do. . . . But I won't change what I do to try to be like someone else just to please the audience, that's what I mean. 'Cause I figure that the people coming to see me come to see me do or hear me do what they have heard me do on record. And I learned that from Muddy Waters."[23]

According to Marshall Chess, Muddy's success at bridging the racial chasm was due to his "fabulous charisma, and he was also a brilliant artist — his playing, his singing. He was special. He was really special. . . . A lot of artists are charismatic on the stage, but they're weak as men. . . . [Muddy] was strong as a man and strong as an artist."[24]

Chess hadn't issued an album by Muddy in two years when it released *Muddy Waters: The Real Folk Blues* in January 1966. While it was titled to appeal to the folk-music market, its content made no concession to contemporary taste. Here is Muddy putting forth what he did best. It's a compilation of previously recorded numbers, spanning from Muddy's 1947 Aristocrat cut "Gypsy Woman" to "Same Thing" and "You Can't Lose What You Ain't Never Had," both recorded in 1964. Only the packaging is new.

From the 27th to the 29th of the same month, the Canadian Broadcasting Corporation held a summit of blues artists in its Toronto television studios. Never before in North America had such an event been televised. Muddy brought along his band, comprising Otis Spann, James Cotton, Sammy Lawhorn, S.P. Leary, bass guitarist Jimmy Lee Morris (who completed only a short stint with Muddy) and his new guitarist James "Peewee" Madison. An Arkansas native and southpaw — also known as "Left-Handed Rabbit" — Madison began as a harmonica player and blew behind vocalist and guitarist Eddie C. Campbell before turning his attention to the guitar.

In addition, the esteemed group gathered in Toronto included Willie Dixon, one-man band Jesse Fuller, Bukka White, Sonny Terry and Brownie McGhee, Big Joe Williams, Georgia singer Mabel Hillary and Sunnyland Slim. Over three days of taping, the musicians displayed the gamut of blues from its country roots to the contemporary electric sound of Muddy Waters. Dixon toted along his camera, saying, "Man, I got to get pictures. There's never been a blues meeting like this here one. We know this is gonna be a document, man."[25]

Backstage Muddy relaxed in his dressing room with Dixon, discussing the universal appeal of their music. In a moment of reflection, Muddy expressed his definition of blues: "The blues is about going up the road, like I come up the road from Mississippi, away from my sadness and bad food, and when things get tough these days I sing about going up the road again."[26]

Muddy and his band performed "Can't Lose What You Ain't Never Had" and "Got My Mojo Working." Spann was granted a frontman role as well. He took the spotlight and a large share of the accolades with his rendition of "Ain't Nobody's Business" and "Blues Don't Like Nobody." As a finale, everyone gathered to sing "Bye Bye Baby Goodbye." Then Spann leapt down from the stage, grabbed Big Joe Williams and joyously cried," We made it, man. We done it. Those blues of yours and those blues of mine is there for posterity and nothing can wipe 'em away."[27] The show, entitled "The Blues," was aired on 23 February 1966.

Muddy's next LP, *Muddy, Brass & The Blues* was recorded on 22 and 23 June 1966 and released on 26 October. Presented as "perhaps a natural culmination of the seeking and the growth of the talent that is Muddy Waters,"[28] it has been decried as one of a series of blunders committed by Marshall Chess in his quest to market Muddy amidst the turbulent tastes of the mid-1960s. Muddy himself disliked it, and hearing him backed by a brass section in a big-band format rankled the sensibilities of many loyal listeners. Nevertheless, as Muddy claimed in a later interview, "If you're an old standard blues singer like me, my changed sound is still the same basic Muddy Waters style."[29]

None of Muddy's own compositions were selected for this album, with the exception of "Trouble," loosely based on his 1955 cut "Trouble No More," and "Hard Loser," which he co-authored. No doubt Muddy felt a certain nostalgia in recording "Corine, Corina," a song he'd performed at country dances on Stovall. In addition to Muddy and the horn section, which was dubbed on later, the personnel on this album were Peewee Madison and Sammy Lawhorn on guitars, Willie Smith, Otis Spann, an unknown bass player and James Cotton blowing harmonica, his last session as a member of Muddy's band.

By the summer of 1966, Cotton believed that he'd gone as far with Muddy as he could go. "I didn't want to disrespect his music," he confesses, "and I wanted to go do something else." Cotton's interests now lay in broaching the more lucrative rock market. It was a tough decision, but as he says, "It's just like anything else, I guess. When your time comes to go, you got to go."[30] He and Francis Clay formed the James Cotton Blues Band. Cotton left Muddy in June and signed on with manager Albert Grossman, but it took Clay longer to extricate himself from the Hoochie Coochie Boys. He claims that Muddy pressured the musicians' union into forcing him to stay on until the next year. Meanwhile, the James Cotton Blues Band successfully melded blues and rock, and Cotton has been a respected frontman ever since.

It was, in fact, a tribute to Muddy's skill as a bandleader that Cotton and so many others honed their talents in his band and went on to forge successful careers as frontmen themselves. It is one of his greatest legacies. Cotton's only criticism of Muddy's leadership was his insistence that his musicians wear tuxedos, which Cotton detested. (Muddy would not relax his dress code until the late 1960s.) Nevertheless, Cotton reflects, "Working with Muddy Waters is working for one of the best. You don't get that chance everyday. I owe him more than I could ever pay him."[31]

That his band served as an apprenticeship for subsequent generations of blues luminaries brought Muddy a great deal of personal satisfaction. "I feels that I did a lot more for blues players than anybody else I know ever lived," he stated quite frankly.[32] "What makes me proud is that, in making a success for myself in Chicago, I was able to open doors for other blues artists to come up."[33]

Muddy must have suspected that Cotton's ambitions were about to lead him elsewhere. That spring he'd seen his former harp player

Little George Smith in Los Angeles and promised him his old job if Cotton left. So after Cotton's departure, Smith moved back to Chicago and took Muddy up on his offer.

By this time 24-year-old Mack Arnold, a Greenville, South Carolina, native who'd previously played for A.C. Reed, had joined Muddy's band on bass, although he stayed only briefly. Despite his acrimonious split with Muddy in 1956, guitarist Hubert Sumlin returned to the band for a short tour in 1966.

Guitarist Luther "Georgia Boy Snake" Johnson also came aboard in 1966. Born Lucius Brinson Johnson in Davisboro, Georgia, on 30 August 1934, Johnson followed in his father's footsteps, learning guitar at age seven. By the end of World War II, he'd moved north and continued to pursue his interest in music in a Milwaukee, Wisconsin, reform school. Following a stint in the army, Johnson performed with a gospel group and with his own blues band. In the early 1960s, he relocated to Chicago where he worked with Elmore James and recorded for the Checker label under the name Little Luther.

Muddy's knack for nurturing developing talent is demonstrated in a session the band fronted on 25 November 1966 in New York City for the Spivey label. Muddy and his guitar stick strictly in the background here, as George Smith, Otis Spann and Luther Johnson trade vocals with Victoria Spivey. It's an impressive showcase for Muddy's musicians, one that highlights the formidable talent in his band.

On 27 January 1967, Chess released another compilation of Muddy's popular early recordings on *More Real Folk Blues*. The songs on the LP range from his 1952 cut "She's All Right" back to the 1948 Aristocrat tracks "Whiskey Blues" ("Sittin' Here And Drinkin'"), "Down South Blues," Train Fare Home Blues" and "Kind Hearted Woman."

The album, *Super Blues*, recorded in January 1967, was a musical summit meeting of three blues greats — Little Walter, Bo Diddley and Muddy Waters — in yet another marketing tactic to appeal to a teen audience. Supporting the luminaries were Buddy Guy, Otis Spann, Frank Kirkland on drums and a recent addition to Muddy's band, bassist Lawrence "Little Sonny" Wimberley. The disc includes the signature songs of the three headliners, but constant chatter and forced joviality mars the musicianship, which never approaches that of the original recordings. Muddy's *Super Blues* contribution is "Long Distance Call," "I'm A Man" ("Mannish Boy") and "I Just Want To Make Love To You."

The album kicks off with Muddy's stinging slide, as he launches into "Long Distance Call." "I'm A Man" is a playful fusion of Bo's hit with Muddy's "Mannish Boy"; the two artists trade verses and toss in a little "Hoochie Coochie Man" for good measure. Of the experience of working with Muddy, his childhood idol, Bo Diddley says, "That was great. It was really good."[34]

After only about a year with Muddy, George Smith returned to his family in California and was replaced by George Buford, another harmonica player who was on his second go-round with the band. Buford had enjoyed a steady gig at a Minneapolis club since he left Muddy in 1963, but after it closed he returned to Chicago to look for work. Minneapolis audiences had insisted he play "Got My Mojo Working" three or four times a night, and although he grew weary of the song, it earned him the nickname Mojo. Muddy approved of Buford's new moniker, and so it stuck.

The band — now called the Muddy Waters Blues Band — was honored that summer with an invitation to appear at the Montreal World's Fair, Expo '67. "Our government sent us there, of course, representing the American music," says Francis Clay. "We were playing Detroit, and we went there in a private plane, with everything you can imagine . . . limos and everything, the whole shebang, you know. . . . We did two numbers, and then the limo rushed us back to the airport. We were brought back to Detroit, didn't miss a night's work. A thousand dollars for two songs. Big time, for once."[35] Buford, who was nervous about flying, was less impressed: "When we came back to land, one of the back wheels wouldn't come out. When the plane dragged to a stop we all hurried off that plane!"[36]

Two 1967 Chicago sessions provided the foundation for the future album *They Call Me Muddy Waters*, which wasn't released until four years later. Joining Muddy and the group on organ for at least one of the sessions was future band member Pinetop Perkins. "When The Eagle Flies" — an ode to the dollar, written by Willie Dixon — and "Blind Man" are two strong, up-tempo numbers, while the hopelessness depicted in "County Jail" and the growling anger of "Another Fool" portray a darker side of blues.

The sequel to *Super Blues*, entitled *The Super Super Blues Band*, was yet another attempt to contemporize blues that only diluted its quality. Recorded in September 1967, the LP featured the headline trio of Howlin' Wolf, Bo Diddley and Muddy. The backup roster included Otis Spann at the piano, guitarist Hubert Sumlin, Frank Kirkland playing drums and possibly Buddy Guy on bass. The musicians' prattle that marred the first album persists here, and the ever-competitive Wolf occasionally steps on the others' solos. Muddy's "Long Distance Call" is virtually unrecognizable, and although the cuts include other blues standards, such as "Sweet Little Angel," "Spoonful," "The Red Rooster" and "Goin' Down Slow," they are shoddy approximations of the originals.

In September 1967, while the Muddy Waters Blues Band was playing a run at New York's Apollo Theatre, Muddy once again proved his generosity and stepped into the role of sideman, lending a hand to his guitarist Luther Johnson on his own recording session. Ten of the numbers they taped that day were later issued on the album, *Mud In Your Ear*. Johnson furnishes vocals for most of the cuts, the Muddy Waters Blues Band contributes several instrumental numbers and Mojo Buford sings "Watch Dog," "I'm So Glad" and "Love Without Jealousy." Despite his good intentions, Muddy began to have second thoughts about backing up his friends: "It ain't too cool for me, man. 'Cause you trying to tell someone something, and maybe they'll think your ideas is too square, you know."[37] He was coming to the conclusion that it was better for everyone if he just stuck to being a bandleader.

After several unsuccessful attempts to recruit a replacement for himself, Francis Clay brought drummer S.P. Leary back into the band and left Muddy for the final time in 1967 to join the James Cotton Blues Band. Although it's been reported that Muddy repeatedly fired Leary onstage for drunkenness, such allegations are false. Muddy remained loyal to S.P. and would just send him home for the night, moving Luther Johnson into the drummer's seat for the balance of the gig. Leary is disarmingly candid about his excessive drinking back then: "[Muddy would] get mad with me and call my wife and tell her that I was drunk. That's what it was all about. I'd be messin' up the show. But mistreat me? He never did that. I do think it was fair. I was the one that was messin' up, not Muddy. I was messin' up his show. You see, you work too hard to . . . let one individual tear it down. That's normal. Muddy was right, yes he was."[38]

Magic Dick and Jay Geils, who would later detonate their amalgam of blues- and soul-based rock in the J. Geils Band, count Muddy as a major influence. "It was shortly after I started playing the harmonica," Magic Dick recalls, "that I picked up an album called *The Best Of Muddy Waters*, which had all the harmonica accompaniment . . . by Little Walter, and I loved him, and I loved Muddy. In fact, I loved that entire band, that whole sound. It was very influential on me and everybody else that I knew. And I still love that record."[39]

Dick and Jay first met Muddy in 1967 when he was touring the coffeehouse circuit and enjoyed the opportunity to sit in with him from time to time. "All the things that are real important as a musician — which is timing, tone, tonality — I can't think of anyone better," Dick says of Muddy. "He had remarkable command over his music. A lot of performers who have done original songs, as the years go by they tend to confuse one melody with another. They round off their songs, you know. I don't want to name any names, but it applies to a whole number of old rock 'n' rollers. But Muddy had a kind of memory that he could retain every nuance of his vocals, even if the band wasn't providing quite the right support for certain tunes. Muddy was very clear about the difference from one tune to another."[40]

Magic Dick also reflects on Muddy as a bandleader: he had "remarkable command over the people in his band. When Muddy gave a command, you listened to him. He had the ability to keep the band at a low [volume], which is something, as a singer myself now, I admire to a very great extent. It's difficult to do, to have such an influence over your musicians that they respect that command of not playing loud. And it suited him very well, because he was so dynamic as a singer."[41] Muddy's method of signaling that the decibel level was creeping too high was to shoot a look at the offending party, described by Dick as "not totally menacing. It was sort of a quick stare, and I think people knew to cool it. I really believe the same thing, that when the music becomes too loud, it's difficult to discern certain essential elements about it."[42]

Otis Spann's contribution to the music was obvious, although he had a playful side that could also be memorable. Dick remembers going to hear the Muddy Waters Blues Band perform in Cambridge, Massachusetts, "and some kids showed up with a big hunk of hash and went over to show it to Otis, and Otis was holding it and goes, 'Nice,' pops the whole thing into his mouth and says, 'Thanks.' Well, about two days later, Jay [Geils] saw Otis Spann at some club . . . and Jay made some mention of it, and Otis said, 'Oh, yeah, I didn't know where I was for a *long* time!' Otis liked to get high, but he was great."[43]

With the exception of hard drugs, Muddy didn't care what substances his band members took as long as they were ready and able to play each night, which was regrettably not always the case. Although Muddy would take an occasional drag of marijuana, alcohol was more to his and the band's taste. For a while they indulged in Old Grand Dad 100-proof bourbon, then a provision for Hennessy Cognac or Chivas Regal was written into their performance contracts. Muddy's was a hard-drinking band, and when one of his musicians got lost in a drunken haze onstage, Muddy would hit him with a drumstick to get him back on track. Spann was known to fall asleep at the piano, but with a swift swipe from Muddy he could pick up the tune without missing a note. No matter how much Muddy drank, however, he never appeared inebriated. "I wasn't a cat to come in with a big bottle of wine in my pocket and talking loud. Not me. . . . I am an intelligent blues singer. . . . I made myself classy with it," he declared.[44]

While Muddy still occasionally teased black audiences with the Coke-bottle routine, his stage persona in white venues was more subdued. He remained seated for most of his performance; his image was decidedly distinguished. Now a mature man in his fifties, Muddy was evoking a less overtly sexual reaction from his female fans. "The response was uniformly wild," Magic Dick recalls," but he was less specifically the studly guy. He was just thought of as being extremely good-looking, a very handsome man, very dignified in the way he carried himself."[45] Muddy himself maintained, "You don't have to have a white face to be a gentleman and up to date with what you're doing. . . . They might say I can't play, or can't sing, but, damn it, they'll say I'm a gentleman."[46]

"Muddy Waters was a very big part of what was happening at that period of time in music," says Dick, referring to Muddy's standing in the late 1960s, "and although he never reached huge mass popularity that he always deserved, to the level like B.B. King is getting to have now, Muddy influenced and continues to influence everybody. I miss him a lot; we all do. He was just such a great, great man."[47]

Mojo Buford was soon lured away from Muddy's group by a lucrative offer to form a house band for the new Key Club in Minneapolis, and Muddy called upon Paul Oscher to fill the harmonica spot. A native of Brooklyn, New York, where he was born on 5 April 1950, Paul was introduced to the harp by his uncle who presented him with one when he was about 12 years old. He became hooked when an older black friend from Georgia said, "Let me see that whistle, boy."[48] The friend blew one note, and the blues sound knocked Paul out. By the time he was 15, Oscher was playing professionally in soul revues at black New York clubs. He first met Muddy in 1964 or 1965 when Muddy was performing at the Apollo. Then in 1967 through his friend Luther "Georgia Boy Snake" Johnson, Paul got the opportunity to sit in with Muddy. Muddy liked what he heard, and Oscher jumped aboard the ride of a lifetime.

Oscher was Muddy's first white band member, but to Paul and the rest of the group, this precedent was not significant in any way. In Muddy's opinion the young harpman was simply the best man for the job. "He always would hire who he thought was the best guy to play the gig with him," says John Hammond, "and if it was a guy who was white, so be it."[49]

The only time race seemed as if it could become a negative factor was one afternoon when the band was booked at a black venue in the Hough neighborhood of Cleveland. It appeared a political disturbance was about to erupt. Blacks in paramilitary garb were gathering outside the club, and Bo noticed automatic weapons being distributed from the trunks of several cars. It occurred to Muddy that Paul and his black date could be in peril. The crowd, Muddy later explained, "was getting a little funny, you know, acting violent. We didn't even let him play that day, we just sent him on over to one of them big restaurants, let him eat and drink coffee till we get through playing."[50]

Paul already knew most of Muddy's repertoire, but he still had to adjust to his live-performance style. "He wasn't doing the songs like the records," says Oscher. "What you really have to learn is Muddy's phrasing, his timing, the way he preached to the crowd. . . . Muddy *preached* the blues, messed with the time."[51] Paul describes how he wrapped his harmonica around Muddy's vocals: "You wait on him, you let him get his words out. You don't want to step on him. You have to adapt your fill-ins to the length of his phrases."[52]

"If you were playing something he didn't like," Oscher recounts, "he'd put his finger in his ear or he'd scratch his head. That would let you know. . . . Muddy hated a loud bass. If a bass player was too loud, he'd say, 'Cut out that bumpty-bump!' 'Cause really, to play that shit Muddy was doing, you had to get that stuff down to a whisper. That's when he could really work the crowd. And S.P. was cool, 'cause he'd play brushes on *everything*. Muddy really liked that."[53]

There was no set play list for club gigs; Muddy would just launch into whatever song he felt like singing, and the band would join in. He liked to work the club from offstage as well. With a long cord Muddy would often perform as he wandered through the audience.

Typically the band would play a couple of tunes — "Chicken Shack" plus "Moanin'," "I Can't Sit Down," "Scratch My Back" or another instrumental — before Muddy came onstage. "I was really getting pretty good with Muddy, in terms of like starring on the show," Oscher recalls, "so what used to happen was the band would play like two numbers, then I'd come out and do like 'Off The Wall' . . . then we started: 'Ladies and gentlemen, right now put your hands together for the one and only, the King of the Blues — Mr. Muddy "Clarksdale, Mississippi, Hoochie Coochie Man" Waters,' and then he'd come out like that. And that was a really powerful presentation."[54]

"He would give everybody a solo," says Paul. "You could play as much as you want, you know. Let's put it this way, he wasn't scared of anybody taking his show, you know what I'm saying? He was Muddy Waters, and everybody knew that. I don't care how good his sidemen could sing, Muddy was Muddy. . . . There are other people in that business who aren't quite as gracious to people if they think that you're gonna cut 'em; you know they're not gonna call you up. Muddy wasn't like that at all. What Muddy was doing nobody could do."[55]

Muddy's generosity in sharing his stage also extended to musicians outside his band. Sam Lay — drummer for Little Walter, Howlin'

Wolf and then the Paul Butterfield Blues Band — remembers sitting in with the man he called his buddy Muddy: "Knowing the caliber of musician Muddy was, it wasn't a thing like, 'Well, I'm afraid to let you come up to the club. They might hire you, and they might not hire us back.' He didn't feel that. He had no reason to feel that, believe me, because nobody could weasel their way in on Muddy's job. He always called me up and anybody else that was a musician, he brought 'em up to the spotlight. Muddy backed off nobody. . . . You want to know what the word Muddy Waters means? That means *great*."[56]

Oscher recalls that when he joined Muddy, the band was still playing primarily for black audiences: "Muddy had a falling-out with his manager, Bob Messinger, and Muddy was booking himself, so we were playing lots of black clubs. We played the Howard Theatre in Washington, D.C., the Regal Theatre in Chicago, we used to play at this place called the White Rose all the time outside of Chicago and at Sylvio's and a place in St. Louis called the Moonlight Lounge. There was a lot of black venues."[57]

Paul remembers the gigs at the Moonlight Lounge with special fondness. "We pulled up to the hotel on Delmar Boulevard," he says, "and there are all these prostitutes on the corner. As soon as the band pulled up, all the girls started shouting, 'Muddy Waters's band is here!' and they'd hike up their dresses."[58] Blues luminaries such as Albert King would often sit in with them at the club, then after the show, the musicians retired to the hotel bar, where Spann played piano until daylight while the rest of the band hit on the women and shot dice.

"When I was playing with Muddy, he was a pretty tough guy," Paul contends, and his musicians were more so. "Spann and Luther — he had some real rough band members. When I was in the band, that band was nothing like those bands he had in his later years. We're talking about some real roughneck blues characters, you know. They're hard drinkers. Everybody carried guns."[59]

Muddy always packed a .25 automatic, as well as a .22 in his shirt pocket and a .38 pushed down the back of his car seat. Oscher maintains that being armed preserved the balance of power in volatile club settings and even within the band itself. Once Luther emptied his gun at S.P.'s feet, demanding, "Dance, motherfucker!" "I've been in the van when Sammy pointed a gun at Sonny, and

Sonny pointed a gun at Sammy, and I was in the middle," Paul recalls. "It was not uncommon for band members to point guns at each other."[60] Oscher explains, "That's the only reason why everybody didn't get killed, because everyone knew everybody else had a gun."[61]

With their penchant for firearms and heavy drinking, all the sidemen were potential sources of trouble. Muddy, however, remained aloof from any turmoil, and the band would protect him if a situation became dangerous. Or, as Paul recalls, he could take defensive action for himself: "I saw somebody pull a gun, and I saw Muddy push somebody in front of it, in the line of fire. But I don't think the person was going to shoot the gun. But Muddy wasn't really one that would take chances with things like that. He was quite a shrewd character."[62]

"Everybody had a big respect for Muddy, a tremendous respect for Muddy," Oscher says of himself and his band mates.[63] Plus Muddy possessed great insight into the personalities of those he worked with. "Muddy had an uncanny sense of the needs of his musicians," Paul remarks. "He knew when we needed a drink, he knew when something was wrong in our love lives. He knew what we were thinking almost before we thought it ourselves."[64] That innate perception of people and their emotions came out in his music as well. "We knew Muddy had lived the words of his songs, and that was part of his understanding," Oscher comments.[65]

Yet according to Paul Oscher, that understanding usually went only one way: "If Muddy Waters was thinking something, you wouldn't really know it. Okay, Muddy wasn't the kind of person who told people how he thought about things that really affected him. You know, he'd be nice to you and be, you know, very cordial, but you really wouldn't really learn anything really deep about how Muddy felt about something. Like if he had a record that he didn't like, he wasn't about to tell you, 'I don't like my record,' because that would be cutting off whatever economic interest he was getting out of the record."[66]

Oscher learned the hard way that when dealing with Muddy it was best to keep certain things private. After confiding to his bandleader that his girlfriend was an incredible lover, Paul was startled to learn that Muddy had immediately called her up for a date.

Not long after he joined the Muddy Waters Blues Band in 1967, Oscher left for a short time and was replaced by Birmingham Jones until Paul returned in February 1968. He was living in a building across South Lake Park Avenue from Muddy, but when Andrew Bolden vacated his room in the front of Muddy's basement, Oscher took up residence there. "They treated me like part of the family," he says of Muddy and Geneva.[67]

As watermelon and hot-tamale vendors hawked their goods around Lake Park and 43rd, a panorama of humanity unrolled in the South Side ghetto. One local character, a ragged wino toting a bottle of booze in his pocket and leading a cat on a rope, was reminiscent of the Pied Piper. Whenever he passed Muddy relaxing on his porch, Muddy would shout, "Hit it, man!" and the piper would blow a few notes of "Chain Gang" on his flute, the signal for all the kids within earshot to line up and dance along behind him.[68]

At the end of a passageway opposite Muddy's house was a down-stairs bar called the Hole in the Wall, which Spann, who was also living in Muddy's basement, adopted as his own. "Otis Spann used to play in there all the time," remembers Oscher. "He used to hang out in there. Sometimes in the summertime he'd set his piano up in that alley and people would come down and drink and play in that alley."[69] On occasion, however, the soulful sound of Spann's blues was punctuated with bursts of violence.

I spent a lot of time sitting on Muddy's porch, you know, just sitting there, hanging out [Paul Oscher reminisces]. A lot of people used to come over there — St. Louis Jimmy, Floyd Jones, Johnny Young was over there all the time . . . Earl Hooker, Roosevelt Sykes, Little Brother Montgomery. . . . There was this liquor store over there on 43rd Street where a lot of people would hang out, you know, on the corner there. Then there was this gang sometimes, the Blackstone Rangers, sometimes they'd have these marches, like about three or four hundred of them walking down the street . . . saying, "Who run it? We run it" . . . carrying sticks and stuff. Then there was a gang on 43rd Street called the Disciples — the Devil's Disciples — called the Ds for short.

You'd hear a lot of gunshots in the neighborhood. I saw a woman get shot in the head there while I was talking to her.

The guy just walked out the doorway, said, "This is for you, bitch," *boom*, shot her. . . . Muddy was very cool with things like that, 'cause I ran across the street to Muddy. I said, "Muddy, this guy just shot this woman," and Muddy just called up the police, and then he just put a gun under his shirt and walked out by the fence of his house, said, "Motherfucker don't scare nobody."[70]

By the mid-1960s, Muddy's blood pressure had begun to sky-rocket, yet he was unaware of the seriousness of his condition until a 1967 tour. During the drive to Detroit, Muddy suffered a danger-ous hemorrhage from his nose and the corners of his eyes. "That's when the doctor told him that he wasn't supposed to drink whiskey anymore," Oscher reports. "He was drinking this Ambassador 25 Scotch. He'd bought that for Christmas, and he had a whole case of it, and he got pretty sick."[71] Muddy himself admitted, "Liquor's the thing that'll get you. . . . Sure, I used to be a good liquor-drinking man. But when the doctor told me to come off the liquor, I said, 'This is it. No more whiskey.' "[72]

That pronouncement didn't mean Muddy had sworn off alcohol, however. Instead, he simply switched his libation from the hard stuff to champagne. It seemed to fit his evolving image, as well. Although he continued to play deep, dirty blues, Muddy increas-ingly portrayed himself as prosperous and elegant. There was an incongruity to it all: the venues he and the band played were still rough joints, but backstage they would be sipping Piper Heidseick, a beverage more likely found in fashionable parlors than grotty backstage dressing rooms.

Throughout the 1960s Muddy's drummers continued their game of musical chairs. S.P. Leary returned to the group in the fall of 1967. He then left Muddy for the last time in late 1968, and Willie Smith reclaimed the drummer's stool, a position he'd hold for the next 12 years.

On Valentine's Day 1968, Little Walter provoked one fight too many. His career had been in a tailspin for a decade, and *Super Blues*, his album with Muddy and Bo Diddley, was too little too late. Walter's voice had roughened, he couldn't keep a band together, and more often than not, he was finding himself relegated to a sideman role. He was a renegade, brandishing a pistol on and off the stage. Heavy drinking exacerbated his quick temper; his compulsion to fight had left him battered and scarred.

Walter and another man were "shooting dice on the sidewalk outside a building," Junior Wells reports, "and Walter grabbed the money, and the guy took an iron pipe and hit him in the head."[73] He didn't seem hurt; all he wanted was an aspirin for his headache. He went to sleep that night and never woke up. A brain hemorrhage had claimed the life of the inimitable master of the harmonica. Little Walter was 37 years old.

Through his years of brawling and boozing, Walter Jacobs had elevated the lowly harmonica from a level of insignificance to its position as a key component of Chicago blues. In his hands it had become an instrument of soaring virtuosity. "Awwwww man," Muddy lamented, "he was another Robert Johnson. It's hard to find them kinds of peoples. . . . You don't run into 'em too often. They *born* with that."[74]

An added aspect of the tragedy is that, according to Willie Smith, Little Walter had just agreed to rejoin Muddy's band. Perhaps under Muddy's paternal influence, Walter could have held his demons at bay and equaled his former triumphs. As it was he died broke and broken; Chess Records paid for his funeral.

At about this time Muddy set aside his trademark Telecaster for a while to promote the Guild line of guitars and musical equipment. As a Guild endorsee, he was provided with a black Guild s-200 Thunderbird guitar and a Guild amp; most of the band members were also furnished with Guild equipment.

The infamous *Electric Mud* album, considered by most to mark the nadir of Muddy's recording career, was cut in May 1968 and released on 5 October that year. By this time Leonard and Phil Chess had put virtually all of the company's popular-music production into Marshall's hands. Marshall outlined his intentions: "What I'm trying to do with the blues is put a modern thing to it."[75] Producers Marshall Chess, Gene Barge and Charles Stepney distorted Muddy's music into a hallucinatory haze of fuzz boxes and wah-wah pedals suggestive of Muddy Waters meets Iron Butterfly. They knocked the dirt off his blues, slapped on a veneer of psychedelia and peddled it to a new generation of consumers eager to groove to blues-encrusted rock.

Muddy's band was not subjected to the session; the guitarists were

Phil Upchurch, Roland Faulkner and Pete Cosey, with Charles Stepney on organ, bass player Louis Satterfield and Morris Jennings on drums. While the album features a photo of Muddy holding his Guild guitar, he didn't play it for this project.

Muddy's vocals were buried in a morass of screeching guitars, malformed rhythm patterns and the incongruous overdubbing of flute, stringed harp and even a tomcat in heat. Most of the cuts are mutilations of such standbys as "I Just Want To Make Love To You," "I'm Your Hoochie Coochie Man," "She's All Right," "I'm A Man" ("Mannish Boy") and "Same Thing." Muddy also pays a dubious tribute to his apprentices, the Rolling Stones, with his rendition of "Let's Spend The Night Together." As a forerunner of the electric-band sound, Muddy was, in *Electric Mud*, a participant in its gross degeneration.

"That's not my music," Ken "Snowman" Minahan remembers Muddy grousing during the session. "I don't like that damn wah-wah thing. I don't like it." Minahan had just delivered a twin reverb amp to the studio and was sticking around to grab a little slice of history in the making. "Muddy Waters was very upset because they were trying to make it way too psychedelic. . . . He grumbled a lot under his breath. You know, he would say stuff to [Marshall] Chess . . . but they were going to do it that way and that was it. It's funny he didn't have that much say in his own recordings. He didn't like it, he didn't like doing it, it wasn't his music, that's what he said."[76]

Muddy later agreed with an interviewer who referred to the album as "dogshit,"[77] and commented that "if you've got to have big amplifiers and wah-wahs and equipment to make your guitar say different things, well, hell, you can't play no blues."[78] He was also concerned that fans coming out to hear him live would expect the band to replicate the psychedelic effects onstage, which it did not do.

Marshall, on the other hand, was delighted with *Electric Mud* and claims Muddy shared his view, at least initially. "Muddy was willing to try things," he explains. "You have to understand, there's another element — Muddy liked money. . . . Things were changing, and he was willing to try it to make money. The psychedelic album, that was his biggest selling album ever at that time. He loved that, even though critics didn't like it, but Muddy loved it."[79] Admitting that Muddy later had a change of heart, Marshall remarks, "What happened was that the publicity was very negative, and all the real blues people hated it, and he sort of just joined in with them rather than defend it. That's the way I always viewed it. But, you know, it was okay. It was just an experiment for him and for me. It wasn't the end of the world. It was just an experiment."[80] Despite this latest offering, the critics' poll of *Down Beat* magazine elected Muddy's band the "best blues/rhythm and blues group" for 1968 and again for 1969.

Surely one of the most difficult transitions Muddy had to endure was Otis Spann's departure from the band in 1968. "He was kinda expecting it," comments Willie Smith, "because Spann was getting a lot of offers to form his own band and go out and do his own thing. Then Spann got him another wife and she — Lucille Spann — she was singing, too, so between the two of them, they just took off."[81] Muddy explained that "everybody looking for a break, you know, when that comes, well let him go. Find somebody else somehow."[82] There was no animosity involved in the split, but Otis left a big bench for Muddy to fill. As his replacement Muddy chose Pinetop Perkins.

Joe Willie Perkins was born outside Belzoni, Mississippi, on 7 July 1913. His two uncles were string musicians and sparked his initial interest in music, but it was the piano players rocking the local juke joint who focused Perkins's sights. He began practicing piano there at age 10, amidst a group of testy gamblers who kept trying to oust the young nuisance. As a teenager Perkins heard the recordings of Leroy Carr and Clarence "Pinetop" Smith, which aroused his determination to become a professional pianist.

At 17 he began his musical career under the name Little Willie Perkins, then earned the moniker Pinetop after gaining renown for his rendition of Pinetop Smith's "Pinetop's Boogie Woogie." He played for a while in Indianola, Mississippi, with another pianist, Willie Love; the two took turns backing each other on drums.

In 1941 the government put Pinetop to work as a tractor driver outside Clarksdale. For the next two years, he played weekend gigs in Clarksdale and in neighboring Marks, and gave a local lad, Ike Turner, a few pointers on the piano. After a short stint backing Robert Nighthawk, Pinetop played with the King Biscuit Boys for five years, then returned to work for Nighthawk in Cairo, Illinois. In 1949 he was living in Chicago, where he played with Earl Hooker, Albert King and Little Milton before joining Muddy's band.

The bad acid trip of *Electric Mud* recurred in January and February 1969 with the recording of Muddy's next LP, *After The Rain*, released on 12 May. Although it is not as severe a shock to the system, it is similarly defaced with misguided attempts to alter Muddy's sound, a failed experiment that surely satisfied very few. In addition to Paul Oscher and former band mate Otis Spann, the other musicians on this album were Charles Stepney on organ, guitarists Phil Upchurch and Pete Cosey, Louis Satterfield on bass and drummer Morris Jennings. Rising out of the psychedelic din, "I Am The Blues" and "Honey Bee" remain passable. Although "Screamin' And Cryin'" features Muddy's tangy slide, it's marred by over-zealous drumming. Referring to this and earlier Chess marketing ploys, Muddy concluded, "They tried to put me over in another bag but I just don't fit no other bag. Exactly I fits one shoe, and that is the blues."[83]

Fortunately the fit was impeccable for Muddy's next undertaking, the splendid *Fathers And Sons*, his most important album since *Muddy Waters At Newport, 1960* and the disc that set him back on the straight-ahead blues track from which he'd veered. Marrying two generations and races of bluesmen and uniting the teacher with his pupils, this project, more than any other, spanned that last hurdle for Muddy in his effort to win over a white audience.

The concept was the creation of producer Norman Dayron and Marshall Chess. Their aim was to restore Muddy's original hits, backed by Muddy's contemporary, Otis Spann, plus a new crop of bluesmen — guitarist Michael Bloomfield, Paul Butterfield on harmonica, bass player Donald "Duck" Dunn and Sam Lay on drums. Also assisting were Jeff Carp on chromatic harp, rhythm guitarist Paul Asbell, Phil Upchurch on bass and drummer Buddy Miles (for the concert encore only).

The double album emerged from three studio sessions in Chicago — on 21, 22 and 23 April 1969 — capped off by a live performance at the Auditorium Theatre the following night. *Fathers And Sons* showcases a reinvigorated Muddy, demonstrating that he'd lost none of his verve in his trip through psychedelia. In a lineup of mostly his own compositions, Muddy serves up his vocals with gusto, while dishing out some savory slide guitar. It's a tour de force, supplemented by Spann's superb piano, and features such numbers as "All Aboard," "Standin' Round Crying," "Twenty Four Hours,"

"Long Distance Call," "The Same Thing" and "Got My Mojo Working." The studio portion of the album was recorded apace, with only a couple of takes required for most songs. Muddy made it clear what he wanted, and his musicians delivered. The young sidemen already knew his repertoire; they'd cut their teeth on the songs of their hero.

For Sam Lay, *Fathers And Sons* was a professional and personal milestone: "It was really an honor and a thrill to be in, and I really appreciate just knowing that I was a part of it," he states with great reverence. "You're talking about a legend. [Muddy] *is* a legend, I won't say *was*. He still is as far as I'm concerned."[84]

Muddy had been Sam's idol ever since he discovered blues. He'll never forget the first time he saw Muddy perform, in the late 1950s at Gleason's in Cleveland. Although Muddy was singing through a small crackerbox PA, Lay describes his voice as frightening. It carried the force of a Texas tornado and the impact of a bolt of lightning. After moving to Chicago, Lay joined Little Walter's band, then played for Howlin' Wolf for six years before becoming a founding member of the Paul Butterfield Blues Band. He got to know Muddy, jammed with him and occasionally filled in for his drummer if he couldn't make a gig.

The live portion of *Fathers And Sons* was taped at a concert on 24 April, dubbed the "Super Cosmic Joy-Scout Jamboree," a benefit for the Phoenix Fellowship of the Academy of Cultural Exploration and Design. Among the acts preceding Muddy that night were Nick Gravenites, Quicksilver Messenger Service and a set performed by Butterfield, Bloomfield and Buddy Miles.

Then Muddy appeared and delivered his first offering, "Hoochie Coochie Man." He galvanized the predominantly white audience of 2,800 — most of them hearing Muddy for the first time — and led them on an orgiastic blues trip that left the crowd howling for more. In response to his last number, "Got My Mojo Working," the rapturous throng rose en masse and demanded an encore. Another set of drums was pushed onstage, and Buddy Miles sprinted out to join Lay in drumming for the finale.

It was a triumph. Almost 10 minutes of pandemonium ensued after Muddy left the stage. "The people had him surrounded," Lay says, describing the bedlam backstage. "They swarmed him like a flight of bumblebees."[85] Obviously pleased, Muddy exclaimed, "It's just like Newport out there."[86] The impact of *Fathers And Sons* would be as momentous.

Now Muddy's tours were almost wholly booked in white venues — coffeehouses, clubs, colleges and festivals. *Fathers And Sons* had made Muddy an icon of white American rock music. His income, however, still lagged far behind what the young white stars were pulling in.

Following the excesses of *Electric Mud* and *After The Rain*, Muddy was relieved to be able to be himself again, and to be increasingly appreciated for it by his growing white audience. "The blacks are more interested in the jumpy stuff," he said. "The whites want to hear me for what I am."[87] Furthermore, Muddy maintained that black crowds were stingy with their praise. "Now with white people when you play something good you really get appreciated for it. You get more of a push-off."[88] The opportunity to perform in venues where there was little dancing also appealed to him. "Because if they're dancing," Muddy explained, "they're not paying too much attention to the way how you're shooting out the good stuff to 'em."[89]

Both Muddy and Howlin' Wolf were primed to detonate some explosive blues at the 1969 Ann Arbor Blues and Jazz Festival in Ann Arbor, Michigan. Hubert Sumlin, still playing guitar for Wolf, remembers that day with fondness: "Wolf and Muddy sat down and talked and made friends. They shook hands and said, 'No more enemies.' That thrilled me so much, I went and got a beer."[90] Nevertheless, once onstage, Wolf prolonged his scheduled 45-minute performance to 80 minutes in an unsuccessful bid to intimidate Muddy and squeeze out his set. "He was trying to cut Muddy," Paul Oscher declares, "but we cut 'em. . . . That was a very good show."[91] Although Muddy had to reduce his set to only 30 minutes, his finale, "Mojo," earned him one of the biggest ovations of the three-day festival.

Luther "Georgia Boy Snake" Johnson left Muddy's band in 1969, joining Bill Dicey's Atlantic Blues Band, then forming his own group in Boston. He credited Muddy with providing the foundation he required to build his own career as a frontman. "I was getting mad at him at the time," Johnson admitted, "but I found out later, everything he told me worked out good. He's like a father to me, just like a father to me."[92] Tragically Luther's promising future was terminated in 1976; he died of cancer in Boston at the age of 42.

In October 1969 Muddy's first and most celebrated album, *The Best Of Muddy Waters*, was resequenced and released under the title *Sail On*, earning him his second Grammy nomination in the category of Best Ethnic or Traditional Recording (Including Traditional Blues). The award, however, was destined to go to T-Bone Walker for "Good Feelin'."

Encumbered with ill health and bored with the business and its attendant hassles, Leonard Chess had sold the Chess Record Corporation in January 1969 to the California-based General Recorded Tape Corporation (GRT) for an estimated $10 million, an offer the family considered too good to refuse. As part of the agreement, Leonard stayed on as president and Phil as vice president. Now on 16 October, Leonard died suddenly, stricken with a heart attack at the wheel of his car. His son Marshall assumed his place as president of Chess.

Muddy was "just very sad and upset," says Marshall, recalling the bluesman's reaction to Leonard's unexpected death. "Everyone was. Bad, bad situation for a few weeks around the office. People crying all the time."[93] But the loss of his dear old friend would not be the only calamity to befall Muddy that month. Ironically, the next blow would also be delivered in an automobile.

On the unusually warm evening of 27 October 1969, Muddy and the band were heading home after playing the last gig of a southern tour in Covington, Tennessee. "Muddy had two drivers. He had Bo [Andrew Bolden] and this guy [James] Warren," Paul Oscher recalls, "and that night Warren said, 'Don't worry about it, when you ride with me you're in the hands of Allstate.' That's what he said, and he made a gesture with his hands."[94]

The musicians were traveling in two cars. Muddy's station wagon took the lead, with Muddy's driver James Warren and Peewee Madison in the front seat and Muddy and Pinetop in the back. The rest of the band — Smith, Oscher, Lawhorn and Wimberley — and driver Andrew Bolden followed in the van. The convoy was moving north along Highway 45, a two-lane road lined with cornfields, just south of Champaign, Illinois.

Disaster was approaching. An oncoming car, speeding at 65 or 70 miles per hour, veered to its right, and its two outer wheels slipped off the shoulder of the road. Later Muddy speculated that perhaps "the guy driving that car was playing around with his girl."[95] Willie Smith vividly recalls the sequence of events from his vantage point in the second vehicle: "The driver who was driving Muddy, he practically stopped, because he seen [the oncoming car] . . . coming so fast. And when he went off the road, Muddy said the driver said, 'Look at that!' But by that time, you know, things happen fast. Muddy said *he* seen it, *everybody* seen it. All but James Madison because he was asleep."[96]

Instead of waiting until the two approaching vehicles had safely gone by, the oncoming driver turned the steering wheel abruptly to his left in order to get back on the pavement. He gravely miscalculated. His vehicle swerved too sharply, placing it directly in the path of the oncoming traffic. "The car just *jumped* back up there," Willie stresses. "It didn't just roll back. It *jumped*. By that time he was sitting right up in the front of the station wagon."[97] There was a head-on collision.

"All of a sudden I hear Bo shout . . . 'Lord, have mercy!' like that," Oscher says. "And all this stuff started spraying over the van, you know, like debris."[98] To avoid rear-ending the station wagon, Bo wrenched his vehicle off the road, where it coasted to a halt in a cornfield. "The only thing I really remember is . . . going up there and Warren was dead behind the wheel with a bone coming out of his leg," comments Oscher. "The two people that were in the car that hit them were gasping, and they died just right there, both of them. . . . Peewee was up against the windshield; he had wound up with broken ribs. We pulled Pinetop out. We pulled Muddy out, and Muddy told Bo . . . 'Man, I'm broken up.' Then he asked Bo is his face messed up."[99] The force of the crash had broken Muddy's pelvis and three of his ribs; Pinetop's leg was injured; Peewee was out cold.

The injured musicians were rushed to the Carle Foundation Hospital in nearby Urbana, where Muddy underwent almost three hours of surgery to repair his pelvis and insert a pin in his hip. His condition was listed as fair. Madison and Perkins were released after a couple of days. Four days after the collision, Muddy was questioned about his immediate future. "I hurt so bad right now, I'm not thinking about no plans," he chuckled, despite the pain. "I ain't dying," Muddy wryly commented, "but I ain't feeling so good."[100]

NOTES

[1] Charles Shaar Murray, "The Blues Had a Baby and They Called It Rock 'n' Roll," *New Musical Express* (30 Apr. 1977): 30.

[2] Bruce Cook, *Listen to the Blues* (New York: Charles Scribner's Sons, 1973), 181.

[3] Keith Richards, "Muddy, Wolf & Me," *Guitar Player*, vol. 27, issue 285, no. 9 (Sept. 1993): 88.

[4] Richards, 88.

[5] Robert Palmer, "Muddy Waters: The Delta Sun Never Sets," *Rolling Stone* (5 Oct. 1978): 56.

[6] Murray, 30.

[7] Murray, 30.

[8] John Hammond, interview with author, 17 Oct. 1991.

[9] Peter Guralnick, *Feel Like Going Home* (New York: Harper & Row, Publishers, 1989), 85.

[10] John Hammond, interview with author, 17 Oct. 1991.

[11] Koko Taylor, interview with author, 27 June 1995.

[12] Koko Taylor, interview with author, 27 June 1995.

[13] Willie Dixon and Don Snowden, *I Am the Blues: The Willie Dixon Story* (London: Quartet Books, 1989), 174.

[14] Charlie Musselwhite, interview with author, 13 Aug. 1995.

[15] Robert Morganfield, interview with author 16 May 1995.

[16] Joseph Morganfield, interview with author, 19 Aug. 1995.

[17] Francis Clay, interview with author, 23 Mar. 1996.

[18] Francis Clay, interview with author, 22 Mar. 1996.

[19] James Cotton, interview with author, 26 Sept. 1995.

[20] B.B. King, interview with author, 24 Aug. 1995.

[21] B.B. King, interview with author, 24 Aug. 1995.

[22] B.B. King, interview with author, 24 Aug. 1995.

[23] B.B. King, interview with author, 24 Aug. 1995.

[24] Marshall Chess, interview with author, 4 Nov. 1996.

[25] Barry Callaghan, "They Came Together, Apprehensive and Trying to Shield Their Excitement," *Toronto Telegram*, Saturday, 19 Feb. 1966, p. 3.

[26] Callaghan, 3.

[27] Callaghan, 3.

[28] Ralph Bass, liner notes, *Muddy, Brass & The Blues*, Chess, 1966.

[29] Tom Wheeler, "Muddy Waters & Johnny Winter," *Blues Guitar: The Men Who Made the Music: From the Pages of Guitar Player Magazine*, ed. Jas Obrecht (San Francisco: GPI Books, 1990), 77.

[30] James Cotton, interview with author, 26 Sept. 1995.

[31] Guy "Doc" Lerner, "Muddy Harps," *Living Blues* 99 (Sept.–Oct. 1991): 35.

[32] Murray, 30.

[33] Alfred Duckett, "I Have a Right to Sing the Blues," *Louisville Defender*, 14 Apr. 1955.

[34] Bo Diddley, interview with author, 26 July 1995.

[35] Francis Clay, interview with author, 23 Mar. 1996.

[36] Jeff Titon, "Mojo Buford, Part 3," *Blues Unlimited* 78 (Dec. 1970): 14.

[37] Peter Guralnick, "Muddy Waters: A Man of the Blues," *Rolling Stone* 91 (16 Sept. 1971): 38.

[38] S.P. Leary, interview with author, 11 June 1996.

[39] Magic Dick, interview with author, 24 Aug. 1995.

[40] Magic Dick, interview with author, 24 Aug. 1995.

[41] Magic Dick, interview with author, 24 Aug. 1995.

[42] Magic Dick, interview with author, 24 Aug. 1995.

[43] Magic Dick, interview with author, 24 Aug. 1995.

[44] James Rooney, *Bossmen: Bill Munroe & Muddy Waters* (New York: The Dial Press, 1971), 147.

[45] Magic Dick, interview with author, 24 Aug. 1995.

[46] Rooney, 149.

[47] Magic Dick, interview with author, 24 Aug. 1995.

[48] Paul Oscher, interview with author, 22 Nov. 1996.

[49] John Hammond, interview with author, 17 Oct. 1991.

[50] Guralnick, *Going Home*, 86–87.

[51] Paul Oscher, interview with author, 18 May 1996.

[52] Tom Townsley, "Paul Oscher: Long Overdue," *Blues Connection*, vol. 3, issue 7 (May 1996): 6.

[53] Townsley, 8.

[54] Paul Oscher, interview with author, 18 May 1996.

[55] Paul Oscher, interview with author, 18 May 1996.

[56] Sam Lay, interview with author, 27 Mar. 1996.

[57] Paul Oscher, interview with author, 18 May 1996.

[58] Townsley, 6.

[59] Paul Oscher, interview with author, 18 May 1996.

[60] Paul Oscher, interview with author, 22 Nov. 1996.

[61] Paul Oscher, interview with author, 18 May 1996.

[62] Paul Oscher, interview with author, 28 Nov. 1996.

[63] Paul Oscher, interview with author, 18 May 1996.

[64] Paul Oscher, interview with author, 10 June 1996.

[65] Paul Oscher, interview with author, 22 Nov. 1996.

[66] Paul Oscher, interview with author, 18 May 1996.

[67] Paul Oscher, interview with author, 22 Nov. 1996.

[68] Paul Oscher, interview with author, 22 Nov. 1996.

[69] Paul Oscher, interview with author, 18 May 1996.

[70] Paul Oscher, interview with author, 18 May 1996

[71] Paul Oscher, interview with author, 18 May 1996

[72] Guralnick, "Muddy Waters," 37.

[73] *Sweet Home Chicago*, film, MCA Records – Initial Film and Television (Chicago) – Vanguard Films, 1993.

[74] Charles Shaar Murray, *Crosstown Traffic* (London: Faber and Faber, 1989), 133.

[75] Pete Golkin, "Blacks, Whites, and Blues, Part Two," *Living Blues* 89 (Dec. 1989): 27.

[76] Ken Minahan, interview with author, 5 May 1995.

[77] Tom Wheeler, "Muddy Waters & Johnny Winter," *Blues Guitar: The Men Who Made the Music: From the Pages of Guitar Player Magazine*, ed. Jas Obrecht (San Francisco: GPI Books, 1990), 74.

78 Jas Obrecht, "The Life and Times of the Hoochie Coochie Man," *Guitar Player* (Mar. 1994): 46.

79 Marshall Chess, interview with author, 4 Nov. 1996.

80 Marshall Chess, interview with author, 4 Nov. 1996.

81 Willie Smith, interview with author, 10 Dec. 1995.

82 Peter Guralnick, "Muddy Waters," 37.

83 Jim O'Neal and Amy O'Neal, "Muddy," *Living Blues* 64 (Mar.–Apr. 1985): 40.

84 Sam Lay, interview with author, 27 Mar. 1996.

85 Sam Lay, interview with author, 27 Mar. 1996.

86 Don DeMichael, "Muddy Waters Week in Chicago," *Rolling Stone* 34 (31 May 1969): 12.

87 "Down Home and Dirty," *Time* (9 Aug. 1971): 46.

88 Guralnick, *Going Home*, 84.

89 O'Neal and O'Neal, 40.

90 Alan Paul, "Of Wolf & Man," *Guitar Legends*, vol. 3, no. 1 (1994): 17.

91 Paul Oscher, interview with author, 18 May 1996.

92 Robert Neff and Anthony Conner, *Blues* (Boston: David R. Godine, 1975), 21.

93 Marshall Chess, interview with author, 4 Nov. 1996.

94 Paul Oscher, interview with author, 18 May 1996.

95 "Car Crash Puts Muddy in Hospital," *Rolling Stone* 47 (29 Nov. 1969): 18.

96 Willie Smith, interview with author, 19 Dec. 1996.

97 Willie Smith, interview with author, 19 Dec. 1996.

98 Paul Oscher, interview with author, 18 May 1996.

99 Paul Oscher, interview with author, 18 May 1996.

100 "Car Crash," 18.

9

*No, I don't have no intention of
giving up. . . . I just want to blow
until I get to be a real old man.*[1]

Late in April 1970, Muddy's Cadillac rolled into a Chicago graveyard. As he shifted uncomfortably from his mending injuries,
Muddy felt a pain that was more than physical. He'd come so close
to death himself, and now he was burying one of his closest friends
and musical alter ego — Otis Spann.

Muddy's convalescence had been tediously slow, a trial for such a
formerly active man. "I was almost destroyed," he admitted. "I love
to travel, but this accident taken a lot out of me. I mean, you don't
never know when it's coming, that's the heck of it."[2] He'd remained
in the Carle Foundation Hospital for almost two and a half months,

until his release on 8 January 1970. He'd had no medical insurance; Chess picked up the tab.

Although he was unable to walk without crutches and was suffering from back pain and a loss of feeling in his hands, his spirit had remained indomitable. "I'm up and around," Muddy declared, "and I ain't runnin' yet."[3] Hundreds of concerned fans overwhelmed him with get-well letters. "I won't be able to answer all of them," he said, "but I want to say thanks to the people for all the nice mail."[4]

Not since his early days in Chicago had Muddy spent so much time in one place. For months he recuperated at home, ever stylish in black silk pyjamas with a matching doo rag around his head and wrapped in a richly colored kimono. Each afternoon he'd be taken on a chauffeur-driven outing. Time dragged by. "It kind of gets on your nerves," Muddy confessed.[5]

At first the swollen, numb condition of his hands cast some doubt on his future as a guitar player. "Some thought I'd never play again, because I couldn't even move my fingers, man."[6] But there were no thoughts of an early retirement for this spirited 55-year-old. "As long as I'm healthy and able, I'm going to send my good friends some blues," he said. "I don't think of the retiring thing yet."[7] Earlier that spring he'd begun making forays into Chicago clubs, such as the Bad Sign and the Burning Spear, shambling onstage with the aid of crutches, performing seated on a bar stool. Due to the condition of his hands, he could only play about a half-hour per night.

Then as he was conquering his own injuries, Muddy was hit with the shock of Otis Spann's death from liver cancer on 24 April 1970, just over a month after the pianist's 40th birthday. While he was upset, Muddy was not one to share his feelings. "Muddy was a very difficult person to read," Paul Oscher comments. "You really would not know Muddy. Even when Spann died, right, well, you could see that Muddy was bothered, but Muddy would just say, 'There'll never be another Otis Spann.' "[8]

John Lee Hooker describes Spann as "one of the greatest blues piano players that ever lived."[9] His death was a blow to the blues world. "It was very sad because it was one of us gone," James Cotton remembers with sorrow. "Down through the years we did a lot of things together, so it was very, very, very, very, very, very sad."[10] Cotton flew to the funeral from San Francisco and had to return three hours later to make his gig that night.

Most of Chicago's bluesmen were there, including Charlie Musselwhite. "I knew Otis real well," Musselwhite remarks, the grief still discernable in his voice. "He was one of my best friends. Yeah, he was really sweet, just the most mellowest guy, not a mean bone in his body. And real deep. His playing was the deepest piano playing I ever heard. In fact after he died, I couldn't even listen to him for years. It was just too painful because he was so sensitive."[11] Muddy was unable to get out of his limo at the graveyard, due to his physical limitations, but his sorrow was also evident. "When I saw Muddy at Spann's funeral, I know he was pretty upset," Mussel-white recalls. "I walked by the car, and Muddy stuck his hand out, and we shook hands, and I said, 'It's a sad day.'"[12]

On 11 June 1970, Muddy made his first major appearance since the car accident. With the aid of one crutch, he picked his way across the stage of Philadelphia's Spectrum, sat gingerly upon a stool and opened with "Hoochie Coochie Man." It was a prudent, constrained performance. Muddy's doctors had informed him that the numbness in his hands would fade at the rate of about a half-inch per month. That meant full recovery would take "about six to eight months," Muddy forecast. "I got big hands."[13] While initially his playing lacked some of its former vitality, his voice retained all its richness and power of projection. Gradually he resumed his touring schedule and was back on the patio of New York's Museum of Modern Art on 6 August, delighting a capacity audience of 2,500, including some admirers who'd perched in the trees for a better view.

By November Muddy was ready to tour Britain, although over a year after the crash, he still needed crutches to walk. As in the past, his manager Bob Messinger was to have most of the band's earnings sent back to Chicago, except what was needed on the road. This time, however, Messinger — who'd described his relationship with Muddy as closer than father and son — failed to meet the group in New York with their money, as arranged. Muddy had to pay his musicians what he could out of his own funds, which amounted to only about half of what they were owed. Although he had been warned about Messinger, Muddy had steadfastly trusted him. Now he searched for his manager in vain. Muddy never saw Messinger again.

It had been an arduous year, and it wasn't over yet. In 1970 Muddy's stepson Dennis, who'd been pursuing a career as a boxer, moved back into the family home and assumed the position of Muddy's valet. During a road trip to Canada, however, he was arrested for possession of marijuana.

By this time Muddy had been embraced by white audiences as the father of Chicago blues. He proudly accepted credit for consolidating the music of the Windy City into one blues personality. In his opinion the great singers of 20 years earlier — such as Memphis Slim, Sonny Boy Williamson and Tampa Red — lacked a unifying style. "They seemed to be going every which way," Muddy believed. "I was able to make a lot of the fellas sing like me."[14]

"It makes me feel very good," said Muddy, commenting on the kudos coming his way. "You know I feel like I deserve it. I've been through quite a bit, and I've paid my dues."[15] He believed the timing was right. "I'm glad all this is happening to me in my old age," admitted the balding 57-year-old, "because if it had happened when I was younger I would have blown it all."[16]

Yet his gratification was tempered by the sorrow he felt at the loss of the original black blues audience. While he enjoyed the support of white fans, he yearned for a more balanced base. "There be's a few blacks around," Muddy commented. "But, you know, to keep your race going, support your peoples, they're not treatin' me fair on that part of it."[17] He blamed their loss of interest on a lack of knowledge: "Most black kids don't understand that what we're doing is mother earth; this is the root to all of it."[18]

Perhaps more than the loss of black fans, however, was what this alienation foretold for the future of blues. "Our people are just nuts," he said candidly. "They don't know how much this music did for the world. They ought to be glad to carry it on."[19] As for black musicians, Muddy stated, "There ain't enough of my peoples trying to get interested in playing the blues and that's what really keeps me kind of worried about it, 'cause they can do it, you know."[20]

They Call Me Muddy Waters was released in February 1971, an album comprising cuts from two 1967 Chicago sessions, plus some earlier recordings. "Howling Wolf," taken from a January 1951 session, and "They Call Me Muddy Waters," recorded in December 1951, give the listener a retaste of Muddy with Little Walter, Jimmy Rogers and Big Crawford. "Making Friends" was recorded in June 1966, and "Crawlin' Kingsnake," from early 1959, features stunning, expressive vocals by Muddy, accompanied by Little Walter.

The LP was nominated for a Grammy Award in the category of Best Ethnic or Traditional Recording (Including Traditional Blues). This time Muddy aced it. On 14 March 1972, Muddy triumphed over diverse competition — Japanese artist Keiko Matsuo, the Esso Trinidad Steel Band and the Javanese Players, as well as bluesmen "Mississippi" Fred McDowell, T-Bone Walker and his old rival Howlin' Wolf — and claimed his first Grammy. Muddy was also the recipient of *Billboard* magazine's 1971 Trendsetter Award for his pioneering contribution to electric blues and for being an important influence on British blues trends.

A two-record set, entitled *McKinley Morganfield A.K.A. Muddy Waters*, was released in June 1971, a compilation issue presenting an overview of Muddy's career to date. It comprises *The Best Of Muddy Waters* in its entirety; a selection of songs from *The Real Folk Blues* and *More Real Folk Blues*; plus two live cuts, "Baby, Please Don't Go," from *Muddy Waters At Newport, 1960*, and "Got My Mojo Working."

With the departure of Sonny Wimberley in 1971, Muddy called upon an old pal, Calvin Jones, to fill the vacancy on bass. A native Mississippian, Jones was born near Greenwood on 9 June 1926. Although he began playing harp at about age 10 or 11, he switched to guitar because, he says, "I never could get nothin' on that harmonica too tough."[21] Shortly after arriving in Chicago in 1947 — where he soon acquired the nickname Fuzzy — he became acquainted with Muddy. Calvin remembers hearing Muddy perform on an acoustic guitar equipped with a pickup, accompanied by only a drummer. Soon Jones was hanging out with Muddy, Jimmy Rogers and Little Walter, enjoying their early cutting contests in South Side clubs.

As he learned guitar, Calvin was fortunate to have some impressive teachers: Freddie King, "Homesick" James Williamson and Jimmy Rogers. In the 1950s he played with Rogers, Junior Wells and Harmonica Slim. As leader of his own band, Jones began to concentrate on playing bass lines on his guitar, and after his brother-in-law gave him an electric bass, he gradually made the switch to playing bass exclusively. He joined Howlin' Wolf in 1964 or 1965, then worked with Fenton Robinson until he was asked to join Muddy.

Jones's recording debut as part of the Muddy Waters Blues Band occurred one night in June 1971, with the taping of a live album at

Chicago's upscale supper club, Mister Kelly's. "Mister Kelly's was a place on the Gold Coast," says Paul Oscher, "and this was more of the kind of place you'd get Las Vegas acts in, like the Copa Cabana was in New York. It was a white place . . . a really fancy place."[22]

The Mister Kelly's gig was, according to Oscher, a pivotal event in Muddy's career, a performance that led to his representation by the booking agency Willard Alexander, Inc., which would in turn open up new opportunities for him. Muddy was cognizant of the possible significance of this outing and warned the band ahead of time to be sober and ready to do its best. While he was uptight going in, Muddy had loosened up by the second set and was dishing out his usual feast of deep-bottom blues.

The resultant album, entitled *Live At Mister Kelly's*, is a fine sample of Muddy's vocals and guitar work, backed by his superb musicians and delivered with seeming effortlessness. James Cotton lends a hand on three cuts, ill disguised on the album credits as Joe Denim. Muddy presented four original compositions never before recorded: "What Is That She Got," the seductive "Strange Woman" (co-written with producer Ralph Bass), an instrumental called "Mudcat" and "C.C. Woman." Another cut, "Country Boy," is a standout — Muddy's voice slides down to the nethermost depths of the blues, echoed by his guitar. Sonny Boy Williamson's "Nine Below Zero" is a strong offering, as is "You Don't Have To Go" by Jimmy Reed and "What Is That She Got."

To Oscher, Muddy's extraordinary talent always remained an enigma. Even though he lived in Muddy's house, Paul never saw Muddy rehearse a new tune before it emerged full-blown in performance or in the recording studio. Muddy did not participate when the band worked through new arrangements. He claimed that he learned his songs by sleeping with the lyric sheets under his pillow.

The only time Oscher recalls Muddy playing at home was when he occasionally taught Paul some licks on the guitar. And once on Geneva's birthday, as they sat around the kitchen table, she said, "Old Man, sing me a song," and Muddy and Cotton serenaded her with "Rock Me" and "Evans Shuffle."[23] It was the first time Oscher had heard Muddy sing without a microphone, and he was awestruck. "I never realized what power he had in his voice," he recalls with reverence. "The whole house shook. His voice filled up the entire house."[24]

It was a fortunate coincidence that, when Oscher was forced to leave Muddy in late 1971 due to a bout of pneumonia, Mojo Buford was in need of another job, so yet again Buford accepted the position of harmonica player in Muddy's band. "Every time I wanted a job, he'd take me on," Mojo says. "He liked me, but I wasn't the greatest harp player he had, but he just liked me. He liked my sound."[25]

Inspired by the success of Howlin' Wolf's LP, *The London Howlin' Wolf Sessions*, Chess decided to apply this winning formula to Muddy. From 4 to 8 December 1971, Muddy stayed at London's Dorchester Hotel while recording a similar album targeted at the lucrative rock-music market. He'd brought along harmonica player Carey Bell and guitarist Sammy Lawhorn; the balance of the supporting musicians were British rockers — guitarist Rory Gallagher, Steve Winwood and Georgie Fame sharing keyboards, Rick Grech on bass and former Jimi Hendrix drummer Mitch Mitchell.

Muddy hadn't known who he'd be playing with until he arrived in London, but he remained unfazed. "I was so proud to go over there and record with a British band," he said, making the best of it. "The sessions were beautiful and the guys were very understanding and they're good musicians."[26] The most memorable cuts to come out of these sessions are Muddy's 1952 number "Who's Gonna Be Your Sweet Man When I'm Gone," "Sad Sad Day," Willie Dixon's "I Don't Know Why" and especially the powerful, yet unadorned, "Walkin' Blues," for which Muddy is accompanied only by Lawhorn.

The album that emerged from this outing, *The London Muddy Waters Session*, was overdubbed with horns and a background vocal in New York and released in April 1972. While not ranking among Muddy's best — the supporting musicians couldn't plumb those bluesy depths he reached with his own band — it was a worthwhile endeavor and brought Muddy to the attention of a wider audience. On 3 March 1973, the LP snared Muddy his second Grammy in the category of Best Ethnic or Traditional Recording (Including Traditional Blues), beating out formidable competition from fellow nominees Lightnin' Hopkins, John Lee Hooker and the late Otis Spann.

Sandwiched between this first London-session album and a second one released in 1974, *Can't Get No Grindin'* was a welcome dose of the more authentic Muddy Waters sound. This LP, recorded in March 1972, reunited Muddy with his regular band, plus James Cotton guesting on harp. The only apparent concession to the times was some occasionally intrusive electric-keyboard work.

The play list reprises several of Muddy's old numbers: "Mother's Bad Luck Child," recorded in 1947 as "Gypsy Woman"; "Sad Letter"; his 1954 cut "Oh Yeah," now entitled "Someday I'm Gonna Ketch You"; "Whiskey No Good," based on his 1948 recording of "Sittin' Here And Drinkin' "; and "Muddy Waters' Shuffle," named "Evans Shuffle" when he recorded it in 1950. The title track, attributed to Muddy, was in fact an adaptation of Memphis Minnie's "What's The Matter With The Mill." Muddy offers two new compositions for this album — the tantalizing "Love Weapon" and an instrumental entitled "Funky Butt."

Can't Get No Grindin' was nominated for a Grammy Award in the category of Best Ethnic or Traditional Recording, along with King Curtis, John Lee Hooker, Leadbelly and Doc Watson. *Then And Now* captured the honor for Watson.

By this time Muddy had to confess that his songwriting output was slowing down, blaming it on the day-to-day administrative headaches of running a band. "I used to come up with some good songs, you know," he reflected, "but I can't get down with it, 'cause I can't think no more. I got too many things on my mind."[27] On another occasion he attributed his mental lethargy to his age, recalling the old days when his songs would spring from a dream or from a catchy phrase. "That's why I tell people I'm getting old. . . . I can't *think* it no more," he said. "You got to be young, young, young. And with a hell of a head on your body."[28] As always, Muddy encouraged his band members to bring their own songs to the group.

Returning to Europe in June 1972, Muddy headlined at the Montreux Jazz Festival in Switzerland, backed by Mojo Buford, guitarist Louis Myers, Dave Myers on bass, Lafayette Leake on piano and drummer Fred Below. On "County Jail," part of his recorded Montreux performance of 17 June, Muddy is outstanding as his seductive slide work builds to a fever pitch. In addition to his own set, Muddy teams with T-Bone Walker for "They Call It Stormy Monday" and "She Says She Loves Me." It was Koko Taylor's first trip to Switzerland, and for her it was a day to remember, especially as she had the honor of calling on Muddy to join her for "I Got What It Takes." Koko's raw, gravelly vocals provide an effective counterpoint for the provocative lushness of Muddy's delivery, as he interjects verses from "The Same Thing" into Koko's number.

Upon his return to the U.S., Muddy was hired to play at Mick Jagger's 29th birthday bash in New York City on 26 July, then was on hand at the Ann Arbor Blues and Jazz Festival on 9 September to pay tribute to Otis Spann. A commemorative plaque in Spann's honor read, "The people of Ann Arbor, Michigan, in recognition of the talent and genius of the late Otis Spann, the sweet giant of the blues, humbly dedicate the Ann Arbor Blues and Jazz Festival 1972, and the ground upon which it stands, to the memory of this great artist." As he presented the plaque to Otis's widow, Lucille, Muddy declared, "One of the greatest guys that ever lived, in the music field, was Otis Spann."[29] As part of his set that day, Muddy performed a stunning version of "Honey Bee"; his seething slide solo thrilled the crowd.

Muddy went upscale in December 1972 when he moved his blues to the Maisonette Room in New York's St. Regis-Sheraton Hotel, the first time a Chicago-blues band had broached the formality of a midtown hotel venue. The Muddy Waters Blues Band shared the program with Sy Oliver's orchestra, a group that played dance numbers its leader had written for Tommy Dorsey and Jimmie Lunceford. "Everything was nice, but it just wasn't what we were used to," comments Willie Smith. "With sophisticated people, you know, you just don't do the things you normally would do."[30] Muddy's demeanor was as restrained as the audience's response. A journalist seemed relieved to report that Muddy had put on "a relatively calm, couth set, avoiding the raw, boiling drive that he usually generates."[31]

Following the inauspicious departure of Bob Messinger, Muddy was in need of new management. After producer Ralph Bass did some preliminary scouting on his behalf, Muddy found a devoted manager and strong advocate in Scott Cameron, former vice-president of Muddy's booking agency, Willard Alexander, Inc. Cameron knew that most older black blues artists had been pressured to sign record contracts without legal counsel; they'd rationalized that a bad deal was preferable to no deal. "They lived from hand to mouth," remarks Cameron. "If they could go sell a song of theirs for $50 to a publisher, they'd sign every right in the world away for 50 bucks."[32] Most blues recording artists knew they were being ripped off; what they didn't know was how to rectify it.

As other artists earned big bucks from Muddy's songs, he was elbowed out of his share of the royalties. Referring to what he considered to be the paternalistic attitude of Chess Records, Cameron reiterated the company's typical excuses: " 'Muddy was bought Cadillacs and Muddy was bought this and that.' Hell, if they'd given him his money, he could have bought his own damn car!"[33] Cameron set out to educate himself about copyrights and royalties. He discovered that in the early 1970s Muddy had unwittingly signed away the rights to his songs in a contract that was retroactive to the 1950s. Although he was being paid a salary, the agreement prevented any renumeration extending to his heirs. Contesting this contract and what he perceived to be Chess's faulty accounting, Cameron filed a lawsuit on Muddy's behalf against the Arc Music Corporation, Chess's music-publishing arm. It was settled out of court to Muddy's partial satisfaction, and on the strength of this success, Willie Dixon also took on Cameron as his manager. Subsequently, Muddy pulled out of Arc Music and formed his own publishing affiliate named Watertoons Music.

"Working-wise, things changed," notes Willie Smith regarding Cameron's management of the band. "I mean it got better, a step up the ladder, I feel."[34] Muddy was booked at larger venues, often opening for superstar groups, which increased both his income and his exposure. On 5 January 1973, the Muddy Waters Blues Band appeared at a concert entitled "Blues Variations" at New York's Philharmonic Hall, along with John Lee Hooker and Mose Allison. Muddy returned to the Big Apple on 4 March for "Blues Variations II," this time at Carnegie Hall, where he topped a bill comprising Lightnin' Hopkins and Bonnie Raitt and rocked a capacity crowd. He returned to Philharmonic Hall on 29 June, where he performed an exemplary set distinguished by slide work that was truly superb.

By the early 1970s, Geneva Morganfield was seriously ill. Those who were closest to Muddy believe that, despite his affinity for young women, he loved his wife deeply. "When she was sick, he used to call home every day," Willie Smith remembers, "and if we had a couple of days off, he'd fly home."[35] Geneva's illness weighed heavily on Muddy, "but he held his head up and kept going," says

Mojo Buford.[36] Finally in early May 1973, Geneva died of cancer at the age of 57.

Muddy immediately moved the children he'd had with his girlfriend Lucille into his home and changed their last name to Morganfield. Now he could assume the responsibilities of a full-time father to Joseph and Renee. Muddy's granddaughter Cookie — whom Geneva and Muddy had raised following the death of her mother — agreed to stay on and run the house. That summer during school vacation, Muddy took his kids on short tours with him, a treat they would enjoy for the rest of their father's life. Nine-year-old Joseph was proud to help out as a roadie, assisting the band members as they set up and took down their equipment.

Muddy's residence on South Lake Park Avenue had been kept spotless and well maintained, but the South Side neighborhood was deteriorating around it. Geneva had been reluctant to relocate, and Muddy himself had declared that he'd never leave. But now the hazards of raising children in such surroundings were likely a major factor in his decision to move that autumn from the community that had been his home for 30 years.

Muddy's new address was at 16 South Adams Street in Westmont, a predominantly white Chicago suburb 20 miles west of his previous home. It was a white, two-story frame house, a modest structure situated on a quiet residential corner lined with trees. Inside it was well appointed with contemporary furniture, plush carpeting and a large modern kitchen, the focal point of activity for the household. In the yard was a toolshed and a small swimming pool. The home provided a comfortable standard of living for the family, much superior to that of most Chicago blacks. Nevertheless, it was still a far cry from the opulent lifestyles enjoyed by the rock stars who'd been influenced by Muddy and grown wealthy performing his music.

Muddy settled into a new life of domesticity in Westmont, concentrating his energies on raising his children to the best of his ability. While Muddy's formative years on Stovall were tough ones, he believed his grandmother had instilled in him valuable life lessons. These he resolved to teach to his own children. Joseph considers himself blessed in "having an honorable father, a wise father, who taught you right from wrong and who showed you the right way and the wrong way of doing things. . . . He was a great musician, but he was a great father, also."[37]

Muddy wasn't a churchgoing man, but he sent Renee and Joseph to church for the religious training that had been so influential in his own upbringing. "I know for a fact he believed in God, and he was a Christian," Joseph declares. Also in the tradition of Della Jones, "He made sure that I had chores," Joseph continues. "Back at the time I didn't understand why I had so many chores, but he wanted to make me responsible." Muddy was a strict but loving parent. "We had a lot of rules in our house," says Joseph. "Some lines we could not cross. . . . I remember I got a whoopin' once, actually a whoopin' Christmas Eve, I think. I think I had punched my sister. That was a no-no. He got me good," Joseph laughs.[38] His son now appreciates Muddy's guidance.

Journalists have often described Muddy as a man of few words, but that was not the case when he was with friends and family. Muddy enjoyed reminiscing with his children about his early life in Mississippi, especially about the grandmother he loved so much. But there were also stories of hurtful racial discrimination and grueling labor on the plantation. "He used to compare that to what I was doing at the time," says Joseph, "and how easy that I had it and how hard that he had it."[39]

Muddy made time to be a good parent. He shared his love of baseball with his son, teaching him to keep his eye on the ball and to stay in front of it. Whenever he could, he'd go to cheer for Joseph at his ballgames. Muddy would frequently relax in his room, watching his beloved White Sox on television, and his son would sometimes join him, especially for the World Series.

The Morganfields often gathered at the kitchen table, and while Muddy sipped champagne, dressed in an elegant smoking jacket or robe, they'd play his favorite card game, casino. "He loved that game," Joseph remembers. "He could play it all day and all night and never get tired of it. . . . He taught me when I was little, and as I got older I got a little better. I got good at it. We had some good games. He used to get me at the end though."[40]

It was an active household. Muddy still possessed abundant energy and danced about the house, only occasionally admitting a twinge from his hip injury. Although he wasn't a swimmer and had never been seen in the pool, he playfully tried to fool his kids by hopping in once and pretending to swim laps, doing the crawl with his hands as he walked across the bottom. Muddy loved dogs and

always kept two German shepherds. His passion for fine cars continued unabated, and there was always a Cadillac parked outside.
By the late 1970s, he also had a Lincoln Continental, which he
called "the big yellow cat," then he added a Mercedes to his fleet
in the 1980s, although Joseph maintains that Cadillacs remained
his father's favorite vehicle.

A typical day in the Morganfield home would begin early. "He
used to be the first one up," Joseph says of his father. "On school
days he used to get us up for school if we overslept or something,
especially my sister Renee. She could never get up on time for
school. I used to wake her up, and if I couldn't get her up, I had to
get my father to get her up, so he was always waking her up."[41]
Muddy would sometimes also make breakfast.

"Ahh, he was the best chef in the world!" sighs Joseph, still
recalling the culinary feasts Muddy prepared.[42] He'd often begin
cooking dinner early in the day, as he puttered around the kitchen,
drinking champagne and playing casino. Such days were pure relax-
ation for Muddy. Down-home soul food was his favorite fare and his
specialty; he'd cook up collard or mustard greens maybe three times
a week. Often the ingredients would come from Muddy's garden,
where he cultivated tomatoes, cabbages, peppers, okra and greens.

Of course, music commanded a significant presence in the
Morganfield household. Muddy listened only to blues, a mix of
old and newer performers. Because most of his friends were white,
rock music was Joseph's passion. Muddy wasn't bothered, however,
explaining to his son that blues was the taproot of all popular music.
Yet Muddy's dream was that some member of his family would carry
on his name in blues. "He used to play [slide guitar] in the basement," says Joseph. "Actually, sometimes he'd sit me down with
him, and he would play something and make me copy him. And I'd
try to copy it, and then if I couldn't get it, I'd practice until I got
it. . . . He was patient with me, very patient. If he got frustrated, I
couldn't tell. I'm sure he did at times."[43] After a year or so, Bob
Margolin, a future member of Muddy's band, became Joseph's music
teacher.

The downside of being Muddy's children was that he had to spend
so much time on the road, and Renee and Joseph would miss him
terribly. Muddy's pal Bo Bolden usually supervised things at home
when Muddy was on tour. "When he was gone there was always

someone in charge of the house," says Joseph. "We had our responsibilities, of course, and he would call and check up on us. . . . Sometimes you'd figure if he was gone you could get away with not doing [your chores], but, no, we couldn't."[44] When Muddy returned from a long road trip, he'd be drained of energy and would need a lot of rest before he could ease himself back into the flow of domestic life. During these periods he'd rarely play his guitar at home.

Muddy's other son, Williams — the child he'd had with Mary Brown — was being brought up by his maternal grandmother in Fort Lauderdale, Florida, and Muddy maintained sporadic contact with him. "He loved his kids," Williams declares, "and he did whatever he could for them, and when he died, he made sure everybody was taken care of."[45] Williams enjoyed his father's fine sense of humor, although he admits that Muddy's good nature was challenged by tardiness. If a family member was late for a planned outing, Muddy would get annoyed and was known to leave the offender behind. When Muddy resumed touring following the car accident, he passed through Florida and presented Williams with his cane.

By this time Peewee Madison had left the band, and Michael Mann, known as Hollywood Fats, joined Muddy on guitar for a few months. Mann, a Los Angeles native, took up guitar at age 10, and four years later was playing as a pro. Along the way he picked up tips from Magic Sam and Freddie King and acquired his moniker from Buddy Guy. Fats's first road tour was with J.B. Hutto and the Hawks, then he worked with Albert King and John Lee Hooker before playing with Muddy in 1973. Fats was Muddy's second white band member.

Not long after Geneva's death, Muddy had no choice but to fire Sammy Lawhorn. Jerry Portnoy, who was to join Muddy's band the following year, elaborates: "He liked Sammy Lawhorn, Sammy was a good guitar player. Sammy was also one of the leading world-class drinkers, and Muddy had to have a word with him on a number of occasions, and finally had to warn him that his job was in jeopardy. Sammy kept messing up and Muddy kept looking the other way. Finally it went on too long, and Sammy was asleep under the stage while they were playing or out sleeping it off in the truck or something while he's supposed to be working. Finally he had to let him go, but he didn't enjoy doing that."[46]

Lawhorn was replaced on lead guitar by 23-year-old Bob Margolin, a native of Brookline, Massachusetts, a suburb southwest of Boston. Chuck Berry had sparked Bob's ambition to learn guitar, but it was Muddy's records that instigated his passion to play blues. "When I heard Muddy," Bob says, "that was just a real revelation to me. . . . For a long time I was probably one of his biggest fans."[47] The first time he saw Muddy live was at Boston's Jazz Workshop. Margolin positioned himself right in front of his icon, intent on studying his technique. "It's the most powerful music I ever heard in my life," he remarks.[48]

Bob was playing in a Boston group with Luther "Georgia Boy Snake" Johnson, Muddy's former band mate, when Johnson introduced Margolin to the great bluesman. In the early 1970s their paths crossed frequently, as Bob played with various bands that opened shows for Muddy. Margolin's zeal and intuitive feeling for Chicago blues were apparent to Muddy. "He was kinda tickled to see somebody that was young that wanted to do it," Bob comments, "because, for the most part, more modern players wanted to play more modern things."[49]

One night at Pall's Mall, a small Boston club, Margolin came backstage to say hello to Muddy, who was performing there. As fate would have it, Muddy had just fired Lawhorn the day before, and he needed a replacement fast. He offered Bob the job that would change his life. "I was very aware of what it would mean," Margolin recalls, "that it was a very big opportunity, and if I didn't do it, it would be like putting a cap on my career. And I knew that it was really the best thing to do, and it was really a great opportunity to learn a whole lot and to take a step up in the blues world."[50]

"Muddy used to say that he would try to find somebody that could play pretty good and then bring him around to his own style," says Margolin, commenting on Muddy's guidance as a bandleader. "He really didn't want to teach anything very specifically. You just got up on the bandstand and played, but you tried to pick it up as well as you could."[51] Margolin adds that "Muddy's idea of constructive criticism, however, was something like, 'Don't ever play that again, it makes my dick sore.'"[52] Bob admits, "The hardest part for me was that Muddy had a very behind-the-beat style of playing that he called delay time. And it wasn't natural to the way I had been playing, and it took me a while before I was really comfortable doing it, but I tried to get with the program, so to speak, and eventually I was able to do that to the point where now it feels unnatural for me to play any other way."[53]

"He was really special," says Bob, reflecting on Muddy's character. "He had charisma. He could affect people spiritually, both with his personality and with his music."[54] Muddy was the type of man who commanded respect the moment he entered a room. Remarkably, it had more to do with the essence of the man than with his renown as a bluesman. The reaction to Muddy was the same whether or not you were aware of his musical achievements. His dignity, his noble bearing and the substance of his personality signaled his uniqueness as a man. Yet Muddy was not a stuffy, one-dimensional character. "When he was with family or close friends, or having a particularly good time on the bandstand," Margolin reveals, "he displayed a loose, good humor that ranged from playful to downright silly."[55]

One of Bob's first gigs with Muddy was in New York's Central Park that summer. "It was exciting for me," he remembers. "The real trip to it was when he'd sing out 'Got my mojo working,' and all those 5,000 people or so would sing it back to him."[56] Bob had played large venues before, but this magnitude of audience response was a new and very exhilarating experience.

Bob was the third white member of Muddy's band, and he recalls hearing a few comments that Muddy should hire only black musicians for his group: "At first I thought nobody would actually be stupid enough to go up to him and tell him that he was making a mistake . . . but there were people who did it. Some, especially European promoters, actually would do that, which is I guess their privilege, but he would respond in a to-the-point, yet vulgar, fashion."[57]

During this time a typical tour for the Muddy Waters Blues Band would be a four-week run, packing the house for six nights each at Toronto's Colonial Tavern, Pall's Mall in Boston, Connecticut's Shaboo Inn and the Cellar Door in Washington, D.C. Age had neither impaired Muddy's desire to perform nor his ability to do so. When questioned about the source of his awesome blues talent, Muddy replied that it was innate. "Sometimes it scares me," he conceded. "I really don't know why it is — just a way I have with the words in a song and having a good strong voice."[58]

Although he'd been singing and playing seated since the car

crash, it hadn't lessened the dynamism of his performance. In fact, it added a new dimension. Now when he was energized by a song, Muddy would rise off his stool; that act alone would earn him explosive cheers. "It's funny, 'cause it's a very cheap way to get a round of applause," Margolin wisecracks. "I'd go, 'Hey, big deal. I was standing up to start with!' . . . I'm sure that [accident] did slow him down, although he could still dance pretty good when he wanted to."[59]

The band continued to drive from gig to gig in two vans, but after the accident Muddy began flying to any engagement that was over a hundred miles from Chicago, meeting his musicians there. He was nervous whenever he rode with the band, but as Willie Smith hastens to add, "After that we *all* was nervous!"[60] "[Muddy] was a very good driver himself," Margolin says. "His driving skills were excellent and his eyes were very good. If he was driving with somebody, which he did with me plenty of times, he'd always be telling you what to do and that you were messing up and asking if you were all right and stuff. He did this to Willie, our drummer, so bad one time when we were driving through Berkeley, California, that Willie stopped the van in the middle of the street and got out, and told him, 'You drive!' Willie just stopped in the middle of the street, put it in park and left. It was pretty funny."[61]

Knowing that their grueling schedule would eventually fray everyone's nerves, Smith would always inaugurate a tour with the same ritual. "When we'd get ready to load up, I would always say, just for a joke, 'Let's all shake hands now,' 'cause we knew we gonna be fighting after a while," he laughs.[62] Small frustrations would build to a boil, erupt, then quickly be forgotten.

"I always liked to follow the leader," says Smith, speaking of his style of drumming, "but if [Muddy] started to lagging, I'd just put him on my back and try to drag him along." Muddy would throw him a look that meant trouble. If he was going to catch hell anyway, Willie reasoned he might as well continue apace. "We used to argue like cats and dogs, behind closed doors, about the way things went," Willie admits as he describes the band's post-performance critiques. "But it never meant nothing. With nothing but five men and four walls, something's gonna hit somewhere."[63]

Some days Muddy would overdo it with the champagne, and at the gig that night he'd be especially difficult to please. "He'd get pretty tore down," Calvin Jones recalls, chuckling. "He'd start off a song, and then he'd come in late singing and he'd be saying, 'I don't know what y'all playing!'" and Jones would suggest another bottle of champagne. "He was a lotta fun," Calvin adds. "Just great."[64]

"Muddy was just like an old good buddy," Jones reminisces. "We'd sit down and gamble; play poker. He'd cuss me out 'n' I'd cuss him. We didn't ever talk to him like no boss."[65] Margolin says, "Yeah, they'd always play the game casino. I heard him say that he wouldn't play for money with our guys, 'cause he had too much to lose. And our guys were pretty rough cardplayers. They could definitely take you down."[66] Members of ZZ Top first met the Muddy Waters Blues Band on tour in 1973, and they remember Muddy and some other musicians playing poker on a Fender bass case balanced across their knees. In front of each man was a stack of bills and a gun.

Despite Muddy's mounting celebrity, on-tour amenities remained scarce. Except for two bottles of Piper Heidseick champagne, stipulated in his contracts, Muddy and his musicians were lucky if they got a sandwich backstage. Kentucky Fried Chicken was a regular stop en route, and soul-food restaurants were a favorite. Whenever the band stayed at a place with cooking facilities, they'd prepare their own meals. Muddy often served as chef, and his dishes sparked as much praise from the band as they did from his children back home.

"A good case could be made that Muddy's goal in life . . . was to get back in bed," says Bob Margolin, recounting Muddy's extracurricular, on-tour activities. "Whether alone or with a young woman, it just seemed like he wanted to spend a lot of time in bed. And he'd try to get to the hotel as quick as possible, or get back home, or wherever he was going . . . and when he got there, he'd get back in bed." Muddy was already known as "the Old Man" to his band members, and as Bob recalls, "He didn't get too wild and crazy, although he still did attract, over that last 10 years of his life, a lot of young women."[67]

A number of awards came Muddy's way in 1973 as well. The readers of *Blues Unlimited* magazine voted him best male blues singer of the year and named his group the best blues band. In addition, an *Ebony* readers' poll bestowed upon Muddy the magazine's Black Music Hall of Fame Award.

Before the end of that year, guitarist Hollywood Fats had left Muddy's band and was replaced by Luther "Guitar Junior" Johnson, no relation to Muddy's previous guitarist, Luther "Georgia Boy Snake" Johnson. This latest Luther Johnson was born in Itta Bena, Mississippi, on 11 April 1939 and raised near Greenwood. As a child he sang in a Baptist choir, and although his father was a harmonica player, Luther chose to teach himself guitar as a teenager. He soon formed his own gospel group and performed as a blues musician at local events before joining various blues bands in Chicago and St. Louis, including those of Magic Sam and Bobby Rush. For the next few years, Johnson worked mainly outside the music field, making occasional forays into Chicago clubs with his own band. In 1972 he recorded for the Big Beat label.

What he may have initially lacked in technical ability, Johnson made up for with the bluesy feel he projected through his instrument. As was his practice, Muddy set to work refining his new protégé's raw talent. "I look for a guy that can play pretty good," Muddy commented, "and then we get him and rehearse him and try to get him to play my sound. The Muddy Waters sound."[68]

Muddy returned to the studio on 29 and 30 January 1974 for the first time since March 1972. Backed by his regular band — and with Paul Oscher and Carey Bell sharing harp duty with Mojo Buford — Muddy revives a few old favorites, such as an extended version of the rollicking Delta theme, "Rollin' And Tumblin'" and "Trouble No More." As well, the lineup includes the far-from-subtle "Electric Man," "Drive My Blues Away," "Katie" and a fun, self-promotional number called "'Unk' In Funk," which became the name of the resultant album, released that March.

January also saw the unreleased tracks from Muddy's 1971 London recordings paired with Howlin' Wolf's own London sessions issued together on the album *Muddy Waters & Howlin' Wolf: London Revisited*. Although lackluster compared with many of his other offerings, the LP was impressive enough to earn Muddy a Grammy nomination. Other nominees for that year's Grammies included Howlin' Wolf, Bukka White, Willie Dixon and Doc and Merle Watson; the Watsons won the award for *Two Days In November*.

Muddy went Hollywood in 1974 when he recorded the soundtrack for the movie *Mandingo*, directed by Richard Fleischer and starring James Mason, Ken Norton, Perry King and Susan George. With a meandering plot that purports to expose the humiliation and degradation of slavery, the movie devolves into a sadistic peep show that sensationalizes the sex and violence of the antebellum South. Nevertheless, Muddy's contribution rings true; his spectacular vocals on "Born In This Time" are saturated with the angst and hopelessness of being in bondage (although, in the pre-Civil War era, blues hadn't yet evolved as a music form). With only a banjo, ukulele and washboard to accompany him, Muddy provides a significant measure of poignancy missing from the film. It's in stark contrast to his other project recorded about this time, a radio jingle for the soft drink Dr. Pepper, in which he half-heartedly exhorts listeners to drink it every day.

Once again Mojo Buford left Muddy, this time to attend to family problems, and his vacancy was filled by harmonica player Jerry Portnoy. Born in Chicago on 25 November 1943, Jerry grew up listening to the musicians of Maxwell Street as they cranked out their blues in front of his father's rug shop each Sunday. Yet it wasn't until the late age of 24 that he picked up a harmonica, and unlike his previous efforts at guitar and piano, Portnoy felt an immediate affinity for the instrument. His path was finally charted when he dropped acid and listened to a recording of Rice Miller blowing harp. In 1970 he joined bluesman Johnny Young, a guitar and mandolin player who'd played with Muddy in the 1940s, then Portnoy went on to work with John Littlejohn and Sam Lay. He forged a close relationship with Big Walter Horton, who years before had instructed Rice Miller and who helped Jerry develop his talent.

Paul Oscher was another pal of Jerry's, and it was through this friendship that Portnoy first met Muddy. "In the afternoons, [Muddy would] lie around in his bed with his doo rag on in his robes with a bottle of champagne and watch the Cubs," says Jerry, who'd visit Oscher's room in Muddy's basement, "and occasionally we'd go up there and he'd offer us a glass of champagne."[69] Subsequently he got to sit in with Muddy, and whenever Portnoy was at a gig, Muddy would graciously introduce him to the audience.

Portnoy kept his day job as a vocational evaluator for inmates at the Cook County Jail while he set about forming his own band. When Johnny Young died in April 1974, both Jerry and Muddy were booked to play a benefit performance for the Young family.

Mojo had just resigned, so Muddy invited Jerry to join the band for their set. He was so impressed by Portnoy's playing that night, that a few days later he asked him to become a permanent member of the Muddy Waters Blues Band.

"I went bananas," says Jerry, recalling it as one of the highlights of his life. "But I mean, this was *the* job. There was only *one*, and the planets had to align pretty good for that, you know. It was a dream come true."[70] No better job existed for a harmonica player, because Muddy made the harp the centerpiece of his band. "All the great players that went through there, it was like being in the royal line of succession," Jerry maintains. "It was a great gig from the standpoint of exposure and getting your credentials in order."[71] He resigned from his job at the jail, and worked on Muddy's repertoire with the band at a gig they were playing at Queen Bee's Lounge while Muddy took three weeks off.

On 25 May 1974 at Roosevelt Stadium in Indianapolis, Jerry Portnoy made his debut as a member of Muddy's band. "When we walked out onstage, and the public-address announcer said, 'Ladies and gentlemen, the Muddy Waters Blues Band,' well, a chill went up my spine," Jerry recounts. "It was just fantastic. I got such a great thrill out of standing next to him."[72]

"I was kind of afraid to step on his toes," he says of his initial outings with Muddy, "but I learned how to weave in and out and work around his voice appropriately. I was fairly confident that I had the goods for the job, so although, you know, I was filling big historical shoes, I knew his material pretty well."[73]

Assessing Muddy's approach as a bandleader, Jerry explains,

I'd have to call him a kind of laissez-faire bandleader, much like Eric [Clapton] now. They basically hire you for what you can do and your skills, and then they let you do it. If there's something egregious that they feel compelled to address, they'll certainly do it, but basically you have freedom to play the job according to your own likes. . . . Basically Muddy let me do my thing, and he was actually a very generous bandleader, as is Eric. He'd push me out in the spotlight and say, "Go get 'em," so it was great. . . .

The only rule was show up and do the job. He was not in any sense a martinet, and you know, it was not some kind of atmosphere where you had all kinds of rules or bed check or anything like that. [laughs] You're dealing with a bunch of pretty wild guys. You were grown; he figured your life's your own. "I'm hiring you to do a job, and as long as you're doing that, we don't have a problem."[74]

Muddy recognized that a boss can't always be popular and that musicians have strong wills of their own. "If I push them too hard," he explained, "they ain't gonna play good. You should leave them *loose*. Like you let a bunch of cows loose in a pasture, say, 'Go get you some grass.' "[75]

Muddy was very loyal to those he employed. "If he hired you, you had a job," declares Portnoy, "unless there was something that went on too long or something really unsolvable, you didn't have to worry about someone taking your job. If you went into some town and there was some incredible guitar player, he wasn't going to fire one of his guitar players. . . . He didn't jump around that way."[76]

"He was a regular guy," says Jerry, describing Muddy's demeanor. "You could have a lot of fun joking around with him. Great story-teller. . . . Muddy was not mad with his own perfume; he didn't have a big head." Yet, on the other hand, "He knew that he was Muddy Waters, and he knew that he really was entitled to a certain amount of respect, [and] he carried himself in a very regal way."[77]

A sojourn in Muddy's band was the equivalent of taking a gradu-ate course in music — in addition to playing, it included exposure to the business of music and guidance on how to behave profession-ally. Those who passed through its ranks were well prepared to become successful frontmen in their own right. Bob Margolin credits Muddy with teaching him "an awful lot musically, about his style of music and playing and singing. And also an awful lot about how to conduct yourself in the world and how to run a band. Musically and socially, I would say, there was quite a bit. It wasn't always by good example, either. Sometimes I felt like I could learn from his mistakes a little bit."[78] Portnoy considers his debt to Muddy to be incalculable. Musically he "learned how to contribute textur-ally without stepping on anybody's toes. I learned how to play ensemble sound. . . . I learned a lot from him personally about being a bandleader."[79]

"The thing that was really special about him," Margolin explains, "was that he gave the sidemen the opportunity to express themselves, to be able to really get to sing some songs each night, if they could. I think as a result of him giving people a chance to do this and not holding them back, a lot of the talented players in his band went on to become well-known frontmen themselves."[80]

By treating band members generously, Muddy recognized that they would play to the best of their ability. Spotlighting the artistry of his sidemen didn't detract from his own performance, it enhanced it. "You can't play music without confidence," Jerry maintains. "You have to have confidence to go out there, and so the more you instill confidence in your band members . . . that helps them gain their own self-confidence, and that lets them flower."[81] Muddy remained open to new ideas from band members, as long as they didn't cause the music to stray from its deep-blues sound.

When Muddy entered Chicago's WTTW television studio on 18 July 1974, he was amazed to encounter an array of blues artists who'd assembled there to offer him their respect, gratitude and affection. The weekly PBS series *Soundstage* was kicking off with a tribute to Muddy. Ken Ehrlich, the instigator and producer of the program, saw it as a way to honor the blues legend for his contribution to music in general and for his role in inspiring many younger musicians who went on to garner immense success. "At this point in time, in a tempered way, he needed [the help of his friends]," Ehrlich comments, "and I felt that I had the opportunity if not the responsibility to tune in five to seven million people to Muddy Waters."[82]

Willie Dixon, Junior Wells, Michael Bloomfield, Johnny Winter, Dr. John, Koko Taylor and Buddy Miles were among those who came out to pay tribute to the godfather of Chicago blues, despite budget limitations that provided for payment of only $500 each with no expenses paid. "You never pass up the chance to pay homage to someone like Muddy Waters," said Michael Bloomfield, "to be able to pay a little bit back for what they give you. The man is literally responsible for many of the different offshoots of the music that you listen to today."[83] For Junior Wells his appearance helped redress a long-standing personal debt: "This man was my guardian, showing me the ropes. He taught me to be an obedient young man, how to get respect from people. . . . I'm a proud person to come back and do it."[84] With deep feeling, Koko Taylor adds, "I was just more than honored to be on that show. And I remember that was the first time I was on TV, and it was just wonderful. . . . I was shown with Muddy Waters, my idol."[85]

The program was filmed before a studio audience. "There was no phony-baloney shit," drawls Dr. John, who presented Muddy with a mojo necklace. "Wasn't nobody trying to go uptown; just staying out in the alley with sally."[86] It was the first time Johnny Winter had worked with Muddy, and it paved the way for their future triumphs together. Muddy and his stellar retinue covered "Blow Wind Blow," "Long Distance Call," "Hoochie Coochie Man" and "Mannish Boy." "When Muddy did 'Mannish Boy,'" exclaims Dr. John, "shit man, that to me is the rattiest of the junky blues."[87] Taking a break backstage, Muddy sighed with contentment: "You don't know how happy I am. . . . It's the thrill of my life, man. Just to think that the kids didn't forget me."[88]

The musicians assembled for several encores of "Got My Mojo Working," and the crowd rose to its feet in jubilation. Muddy kicked up his heels and executed a suave dance step, then left the stage. The musicians departed one by one until only Dr. John was left playing a quiet piano solo. The hour-long production, entitled "Muddy and Friends," aired on 3 December 1974.

Following the taping of *Soundstage*, Muddy departed on another European tour. He headlined the opening night of the Montreux Jazz Festival accompanied by Buddy Guy, Junior Wells, Rolling Stone bassist Bill Wyman, Pinetop Perkins, Dallas Taylor on drums and rhythm guitarist Terry Taylor. Then with his regular band, he also received top billing at the Juan les Pins Festival in Antibes and at the 1-Jazz Festival in Dijon. Well pleased with the welcome he'd received on his first tour of Australia the year before, Muddy returned with his band in September 1974 to perform at eight major venues in Australia and three in New Zealand. "The people loved him, I tell ya," Mojo remembers. "They's crazy about Muddy Waters, they sure enough was. It was the biggest crowd I ever saw, I'm telling you. I was nervous, but I come on through."[89] When asked if he liked performing overseas, Muddy was disarmingly candid: "I like working any place where the peoples like me."[90]

Riding high on a crest of popular appeal, The Band had emerged from blues-based origins to become one of the superstar groups of the decade. Singer, songwriter and multi-instrumentalist Levon Helm, who'd grown up in Helena, Arkansas, had drawn much of his early inspiration from Muddy Waters and his band. "Right there in the Mississippi Delta region around Helena and Clarksdale, Mississippi, and West Memphis, Arkansas, in that area, Muddy was one of the *big* record sellers," Helm explains. "Muddy was a big radio star, and Muddy was a big jukebox star also. You couldn't miss Muddy Waters's music, it was that strong, and it was on the good radio stations and you could find it on those big Wurlitzer juke-boxes. It was great."[91] Until he set out on the road to establish his own career, in about 1957, Levon would make sure he was in attendance whenever Muddy played nearby.

Henry Glover — songwriter, arranger and record producer, formerly with King Records, then with his own label and with Roulette — initially conceived the idea of recording Muddy with members of The Band. It seemed a logical step — one that must have had the Chess marketing department salivating — to follow the past successes of partnering Muddy with more commercial rock stars by cutting an album with The Band. "I would give Henry Glover the credit for most of it," says Levon,

and I would say also that the people at Chess Records at the time, and their president . . . a gentleman named Marvin Schlachter . . . really got behind the project, and Mr. Schlachter's enthusiasm made it one of the last big records for the Chess Company before they were conglomerated into the big organization that happened years ago. So he made that happen, and the next thing you know, a dream had certainly come true. You know, I'm down at the airport picking up Muddy and Bob Margolin and Pinetop, man, and we're goin' to Woodstock [New York] in a hurry! It was fantastic.[92]

Joining Muddy, Bob and Pinetop for the sessions of 6 and 7 February 1975 were two members of The Band — Levon Helm on drums and bass, and keyboard player Garth Hudson — plus Howard Johnson on saxophone, and guitar and bass player Fred Carter. Jerry Portnoy was nudged aside to make way for Muddy's disciple — and a drawing card in his own right — harmonica player Paul Butterfield. The album was cut at Bearsville's Studio, a converted chestnut-timbered barn on Turtle Creek Farm in Woodstock.

The Muddy Waters Woodstock Album was a live-in-the-studio project, an attempt to recreate the fabled Chess sound of the 1950s.
Muddy was given a transistorized German mike. "After we made
sure he had a big Neumann microphone to sing in, so we had his
voice covered," Levon says,

> then everybody just got right in his lap nearly. I got up real
> close with the drums so that I could really hear his guitar and
> everything and hear his voice and try my best to play with
> him. And it just made it a whole lotta fun to get up that close
> and, you know, tie right in to what he was pulling off. . . . The
> Neumann microphone we used on his voice certainly captured
> some of the depth that was in Muddy's voice. Muddy had a
> great voice, and he had a lot of the Brook Benton smoothness
> and depth to his voice. His voice could make one of those echo
> chambers ring like a bell.[93]

Although he asked for everyone's input, the final song selection
was up to Muddy. Surprisingly, he decided to stray slightly from his
deep-blues repertoire, although he did choose numbers that he
often performed live.

> It kind of came off as a show unto itself, you know [Helm
> recalls] and we played it that way. We ended up playing some
> of those good show tunes by Louis Jordan and just things you
> would want to hear the Muddy Waters Woodstock Band play,
> just some of those songs, blues standards. At the same time, I
> wasn't disappointed because when you listen to . . . some of
> the deeper and heavier things that Muddy pulled on the
> album, I get real satisfied with it.
> And the way that the melody line — the horn spaces — the
> way that Butterfield and Garth with the accordion played
> the harmonica and the accordion as a section almost. And it
> really did sound good, a real country kind of a horn section
> sound to it. . . .
> Muddy Waters certainly called the shots . . . and at the same
> time, gave us a whole lotta freedom on how we wanted to do
> it, and just let everybody have a good time. It really did happen
> like you would want a dream come true to happen. It was just
> that much fun.[94]

The LP delivers a foot-stompin' good time with such standards as "Caledonia," "Let The Good Times Roll" and "Kansas City," the latter two cuts featuring Muddy and Pinetop sharing vocals. Muddy resurrects his 1952 recording, "Gone To Main Street," in a rollicking version now called "Going Down To Main Street." "Born With Nothing," newly penned by Muddy, combines his robust voice with his signature slide patterns; the tune is similar to "Blow Wind Blow." Levon comments that "[Muddy] basically has got that guitar owned. He played guitar on just about all the tracks . . . and a lot of those licks are those famous licks that when you hear one of them you know that's one of them rock 'n' roll builder licks. You know it's Muddy."[95]

Although he had been to see Muddy play many times over the years, Levon had never actually met him until they were brought together for the Woodstock sessions. He had high expectations, but Muddy was "better than I had hoped, more of a gentleman. It made you tighten up a little to be around Muddy!" he laughs. "I never heard him use a curse word, never. And you never did get Muddy's goat — he didn't have one to get, you know — and was always a gentleman. It wasn't like he was quiet. You know we'd sit down and eat and have a hell of a good time, laugh and talk and go on, you know, easy thataway. But a real gentleman, one of those self-educated, self-made men for sure. And a gentleman of the first degree."[96]

Muddy's sense of humor delighted him as well:

That's what made it so much fun. We got to eat supper with him for about two nights down at a restaurant down in Woodstock there, and, boy, that was fun. You know between him and Butterfield and Henry Glover and everybody else, there was a lot of laughs going on. . . . We spent most of our free time eating and laughing and talking. We never would get very serious, unless we were playing. . . . I hung out with him every minute that I could, without just bringing him down and making a nuisance of myself. I hope I didn't do that, but I sure did enjoy.[97]

The Muddy Waters Woodstock Album was released that April to enthusiastic reviews. At the Grammy Awards on 28 February 1976,

Muddy shut out Koko Taylor, Memphis Slim, the Sam Lucas Band of Guatemala and Rounder Records with its collection of black convict songs to win his third Grammy for this LP in the now-familiar category of Best Ethnic or Traditional Recording.

On Monday, 30 June 1975, Muddy played a club date in New York and attracted more than his usual audience. Jerry Portnoy recalls that night with a fair bit of amusement:

Muddy was a real icon of American music, and his appeal, especially to musicians, went across the board. The greatest players in jazz, in rock 'n' roll, in country and western, in blues and pop, it didn't matter what the field was, they knew about Muddy and they were fans of Muddy's, and they would come out to see him play. And frequently, you know, they would come up on the bandstand and do something with him. . . . Although they knew who Muddy was, Muddy didn't really know sometimes who they were. I mean if they were blues people, he knew, but in some of the other fields, he really wasn't up on who was doing what.

At any rate, one night we were playing at the Bottom Line in New York, which is a showcase club, and it was sold out — two shows, standing room only — and his manager was there, Scott Cameron. . . . I went backstage, and I hear Scott tell Muddy that "Bob Dylan's in the audience tonight, and he's sent word that he'd like to join you onstage. Now he's a really, really big star, and you know there's all kinds of photographers here, and we might get some photos in *Rolling Stone* or something. You should really call him up. Don't forget — *Bob Dylan*, he's really, really big. Don't forget now. You call him up in the next set — *Bob Dylan*."

So Muddy looked over at Scott and said, "Uhhh, gotcha!" He had this little habit: with his right hand he'd kind of wave it in front of his mouth and stutter a little bit, and when he was doing it he said, "Gotcha," and when he said it his finger would point out.

So we go up to play the second set, and we do our three opening numbers . . . then Junior [Luther Johnson] starts with the intro and brings Muddy out to the front of the stage. And Muddy's perched right at the front of the stage on his bar stool, and we segue right into "Stormy Monday," and Muddy sings a couple of verses, finishes the song, then he gets on the mike, and he says, "Ladies and gentlemen, we got a big surprise for you tonight. We got a very special guest in the house tonight. Uhh, uhh, uhh, *Dylan's* here! Come out here, *John!*"[98]

Unfazed by the botched introduction, Dylan shuffled onto the stage to sit in with the band. "To me he was blowing a funny-type harmonica," says Willie Smith. "Muddy's singing one thing, and he's blowing something that we wasn't used to, you know, and I got pissed. Muddy asked me, he said, 'Do you know who he is?' and I said, 'I don't give a damn who he is,' I said. 'He ain't playing shit.'"[99]

Dylan began his career performing songs by Woody Guthrie and Muddy Waters. "Bob Dylan was definitely influenced by blues, as well as many other things," says Bob Margolin, "and he was very interested in understanding Muddy and his music. He asked me a lot of technical questions about his guitar and his amplifier, and I think he just wanted to be around Muddy and kind of pick up on it a little bit."[100]

Under the ownership of the GRT Corporation, the blues division of Chess Records had stagnated. Phil Chess had left in 1971 to devote his attention to his radio-broadcast interests, the same year Marshall also departed to form the Rolling Stones's new record label. In August 1975 GRT sold its entire catalog of Chess, Checker and Cadet recordings to All Platinum Records of Englewood, New Jersey. "Yeah, they sold it all," said Muddy, chafing at the impersonality of corporate tactics. "I'm getting a little old and I don't think I should be pushed around like that."[101]

Muddy had promised he'd stay with Chess as long as a family member was involved, but that was no longer the case. On 20 November when he learned that All Platinum would not hold him to his renewal option, Muddy officially ended his 28-year association with Chess Records. "I ain't in no hurry to sign with another record company," Muddy valiantly proclaimed. "Somebody will grab me."[102]

But blues wasn't selling. No one was grabbing.

NOTES

1 Bruce Cook, *Listen to the Blues* (New York: Charles Scribner's Sons, 1973), 186.

2 Peter Guralnick, *Feel Like Going Home* (New York: Harper & Row, Publishers, 1989), 63.

3 "Muddy's Back on His Feet Again," *Rolling Stone* 57 (30 Apr. 1970): 12.

4 "Muddy's Back," 12.

5 Guralnick, 64.

6 Charles Shaar Murray, "The Blues Had a Baby and They Called It Rock 'n' Roll," *New Musical Express* (30 Apr. 1977): 30.

7 Tony Stewart, "Muddy Waters Now Records in London with the British Blues-Rockers," *Hit Parader* (July 1972): 18.

8 Paul Oscher, interview with author, 18 May 1996.

9 John Lee Hooker, interview with author, 9 Aug. 1995.

10 James Cotton, interview with author, 26 Sept. 1995.

11 Charlie Musselwhite, interview with author, 13 Aug. 1995.

12 Charlie Musselwhite, interview with author, 13 Aug. 1995.

13 "Random Notes," *Rolling Stone* 63 (23 July 1970): 4.

14 Hamilton Bims, "Blues City," *Ebony* 27 (Mar. 1972): 80.

15 "Muddy Waters," *Blues Guitarists From the Pages of Guitar Player Magazine* (Saratoga, CA: Guitar Player Productions, 1975), 70.

16 Vernon Gibbs, "Muddy Waters," *Essence* (Dec. 1972): 85.

17 Jim O'Neal and Amy O'Neal, "Muddy," *Living Blues* 64 (Mar.–Apr 1985): 40.

18 Gibbs, 85.

19 Cliff Radel, "Muddy Waters is the Blues," *Cincinnati Enquirer*, 6 July 1976.

20 James Rooney, *Bossmen: Bill Munroe & Muddy Waters* (New York: The Dial Press, 1971), 146.

21 Calvin Jones, interview with author, 29 May 1996.

22 Paul Oscher, interview with author, 18 May 1996.

23 Paul Oscher, interview with author, 5 Nov. 1996.

24 Paul Oscher, interview with author, 5 Nov. 1996.

25 Mojo Buford, interview with author, 7 Mar. 1996.

26 Stewart, 17.

27 Guralnick, 80.

28 Robert Neff and Anthony Conner, *Blues* (Boston: David R. Godine, 1975), 104.

29 *Ann Arbor Blues & Jazz Festival 1972*, Atlantic Recording Corp., 1973.

30 Willie Smith, interview with author, 10 Dec. 1995.

31 John S. Wilson, "Blues Band," *New York Times*, Thursday, 21 Dec. 1972, p. 30.

32 Willie Dixon and Don Snowden, *I Am the Blues: The Willie Dixon Story* (London: Quartet Books, 1989), 192.

33 Dixon and Snowden, 187.

34 Willie Smith, interview with author, 10 Dec. 1995.

35 Willie Smith, interview with author, 10 Dec. 1995.

36 Mojo Buford, interview with author, 7 Mar. 1996.

37 Joseph Morganfield, interview with author, 19 Aug. 1995.

38 Joseph Morganfield, interview with author, 19 Aug. 1995.

39 Joseph Morganfield, interview with author, 19 Aug. 1995.

[40] Joseph Morganfield, interview with author, 19 Aug. 1995.

[41] Joseph Morganfield, interview with author, 19 Aug. 1995.

[42] Joseph Morganfield, interview with author, 19 Aug. 1995.

[43] Joseph Morganfield, interview with author, 19 Aug. 1995.

[44] Joseph Morganfield, interview with author, 19 Aug. 1995.

[45] Williams Morganfield, interview with author, 2 Sept. 1995.

[46] Jerry Portnoy, interview with author, 13 Nov. 1995.

[47] Tut Underwood, "Bob Margolin: Remembering Muddy Waters," *Living Blues* 99 (Sept.–Oct. 1991): 22

[48] Underwood, 22.

[49] Underwood, 23.

[50] Bob Margolin, interview with author, 6 June 1995.

[51] Bob Margolin, interview with author, 6 June 1995.

[52] Bob Margolin, "Can't Be Satisfied," *Blues Revue* 20 (Dec. 1995–Jan. 1996): 12.

[53] Bob Margolin, interview with author, 6 June 1995.

[54] Bob Margolin, interview with author, 6 June 1995.

[55] Margolin, 13.

[56] Bob Margolin, interview with author, 6 June 1995.

[57] Bob Margolin, interview with author, 6 June 1995.

[58] Cook, 186.

[59] Bob Margolin, interview with author, 6 June 1995.

[60] Willie Smith, interview with author, 10 Dec. 1995.

[61] Bob Margolin, interview with author, 6 June 1995.

[62] Willie Smith, interview with author, 10 Dec. 1995.

[63] Emily Tidwell, "Going Back to Where I Had Been," *Living Blues* 99 (Sept.–Oct. 1991): 20.

[64] Tidwell, 20.

[65] Tidwell, 20.

[66] Bob Margolin, interview with author, 6 June 1995.

[67] Bob Margolin, interview with author, 6 June 1995.

[68] Guralnick, 79.

[69] Kim Field, "The Resurrection of Jerry Portnoy," *Blues Revue* 18 (July–Aug. 1995): 43.

[70] Field, 43.

[71] Guy "Doc" Lerner, "Muddy Harps," *Living Blues* 99 (Sept.–Oct. 1991): 32.

[72] Jerry Portnoy, interview with author, 13 Nov. 1995.

[73] Jerry Portnoy, interview with author, 13 Nov. 1995.

[74] Jerry Portnoy, interview with author, 13 Nov. 1995.

[75] Neff and Conner, 84.

[76] Jerry Portnoy, interview with author, 13 Nov. 1995.

[77] Jerry Portnoy, interview with author, 13 Nov. 1995.

[78] Bob Margolin, interview with author, 6 June 1995.

[79] Lerner, 36.

[80] Bob Margolin, interview with author, 6 June 1995.

[81] Jerry Portnoy, interview with author, 13 Nov. 1995.

[82] Jim Litke, "TV Tribute: Blues for Muddy Waters," *Rolling Stone* 174 (21 Nov. 1974): 15.

[83] Litke, 15.

[84] Litke, 15.

[85] Koko Taylor, interview with author, 27 June 1995.

[86] Litke, 15.

[87] Litke, 15.

[88] Litke, 15.

[89] Mojo Buford, interview with author, 7 Mar. 1996.

[90] O'Neal and O'Neal, 40.

[91] Levon Helm, interview with author, 3 July 1996.

[92] Levon Helm, interview with author, 3 July 1996.

[93] Levon Helm, interview with author, 3 July 1996.

[94] Levon Helm, interview with author, 3 July 1996.

[95] Levon Helm, interview with author, 3 July 1996.

[96] Levon Helm, interview with author, 3 July 1996.

[97] Levon Helm, interview with author, 3 July 1996.

[98] Jerry Portnoy, interview with author, 13 Nov. 1995.

[99] Willie Smith, interview with author, 10 Dec. 1995.

[100] Bob Margolin, interview with author, 6 June 1995.

[101] Mark von Lehmden, "Muddy Waters' Winter of Content," *Rolling Stone* 239 (19 May 1977): 27.

[102] Radel.

1 0

What makes me happy
is to see how many kids
been influenced by me.[1]

"They've been trying to get blues to leave all of my life," said Muddy, responding to the latest slump in blues popularity. "But blues ain't goin' no where as long as somebody carries it on."[2] Muddy had weathered too many oscillations of public taste to experience a crisis of faith now; he remained optimistic about signing with another record company. The emotions portrayed through blues were universal, he reasoned. It spoke to everyone. Blues — and Muddy — would enjoy another day.

"If my records don't sell a million copies, it don't make no difference," admitted Muddy contentedly.[3] "I paid my dues, so I'm happy with it. I don't look for no hit record no more."[4] For him $15,000 to $25,000 a year was enough to ensure a comfortable lifestyle, one that kept him supplied with French champagne.

The night before his 61st birthday, Muddy was playing at Antone's in Austin, Texas, one of the foremost blues clubs in North America. As midnight approached he made an announcement from the bandstand: "This is a big time for me tonight. I'm gonna be 40 years old tonight, and I guess that makes me about the oldest young person I know of."[5] When the clock struck twelve, Margolin led the packed house in a rousing chorus of "Happy Birthday." Suddenly Junior Wells and Buddy Guy appeared onstage — flown in by Clifford Antone for the occasion — and Muddy let out a whoop of surprise, obviously delighted. They joined Muddy in an unforgettable rendition of "Got My Mojo Working." When questioned backstage about his search for a record label, Muddy seemed unconcerned, saying that he'd written some new songs in preparation for his next album. "Knowing that young people are keeping my music playing is what I'm living for today," he added. "I feel like I was put here to influence others."[6]

In Scott Cameron's quest to secure a recording contract for Muddy, he received some interest from CBS Records, although it was tempered with concern as to how to produce him. It was suggested that Blue Sky Records, which was distributed by CBS, might be a better fit. When Muddy learned that Blue Sky was the label with which Johnny Winter was associated, he felt he'd found a home. A deal was struck. "I figured that this was the greatest chance, man, of all my days," Muddy enthused, "to get with someone who's still got it, got that early '50s sound."[7]

Muddy knew that Winter was committed to old-time blues. Born on 22 February 1944 in Leland, Mississippi, Johnny was also a child of the Delta, although he was raised in Beaumont, Texas. When he discovered black radio at age 11, the blues claimed his soul. It was Delta and Chicago blues more so than the blues of Texas that influenced the young guitar player, so of course, the path he followed led invariably to Muddy. Ever since Johnny first slapped *The Best Of Muddy Waters* on his turntable, the great bluesman's style and stinging slide had enormously affected his own musical direction.

Many years later the two musicians met at the Vulcan Gas Company, an Austin, Texas, club where they both were booked. "I can't tell you how excited I was to be on the bill with Muddy Waters," Winter exclaims. "He's been my idol since I was 11 or 12, so I was there with my camera and my tape recorder."[8] So awed was he at finally meeting his hero that Johnny didn't dare ask to jam with him, but Muddy, impressed with what he'd heard, asked instead. When their paths crossed again in 1974, at the taping of the PBS *Soundstage* show, the two bluesmen knew they'd like to work together. Now under the Blue Sky label, Muddy and Johnny would finally get that chance.

Winter, the producer of all Muddy's recordings on Blue Sky, possessed the key components for the task: he understood Muddy's music and knew how it should sound, plus he had the commitment to the project to ensure it was done right. Throughout the 1960s and 1970s, marketing considerations had reshaped, redefined and revamped Muddy's albums. Johnny knew his mentor sounded better than that. He set out to capture the real Muddy Waters on disc.

"My whole thing was to make the record that Muddy wanted to make, with the musicians he wanted to work with," says Johnny. "If Muddy gets pissed off, things change. He's the boss."[9] From the outset the two principals agreed on the recording strategy. Contemporary studio technology had sanitized the sound of blues, tidied up its tatters, polished its rough edges. Now Winter's mission was to regain the primitive sound of the 1950s. To achieve that, he selected a studio in Westport, Connecticut, with a room large enough to accommodate the entire band at once. There would be few overdubs here; they were live-in-the-studio sessions. Each musician would be miked, with one large microphone in the center of the room. In this way Johnny sought to recapture the echo that had been a hallmark of early Chess cuts.

In addition to Winter, who doubled as producer and musician, the personnel backing these two sessions between 4 and 10 October 1976 were Muddy's regular sidemen — Bob Margolin, Pinetop Perkins and Willie Smith — plus special guest James Cotton, who brought along his bass player Charles Calmese. "And we didn't practice," Muddy remarked. "We just got in there, and we'd run over a song and put it down. We caught it."[10]

Keeping up with Muddy in the studio almost wore Johnny out. Muddy wouldn't consider stopping for a break. They'd run through a song once, then Winter would rush upstairs to the control room to listen to the tape. He remembers, "I was running back and forth saying to myself, 'God *damn*, Muddy, you're gonna kill me.'" The first take was generally sufficient. "That's so rare," Johnny says, "when everything's *right* the first time."[11]

The studio atmosphere was "loose and fun," according to Margolin. "But the real weird part of that record is that Muddy didn't pick up a guitar through the whole thing, for no particular reason. It was sitting there tuned up right next to him, but for the most part, he just had other people play the parts and he sang. Of course, on some of the reviews for the record they say, 'Wow, Muddy's guitar really sounds great,' but it was Johnny."[12] Most times, however, Johnny's slide can be recognized by his signature licks and his irrepressible propensity for throwing in a few extra notes.

The resulting cuts were a raucous, unconstrained celebration of Muddy and his raw, fervid blues. Winter's understanding of Muddy's music, and his devotion to it, were key factors in capturing its essence. "My sound was pretty hard to get into," said Muddy. "It's simple and there's not a lot of notes going on, but it's got a heck of a sound, man."[13] Delighted at the outcome of his collaboration with Johnny, Muddy quipped, "It made my little pee pee hard again."[14] Thus *Hard Again* became the title of the LP.

The album kicks off with a rowdy version of "Mannish Boy," then "Bus Driver," a new Muddy Waters composition, features his sumptuous vocals punctuated with sizzling solos by Johnny, Cotton and Pinetop. The potent pairing of Winter's guitar and Cotton's harp is a standout in "Jealous Hearted Man," and "The Blues Had A Baby And They Named It Rock And Roll" is an upbeat offering with all the vigor of a Saturday-night fish fry.

"I Can't Be Satisfied" is a savory morsel that Johnny almost didn't bag for *Hard Again*. At the end of the two-day session, when Muddy was preparing to leave, Johnny implored him to do a couple of acoustic numbers. Despite his initial reluctance, Muddy gave in and recut the songs from his first hit 78 — "I Can't Be Satisfied" and "I Feel Like Going Home" — accompanied by Margolin and Winter on guitar. The metallic ring of Johnny's steel-bodied National guitar gives these tracks the flavor of old-time, juke-joint blues. The sound here is grittier and cruder than Muddy's original recordings of them 28 years earlier. Although they suffer somewhat in comparison with their predecessors, the later versions are still very satisfying blues ("I Can't Be Satisfied" more so than "I Feel Like Going Home"). Unfortunately, Muddy would only play one take of each, concerned that extra tapes would end up on bootleg discs from which he'd see no royalties.

Muddy believed that *The Best Of Muddy Waters*, his 1958 Chess LP, and *Hard Again* were the two best albums of his career. He was also pleased that CBS, Blue Sky's parent corporation, was willing to spend money to promote the release, demonstrating a commitment he claimed Chess had let slide in recent years. "That makes me feel right, right," commented Muddy on the marketing of his album. "They make me feel like somebody is thinkin' about me."[15]

The celebrated photographer Richard Avedon was commissioned to take the album-cover shot of Muddy. Upon arriving at Avedon's studio, Muddy began to peel off his coat. Avedon asked him to keep it on, and had captured the photo he was after in short order. In it Muddy looks dapper and lovable in his camel coat and homburg. "He's a killer at takin' pictures," Muddy said of Avedon. "They had one of them coffee-makers there. You know the kind that make it in a minute. Well, before they could get the pot made, he done took my picture."[16]

It wasn't only Muddy's record company that was excited about the bluesman's latest offering. Sales figures climbed beyond any he'd achieved at Chess. In 1977 Muddy won the *Rolling Stone* Critics Award for *Hard Again*, and the same album earned him a nomination for a Grammy Award in the category of Best Ethnic or Traditional Recording. On 23 February 1978, Muddy defeated a distinguished roster of nominees — Junior Wells, Otis Rush, Joe Turner and Willie Dixon — to win his fourth Grammy. And in recognition of his lifetime contribution to blues and popular music, Muddy was inducted into the Rock and Roll Hall of Fame at a banquet held at New York's Waldorf-Astoria Hotel on 21 January 1977.

The Band, in the meantime, had run its course and Robbie Robertson, Levon Helm, Garth Hudson, Richard Manuel and Rick Danko decided to wrap up operations with a celebratory bash entitled "The Last Waltz." The coup de grace was held on Thanksgiving Day, 25 November 1976, and included performers who'd influenced the group in its varied musical odyssey. Anybody who was anybody was there, and the guest list included Muddy. "That started off to be the main thing to, you know, present as many of the heroes as we could," Helm explains. "Muddy knew early on that we certainly wanted him to be in the show with us."[17]

With a lineup that encompassed Bob Dylan, Eric Clapton, Neil Diamond, Van Morrison, Joni Mitchell, Neil Young, Emmylou Harris, Ringo Starr, Ron Wood and more, the musical bases were covered. With a subsequent album release and movie, directed by Martin Scorsese, the event was a rock happening. For Muddy it meant instant exposure to worldwide audiences of every popular-music genre. For The Band it was a way to pay tribute to an icon, to acknowledge Muddy as a wellspring for contemporary music.

When Muddy strode onstage at San Francisco's Winterland Arena for "The Last Waltz," he separated the man from the boys. He looked every bit the elder statesman, dignified in a classic gray suit, a narrow moustache hugging the top of his upper lip, his age apparent with his double chin and balding crown. If there'd ever been doubts about his right to be there, he dispelled them with his rendition of "Mannish Boy." Accompanied by The Band, Paul Butterfield, Bob Margolin and Pinetop Perkins, Muddy proclaimed his manhood before 5,000 believers. Singing from a place so deep it reverberated throughout his body, he wagged his finger at the crowd and shook his head as he delved down to his soul. As he declared he was "full-grown," Muddy stretched up to his full height, waved his hands as though he were wringing every drop of feeling from the atmosphere, then bounced up and down as he brought the song to a rapturous close. Robbie Robertson announced the obvious: "Wasn't that a *man*, Muddy Waters!"[18]

Helm would like to have seen more of Muddy's performance included in the Scorsese film: "I'm kinda disappointed because of the shortness of time that the camera is on Muddy. I could have personally took another song or two [of Muddy's] myself; a couple or three songs wouldn't have been too much for me."[19] Nevertheless, it was a privilege for these esteemed performers to share their stage with Muddy. "He was just a master musician," Helm comments.[20] According to Levon, there was only one downside to performing with Muddy: "When you did get to play with Muddy, it was a short ride, right. You know, you were so into it . . . that it was over way too quick."[21]

Sometime later when Levon was in Chicago, he called Muddy at home:

He invited me [to his house] and fed me a good home-cooked dinner. Muddy understood, Muddy was a musician himself and knew that when he could put one of them corn-bread dinners on you, he had done you a good favor. . . . I carried us two big bottles of [champagne], and we sat in the shade and just relaxed, and I hung with him as much as I could until I knew it was time to get back on the road. But I got to . . . hang out with him for a couple of hours. I sure did enjoy it. I almost got to introduce him to Jane Fonda, too. We were in Chicago working on a show and that was going to be fun. They wanted to meet each other. . . .

Muddy was a gentleman's gentleman when I did get to be around him. He was just always one of the best dressed, best acting, best talking, you know, best laughing people there. Muddy was a gent.[22]

Following an autumn 1976 tour of Europe, Muddy set off to promote *Hard Again* throughout North America in March 1977. With him on the road were Johnny Winter, James Cotton, Charles Calmese, Bob Margolin, Willie Smith and Pinetop Perkins. Calvin Jones and Jerry Portnoy were temporarily laid off and paid small retainers for the interim.

Winter, Cotton and the rest of the band played for the first half of each gig, then Muddy took charge after the intermission. "He'd usually just pick a couple of songs a night and play some really burning leads on that," Winter says of Muddy's guitar work during the tour, "but he didn't seem to want to play all the time like he used to."[23] Still, that coupled with his powerhouse vocals was more than enough to satisfy. Critics raved and audiences roared their approval. At New York's Palladium, Muddy was given four standing ovations in one night.

Muddy's red Telecaster continued to be his performance guitar, although after Billy Gibbons of ZZ Top presented him with a custom-made instrument, he would bring the new guitar out for a song or two just to show it off. His amp of choice was a mid-'60s Fender Super Reverb. "Even if I forgot my guitar and had to borrow one, I could make the sound come out of that amplifier," Muddy claimed.[24] "After it was stolen," says Margolin, "he replaced it with a stock late-'70s Super Reverb that sounded just the same. He ran his amps with all the knobs set on '9' and no reverb or tremolo, controlling his volume from the guitar."[25]

The action still seemed impossibly high on Muddy's guitar. He now used medium-weight Gibson strings, ranging from .012 to .056, substituting the wound third string with a plain .022-gauge. As it would have been inconvenient to retune several times a set, he generally played in regular tuning or clamped a capo across the fretboard to set up the guitar in whatever other key he desired. Unfortunately, Muddy rarely played in the open tunings he'd utilized earlier in his career. "It's tough if you're waiting in between songs to tune to G or A. And I'm too lazy to carry two or three guitars around like Johnny," laughed Muddy.[26]

As he'd done since his early days in Chicago, Muddy played with a metal slide on his little finger and a thumbpick, although he'd switched from a metal to a plastic plectrum. Muddy's slide was unusually short, as he generally slid along one string at a time, or two at the most. It had become rare for him to fingerpick a solo. He could do it; he just chose to leave the finger-style guitar work to his supporting musicians.

"People don't realize that he was a monster that just couldn't be messed with on the guitar. I never heard anybody play better," says Margolin, referring to the fact that Muddy's guitar virtuosity tended to be overshadowed by his colossal contribution to music, as well as his songwriting skill and blockbuster voice.[27] His mastery of the instrument continued to surprise Bob throughout the seven years they worked together: "You know, he'd throw out some little hot lick and look around to see if I'd caught it. . . . Some of 'em were subtle, but in a lot of ways they were all spectacular musicianship."[28]

Muddy, however, still insisted that others had more technical skill: "I'm no hell of a guitar player, not the best guitar walkin' around the streets, but one thing I have tried is to make the guitar sound like my voice." In addition, Muddy possessed an unerring sense of how to put it all together, how to emanate the deepest feelings in one's soul through his guitar. "That one note of mine will say something that the other guy can't say. The tone that I lay in there, the other guy can't get it out with 12 notes."[29] He still called on the essence of the Delta for his brand of Chicago blues. And he had to strive relentlessly to bring his band down to his level of deep blues; he claimed that without his leadership, their sound would drift into something else.

A year after his triumphant Blue Sky sessions, Muddy returned with Johnny Winter to the Westport, Connecticut, studio. This time he included two esteemed guests from the past — Big Walter Horton and Jimmy Rogers, who'd ended his musical retirement in 1971. "I'd like to take some credit on that one, because getting those guys in there was an idea I had that I was able to help make happen," Margolin reveals.

I guess it would have been in about April of '77. We were getting ready to record the next album. We had just done a tour for the *Hard Again* stuff, and we were off the road a little bit. Jimmy Rogers played in, I guess, Rhode Island or something, which is not too far from Boston. I went down to see him, and I told him I was going to be talking to Muddy on the phone the next day, and I asked Jimmy if there was anything he wanted me to tell him, and he said, "Well, just tell him anytime he wants to get together and play those old blues like we used to, I'd really like to do that again sometime." That just sent shivers down my back because Muddy and Jimmy playing together was something really special, and it hadn't happened really since the '50s.

And I gave Muddy that message and he said, "Well, maybe we could put him on the next record or something like that," kind of casually. . . . I got excited about it 'cause it seemed like there was no reason not for them to have a little reunion. And I told Johnny Winter right away, and he took it from there and made it happen. Since we were doing that, we thought it would be cool to get Big Walter in there too as one of the last of the old school. It did work out real, real well. It was successful musically and was wonderful to get to see them play together.[30]

The music that came out of these sessions — recorded between 31 October and 5 November 1977 — was more polished and intricate than that of *Hard Again*. Pinetop manned the piano, Willie was on drums, Bob switched to bass — relinquishing his usual place to Jimmy Rogers and Johnny Winter — and Jerry shared harp duty with Big Walter. "It was great fun to do that," remembers

Portnoy, "because it's always great to play with Jimmy, who played so wonderfully with the harmonica. And of course Big Walter was a great friend of mine, and I learned a lot from him. It was actually a terrific thing to be able to do the record with those guys, and especially with Big Walter."[31] In an unusual treat, the two harmonica dynamos trade licks on "I'm Ready" and on "I'm Your Hoochie Coochie Man," a slightly revised arrangement of Muddy's original.

Having decided against playing guitar on the *Hard Again* sessions, Muddy now served up some searing slide on "33 Years," "Mamie" and one of his favorites, "Screamin' And Cryin'," in which he plays a tasty chorus with Big Walter. Johnny, Walter and Muddy swap solos in "Who Do You Trust," which features a rare sample of Muddy's finger-style guitar. "I remember [Muddy] saying, 'Well, even an old man probably can outplay me, but I got something that works,'" Winter recalls. "He knew what he did was cool, but it wasn't about technique. He just had a way of putting it all together."[32]

This second Blue Sky album, entitled *I'm Ready*, was yet another success for the team of Waters and Winter, and Muddy set out on tour again. On 27 September 1978, he was honored in a Chicago ceremony with the Governor's Award for the Arts. *I'm Ready* earned him his fifth Grammy Award on 15 February 1979 in the category of Best Ethnic or Traditional Recording (the same year the Grammys saw the Bee Gees sweep the awards with *Saturday Night Fever*). "When you win something like that," said Muddy, reflecting on his Grammy successes, "every time you win you be proud. There's a lot of people out there and you came in first place. That's something to think about." Yet Muddy's greater concern — about the future of blues — prevailed. "Listen," he exclaimed, "somebody new better get out there and start singin' blues or I'm goin' to win them all. . . . I'll need a new house for my Grammys."[33]

Throughout 1978 the Muddy Waters Blues Band crisscrossed the United States. "I love the road," Muddy proclaimed. "People all over the world say, 'Who is this Muddy Waters?' and as long as I feel good and stay healthy, I'm going to keep out there and give 'em a look."[34] Although his fans always screamed out for more, Muddy limited his playing time to 45 or 50 minutes per night, following an opening set by his band. "I'm trying to protect this one body," he explained. "The kids be hollerin' for more all night, but if I did in a coupla weeks I be lyin' on my back in a bed somewhere."[35] In the summers he still took Renee and Joseph with him on tour dates close to home. When it came time to close the show, he'd bring them out to join him in singing "Got My Mojo Working." "It was exciting," his son says, still savoring the memory, "especially at that age going onstage like that."[36]

Muddy was resolute in his opposition to hard drugs, perhaps in reaction to witnessing the self-destruction of his daughter Isoline or from seeing too many young musicians lose their way. "Muddy was really very, very much against cocaine," Margolin states. "He didn't use it himself and thought it was a very destructive thing. On the other hand, you know, he loved reefer himself, and he loved to drink."[37] He was never far from a bottle of champagne. Patrick Day, a young harmonica player who was taking lessons from Portnoy, remembers Muddy referring to his favorite libation as "payne." One night Day was backstage with Muddy and several journalists at the Cellar Door in Washington, D.C. The band was onstage playing its set, when Muddy realized he was about to go on. Suddenly he announced, "I need my payne. Where's my payne?" and left the room. The journalists looked at each other, then started writing furiously, assuming they'd just observed the great man delving for inspiration with which to play the blues.[38]

Despite his age, Muddy continued to appreciate young ladies and pursue them whenever he could. "When there was an opportunity for Muddy to go to bed with an older woman," Margolin divulges, "he had a formula whereby if their ages added up to more than a hundred, then she was too old, 'cause apparently more than a hundred years in the bed was too many years."[39] According to Portnoy, Muddy also devised another rule for dealing with his sexual escapades: "He told me that if I was ever cheating on my woman, never to admit it, even if you're caught in the act."[40]

On 9 August 1978, the man from a sharecropper's shack on Stovall made it all the way to the lofty heights of the White House. While he was in town for a week-long gig at Washington's Cellar Door, arrangements were made for Muddy and the band to appear at the annual White House staff picnic. "*They* wanted *me* and *my* band," Muddy stated proudly, incredulous at the great honor. "From where I'm from a black man couldn't even get inside a white man's front room."[41] A driver with a White House van and two Secret

Service agents were dispatched to pick up the musicians and their equipment. When Muddy and the band arrived at the White House, they were given a private tour.

A stage had been erected on the south lawn, and from it President Jimmy Carter introduced Muddy to the 700 assembled staff members: "As you know, Muddy Waters is one of the great performers of all time. He's won more awards than I could name. His music is well known around the world, comes from a good part of the country, and represents accurately the background and history of the American people."[42] In the baking summer sun, the band delivered a torrid 40-minute set of blues. Even at this historic gig, Muddy highlighted his sidemen, giving Portnoy the opportunity to perform "Scratch My Back." Afterwards the President and Rosalyn Carter chatted with Muddy and the band as they were served hamburgers and lemonade. Muddy savored the memory: "To think I got a chance to walk in the White House and then out on the lawn, play for the President and afterwards, shake hands with him and his wife."[43]

"I think there were a lot of those moments for Muddy," says Jerry, referring to the recognition that was now embracing the great bluesman.

I think the awareness of his so-called humble origins never left him, and he found a lot of moments like that later on in his life. One of my favorite things that Muddy said, I remember he was being interviewed by some journalist, and the fellow asked him, "At this point in your life, Muddy, you're doing pretty well. You probably got some money in the bank, you got a nice house out in the suburbs, you're driving a big Lincoln Town Car." He said, "Can you still play the blues with that old feeling?" I'll never forget, Muddy looked at the guy and said, "Man, I got me a *long* memory."[44]

Other recollections, those of his early influence Robert Johnson, were brought to mind later that August. At a gig at Pall's Mall in Boston, a woman named Anne Anderson asked Bob Margolin to introduce her to Muddy. She was Johnson's younger sister and was curious if Muddy had known her brother in Mississippi. "Muddy went nuts," says Bob. He told her that Johnson and Son House had been his main sources of inspiration. In the next set, Muddy introduced Anne to the audience and serenaded her with some of her brother's own songs.[45]

Also in 1978 the Rolling Stones dropped by unexpectedly to jam with Muddy and Willie Dixon at Muddy's regular club date at the Quiet Knight in Chicago. "It was pretty exciting for me, getting to be around those guys and play with them," Margolin confides. "When they came in, somehow the place got about five times as crowded. I don't know how the word gets out, but it does. . . . They were all there except for Bill Wyman, who was sick that night."[46] As pleased as he was to see old friends, Muddy was never impressed by superstar status. In fact, it was the other way around. "I used to do . . . sit-in gigs with Muddy Waters," Mick Jagger relates, "and I was a little bit in awe of Muddy Waters at that point."[47]

When Eric Clapton first heard *The Best Of Muddy Waters* at a meeting of the *Blues Unlimited* record club, the teenager was rocked by an impact that would reverberate throughout the rest of his life. "I couldn't believe it," Clapton remarks. "It changed everything."[48] Robert Johnson's music had first motivated young Clapton to try his hand at Spanish guitar, but he abandoned it after a year and a half. Now Muddy's blues convinced him to try again, this time on electric. Clapton had found his instrument; with it he'd reap the fruit of great bluesmen and hack his own trail through unexplored musical terrain. It was the subtlety of Muddy's guitar playing that he responded to. Muddy wasn't flashy or fast; he was simply the deepest. "He was the first that really got to me," Clapton says of Muddy's influence, "and his is still the most important music in my life."[49]

Although Clapton had played a session with Muddy and Otis Spann in London in 1964 and appeared with Muddy at "The Last Waltz," Muddy had no recollection of who this rock icon was. Bob Margolin remembers Muddy's announcement to the band in November 1978: " 'Oh, something new just came up. I'm sorry there's not much notice on this, but we're going overseas next week to open up a tour for some rock guys.' And I said, 'Well, who is it?' And he says, 'One of those people who was at "The Last Waltz," but I can't remember who.' So I mentioned a bunch of names, and when I got to Eric Clapton, he said, 'Yeah, that's it.' But he didn't know who Eric was."[50]

The tour got underway in Lyons, France, with a mediocre opening-night performance by Clapton and an incendiary set by Muddy the following evening. Bob describes Clapton as "shaken by the power of Muddy's performance. He told me, 'I was thinking about getting Paul Butterfield to open the shows, and I could deal with that, but how do I follow this?'"[51] Margolin advised him not to try to beat the master at his own game. Clapton regrouped and went on to deliver strong performances for the rest of the tour. Early in their travels, Muddy asked Bob about this rock phenomenon, and Margolin explained Clapton's roots in the blues. Curious, Muddy stuck around to hear Clapton play one night and was impressed with his version of Big Maceo Merriweather's "Worried Life Blues"; he was especially delighted with one of Eric's turnarounds in "Early One Morning," a signature lick he'd borrowed from Muddy.

Yet again, Muddy's music had furnished the catapult to launch a superstar's career. The master was opening for the apostle. "That's just the way the world works, and Muddy understood that," Jerry Portnoy explains. "If Eric Clapton or the Rolling Stones or anybody else you want to name could help get his music out to a wider audience than he was reaching, then as far as he was concerned, they were doing him a great service. I don't think he had any of that sense that 'I should be the headliner' or 'I should be making the money he is' or anything like that. I think that he was glad that those guys had enough respect for him to pay him his propers and to help when they could to expose him and his music to the audiences."[52]

Muddy had a half-hour set on the Clapton tour. The band would begin with an instrumental, then Muddy came on with "Hoochie Coochie Man," "Baby Please Don't Go" and a slow blues, finishing off with "Got My Mojo Working" and "Mannish Boy." The response was phenomenal; even the young teens who'd come out solely to hear Clapton perform his latest hits were elated.

Before long Eric and Muddy were fast friends. Muddy sensed that Clapton was wrestling to define his identity amid the seductions and distractions of commercial success. "He always kept an eye on me," recalls Eric, "and put me in my place if he thought I was slipping in the wrong direction or not really paying attention." Clapton likens Muddy to a Buddha-type figure, a tranquil patriarch who would encourage those with promise. "I felt so much love for him," he says. "I felt like he was my father and I was his adopted son. It was honor bound."[53]

In 1979 a dazzling tribute to Muddy's greatness was released in the form of his third Blue Sky album, *Muddy "Mississippi" Waters Live*. A compilation of two concert recordings — at Detroit's Masonic Temple on 18 March 1977 and at Harry Hope's Club in Chicago on 27 August the following year — the LP is testament that this 63-year-old was still a ferocious force in blues. Opening with the raunchy vitality of "Mannish Boy," played to a frenzied crowd, Muddy's devastating slide then delivers the goods in "She's Nineteen Years Old." Cotton and Pinetop are superb on the Sonny Boy Williamson standard "Nine Below Zero," and in "Streamline Woman" and "Howling Wolf," Muddy plumbs the depths of blues with his down-and-dirty guitar. Portnoy's harp and Winter's guitar are exquisite in a rousing version of Big Joe Williams's "Baby Please Don't Go," and "Deep Down In Florida" features Johnny's knockout slide. Muddy's vocals seethe with emotion throughout; his gut-wrenching blues have never been better, as he drives the audience to near delirium.

"Since *Hard Again*, I've been goin' up the ladder. Up, up, up I go," remarked Muddy with obvious pride.[54] On 27 February 1980, yet another Grammy Award was bestowed upon him for *Muddy "Mississippi" Waters Live*. It was his sixth Grammy, his third in a row.

In spring 1979 Clapton engaged the Muddy Waters Blues Band for his 47-city North American tour, slated to begin on 28 March. When they hit Minneapolis, Muddy's erstwhile guitar player Pat Hare arranged an escorted leave from prison to surprise his former bandleader backstage. Without the influence of alcohol, Hare was a model prisoner and had initiated a musical program for inmates. His health was poor, however; in 1975 he was diagnosed with lung cancer and two years later he learned he had cancer of the throat. After undergoing surgery to remove part of a lung, a portion of his jaw and the muscles on one side of his neck and underneath his tongue, he had been transferred to a minimum-security ward and was permitted to perform outside prison under supervision.

Muddy invited Pat onstage for the encore of his set, and borrowing Margolin's guitar, Hare joined the band in "Got My Mojo Working." It would be the last time he'd perform with Muddy. His plans to sit in with Muddy for a Minneapolis gig the following year were thwarted by the recurrence of his lung cancer. Hare died in St. Paul's Ramsey Hospital on 26 September 1980, one day after learning he was to receive a medical pardon.

"I tell you Muddy really got up for those shows," says Jerry, reminiscing about the Clapton tour. "He really took them seriously, and he really turned on the juice for them. He'd go out there in front of a few thousand people . . . and he'd show them why he was Muddy Waters. I'll tell you we got a phenomenal, phenomenal response on both the European tour and especially the U.S. tour that we did in '79."[55] Often Clapton would call Muddy and Portnoy onstage to join him at the conclusion of his performance.

Betrothal was in the air, and it was contagious. Eric took the first walk down the aisle in March, marrying his longtime love, Pattie Harrison, former wife of George Harrison. Then on 5 June 1979, during a hiatus from the tour, 64-year-old Muddy Waters tied the nuptial knot for the fourth time. For the bride, Marva Jean Brooks, the occasion was a double celebration — it was also her 25th birthday.

A stopover in Gainesville, Florida, the previous year had proven especially fortuitous for Muddy. That afternoon he had met his future wife, an attractive young woman from nearby Newberry who was employed as a maid at the hotel where the band was staying. Bob Margolin had been out running an errand for Muddy, "and when I came to his room, he was sitting in bed in a fancy bathrobe and there was three or four of the maids just sitting around him on the bed, and the room was kind of semidark, and as my eyes were getting adjusted to the darkness . . . he said about Marva, 'Don't look at this one. I'm gonna marry this one.' "[56]

The wedding ceremony was held at Muddy's Westmont home, and guests included his immediate family, his oldest friend Andrew Bolden, Scott Cameron and his wife Jean, Eric and Pattie Clapton and Eric's manager Roger Forrester. Word of Clapton's presence at the Morganfield home got out, and a steady stream of Joseph's awestruck teenaged friends stopped by to catch a glimpse of their hero.

The 39-year age gap between himself and his wife didn't trouble Muddy; he was proud of it. Marva found him to be the most generous and loving person she'd ever known. While Joseph admits that Marva was "like a trophy" for Muddy, he hastens to add that

Muddy "really loved her. . . . She made him happy, so that made us happy."[57] Joseph and Renee continued to live with the newlyweds in Westmont.

One of the highlights of the second leg of Clapton's North American tour occurred a few nights later on 12 June at the Chicago Stadium. Although many in the crowd weren't familiar with blues, Muddy's status as a legend had created an aura of excitement. When the senior statesman of popular music stepped onstage, the audience offered him a tumultuous greeting. Then Johnny Winter surprised the crowd by joining Muddy for "Mannish Boy." Muddy rose from his stool and prowled the stage as he "pulled the lyrics from his throat and forcefully pushed them over the audience, raw edges intact, power unalloyed." A reporter for the *Chicago Sun-Times* observed, "Waters not only captivated the crowd, he captured them."[58] With thousands of lit matches, the audience enticed Muddy to return for an encore, and he called on another unexpected guest, Willie Dixon, and then Clapton, to lend a hand on "Got My Mojo Working," as he energetically bopped around the stage. It was a stunning 45-minute tour de force — and a tough act for Eric to follow. At the end of his show, Clapton invited Muddy and Johnny onstage for the finale.

Muddy luxuriated in the accolades now generously bestowed upon him. "I paid my dues, thank God," he declared, "and I'm so thankful that I lived long enough to understand it, you know, and got a little payback for some things that I did."[59] While Muddy's earning power was far surpassed by that of the rock stars he'd influenced, he was content to be making a good living and rationalized, "I may enjoy my little dollars better than they do their big ones."[60] He also relished the satisfaction derived from his contribution to the development of blues and later forms of popular music. "I did good for the music field, you know," he proclaimed. "I feel good with that, man."[61] But on another occasion, Muddy wistfully looked back to what might have been: "I'm sorry the world didn't know me before they did. . . . They could have come around a lot earlier, you know. When I was younger and could put out more."[62]

Yet despite his years, Muddy could still deliver the goods. He intoxicated a capacity audience in Mexico City in November 1979 and thrilled concertgoers the following year in Tokyo, Nagoya and Osaka on his first tour of Japan. After recording a Miller Beer jingle for a nationally televised ad, Muddy returned to the studio in May 1980 to cut another album with Johnny Winter. Although it's the weakest of his Blue Sky recordings, the disc, entitled *King Bee*, is still a worthwhile offering. Muddy brought to the sessions a number of original compositions never previously recorded: the plaintive "Too Young To Know," "Forever Lonely," the provocative "Champagne And Reefer" and a song he co-wrote with his stepson Charles Williams, "No Escape From The Blues." "(My Eyes) Keep Me In Trouble" and "I Feel Like Going Home" were taken from the October 1976 sessions that produced *Hard Again*.

Jerry Portnoy believes that an overabundance of musicians in the studio was *King Bee*'s chief shortcoming. "Muddy's best stuff, as far as I'm concerned, was done with a small band where there was a lot of space and you could communicate musically much easier. The more pieces you have on a recording, the more the music has to be arranged, so that the music dovetails. I think his best stuff was done with two guitars, a drum and a harp. Now this particular record had four guitars, drums, bass, piano and harp, and I thought it was too much."[63]

"[*King Bee*] didn't really come out very good," Margolin admits, "and it took a long time doctoring it up and going back and getting out-takes from other albums before they put that out. . . . That was by far the worst of that batch of albums for the Blue Sky ones. It was the only one that didn't win a Grammy. . . . I was surprised it came out at all."[64] Winter concedes that *King Bee* had its weaknesses, but because Muddy refused to play extra takes of each song, Johnny was left with little to work with. "If we would have had a few extra things to choose from," he says, "it definitely could have been better."[65] It was a pity. This would be Muddy's last studio session.

King Bee was not released until 1981. When asked to comment on what made the record unique, Muddy replied frankly: "It's the same thing. What the hell can I do? The only thing else I can do for an album is play rock 'n' roll or play disco, and that's really another thing."[66]

Paul Oscher, Muddy's harmonica player from 1967 to 1971, noticed a significant change in his former bandleader at about this time. "I think that when he got older, he was much more open," remarks Oscher. "Muddy was [now] more outspoken and more sure of what he liked or what he didn't like. There's a big difference between the Muddy Waters that I knew when I was playing in the band and, let's say, the Muddy Waters from like around 1980, after having received all these accolades and Johnny Winter and all that stuff. You know, it was a different Muddy."[67]

Paul cites Muddy's car accident as the catalyst that began the change, followed by his shift, both professional and personal, into the white world. In interviews, for example, he now knew the standard blues rap that music journalists expected to hear, so he obligingly delivered it. "I think there were changes in the intensity of the music," Oscher continues. "Changes for performing to a different audience, like this song, 'Champagne And Reefer' — just a different approach to the audience that was slightly different."[68] Oscher hastens to add, however, that Muddy's blues remained as deep.

Perhaps that's because, as Bob Margolin believes, a profound sadness continued to tug at Muddy's psyche, despite his fame and good fortune. Margolin maintains that Muddy's first hit, "I Can't Be Satisfied," aptly characterized the bluesman, although the fact that he was troubled was rarely apparent, even to his band mates. Bob remembers one evening after a gig when Muddy was obviously depressed and had had more to drink than usual. Driving back to the hotel with Bob and Luther Johnson, Muddy unburdened his soul. "With Luther and me, his caring friends, he ran down a long list of problems with his health, personal life, and business that were really weighing on him," Margolin relates. "It was heartbreaking to see Muddy so down, and to know that all of his success and greatness, and the world's love couldn't comfort him."[69]

By 1980 Muddy's health had become an issue. "He was beginning to have illnesses that would keep him off the road," Bob recalls, "stomach blockages and pneumonia, things like that, which would cause him to have to cancel gigs. And we weren't working quite as intensely, which was kind of rough on the people in the band, because if we didn't work, we just didn't make any money, and that was it."[70] Willie Smith has another take on the situation: "As far as the band was concerned, the management wasn't right. . . . It was just the little b.s. that was going on in between, that's what it was. . . . Not only that, some things that went down that I wasn't happy with. . . . That didn't have nothing to do with Muddy, but we kinda blamed Muddy for not, at that time, for not speaking up, I'll put it that way."[71]

That June Muddy's entire band left him en masse. The split was the result of a dispute with Muddy's management and not, they all emphasize, with Muddy personally. Nevertheless, it hurt Muddy deeply. Bob struck off on his own to become a bandleader; the rest of the musicians formed the Legendary Blues Band and shortly afterwards signed a deal with Rounder Records. "We never did stop speaking," says Willie, commenting on the band's relationship with Muddy after the breakup. "It wasn't nothing personal or nothing like that. We were still the same about one another as we always had been."[72] Jerry recalls that "while [Muddy] wasn't happy about it, and it was a little touchy for a bit, when we went on to prove we had the goods to make it on our own, he took — as I knew he would — he took great pride in that."[73]

For those who played with Muddy, that's the tag that will always lead off their musical credentials. "I'm real proud of it," Margolin says of his association with Muddy. "It was a wonderful experience and I keep it with me inside. And it comes out, I hope, in the music."[74] Portnoy knows that no matter what else he accomplishes in his career, "when they lay me in the ground, the first line in the obituary is going to be, 'Jerry Portnoy, one-time harmonica player for the Muddy Waters Blues Band, blah, blah, blah.' Muddy put me on the map."[75]

NOTES

[1] Don DeMichael, "Father and Son: An Interview with Muddy Waters and Paul Butterfield," *Downbeat*, vol. 36, no. 16 (7 Aug. 1969): 12.

[2] Cliff Radel, "Muddy Waters Is the Blues," *Cincinnati Enquirer*, 6 July 1976.

[3] Radel.

[4] Jim O'Neal and Amy O'Neal, "Muddy," *Living Blues* 64 (Mar.–Apr. 1985): 35.

[5] *Rolling Stone* 213 (20 May 1976): 28-30.

[6] *Rolling Stone* 213 (20 May 1976): 30.

[7] Charles Shaar Murray, "The Blues Had a Baby and They Called It Rock 'n' Roll," *New Musical Express* (30 Apr. 1977): 30.

[8] Tom Wheeler, "Muddy Waters & Johnny Winter," *Blues Guitar: The Men Who Made the Music: From the Pages of Guitar Player Magazine*, ed. Jas Obrecht (San Francisco: GPI Books, 1990), 70.

[9] Wheeler, 72.

[10] Wheeler, 72.

[11] Obrecht, "Mudslide," *Guitar Player* (Nov. 1992): 60.

[12] Bob Margolin, interview with author, 6 June 1995.

[13] Jas Obrecht, "The Life and Times of the Hoochie Coochie Man," *Guitar Player* (Mar. 1994): 72.

[14] Peter Guralnick, "Muddy Waters (1915–1983), *Living Blues* 57 (Autumn 1983): 54.

[15] Cliff Radel, "The Blues Are Nothing to Mess Around With," *Cincinnati Enquirer*, 3 June 1979, p. 4.

[16] Radel, "Nothing to Mess Around With," 4.

[17] Levon Helm, interview with author, 3 July 1996.

[18] *The Last Waltz*, film.

[19] Levon Helm, interview with author, 3 July 1996.

[20] Levon Helm, interview with author, 3 July 1996.

[21] Levon Helm, interview with author, 3 July 1996.

[22] Levon Helm, interview with author, 3 July 1996.

[23] Obrecht, "Mudslide," 60.

[24] Art Thompson with Dan Forte, "Smokestack Lightnin'," *Guitar Player* (Aug. 1992): 102.

[25] Jas Obrecht, "Muddy Waters: The Life & Times of the Hoochie Coochie Man," *Blues Revue* 20 (Dec. 1995–Jan. 1996): 37.

[26] Wheeler, 76.

[27] Tut Underwood, "Bob Margolin: Remembering Muddy Waters," *Living Blues* 99 (Sept.–Oct. 1991): 22.

[28] Underwood, 22.

[29] Wheeler, 75.

[30] Bob Margolin, interview with author, 6 June 1995.

[31] Jerry Portnoy, interview with author, 13 Nov. 1995.

[32] Obrecht, "Life and Times," 72.

[33] Radel, "Nothing to Mess Around With," 4.

[34] Chip Lovitt, "Muddy Waters: The Real Blues Brother," *Senior Scholastic* (5 Apr. 1979): 34.

[35] Murray, 30.

[36] Joseph Morganfield, interview with author, 19 Aug. 1995.

[37] Bob Margolin, interview with author, 6 June 1995.

[38] Patrick Day, interview with author, 17 July 1995.

[39] Bob Margolin, interview with author, 6 June 1995.

[40] Jerry Portnoy, interview with author, 13 Nov. 1995.

[41] Radel, "Nothing to Mess Around With," 4.

[42] Obrecht, "Life and Times," 72.

[43] Radel, "Nothing to Mess Around With," 4.

[44] Jerry Portnoy, interview with author, 13 Nov. 1995.

[45] Bob Margolin, "Blues Fans," *Blues Revue* 15 (Winter 1994): 12

[46] Bob Margolin, interview with author, 6 June 1995.

[47] *Sweet Home Chicago*, film, MCA Records – Initial Film and Television (Chicago) – Vanguard Films, 1993.

[48] Robert Palmer, "Muddy Waters: 1915-1983," *Rolling Stone* 398 (23 June 1983): 40.

[49] *TV Guide* (6 May 1995): 3.

[50] Bob Margolin, interview with author, 6 June 1995.

[51] Bob Margolin, "Clapton's Blues," *Blues Revue* 16 (Mar.–Apr. 1995): 10

[52] Jerry Portnoy, interview with author, 13 Nov. 1995.

[53] Palmer, 40.

[54] Radel, "Nothing to Mess Around With," 4.

[55] Jerry Portnoy, interview with author, 13 Nov. 1995.

[56] Bob Margolin, interview with author, 6 June 1995.

[57] Joseph Morganfield, interview with author, 19 Aug. 1995.

[58] *Chicago Sun-Times*, 14 June 1979, p. 90.

[59] O'Neal and O'Neal, 40.

[60] Radel, "Waters Is the Blues."

[61] O'Neal and O'Neal, 40.

[62] Peter Guralnick, "Muddy Waters, 1915–1983," *The Boston Phoenix*, 10 May 1983, sec. 3, p. 12.

[63] Jerry Portnoy, interview with author, 13 Nov. 1995.

[64] Bob Margolin, interview with author, 6 June 1995.

[65] Obrecht, "Mudslide," 62.

[66] Dave Haynes, "Life's Good But Muddy Waters Still Has the Blues," *Winnipeg Free Press*, 22 Aug. 1981, p. 29.

[67] Paul Oscher, interview with author, 18 May 1996.

[68] Paul Oscher, interview with author, 18 May 1996.

[69] Bob Margolin, "I Can't Be Satisfied," *Blues Revue* 20 (Jan. 1995–Dec. 1996): 14.

[70] Bob Margolin, interview with author, 6 June 1995.

[71] Willie Smith, interview with author, 10 Dec. 1995.

[72] Willie Smith, interview with author, 10 Dec. 1995.

[73] Jerry Portnoy, interview with author, 13 Nov. 1995.

[74] Underwood, 23.

[75] Kim Field, "The Resurrection of Jerry Portnoy," *Blues Revue* 18 (July–Aug. 1995): 44.

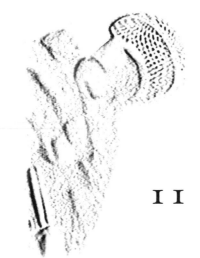

I I

*I don't mind being
called a legend, as long
as it's a living legend.
I don't want to go yet.*[1]

Some 65-year-olds settle into their slippers, snuggle in a deep armchair and resign themselves to a sedate retirement; Muddy wanted none of that. This senior citizen relished the road, wielding his Telecaster and belting out the blues. What he sought for his golden years was more of the same. His acclaim was hard won, but he reveled in its fruits: the acknowledgment of his contribution, increased paychecks and eager young musicians paying homage to their icon. "I'll tell you the truth: This is the best point of my life that I'm livin' right now," Muddy confessed. "I'm glad it came before I died, I can tell you. Feels great."[2]

Although he'd been stranded without a band, fortuity arose in the personage of Mojo Buford, Muddy's recurrent harmonica player. Mojo was back in Chicago and once again he signed on with Muddy, helping him form a new group in short order. John Primer, a native of Camden, Mississippi, who'd been playing with Junior Wells, joined Muddy on guitar. Fellow Mississippian Lee Thomas "Earnest" Johnson, who'd had experience backing Earl Hooker, Junior Wells, A.C. Reed, Sam Lay and Buford, came aboard on bass. Muddy had approached Lovie Lee, from Meridian, Mississippi, with an offer to be his piano player two years before; Lee had turned him down then, but now the timing was right. Jesse Lee Clay initially manned the drums, but was soon replaced by Ray Allison. Almost immediately the new Muddy Waters Blues Band departed on a West Coast tour with Jimmy Rogers also on guitar. Upon their return Rogers formed his own band, and guitarist Rick Kreher stepped in to fill the vacancy.

As had been the case throughout his career, Muddy's band members were devoted to him. "Oh, Muddy was a fine man," Lovie Lee remarks. "If you're nice to him, he nice to you. . . . You couldn't help but be nice to him, because he was nice at all times.[3] John Primer maintains that "playing with Muddy was one of my greatest experiences."[4] Ray Allison echoes a familiar sentiment when he says, "He was like a father to me. He taught me how to be a professional. I loved the man."[5]

By this time Muddy was being booked exclusively by Mike Kappus of the Rosebud Agency in San Francisco. Says Kappus, "I think that anybody that had any association or friendship with Muddy, [that] was the highlight of their life probably." He characterizes Muddy as a cross between a majestic king and a loving grandfather. "He had this amazing aura about him, just a regal aura. You just felt it when you walked in a room, that all the energy was coming from him, that he was just naturally the person you were going to be paying attention to and respecting. He just commanded respect. At the same time, he had such a wonderful smile and . . . he could be such a sweetheart. And I think that everyone that knew him was just very, very proud to know him."[6]

According to Mojo, who'd played with Muddy over the preceding two decades, the great bluesman only improved with age: "He was bending them strings and singing them blues with tears in his eyes."[7] The band would open his show, then Muddy would claim the stage for 25 or 30 minutes. His desire to perform never wavered; there was no mention of retirement.

As Muddy's audiences continued to grow, he began to detect more black faces among them, and this gratified him enormously. "They have a good time, too," he said of all his fans, "standing up on their seats, stomping their feet and clapping their hands. I get a real kick-bang out of that."[8] Champagne remained his beverage of choice; pretty young women, his weakness and delight.

In July 1980 the Muddy Waters Blues Band embarked upon a festival tour of Europe that encompassed the Pori Jazz Fest in Finland, the North Sea Jazz Fest in The Hague, the Velden Jazz Fest in Austria and the Blues Fest in Pistoia, Italy. The next month Muddy performed at home, at the Petrillo Music Shell during the Chicago Jazz Festival. "They didn't want to let him off the stage, they didn't," Mojo says of Muddy's hometown crowd. "That old man could play the blues."[9] By September the band was touring the West Coast, where it was the highlight of the Sacramento Area Blues Festival. Muddy, it was reported, had a high ol' time, prancing around the stage and kissing babies. Twenty thousand fans roared their approval.

When the fledgling Blues Foundation — the only international organization devoted to celebrating the history of blues and ensuring its perpetuation — came to select the greatest artists of the genre with which to inaugurate its Hall of Fame, Muddy was a requisite choice. On 16 November 1980, he was inducted into the hall at the foundation's first annual W.C. Handy Blues Awards Show at the Orpheum Theatre in Memphis. Accompanying him on the honor roll were many of Muddy's confreres from the early days: Little Walter, Otis Spann, Rice Miller, John Lee "Sonny Boy" Williamson, Big Bill Broonzy, John Lee Hooker, Willie Dixon and Howlin' Wolf.

Before a sold-out crowd at New York City's Beacon Theater on 28 March 1981, Muddy once again conquered the Big Apple. In a show opened by James Cotton and featuring special guest star Johnny Winter, Muddy steamrolled all comers and dominated the stage with his lethal vocals and savage guitar. In May he made a triumphant return to New York's Savoy, where he dazzled a standing-room-only crowd that included Johnny and Edgar Winter, Memphis Slim, John Belushi and Christopher Reeve.

Muddy's yearning for the road did not abate with the years. "As long [as] I'm feeling good I'll keep on going out," he stated. "Just staying at home would drive me crazy."[10] Claiming that his modest financial success hadn't hampered his ability to dig deep for the blues, Muddy said, "Just having a couple of dollars don't excite me. I can buy a steak now, but I'm still who I was when I couldn't buy a hamburger."[11]

Following a grueling schedule that would have exhausted a man a third his age, the 66-year-old bluesman set out on tour to promote the *King Bee* album, released in April 1981. After a couple of gigs on the East Coast, Muddy played several dates in eastern Canada, Illinois and Wisconsin before working his way through Europe in July. August saw him performing in Chicago, Ottawa, Quebec City and Geneva, Ohio, and Canada's western provinces. Cotton opened for Muddy's Alaskan debut in Fairbanks and Anchorage. Of Muddy's performance in the far north, Mojo exclaims, "He tore 'em down!"[12] The band then appeared with Willie Dixon as they toured the American West Coast. Next Muddy and his retinue headed east again, playing in Arizona, New Mexico, Texas, Mississippi, Louisiana, Kansas, Iowa, Wisconsin, Illinois and Tennessee.

This marathon road trip also led to a place that Muddy, as a young sharecropper, could never have foreseen. On 18 September, Mississippi Governor William Winter paid tribute to Muddy at a reception given in his honor at the governor's mansion in Jackson. The following day Muddy headlined the 1981 Delta Blues Festival held in a cotton field in Freedom Village, near Greenville, Mississippi. Looking jaunty in a white suit and Hawaiian shirt, Muddy renewed old acquaintances backstage before his evening performance. Then, stepping onstage under the bright stars of a Delta night, he dished up a potent serving of blues in the heartland of its birthplace. Afterwards Muddy invited the band to meet his family in Rolling Fork. It would be Muddy's final glimpse at the town of his birth.

Muddy's last known recording was made on 22 November 1981 in a videotaped performance with his apprentices, the Rolling Stones. The show took place at the Checkerboard Lounge, Buddy Guy's South Side Chicago club, before an audience of invited guests. Muddy's band played several numbers, then Muddy — looking every inch the patriarch in a gray vest and trousers and black tie — climbed onstage, settled onto a stool and launched into "Down The Road I Go." His extended version of "Country Boy" is a knockout, testifying to the fact that his vicious slide had lost none of its bite.

The Rolling Stones, minus Charlie Watts and Bill Wyman, joined Muddy during "Baby Please Don't Go" and stayed to jam behind him for "Hoochie Coochie Man" and "Long Distance Call." While the Stones could add nothing to Muddy's arrangements, the mix of musicians makes this an intriguing performance. "Mannish Boy" is the highlight of the set, as Muddy trades vocals with Mick Jagger before Buddy Guy, Junior Wells and Lefty Diz come aboard to add yet more spice to the musical melange.

Muddy was diagnosed with lung cancer in the spring of 1982. While he hadn't had a cigarette for many years, a lifetime exposure to smoky clubs was likely a contributing factor of his illness. Few people outside the family were told of his condition; his band members were only informed that he'd be spending some time in hospital. Muddy had surgery for the removal of one lung, then underwent radiation therapy. His booking agent, Mike Kappus, recalls that Muddy's attitude was upbeat: "He was laying in the hospital bed, and we were talking about John Lee Hooker, and he was imitating John's voice and joking about how each of them would try to one-up the other with the first one to get a Cadillac, the first one to get a Mercedes, the first one to get a phone in the Mercedes, each one calling the other back with the last one-upsmanship."[13]

Muddy recovered satisfactorily; he regained the weight he'd lost and was looking healthy again. He felt well enough to catch some shows by his own band, which during his illness was performing independently as Mojo Buford and the Hoochie Coochie Boys. (Earnest Johnson would die unexpectedly on Christmas Eve 1982.) Muddy was optimistically planning his comeback. Another album with Johnny Winter was in the offing.

"Blow Wind Blow" was Muddy's final offering on 30 June 1982, the last time the great bluesman graced the stage that was his lifeblood. He, Marva and Scott Cameron had flown to Miami for an Eric Clapton concert, and Muddy surprised Clapton by joining him for this one number. As Muddy sang the last verse bidding farewell to his woman, it would, in fact, be his departing message to the fans he cherished. According to Buford and Primer, it was too much too soon. "He come back home and went on down from there," says Mojo sadly. "Went all the way down. We were getting ready to go on a tour."[14] Muddy's weight plummeted. "The cancer just ate him up," Joseph recalls with immense sorrow.[15]

Muddy maintained a valiant spirit and sustained hopes for recovery, but life without performing was a tremendous adjustment. Waking up in his own bed each day was especially odd for a man who'd been on the road for over three decades. When Bob Margolin asked if he still played guitar at home, Muddy answered, "Naw, I been playing 50 years."[16]

In spring 1983 Jerry Portnoy paid a visit to his former boss:

> He threw his arms around me, ordered up a bottle of champagne from his wine cellar, and we had a great time, and he told me he was really proud of us [the Legendary Blues Band]. Muddy always took great pride in the fact that so many people . . . trained under his tutelage and went on to have successful careers on their own. He was very, very proud of that fact. Because you take a guy like B.B. King — absolutely a great artist — and there were people who were with him for many years and nobody knows their names. None of them really did anything after that or wound up making names as stars in their own right. But with Muddy, Muddy was like the Duke Ellington of the blues in the sense that people knew who was in Duke Ellington's band. They knew Harry Carney and Johnny Hodges and Ray Nance and Cat Anderson, people who were stars in their own right, and the same was true of Muddy's band.[17]

Margolin knew that Muddy had taken a serious turn for the worse when he confessed that he now had good and bad days. Mojo recalls, "He just seemed unhappy and down-and-out. No, he wasn't spry like he was. . . . The last meal I seen him eat was two hotdogs and scrambled eggs, and I knew then he was a sick man, 'cause he was a heavy eater."[18] More surgery was ruled out; Muddy no longer had the strength. That April, Buddy Guy and Junior Wells, alarmed by reports of Muddy's decline, called to say they were coming by for a visit. "Don't come, because I'm doing fine," Muddy assured them, but then added, as if he knew it was time to pass the torch, "Just don't let the blues die."[19]

Muddy's heart finally gave out in the early hours of 30 April 1983. The 68-year-old had been asleep at home with Marva. He was taken to the Good Samaritan Hospital in the neighboring suburb of Downers Grove, where he was pronounced dead from cardiac arrest at 2:17 in the morning.

Eulogies from Chicago's newly elected mayor, Harold Washington, musicians, Muddy's friends and fans crammed the media and descended upon the family. *The Times* of London lauded Muddy as "the most notable of postwar blues singers."[20] He was extolled in the *New York Times* as a musical pioneer "who played a key role in the development of electric blues and rock-and-roll and was the greatest contemporary exponent of the influential Mississippi Delta blues style."[21] Two radio stations battled in court over the rights to Muddy's interview tapes. Blues clubs throughout the city staged tribute shows, and Muddy Waters enthusiasts gathered to mark their loss and to celebrate the music and the man.

Musicians such as B.B. King, Buddy Guy, Johnny Winter and Eric Clapton felt as if they had lost a parent, a guiding light in both their professional and personal lives. "It's like losing your father," King sadly noted. "It's going to be years and years before most people realize how great he was to American music."[22] "My feelings toward Muddy is like a father, you know," Guy commented, "and my tears have been running."[23] Winter declared, "I loved him, man, and it was real mutual. I wish he was still around."[24] A bereaved Clapton kept the positive aspect of Muddy's legacy in mind: "I was in love with Muddy before I ever met him. And that's the great thing. His records will always be there."[25]

Junior Wells remembers the man who stood before a judge and swore to get young Junior back on track. "I just want everybody to know that Muddy was an incredible blues artist, and there won't be another Muddy Waters, period," he states. "He was born with a blues voice, and he had so much soul in his voice. There won't be no more Muddy Waters. That's the onliest one."[26] Longtime friend John Lee Hooker, who considers Muddy to be his idol, sums up his feelings regarding the loss: "I miss him and I wish he was here, but he ain't. And we all gotta go, and he was a really, really good man. It's just too bad he left so soon."[27]

The King of Chicago Blues lay in state for three days at the Metropolitan Funeral Parlor at 4445 South King Drive on Chicago's South Side — the turf on which he'd earned his title. He rested in an open casket, lined symbolically in a deep shade of blue, dressed in a dark brown shirt and a beige leisure suit. "His features remained dignified and statesmanlike in death," a reporter noted, "and just a hint of a smile creased his lips."[28]

Crowds of Chicagoans and blues aficionados filed past the coffin for a last view of the man who had so influenced blues and popular music. "This is overwhelming," said Scott Cameron, "an incredible outpouring of admiration. These were Muddy's stomping grounds. We couldn't close it to the public."[29] Dozens of large flower arrangements clogged the two side aisles of the chapel and extended around behind the casket. Floral tributes arrived from blues societies throughout the United States, from Mayor Harold Washington and from fellow musicians, such as rock star Gregg Allman. Country singer Hank Williams, Jr., attached this message to his bouquet: "I'm sure you never knew, but I loved your music and learned a lot from you."[30] A huge arrangement was sent from the Rolling Stones with a note that read, "In memory of a wonderful man dear to us all. We shall never forget you Muddy."[31]

The funeral was held on 4 May. The visitation was at seven o'clock that evening and the service began a half-hour later. Outside, the press swarmed over the side lawn and front drive of the funeral home, eager to catch a photo or snare a quote from the celebrities in attendance. Johnny Winter, Bob Margolin, Jerry Portnoy, Paul Oscher, Willie Smith, S.P. Leary, John Hammond, B.B. King, George Thorogood, Rick Kreher and many more of Muddy's musical apostles were there. Winter stayed secluded in his limousine, parked behind the chapel, until the service began, reportedly too shaken to talk. "The place was packed," recalls Portnoy. "They were lined up outside. There were all kinds of people there. . . . All kinds of musicians and producers and record people, fans. . . . It was a very moving day."[32] Margolin adds, "It was really sad, 'cause while his music will always live on, it was really sad to lose the man himself, and people were pretty torn up."[33]

As the service began, the melancholy atmosphere of the chapel was suddenly permeated with the sounds of happier times. Muddy's slide and Little Walter's harmonica resonated over the PA system as they launched into the opening bars of "They Call Me Muddy Waters," accompanied by Jimmy Rogers and Big Crawford. Muddy's vocals never struck a more poignant note. Recordings of "Hoochie Coochie Man" and "Got My Mojo Working" followed.

Reverend C.W. Hopson officiated at the service, and according to John Hammond, he delivered "a really lame sermon over an open casket, which was really shocking. This guy didn't even know Muddy, and so I felt really weird."[34] But then Pops Staples, the patriarch of the Staple Singers, stepped up to the coffin and sang "Glory, Glory" as a tribute to his dear old friend. "Tears just started to come," recalls Hammond, "and didn't stop at that point. Pops Staples was so great, and he knew Muddy really well. Just Pops playing the guitar and singing. It was wild. That's what made it. I'm sure Muddy was there and checked it out. It was wonderful."[35]

Afterwards knots of friends gathered at the back of the funeral parlor and outside, reminiscing about the man who'd brought them together that day. "So many of the discussions centered around the good times with Muddy and Muddy playing practical jokes on people and things like that," Mike Kappus recalls. "I just thought it was a wonderful way to be remembered with everybody smiling and talking about how much joy somebody brought into their lives."[36]

The following morning at ten o'clock, Muddy was interred at the Restvale Cemetery at 115th Street and Laramie, southeast of Chicago, just outside the city limits. Serving as pallbearers were Mojo Buford, Lovie Lee, Ray Allison, Rick Kreher, Mike Kappus and Tim Rosner, Muddy's road manager. All those except for family members or close friends — which included Willie Dixon, B.B. King, Jerry Portnoy and Paul Oscher — were kept back from the grave site. Surrounding the burial plot was a profusion of floral arrangements brought from the funeral home, including one in the shape of a guitar. As the casket was placed above the grave, a sharp crack shattered the reverie. Mourners gasped at the eerie symbolism: the floral guitar had split in two.

As everyone was leaving, a reporter asked Willie Dixon to speculate on the future of the music he and Muddy had helped to define. "The blues has no way to go but up," he proclaimed. "It's been down too long."[37]

"I'll tell you Muddy meant a whole lot to me," Oscher declares from his heart, "and he's always with me, every day. I always think about Muddy Waters. He's in my music; he's in everything. My whole life has to do with Muddy Waters. He's the most important thing that ever happened to me."[38]

Oscher and Portnoy were the last to leave the burial site. Here at rest was one of the primary forces of blues and popular music. Here also was a loyal and generous friend, a champion of other musicians, a loving father, a man of humor and respect. Yet some things never die. In many ways, the music and the man live on.

NOTES

[1] Dave Haynes, "Life's Good But Muddy Waters Still Has the Blues," *Winnipeg Free Press*, 22 Aug. 1981, p. 29.

[2] Robert Palmer, *Deep Blues* (New York: Penguin, 1982), 260.

[3] Lovie Lee, interview with author, 20 Aug. 1996.

[4] John Primer, interview with author, 23 May 1996.

[5] *Relix* (Aug. 1993): 20.

[6] Mike Kappus, interview with author, 22 Aug. 1996.

[7] Mojo Buford, interview with author, 7 Mar. 1996.

[8] Robert Palmer, "Muddy Waters is Singing the Real Deep Blues," *New York Times*, 27 Mar. 1981, sec. C6.

[9] Mojo Buford, interview with author, 7 Mar. 1996.

[10] Haynes, 29.

[11] Haynes, 29.

[12] Mojo Buford, interview with author, 7 Mar. 1996.

[13] Mike Kappus, interview with author, 22 Aug. 1996.

[14] Mojo Buford, interview with author, 7 Mar. 1996.

[15] Joseph Morganfield, interview with author, 19 Aug. 1995.

[16] Bob Margolin, interview with author, 6 June 1995.

[17] Jerry Portnoy, interview with author, 13 Nov. 1995.

[18] Mojo Buford, interview with author, 7 Mar. 1996.

[19] Jas Obrecht, "Buddy Guy," *Blues Guitar: The Men Who Made the Music: From the Pages of Guitar Player Magazine*, ed. Obrecht (San Francisco: GPI Books, 1990), 143.

[20] *The Times*, 2 May 1983, p. 12.

[21] Robert Palmer, "Muddy Waters, Blues Performer, Dies," *The New York Times*, Sunday, 1 May 1983, p. 44.

[22] Rafael Alvarez, "Muddy Waters, 1915–1983: Young Guitarists Pay Homage to a Blues Giant," *Guitar World*, vol. 4, no. 4 (Sept. 1983): 12.

[23] "Waters Changed Music World," *The Clarion-Ledger*, 3 May 1983, p. 4B.

[24] Jas Obrecht, "Mudslide," *Guitar Player* (Nov. 1992): 146.

[25] Robert Palmer, "Muddy Waters: 1915–1983," *Rolling Stone* 398 (23 June 1983): 40.

[26] Junior Wells, interview with author, 9 Dec. 1995.

[27] John Lee Hooker, interview with author, 9 Aug. 1995.

[28] Rafael Alvarez, "Great and Small Paid Tribute at Muddy's Funeral," *The Sun* (Baltimore), Friday, 6 May 1983, p. B1.

[29] Alvarez, "Great and Small," p. B1.

[30] Alvarez, "Great and Small," p. B2.

[31] Alvarez, "Great and Small," p. B2.

[32] Jerry Portnoy, interview with author, 13 Nov. 1995.

[33] Bob Margolin, interview with author, 6 June 1995.

[34] John Hammond, interview with author, 17 Oct. 1991.

[35] John Hammond, interview with author, 17 Oct. 1991.

[36] Mike Kappus, interview with author, 22 Aug. 1996.

[37] Alvarez, "Muddy Waters," 12.

[38] Paul Oscher, interview with author, 18 May 1996.

EPILOGUE

After-Death Experiences

Since his death in 1983, Muddy has been the recipient of numerous awards and honors, acknowledgments that would have gratified him. The international Blues Foundation has acknowledged his greatness by presenting him posthumously with several of its W.C. Handy Awards. Muddy's "Got My Mojo Working," coupled with Jackie Brenston's "Rocket 88," won in the category of Blues Single in 1983. In 1985 Muddy's *Rare And Unissued* received a Handy Award as U.S. Vintage/Reissue Blues Album of the Year, and *The Chess Box* (P-Vine Special, Chess/Japan) took the organization's prize for Best Foreign Vintage/Reissue Blues Album. *Muddy Waters – The Chess Box* was honored as the American Vintage/Reissue Album of 1990, Muddy's *The Complete Plantation Recordings* was the

1994 Reissue Album of the Year, and in 1995 his *One More Mile* won a Handy award as Best Reissue Album.

In addition to his inclusion on the honor roll of the Blues Foundation's W.C. Handy Hall of Fame as an individual who perpetuated the blues, many of Muddy's recordings have been inducted into the hall. "I'm Your Hoochie Coochie Man," "Got My Mojo Working," "I'm Ready," "Mannish Boy" and "Long Distance Call" are listed in the category of Hall of Fame Classics of Blues Recordings, Singles. As Classics of Blues Recordings, Albums, *The Best Of Muddy Waters*, *McKinley Morganfield A.K.A. Muddy Waters* and *Muddy Waters – The Chess Box* have also won berths for Muddy in the foundation's Hall of Fame.

A year after Muddy's passing, Willie Dixon's Blues Heaven Foundation established the Muddy Waters Scholarship in recognition of Muddy's exceptional contribution to blues. This annual award is presented to a Chicago college student for further study in history, African-American studies, music, journalism or a related discipline and is based on financial need and academic achievement. As someone who learned the value of education too late, Muddy would have been proud of the scholarship that bears his name.

On 2 August 1985, the city from which Muddy made his impact on the world showed its appreciation by renaming East 43rd Street — extending from State Street to its eastern end at South Oakenwald Avenue — Muddy Waters Drive. Mayor Harold Washington proclaimed, "Chicago is very proud of the contributions made by Muddy Waters in the advancement of blues as a musical artform, and the permanent renaming of 43rd Street will serve as a lasting memorial to this great musician."[1] Bobby Rush, alderperson of the Second Ward, stated, "this occasion marks a significant event to remember one of Chicago's greatest entertainers, Muddy Waters, who meant so much to Chicago. It's very appropriate that Chicago demonstrates its appreciation for Muddy's contribution to music and blues."[2]

As Marva Morganfield, Jimmy Rogers, Sunnyland Slim and other friends and fans of Muddy looked on, the mayor supervised the raising of the first new street sign on 43rd near Martin Luther Drive. Alderperson Dorothy Tillman of the Third Ward remarked that Muddy "took the history and plight of black people not only throughout America, but throughout the world."[3] That evening, in conjunction with the Douglas-Grand Neighborhood Festival on South King Drive, Albert King headlined a concert in Muddy's honor.

The citizens of Muddy's hometown of Rolling Fork, Mississippi, have erected a plaque and built a gazebo in the town square to commemorate their most notable native son. Clarksdale, Mississippi, where Muddy spent his formative years, also acknowledged Muddy's greatness by declaring 21 April 1988 and every 21 April thereafter as McKinley "Muddy Waters" Morganfield Appreciation Day. The Delta Blues Museum, located in Clarksdale, has devoted one room of its exhibition space to Muddy. On display is the "Muddy-Wood" guitar, a white electric model made of a cypress timber from Muddy's Stovall cabin. Prevailing over the exhibition is a life-sized sculpture of Muddy onstage, created and donated by Mary and Ray Daub of Wilmington, Delaware. Seated on a bar stool, dressed in his suit and hat and holding a guitar, his eerie likeness dominates the bandstand still.

On 25 February 1992, Muddy was honored with a Lifetime Achievement Grammy Award, presented to performers "who, during their lifetimes, have made creative contributions of outstanding artistic significance to the field of recordings."

It is a testament to those contributions that the awards and acknowledgments have transcended the lifespan of the man. But for Muddy the greatest possible honor would be the knowledge that, long after his death, his music continues to touch souls, that generations of musicians still carry the legacy of his blues.

NOTES

[1] Mayor's Office of Special Events, Chicago, press release, 31 July 1985.
[2] Mayor's Office of Special Events, Chicago, press release, 31 July 1985.
[3] Larry Cose, "Street Name Honors Blues Great," *Chicago Sun Times*, 3 Aug. 1985.

MUDDY WATERS
DISCOGRAPHY

Compiled by Phil Wight and Fred Rothwell

ORIGINALLY PUBLISHED BY BLUES AND RHYTHM PUBLICATIONS

The following discography is used with the generous permission of the authors Phil Wight and Fred Rothwell and of Blues and Rhythm Publications:

Blues and Rhythm magazine first published this discography in 1991, and since then the Muddy Waters legend has rolled on. There have been tribute albums and tribute bands, blues and rock musicians worldwide cite his influence, and every blues magazine worth its salt contains at least some reference to him in every issue.

In the meantime there has been a revolution in audio recording; the CD now prevails. This discography has, therefore, been updated. New Muddy sessions and previously unissued material have been added, corrections and amendments have been made as new information has come to light, and significant (but by no means all) CD issues have been included.

Acknowledgments

In compiling the discography, the following publications were consulted:

Blues Records 1943–1970 A to K by Mike Leadbitter and Neil Slaven
Blues Records 1943–1970 L to Z by Mike Leadbitter, Leslie Fancourt and
    Paul Pelletier
Blues and Gospel Records 1902–1942 by R.M.W. Dixon and J. Godrich
    (with acknowledgment to John Cowley for the Library of Congress
    information)
The Chess Labels, Vol. 1 and 2 by Michel Ruppli
Chess Blues Discography by Leslie Fancourt
Prestige Jazz Records by Michel Ruppli
Jazz Records by J.G. Jepsen
Chicago Breakdown by Mike Rowe
Jazz On Record by McCarthy, Morgan, Oliver and Harrison
The Complete Bo Diddley Sessions by George R. White
plus dozens of LP sleeves and CD booklets

The following periodicals were consulted:

Blues Unlimited, Living Blues, Blues and Rhythm, Juke Blues, Pickin' the Blues, Blues World, Jazz Journal, Guitar Player, Downbeat, Melody Maker, Soul Bag, Red Lick catalogues and *Sailor's Delight* catalogues

And the following individuals provided help and information:

Mike Rowe, Mark Harris, Don Tarrent, Klaus Killian, Jorma Kempas, Mary Katherine Aldin, Norman Darwen, Tony Burke, David Lees, Dave Moore, Reinhard Scheding, Keith Smith, Ken Smith, Don Zijlstra, Max Sievert, Wolfgang Behr, Bernd Kulla, Dave Everitt, Neil Slaven, Bill Pearson, Alan Balfour, Bill Greensmith, John Bruce, Dan Kochakian, Brian Smith, Cilla Huggins, Tommy Holmstrom, Gorgen Antonsson, Manfred Borggreve, Alasdair Blaazer, Paul Jones, Bill Wyman, Steve Franz, Richard Shurman, Ian Jones, Bert van Oortmarssen, Scott Dirks and Sandra Tooze

Instrument Abbreviations

gtr – guitar; hca – harmonica; pno – piano; tpt – trumpet; tb – trombone; unk – unknown; vcl – vocal; vcl grp – vocal group

Label Abbreviations

BD – Boogie Disease; BGO – Beat Goes On; BM – Blue Moon; COL – Columbia; DO – Document; DV – Deja vu; FCD – France's Concert; GL – Greenline; HB – Happy Bird; JS – Jazz Selection; K/G – Kent Globe; LRdB – Le Roi du Blues; LEB – Les Editions Blues; LC – Library of Congress; MAC – Castle Communications; M. Arch – Marble Arch; MW – Interstate Music; NW – New World; Pye Int. – Pye International; SC – Syndicate Chapter; SEE – See For Miles; SMP – Stylus; SOH – Stack-O-Hits; SFM – See For Miles; Tran – Transatlantic; TR – Tobacco Road

MCKINLEY MORGANFIELD
Stovall, MS, c. 24–31 August 1941

• McKinley Morganfield vcl ①, speech ②, gtr ③; Son Simms speech ④, gtr ⑤; Alan Lomax speech ⑥; John Work speech ⑦

4769-A-1(a)	Country Blues ① ③	LC, AAFS 18, AFSL4, Testament LP2210, Bounty LP6031, Polydor LP236574, MCA CD9344, DOCD-5146
4769-A-1(b)	Interview no. 1 ② ③ ⑥	LC, MCA CHD9344
4769-A-2(a)	I Be's Troubled ① ③	LC, MFS 18, AFSL4, Testament LP2210, Bounty LP6031, Polydor LP236574, Blues Document LPBD-01, MCA CD9344, DOCD-5146
4769-A-2(b)	Interview no. 2 ② ④ ⑥ ⑦	LC, MCA CHD9344
4770-B-1	Burr Clover Farm Blues ① ② ③ ④ ⑤	LC, MCA CHD9344
4770-B-2	Interview no. 3 ② ④ ⑦	LC, MCA CHD9344

SON SIMMS FOUR
Stovall, MS, Friday, 24 July 1942

• McKinley Morganfield gtr, vcl ①; Percy Thomas gtr, vcl ②; Son Simms violin; Louis Ford mandolin, vcl ③; group members foot-tapping, vcl interjections ④

	Ramblin' Kid Blues (partial) ① ④	MCA CHD9344
6628-A-6	Ramblin' Kid Blues ① ④	LC, Testament LP2210, Bounty LP6031, Polydor LP236574, MCA CHD9344, DOCD-5146
6628-A-7	Rosalie ① ④	LC, Testament LP2210, Bounty LP6031, Polydor LP236574, MCA CHD9344, DOCD-5146
6628-A-8	Joe Turner ③ ④	LC, Testament LP2210, Bounty LP6031, Polydor LP236574, MCA CHD9344, DOCD-5146
6628-B-1	Pearlie May Blues ②	LC, Testament LP2210, Bounty LP6031, Polydor LP236574, MCA CHD9344, DOCD-5146

MCKINLEY MORGANFIELD
Stovall, MS, Friday, 24 July 1942

• McKinley Morganfield vcl, gtr, speech ①; Son Simms gtr ②; Charles Berry gtr ③

6628-B-2	Take A Walk With Me ②	LC, Testament LP2210, Bounty LP6031, Polydor LP236574, MCA CHD9344, DOCD-5146
6628-B-3	Burr Clover Blues ②	LC, Testament LP2210, Bounty LP6031, Polydor LP236574, MCA CHD9344, DOCD-5146
	Interview no. 4 ①	MCA CHD9344
6629-A-1	I Be Bound To Write To You ③	LC, Testament LP2210, Bounty LP6031, Polydor LP236574, MCA CHD9344, DOCD-5146
6629-A-2	I Be Bound To Write To You ③	LC, MCA CHD9344 6629-A-3
	You're Gonna Miss Me When I'm Gone	LC, Testament LP2210, Bounty LP6031, Polydor LP236574, MCA CHD9344, DOCD-5146

MCKINLEY MORGANFIELD
prob. Clarksdale, MS, poss. 20–24 July 1942

• McKinley Morganfield vcl, gtr; prob. Charles Berry gtr ①

6666-A-3	You Got To Take Sick And Die Some Of These Days	LC, Testament LP2210, MCA CHD9344, DOCD-5146
6666-B-1	Why Don't You Live So God Can Use You	LC, Testament LP2210, MCA CHD9344, DOCD-5146
6666-K2	Country Blues	LC, Testament LP2210, MCA CHD9344, DOCD-5146
6667-A-1	You're Gonna Miss Me When I'm Gone	LC, MCA CHD9344
6667-F3	32-20 Blues ①	LC, MCA CHD9344

JAMES "SWEET LUCY" CARTER AND HIS ORCHESTRA
Chicago, 1946

- Muddy Waters vcl, gtr; prob. Alex Atkins alto sax; prob. Lee Brown pno; unk. clarinet; Ernest "Big" Crawford bass

| 1597 | Mean Red Spider | 20th Century 20-51 B, Krazy Kat LP820, DOCD-5146 |

NOTE: Reverse by James "Sweet Lucy" Carter.

HOMER HARRIS
Chicago, Friday, 27 September 1946

- Homer Harris vcl; Muddy Waters gtr; poss. Leroy Foster gtr; James Clarke pno; poss. Ransom Knowling bass; prob. Judge Riley drums

cco4649	I'm Gonna Cut Your Head	Testament LP 2207, DOCD-5146
cco4650	Atomic Bomb Blues	Testament LP 2207, DOCD-5146
cco4651	Tomorrow Will Be Too Late	Testament LP 2207, DOCD-5146

MUDDY WATERS
Chicago, Friday, 27 September 1946

- Muddy Waters vcl, gtr; poss Leroy Foster gtr; poss. Ransom Knowling bass; James Clarke pno; prob. Judge Riley drums

cco4652-1	Jitterbug Blues	Testament LP 2207, Epic LP 22123, LP 37318, DOCD-5146
cco4653-1	Hard Day Blues	Testament LP 2207, Epic LP 22123, LP 37318, DOCD-5146
cco4654-1	Burying Ground Blues	Testament LP 2207, Epic LP 22123, LP 37318, DOCD-5146

JAMES (BEALE STREET) CLARKE
Chicago, Friday, 27 September 1946

- James Clarke pno, vcl; Muddy Waters gtr; poss. Leroy Foster gtr; poss. Ransom Knowling bass; prob. Judge Riley drums

| cco4655-1 | Come To Me Baby (What Evil Have I Done) | Columbia 37391, 30020, Testament LP 2207, DOCD-5146 |
| cco4656-1 | You Can't Make The Grade | Columbia 37391, 30020, Testament LP 2207, DOCD-5146 |

SUNNY LAND SLIM WITH MUDDY WATER
Chicago, 1947

• Sunnyland Slim vcl, pno; Muddy Waters gtr; Ernest "Big" Crawford, bass; unk. drums

| U7056 | Johnson Machine Gun | Aristocrat 1301, Chess LP 6641047, GL LP 8105, Chess CD CHD4-9340 |
| U7057 | Fly Right, Little Girl | Aristocrat 1301, Chess LP 6641047, GL LP 8105, Chess CD CHD4-9340 |

MUDDY WATER WITH SUNNY LAND SLIM
Chicago, 1947

• Muddy Waters vcl, gtr; Sunnyland Slim pno; Ernest "Big" Crawford, bass; unk. drums

| U7058 | Gypsy Woman | Aristocrat 1302, Chess LP1501, LP4000, LP6641047, LPS6040-6050, LP680002, SMP LP850, Chess CD CHD3-80002, CHD9274, Charly CD Red Box 3, Charly CD Red 17 |
| U7059 | Little Anna Mae | Aristocrat 1302, Chess LP6641047, LP2057, LPS6040-6050, LP515040, GL LP8010, Chess CD CHD4-9340, CHD9180, Charly CD Red Box 3 |

MUDDY WATERS
Chicago, April 1948

• Muddy Waters vcl, gtr; Alex Atkins alto sax; Ernest "Big" Crawford bass; Sunnyland Slim pno

| U7108 | Good Lookin' Woman | Chess LP 680002, CHD3-80002, Charly CD Red Box 3 |
| U7109 | Mean Disposition | Chess LP2057, LPS6040-6050, LP680002, LP515040, GL LP8010, Chess CD CHD3-80002, CHD9180, Charly CD Red Box 3 |

SUNNYLAND SLIM WITH MUDDY WATERS
Chicago, April 1948

• Sunnyland Slim vcl, pno; Muddy Waters gtr; Alex Atkins alto sax; Ernest "Big" Crawford bass

| U7110 | She Ain't Nowhere | Aristocrat 1304, Chess CD Chd4-9340 |
| U7111 | My Baby, My Baby | Aristocrat 1304 |

MUDDY WATERS WITH RYTHM [sic] ACCOMPANIMENT
Chicago, April 1948

• Muddy Waters vcl, gtr; Ernest "Big" Crawford bass

| U7112 | I Can't Be Satisfied (Looking For My Baby — Chess 1514) | Aristocrat 1305, Chess 1514, EP6006, Vogue EP1046, Chess LP1427, LP203, LP624801, LP4000, LP6641047, LP1539, LP628622, LPS6040-6050, SOH LP9032, K/G LP8156, Cleo LP14983, TR LP2632, BM LP1014 ASTAN LP 20027, Showcase LP 141, Instant LP5001, Chess CD CHD4-9340, CHD3-80002, CHD31268, Charly CD Red 1, Charly CD Red Box 3, Charly CD RB 15 |
| U7113 | I Feel Like Going Home | Aristocrat 1305, Vogue EP1046, Python LP18, SC LP1/2, K/G LP8156, Chess LP4006, LP2057, LPS6040-6050, LP51540, LP 68002, GL LP8010, Chess CD CHD4-9340, CHD3-80002, CHD9180, Charly CD Red Box 3, Charly CD Red 17 |

ST. LOUIS JIMMY WITH MUDDY WATERS AND HIS BLUES COMBO
Chicago, 1948

• St. Louis Jimmy Oden vcl; Oliver Alcorn tenor sax; Sunnyland Slim pno; Muddy Waters gtr; Ernest "Big" Crawford, bass

| UB9290A | Florida Hurricane | Aristocrat 7001, Blues Document LP2058, Chess CD CHD4-9340, Blues Document CD DOCD-5235, Story Of Blues CD3508-2 |
| UB9293A | So Nice And Kind | Aristocrat 7001, Blues Document LP2058, Blues Document CD DOCD-5235, Story Of Blues CD3508-2 |

SUNNY LAND SLIM AND MUDDY WATER
Chicago, 1948

• Little Walter vcl, hca; Muddy Waters vcl ①, gtr; Sunnyland Slim vcl ①, pno; Floyd Jones gtr, Leroy Foster drums

| A | Blue Baby | Tempo Tone 1002, BD LP101/2, Official LP6043 |
| B | I Want My Baby ① | Tempo Tone 1002, Nighthawk LP102, Official LP6043 |

MUDDY WATERS AND RHYTHM ACCOMPANIMENT
Chicago, Autumn 1948

• Muddy Waters vcl, gtr; Ernest "Big" Crawford bass

U7131	Train Fare Home (Train Fare Home Blues)	Aristocrat 1306, Chess LP1511, LP680002, LP4006, LPS6040-6050, SOH LP9032, Cleo LP14983, TR LP2633, BM LP1014, Showcase LP141, Chess CD CHD3-80002, CHD9279, Charly CD Red Box 3, Charly CD Red 17
U7132	Down South Blues	Chess LP1511, LP4006, LPS6040-6050, CD CHD9279, Charly CD Red Box 3, Charly CD Red 17
U7133	Kind Hearted Woman	Chess LP1511, LP4006, LP60006, LP628622, LP203, LPS6040-6050, CD CHD9279, Charly CD Red 1, Charly CD Red Box 3
U7134	Sittin' Here And Drinkin' (Whiskey Blues)	Aristocrat 1306, Chess LP1511, LP4006, LP SOH LP9032, LPS6040-6050, Cleo LP14983, TR LP2633, BM LP1014, Showcase LP141, Chess CD CHD9279, Charly CD Red Box 3, Charly CD Red 17

MUDDY WATERS WITH RHYTHM ACCOMPANIMENT
Chicago, Tuesday, 30 November 1948

• Muddy Waters vcl, gtr; Leroy Foster gtr; Ernest "Big" Crawford bass

| U7148R | You're Gonna Miss Me (When I'm Dead And Gone) | Aristocrat 1307, Chess LP6641047, LP4006, LP2057, LP515040, LP1023, LPS6040-6050, DV LP2034, GL LP8010, Cleo LP30683, TR LP2633, BM LP1023, SC LP1/2, Sunnyland LP100, SOH LP9015, Astan 20028, Chess CD CHD9180, Charly CD Red Box 3 |

U7149R	Mean Red Spider	Aristocrat 1307, Chess LP6641174, LP680002, LP4006, LPS6040-6050, SC LP 1/2, Sunnyland LP100, Python LP12, DV LP2034, BM LP1023, SOH LP9015, Cleo LP30683, TR LP2633, ASTAN LP20028, Chess CD CHD3-80002, Charly CD Red Box 3, Charly CD Red 17
U7150	Standin' Here Tremblin'	Chess LP2057, LP515040, LPS6040-6050, Sunnyland LP100, GL, LP8010, Chess CD CHD9180, Charly CD Red Box 3
U7151R	Streamline Woman	Aristocrat 1310, SC LP1/2, Sunnyland LP100, Chess LP680002, LPS6040-6050, CD CHD-3-80002, Charly CD Red Box 3, Charly CD Red 17
U7152	Hard Days	Chess LP6641174, LPS6040-6050, CD CHD2-9348, Charly CD Red Box 3
U7153R	Muddy Jumps One (inst.)	Aristocrat 1310, Chess LPS6040-6050, SC LP1/2, Chess CD CHD2-9348, Charly CD Red Box 3

LEROY FOSTER AND MUDDY WATERS
Chicago, Tuesday, 30 November 1948

• Leroy Foster vcl, gtr; Muddy Waters gtr; Ernest "Big" Crawford bass

| U7154R | Locked Out Boogie | Aristocrat 1234, Chess LP6641047 |
| U7155R | Shady Grove Blues | Aristocrat 1234, Chess LP6641047 |

MUDDY WATERS AND HIS GUITAR
Chicago, c. July 1949

• Muddy Waters vcl. gtr; Ernest "Big" Crawford bass

U7199	Little Geneva	Aristocrat 1311, Chess LP1501, LP4000, LPS6040-6050, LP680002, CD CHD3-80002, CHD9274, Charly CD Red Box 3, Charly CD Red 17
U7200	Canary Bird	Aristocrat 1311, Chess LP1501, LP4000, LPS6040-6050, SMP LP850, Chess CD CHD9274, Charly CD Red Box 3, Charly CD Red 17
U7201	Burying Ground	Chess LP6641174, LP4006, LPS6040-6050, CD CHD2-9348, Charly CD Red Box 3
U7202	You Gonna Need My Help	Chess CHD2-9348

LITTLE JOHNNY (JONES)
Chicago, Summer 1949

• Johnny Jones vcl, pno; Muddy Waters gtr; Leroy Foster gtr, bass drum, hi-hat

| U7213 | Big Town Playboy | Aristocrat 405, Chess LP6641047, LP4013, EP6145011, GL LP8105, Chess CD CHD4-9340 |
| U7214 | Shelby County Blues | Aristocrat 405, Chess LF6641047, LP4013, LP8105 |

MUDDY WATERS AND HIS GUITAR
Chicago, Summer 1949

• Muddy Waters vcl, gtr; Johnny Jones pno; Leroy Foster gtr, bass drum, hi-hat ①

U7215	Screamin' And Cryin' ①	Aristocrat 406, Chess LP1501, LP4000, LP4006, LP6641174, Vogue LP60100358, Chess CD CHD9274, Charly CD Red 1, Charly CD Red Box 3
U7216	Where's My Woman Been ①	Aristocrat 406, Chess LP6641174, LP2057, LP515040, GL LP8010, Chess CD CHD9180, Charly CD Red Box 3
U7217	Last Time I Fool Around With You	Chess LP6641174, LP4006, LP2057, LP515040, GL LP8010, Chess CD CHD9180, Charly CD Red Box 3

NOTE: Although Chess LP4006 lists "Where's My Woman Been," the track that plays is "Screamin' And Cryin'." It has been suggested that the 2nd gtr on mx U7217 may be Tampa Red. All titles on Chess LPS6040-6050.

JIMMY ROGERS
Chicago, 1949

• Jimmy Rogers vcl, gtr; Little Walter hca; Muddy Waters gtr; Ernest "Big" Crawford bass; poss. Sunnyland Slim or Little Johnny Jones pno; unk. drums

| 1218-2 | Ludella | Biograph LP12035, BD LP101/2, BM LP1073 |

BABY FACE OR BABY FACE LEROY TRIO OR LITTLE WALTER OR LITTLE WALTER TRIO (PARKWAY 502, REGAL)
Chicago, January 1950

• Leroy Foster vcl ①, drums; Little Walter vcl ②, hca ③, gtr ④, Muddy Waters vcl ⑤, gtr, vcl comment ⑥

R-1357	Bad Acting Woman ② ④	Regal 3296, Highway 51 LP100, Muskadine LP 100, Xtra LP1133, Delmark CD DD-648
H-511	I Just Keep Loving Her ② ③	Parkway 502, Herald 403, Nighthawk LP102, Delmark CD DD-648
H-512	Boll Weevil ① ③	Parkway 104, Herald 404, Blues Classics LP8, Delmark CD DD-648
H-513	Rollin' And Tumblin' Part 1 (Rollin' Blues) ① ② ④ ⑤	Herald 404, Parkway 501, Blues Classics LP8, Document LP BD-01, DOCD-5146, Delmark CD DD-648
H-514	Rollin' And Tumblin' Part 2 ① ② ③ ⑤	Parkway 501, Blues Classics LP8, DOCD-5146, Delmark CD DD-648
H-515	Red Headed Woman ① ③	Parkway 104, Savoy 1122, 1501, Xtra LP1133, Highway 51 LP100, Muskadine LP100, Delmark CD DD-648
H-516	Muskadine Blues (Take A Walk With Me) ② ④	Regal 3296, Herald 403, Blues Classics LP8, Delmark CD DD-648
H-517	Moonshine Blues (Moonshine Baby) ② ④ ⑥	Parkway 502, Savoy 1122, 1501, Xtra LP1133, Highway 51 LP100, Muskadine LP100, Delmark CD DD-648

NOTE: H-511 remastered as H-1004; H-512 as H-1007; H-514 as H-1006; H-515 as SBL-4460; H-516 as R-1356, H-1005; H-517 as SBL-4459. Although Herald 404 has matrix H514 in the wax, it is matrix H513 that plays. All titles reissued on P-Vine Special LP9038, Delmark LP648.

MUDDY WATERS AND HIS GUITAR
Chicago, February 1950

• Muddy Waters vcl, gtr; Ernest "Big" Crawford bass ①; drums ② (poss. Elgin Evans)

U7235	Rollin' And Tumblin' Part 1 ① ②	Aristocrat 412, Chess LP1501, LP680002, LP6641174, LP8203, LP624474, LPS6040-6050, GL LP8001, DV LP2034, K/G LP8156, BM LP1006, Cleo LP15983, TR LP2632, SMP LP850, Astan LP20027, Chess CD CHD3-80002, CHD9274, Charly CD Red Box 3, Charly CD Red 17
U7236	Rollin' and Tumblin' Part 2 ① ②	Aristocrat 412, Chess LP6641174, LP628622, LPS6040-6050, CD CHD2-9348 Charly CD Red Box 3
U7237	Rollin' Stone	Chess 1426, JS 751, Vogue 2101, Chess LP1427, LP60006, LP203, LP680002, LP6641047, LP4004, LP1539, LPS6040-6050, Argo LP4034, Pye Int. LP28045, Marble Arch LP804, K/G LP8156, BM LP1006, Chess LPCS1, Cleo LP15983, TR LP2632, DV LP2034, Vogue 17002 GL LP6023, LP8044, SMP LP850, Astan LP20027, Instant LP5003, LP5011, Chess CD CHD4-9340, CHD3-80002, CHD31268, Charly CD Red 1, Charly CD Red Box 3, Charly CD RB 15
	Rollin' Stone (alt. take)	Chess LP624474, LP8202, LP628622, LP9101, LPS6040-6050, CD CHD2-9348, Charly CD Red Box 3
U7238	Walkin' Blues ①	Chess 1426, JS 751, Vogue 2101, 17002, Chess LP1501, LP4010, LP680002, LPS6040-6050, K/G LP8156, SMP LP850, Instant LP5003, Chess CD CHD3-80002, CHD9274, Charly CD Red Box 3

MUDDY WATERS (1434) OR MUDDY WATERS AND HIS GUITAR
Chicago, Summer 1950

• Muddy Waters vcl, gtr; Little Walter hca; Ernest "Big" Crawford bass, speech ①

U7261	You're Gonna Need My Help I Said (Gonna Need My Help)	Chess 1434, LP1511, LP60006, LP203, LP4006, LPS6040-6050, BM LP1023, K/G LP8156, SOH LP9015, Cleo LP30683, TR LP2633, Astan LP20028, Chess CD CHD9279, Charly CD Red Box 3, Charly CD Red 17
U7262	Sad Letter Blues	Chess 1434, LP1511, LP4006, LPS6040-6050, SOH LP9032, Cleo LP14983, TR LP2632, BM LP1014, Astan LP20027, Showcase LP141, Chess CD CHD9279, Charly CD Red Box 3, Charly CD Red 17
U7263	Early Morning Blues (Before Daybreak) ①	Chess 1490, LP1511, LP4006, LPS6040-6050, Charly CD Red Box 3
U7264	Appealing Blues (Hello Little Girl)	Chess 1468, LP1511, LP4006, LPS6040-6050, Vogue 2273, Chess CD CHD9279, Charly CD Red 1, Charly CD Red Box 3

MUDDY WATERS (LITTLE WALTER — LEB LP2017)
Chicago, Monday, 23 October 1950

• Muddy Waters vcl ①, speech ②, gtr; Little Walter speech ①, hca; Ernest "Big" Crawford bass; Elgin Evans drums ①

U7275	Louisiana Blues ①	Chess 1441, Vogue 2101, 133, EP1046, EP6022, Chess LP1427, LP60006, LP203, LP6641047, LP680002, LP1539, LP4000, LP628622, LPS6040-6050, Festival LP1008, SMP LP850, Instant LP5003, GL LP8044, Chess CD CHD3-80002, CHD31268, Charly CD Red 1, Charly CD Red Box 3
U7276	Evans Shuffle (Ebony Boogie; inst.) ②	Chess 1441, Vogue 2101, 133, EP1046, Chess LP6641047, LP8203, LP680002, LPS6040-6050, Python LP1, LP12, SCLP1/2, LRdb LP2017, GL LP8001, Chess CD CHD3-80002, Charly CD Red Box 3

NOTE: Elgin Evans or Elgar (Elga) Edmonds's correct name unknown. Part of the intro to U7275 is missing on some issues.

JIMMY ROGERS
Chicago, Monday, 23 October 1950

• Jimmy Rogers vcl, gtr; Little Walter hca; Muddy Waters gtr; Ernest "Big" Crawford, bass

U7277	Going Away Baby	Chess 1442, LP407, LP60012, LP624807, LP50011, LP813, LP6641047, Python LP6, Bellaphon LP4002, Charly CD Red 16, MCA CHD2-9372
U7278	Today, Today Blues	Chess 1442, LP427012, LP4008, LP6641174, LP207, Python LP21, GL LP2-6027, Charly CD Red 16, MCA CHD2-9372

MUDDY WATERS
Chicago, Tuesday, 23 January 1951

• Muddy Waters vcl, gtr; Little Walter hca ①, gtr ②, speech ③; Ernest "Big" Crawford bass

U7304	Long Distance Call ① ③	Chess 1452, LP1427, LP60006, LP680002, LP203, LP6641047, LP1539, LP4000, LP8202, LP628622, LP9101, LPS6040-6050, Vogue 2273, SMP LP850 Instant LP5003, GL LP 8044, Chess CD CHD3-80002, CHD31268, Charly CD Red Box 3
U7305	Too Young To Know ①	Chess 1452, LP1511, LP60006, LP203, LP40006, LPS6040-6050, Vogue 2372, Chess CD CHD9279, Charly CD Red Box 3, Charly CD Red 17
U7306	Honey Bee ②	Chess 1468, Vogue 2372, Chess LP1427, LP1511, LP4512, LP628622, LP60006, LP203, LP6641047, LP680002, LP1539, LP4000, LPS6040-6050, SMP LP850, Cadet LP4051, K/G LP8156, Vogue LP60100358, Instant LP5003, GL LP8044, Chess CD CHD3-80002, CHD31268, Charly CD Red 1, Charly CD Red Box 3
U7307	Howling Wolf ① ③	Chess LP1553, LP6641047, LP 515036, LPS6040-6050, GL LP 8109, Charly CD Red Box 3, Charly CD Red 17

MUDDY WATERS
Chicago, Wednesday, 11 July 1951

• Muddy Waters vcl, gtr; Little Walter hca ①, speech ②, gtr ③; Len Chess bass drum

U7357	Country Boy (All Night Long) ① ②	Chess 1509, LP1528, LPS6040-6050, Python 04, SC LP1/2, Chess CD CHD2-9348, Charly CD Red Box 3
U7358	She Moves Me ①	Chess 1490, **LP1427**, LP60006, **LP203**, LP8202, LP9101, LP628622, LP680002, LP6641047, LP1539, LP4000, LPS6040-6050, EP6006, BM LP1006, Cleo LP15983, TR LP2632, SMP LP850, Astan LP 20027, Instant LP5003, GL LP8044, Chess CD CHD3-80002, CHD31268, Charly CD Red 1, Charly CD Red Box 3
U7359	My Fault ① ②	Chess 1480, LP6641047, LP4015, LPS6040-6050, SC LP1/2, Python LP19, Charly CD Red Box 3
U7360	Still A Fool ② ③	Chess 1480, 1921, **LP1427**, LP60006, LP680002, **LP203**, LP6641047, LP1539, LP8203, LP4000, LP8202, LP9101, LPS6040-6050, EP6022, Instant LP5003, LP5011, GL LP8044, Chess CD CHD3-80002, CHD31268, Charly CD Red 1, Charly CD Red Box 3

MUDDY WATERS
Chicago, Saturday, 29 December 1951

• Muddy Waters vcl, gtr; Little Walter vcl ①, hca; Jimmy Rogers vcl ①, gtr ②; Elgin Evans drums ②

U7413	They Call Me Muddy Waters ②	Chess LP1553, LP6641047, LP624474, LP4015, LPS6040-6050, EP6145011, LP515036, GL LP8109, Charly CD Red Box 3
U7414	All Night Long	Chess 1509, LPS6040-6050, SC LP1/2, Python LP04, Charly CD Red Box 3
	All Night Long (alt. take) ②	Chess LP6641047, LP4015, LPS6040-6050, CD CHD4-9340, Charly CD Red Box 3
U7415	Stuff You Gotta Watch (Gal You Gotta Watch LP 2057) ① ②	Chess LP6641174, LP4006, LP680002, LP2057, LP515040, LPS6040-6050, SOH LP9015, Cleo LP30683, GL LP8010, DV LP2034, BM LP1023, TR LP2633, Astan LP20028, Chess CD CHD3-80002, CHD9180, Charly CD Red Box 3
U7416	Lonesome Day ②	Chess LP6641174, LP4006, LP2057, LP515040, LPS6040-6050, GL LP8010, Chess CD CHD9180, Charly CD Red Box 3

LITTLE WALTER AND HIS NIGHT CATS
Chicago, May 1952

• Little Walter vcl ①, hca; Muddy Waters, Jimmy Rogers gtr; Elgin Evans drums

U7437	Juke (Your Cat Will Play)	Checker 758, LP2973, LP3004, Chess 114, Chess LP50012, LP6641174, LP60014, LP4002, LP5002, LP1428, LP802, LP202, LP427001, LP1522, LP624805, LP624835, LP515005, M.Arch LP815, LP813, Pye Int. LP28043, EP44035, Pye Golden Guinea LP0280,

		Bellaphon LP5552, Argo LP4026, GL LP6023, LP8018, Instant LP5011, Chess CD CHD2-9342, CHD4-9340, Charly CD Red Box 5
	Juke (alt. take 3)	Chess MCA CD 2-9357
	Juke (alt. take 4)	Chess CHD 9330, Charly CD Red Box 5
U7438	Can't Hold Out Much Longer (Think Of Me) ①	Checker 758, LP3004, Chess LP60014, LP4002, LP802, LP202, LP50012, LP14248, LP427001, Pye Int. LP28043, M. Arch LP815, Bellaphon LP5552, GL LP8018, Chess CD CHD2-9342, Charly CD Red Box 5
	Can't Hold Out Much Longer (alt. take) ①	Chess CD CHD2-9357

MUDDY WATERS AND HIS GUITAR
Chicago, May 1952

• Muddy Waters vcl, gtr; Little Walter hca; Jimmy Rogers gtr; Elgin Evans drums

U7439	Please Have Mercy	Chess 1514, LP6641047, LP4015 Python LP1, LP18, SC LP1/2, Chess LPS6040-6050, DV LP2034, Charly CD Red Box 3

MUDDY WATERS AND HIS GUITAR
Chicago, Wednesday, 17 September 1952

• Muddy Waters vcl, gtr; Little Walter hca; (poss. Junior Wells hca); Jimmy Rogers gtr; Elgin Evans drums

U7476	Who's Gonna Be Your Sweet Man	Chess 1542, LP6641047, LP4006, LPS6040-6050, SC LP1/2, Python LP12, Chess CD CHD4-9340, Charly CD Red Box 3
U7477	Standing Around Crying	Chess 1526, **LP1427**, P60006, LP680002, **LP203**, LP1539, LP4000, LP8202, EP6022, LPS6040-6050, BM LP1006, Cleo LP15983, TR LP2632, Astan LP20027, GL LP8044, Chess CD CHD3-80002, CHD31268, Charly CD Red 1, Charly CD Red Box 3
U7478	Gone To Main Street	Chess 1526, LP4006, LP8202, LP9101, LPS6040-6050, Python LP1, LP18, SC LP 1/2, Charly CD Red Box 3
U7479	Iodine In My Coffee	Chess LP6641174, LP4006, LP2057, LP515040, LPS6040-6050, SOH LP9015, Cleo LP30683, TR LP2633, GL LP8010, DV LP2034, BM LP1023, Astan LP20028, Chess CD CHD9180, Charly CD Red Box 3

MUDDY WATERS
Chicago, poss. 9 January 1953

• Muddy Waters vcl, gtr; Walter Horton hca; Jimmy Rogers gtr; poss. Willie Nix drums

U4332	Flood	Chess LP6641174, LP4006, LP680002, LPS6040-6050, Sunnyland LP100, Chess CD CHD3-80002, Charly CD Red Box 3
U4333	My Life Is Ruined (Land Lady)	Chess **LP1511**, LP60006, **LP203**, LP624801, LP4006, LPS6040-6050, CD CHD9279, Charly CD Red Box 3, Charly CD Red 17

U4334	She's All Right	Chess 1537, LPS6040-6050, SC LP1/2, Charly CD Red Box 3
	She's All Right (alt. take)	Chess LP1511, LP60006, LP203, LP4006, LPS6040-6050, SOH LP9015, Python LP12, Cleo LP30683, TR LP2633, BM LP1023, DV LP2034, Instant LP5003, Chess CD CHD9279, Charly CD Red 1, Charly CD Red Box 3, Charly CD RB15
U4335	Sad, Sad Day	Chess 1537, LP4015, LPS6040-6050, Python LP1, LP12, SC LP1/2, DV LP2034, Charly CD Red Box 3

MUDDY WATERS
Chicago, Monday, 4 May 1953

• Muddy Waters vcl, gtr; Little Walter hca; Jimmy Rogers gtr; Ernest "Big" Crawford bass; Elgin Evans drums

U7501A	Turn The Lamp Down Low (Baby Please Don't Go)	Chess 1542, LPS6040-6050, Python LP12, SC LP1/2, Charly CD Red Box 3, Charly CD Red 17
	Baby Please Don't Go (alt. take)	Argo LP4034, Chess LP4006, LP8202, LP680002, LP628622, LPS6040-6050, Python LP19, DV LP2034, SOH LP9032, Pye Int. LP28045, Cleo LP14983, TR LP2633, BM LP1014, Astan LP20027, Showcase LP141, Chess CD CHD3-80002, Charly CD Red Box 3
U7502	Loving Man	Chess 1585, LPS6040-6050, SC LP1/2, Python LP18, Charly CD Red Box 3

JIMMY ROGERS
Chicago, Monday, 4 May 1953

• Jimmy Rogers vcl, gtr; Muddy Waters gtr; Little Walter hca; Ernest "Big" Crawford bass; Elgin Evans drums

U7503	Left Me With A Broken Heart	Chess 1543, LP4008, LP427012, LP207, GL LP2-6027, Charly CD Red 16
U7504	Act Like You Love Me	Chess 1543, LP4008, LP6641047, LP407, LP813, Bellaphon LP4002, Charly CD Red 16
	Act Like You Love Me (alt. take)	MCA CHD 2-9372

MUDDY WATERS
Chicago, Thursday, 24 September 1953

• Muddy Waters vcl, gtr; Little Walter hca; Jimmy Rogers gtr; Otis Spann pno; Elgin Evans or Fred Below drums

| U7551 | Blow Wind Blow | Chess 1550, LP4015, LPS6040-6050, LP680002, SC LP1/2; Python LP12, GRT LP903360003, Chess CD CHD3-80002, Charly CD Red Box 3, Charly CD Red 17 |
| U7552 | Mad Love (I Want You To Love Me) | Chess 1550, LP1427, LP60006, LP203, LP1539, LPS6040-6050, LP 4000, LP628622, LP9101, EP6008, Argo LP4026, Instant LP5003, GL LP8044, Chess CD CHD31268, Charly CD Red 1, Charly CD Red Box 3 |

U7553	Too Deep Blues	unissued
U7553A	Tell Me How	unissued

ROCKY FULLER
Metropolitan Studios, Pittsburgh, 1953

• Iverson Minter (Louisiana Red) vcl, gtr; Muddy Waters gtr; Little Walter hca

	Gonna Play My Guitar	unissued
	Sweet Geneva	unissued

NOTE: The existence of this session is unsubstantiated.

MUDDY WATERS
Chicago, Thursday, 7 January 1954

• Muddy Waters vcl, gtr; Little Walter hca; Jimmy Rogers gtr; Otis Spann pno; Willie Dixon bass; Fred Below drums

U7589	I'm Your Hoochie Coochie Man	Chess 1560, LP1427, LP60006, LP203, LP1539, LPS6040-6050, LP6641174, LP624825, LP1522, LP4000, LP515005, LP628622, Argo LP4026, Barclay LP84405, Pye Int. LP28030, EP44035, K/G LP8156, NV LP261, Festival LP1008, RCA LP85463, SMP LP850, GL LP SAM500, Instant LP5003, 5011, GL LP8027, GL LP8044, Roots LP113002, Chess CD CHD4-9340, CHD31268, Charly CD Red 1, Charly CD Red Box 3, Charly CD RB 15
	I'm Your Hoochie Coochie Man (alt. take)	Chess LP624474, LPS6040-6050, LP680002, 316500, CD CHD3-80002, Charly CD Red Box 3
15035	Hootchie Kootchie Man (U7589 with brass dubbed on)	Chess 1973
U7590	She's So Pretty	Chess 1560, LP4015, LPS6050-6050, SC LP1/2, Python LP12, Chess CD CHD2-9348, Charly CD Red Box 3

NOTE: The alt. take of U7589 may have been issued on a "light blue" repressing of Chess 1560.

JIMMY ROGERS (AND HIS ROCKING FOUR — CHESS 1574)
Chicago, Thursday, 7 January 1954

• Jimmy Rogers vcl, gtr; Muddy Waters gtr; Little Walter hca; Otis Spann pno; Willie Dixon bass; Fred Below or Elgin Evans drums

U7591	Blues All Day Long (Blues Leave Me Alone)	Chess 1616, LP407, LP6641047, LP4008, LP207, LP813, LP427012, LP624807, Bellaphon LP4002, GL LP2-5027
U7592	Chicago Bound	Chess 1574, LP407, LP6641047, LP4008, LP813, LP60012, LP50011, LP624807, LP4053, Python LP6, Bellaphon LP4002, Charly CD Red 16

MUDDY WATERS
Chicago, Tuesday, 13 April 1954

• Muddy Waters gtr ①, vcl; Jimmy Rogers gtr; Little Walter hca; Otis Spann pno; Willie Dixon bass; Fred Below drums

U7630	Just Make Love To Me (I Just Want To Make Love To You)	Chess 1571, **LP1427**, LP60006, LP680002, LP16500, **LP203**, LP9101, LP1539, LP4000, LP6641174, LP8202, LPS6040-6050, EP6022, EP4006, Pye Int. EP44029, Chess LP628622, KG LP8156, Argo LP4026, SMP LP850, GL LP Sam 500, LP8027, Instant LP5003, LP5011, Ocean LP2044, GL LP8027, LP 8044, Chess CD CHD3-80002, CHD31268, Charly CD Red 1, Charly CD Red Box 3, Charly CD RB15
U7631	Oh Yeh (Oh Yeah) ①	Chess 1571, LP6641174, LP4015, LPS6040-6050, SC LP1/2, Python LP19, DV LP2034, Chess CD CHD2-9348, Charly CD Red Box 3

JUNIOR WELLS
Chicago, Thursday, 15 April 1954

• Junior Wells vcl, hca; Louis Myers, Muddy Waters gtr; Otis Spann pno; Willie Dixon bass; poss. Dave Myers bass; Fred Below drums

1441-4	'Bout The Break Of Day (Early In The Morning)	States 139, Delmark LP640, Red Lightnin LP007, XX EP715
1442-2	Lord Lord (Lawdy Lawdy)	States 139, Delmark LP640, Red Lightnin LP007, XX EP715
1442-2	So All Alone (Baby So Long) (Prison Bars All Around Me)	States 143, Delmark LP640, Red Lightnin LP007, XX EP715
1444-3	Blues Hit Big Town (slow) (Goin' Back To Tennessee)	Delmark LP640
1444-5	Blues Hit Big Town (fast) (Goin' Back To Tennessee)	Delmark LP640

NOTE: On LP640, 1443-7 uses intercut intro from unissued take 6. Muddy Waters probably does not play on all tracks.

MUDDY WATERS
Chicago, Wednesday, 1 September 1954

• Muddy Waters vcl; Little Walter hca; Jimmy Rogers gtr; Otis Spann pno; Willie Dixon bass; Fred Below drums

U7697	I'm Ready	Chess 1579, **LP1427**, LP60006, **LP203**, LP1539, LP4000, LP4010, LP580002. LP16500, LP624474, LPS6040-6050, EP6006, LP628622, BM LP1006, K/G LP8156, TR LP2632, Cleo LP15983, DV LP2034, SMP LP850, Astan LP20027, Ocean LP2044, Instant LP 5003, GL LP8044, Chess CD CHD3-80002, CHD31268, Charly CD Red 1, Charly CD Red Box 3
U7698	Smokestack Lightning	Chess LP6641174, LPS6040-6050, LP680002, LP515040, LP2057, Sunnyland LP100, GL LP8010, Chess CD CHD3-80002, CHD9180, Charly CD Red Box 3

U7699	I Don't Know Why	Chess 1579, LP4015, LPS6040-6050, SC LP1/2, Python LP12, Chess CD CHD2-9348, Charly CD Red Box 3
U7700	Shake It Baby	unissued

NOTE: U7700 may not be by Muddy Waters.

MUDDY WATERS
Chicago, September 1954

• Muddy Waters vcl; Little Walter hca; Jimmy Rogers gtr; Otis Spann pno; Willie Dixon bass; Fred Below drums

U7746	I'm A Natural Born Lover	Chess 1585, LP4015, LPS6040-6050, Python LP 18, SC LP1/2, Charly CD Red Box 3
U7747	Ooh Wee	Chess 1724, LP4015, LPS6040-6050, Python LP18, SC LP1/2, Charly CD Red Box 3

NOTE: Probably from a previous session mastered at a later date.

MUDDY WATERS
Chicago, Thursday, 3 February 1955

• Muddy Waters vcl; Little Walter hca; Jimmy Rogers gtr; unk. gtr ①; Otis Spann pno; Willie Dixon bass ②; poss. Fred Below drums

U7783	This Pain ②	Chess LPS6040-6050, Charly CD Red Box 3
U7784	Young Fashioned Ways (Old Fashioned Ways) ②	Chess 1602, LP4015, SC LP1/2, Python LP12, London EP 1060, Chess LPS6040-6050, LP680002, LP316500, Chess CD CHD3-80002, Charly CD Red Box 3, Charly CD Red 17
U7785	I Want To Be Loved	Chess 1596, LP4015, SC LP1/2, Python LP18, Chess LPS6040-6050, CD CHD2-9348, Charly CD Red Box 3
U7797	My Eyes (Keep Me In Trouble) ①	Chess 1596, LP8202, SC LP1/2, Python LP18, Chess LPS6040-6050, CD CHD4-9340, Charly CD Red Box 3

MUDDY WATERS
Chicago, Tuesday, 24 May 1955

• Muddy Waters vcl; Junior Wells hca; Jimmy Rogers gtr; Willie Dixon bass; poss. Fred Below drums; vocal chorus

U7846	Mannish Boy	Chess 1602, LP1501, LP8203, LP4000, LP624474, London EP1060, Chess LP628622, LPS6040-6050, GL LP8001, Chess LP7250, LP680002, SMP LP850, Connoisseur Collection LP130, Instant LP5003, Chess CD CHD3-80002, CHD9274, Charly CD Red 1, Charly CD Red Box 3, Charly CD RB 15

SONNY BOY WILLIAMSON
Chicago, Friday, 12 August 1955

• Sonny Boy Williamson vcl, hca; Muddy Waters, Jimmy Rogers gtr; Otis Spann pno; Willie Dixon bass; Fred Below drums

U7889	Work With Me	Chess LP6641125, LP417, LP9033417 LP516015, LP4012, LP2015, GL LP8006, Charly LP Chess Box 1, Chess CD CHD2-9343, Charly CD Red Box 1
U7890	Don't Start Me To Talkin'	Checker 824, LP1437, EP 1437, Chess LP427004, LP206, LP624825, LP4001, LP6641125, LP50027, LP817, LP628537, LP4004, LP1522, LP817, LP515005, LP50020, Pye Int. LP28036, LP28030, EP44029, M. Arch LP662, LP813, Argo LP4026, Barclay LP84405, Festival LP1008, Bellaphon LP6542, LP5548, Vogue LP60100358, GL LP8027, Roots LP113002, Charly LP Chess Box 1, Chess CD CHD2-9343, CHD19106, Charly CD Red Box 1
U7891	All My Love In Vain	Checker 824, LP1437, EP1437, Chess LP6641125, LP427004, LP206, LP4001, LP50027, LP50020, Pye Int. LP28036, Bellaphon LP6542, LP5548, Chess LP817, Charly LP Chess Box 1, Chess CD CHD2-9343, CHD19106, Charly CD Red Box 1
U7892	Good Evening Everybody	Chess LP6641125, LP9033417, LP417, LPS15015, LP4012, LP2015, GL LP8006, Charly LP Chess Box 1, Chess CD CHD9116, CHD2-9343, Charly CD Red Box 1
U7893	You Killing Me (On My Feet)	Chess LP6641125, LP9033417, LP417, LPS15015, LP4012, LP2015, GLLP8006, Charly CP Chess Box 1, Chess CD CHD9116, CHD2-9343, Charly CD Red Box 1

MUDDY WATERS (AND HIS GUITAR — CHESS 1612)
Chicago, 3 November 1955

• Muddy Waters vcl; Little Walter hca; Jimmy Rogers gtr; Otis Spann or Lafayette Leake pno; Willie Dixon bass; poss. Fred Below drums

U7937	I Got To Find My Baby	Chess 1644, LPS6040-6050, SC LP1/2, Python LP18, Chess CD CHD2-9348, Charly CD Red Box 3
U7938	Sugar Sweet (I Can't Call Her Sugar LP20027, LP141)	Chess 1612, LP9291, LPS6040-6050, Python LP1, LP18, SC LP1/2, SOH LP9032, LP14983, LP2034, LP9032, Cleo LP14983, TR LP2632, DV LP2034, Astan LP20027, Showcase LP141, Chess CD CHD9291, Charly CD Red Box 3, Charly CD BM 10
U7939	Trouble No More	Chess 1612, SC LP2, Python LP18, GRT LP903360003, Chess LP680002, LP9291, LPS6040-6050, CD CHD3-80002, CHD9291, Charly CD Red Box 3
U7940	Clouds In My Heart	Chess 1724, LPS6040-6050, SC LP1/2, Python LP12, GRT LP903360003, Charly CD Red Box 3

MUDDY WATERS (AND HIS GUITAR — CHESS 1620)
Chicago, 1956

• Muddy Waters vcl; Little Walter hca; James Cotton 2nd hca ①; Jimmy Rogers gtr; Pat Hare gtr; Otis Spann pno ②; Willie Dixon bass; poss. Fred Below drums

8012	Forty Days And Forty Nights ②	Chess 1620, LP1501, LP4000, LP680002, LP624802, LP1528, LP9101, LP628622, LPS6040-6050, Cleo LP15983, TR LP2632, DV LP2034, BM LP1060, London EP1060, SMP LP850, Astan LP20027, Instant LP5003, Chess CD CHD3-80002, CHD9274, Charly CD Red 1, Charly CD Red Box 3
8013	All Aboard ①	Chess 1620, LP9291, LP4015, LPS6040-6050, SC LP2, Python LP12, BM LP1006, London EP1060, Cleo LP15983, TR LP2632, DV LP2034, Club LP Bootleg, Astan LP20027, Chess CD CHD9291, Charly CD Red Box 3, Charly CD BM 10
8014	Tears Of Joy	unissued
8015	Three Time Loser	unissued
8016	Is This Goodbye	unissued
8017	Get Off My Wagon	unissued

NOTE: 8014 may not be by Muddy Waters.

MUDDY WATERS
Chicago, 1956

• Muddy Waters vcl; Little Walter hca; Jimmy Rogers or Pat Hare gtr; Otis Spann pno; Willie Dixon bass; Odie Payne drums

8147	Just To Be With You	Chess 1644, LP1501, LP60006, LP680002, LP203, LP8203, LP4000, LPS6040-6050, GL LP8001, SMP LP850, Chess CD CHD3-80002, CHD9274, Charly CD Red Box 3, Charly CD Red 17
8148	Don't Go No Farther	Chess 1630, LP4015, LP680002, LP9291, LPS6040-6050, GRT LP903360003, SC LP2, Python LP18, Chess CD CHD3-80002, Charly CD Red Box 3, Charly CD Red 17, Charly CD BM 10
8149	Diamonds At Your Feet	Chess 1630, LP680002, LPS6040-6050, SC LP2, Python LP18, SOH LP9015, Cleo LP30683, TR LP2633, BM LP1023, Astan LP20028, Chess CD CHD3-80002, Charly CD Red Box 3

MUDDY WATERS
Chicago, Saturday, 1 December 1956

• Muddy Waters vcl; Little Walter hca ①; James Cotton hca ②; Jimmy Rogers gtr; Pat Hare gtr ②; Otis Spann pno; Willie Dixon bass; poss. Fred Below drums

8388	I Live The Life I Love (I Love The Life I Live) ②	Chess 1680, LP4015, SC LP2, Python LP19, Chess LP680002, LP9291, LPS6040-6050, CD CHD3-80002, Charly CD Red Box 3, Charly CD Red 17, Charly CD BM10
8389	Rock Me ②	Chess 1652, LP4013, LP624474, LP680002, LP9291, LPS6040-6050, SC LP2, Python LP19, GRT LP903360003, BM LP 1006, Cleo 15983, TR LP2632, DV LP2034, Astan 20027, Chess CD CHD3-80002, Charly CD Red Box 3, Charly CD BM 10
8390	(Not by Muddy Waters)	
8391	(Not by Muddy Waters)	

| 8392 | Look What You've Done ① | Chess 1758, LP624474, LP628622, LP680002, LPS6040-6050, Python LP19, Chess CD CHD3-80002, Charly CD Red Box 3 |
| 8393 | Got My Mojo Working ① | Chess 1652, LP4015, LP680002, LP9291, LPS6040-6050, Python LP19, K/G LP8156, GRT LP903360003, Chess CD CHD4-9340, CHD3-80002, CHD9291, Charly CD Red Box 3, Charly CD BM 10, Charly CD RB 15 |

MUDDY WATERS (AND HIS GUITAR — CHESS 1667)
Chicago, May–June 1957

• Muddy Waters vcl; Marcus Johnson tenor sax; unk. tenor sax; James Cotton hca ①; Otis Spann pno; Pat Hare gtr; prob. Robert Lockwood gtr ②; Willie Dixon bass; poss. Fred Below drums

8510	Good News	Chess 1667, LP680002, LPS6040-6050, SC LP2, Chess CD CHD3-80002, Charly CD Red Box 3
8511	Evil ①	Chess 1680, LP680002, LPS6040-6050, SC LP2, Chess CD CHD3-80002, Charly CD Red Box 3
8512	Come Home Baby, I Wish You Would	Chess 1667, LPS6040-6050, SC LP2, Charly CD Red Box 3
8513	Let Me Hang Around ① ②	Chess LP2057, LP515040, LPS6040-6050, GL LP8010, Chess CD CHD9180, Charly CD Red Box 3

MUDDY WATERS
Chicago, 1958

• Muddy Waters vcl; James Cotton hca; Otis Spann pno; Pat Hare gtr; Willie Dixon bass; poss. Fred Below drums

8732	I Won't Go On	Chess 1692, LPS6040-6050, SC LP2, Python LP19, Charly CD Red Box 3
8733	She's Got It	Chess 1692, LP9291, LPS6040-6050, SC LP2, Python LP 19, Chess CD CHD9291, Charly CD Red Box 3, Charly CD BM 10
8734	Born Lover	Chess LP2057, LP515040, LPS6040-6050, GL LP8010, Chess CD CHD9180, Charly CD Red Box 3

MUDDY WATERS
Chicago, August 1958

• Muddy Waters vcl; Little Walter hca; Otis Spann pno; Pat Hare gtr; Luther Tucker gtr; Willie Dixon bass; Francis Clay drums

| 8979 | She's Nineteen Years Old | Chess 1704, LP4003, LP4015, LP680002, LPS6040-6050, Argo LP4042, Python LP19, Chess CD CHD3-80002, Charly CD Red Box 3 |
| 8980 | Close To You | Chess 1704, LP4015, LPS6040-6050, LP680002 LP9291, SC LP2, SOH LP9015, Cleo LP30683, TR LP2633, BM LP1023, Astan LP20028, Chess CD CHD3-80002, CHD9291, Charly CD Red Box 3, Charly CD BM 10 |

LITTLE WALTER AND HIS JUKES
Chicago, August 1958

• Little Walter vcl ①, hca; Muddy Waters slide gtr; Luther Tucker gtr; Otis Spann pno; Willie Dixon bass; Francis Clay drums

8981	Key To The Highway ①	Checker 904, Chess LP1535, LP4011, LP1528, LP624805, EP6011, Argo LP4027, GL LP8035, M. Arch LP804, Bellaphon LP4007, Chess CD CHD4-9340, CHD2-9342, Charly CD Red Box 5
8982	Rock Bottom	Checker 904, Chess LP50043, LP416, Python LP20, SC LP4, Pye Int. LP28035, Charly CD Red Box 5
	Rock Bottom (alt. take)	LRDB LP2017, Charly CD Red Box 5
9141	Walkin' On	LRDB LP2012, Chess LP624805, CD CHD2-9342, Charly CD Red Box 5
	(Rock Bottom; alt. take) Instrumental (poss. Juke; incomplete take)	unissued

NOTE: An alt. take of 8982 appeared on a "light blue" repressing of Checker 904, but not all "light blue" repressings are alt. takes, 8982 extended on some LP issues. On 9141 "Walkin' On" and "Instrumental, " possible change of personnel from Tucker, Dixon and Hunter to Pat Hare, Andrew Stephenson and Francis Clay.

MUDDY WATERS
Chicago, poss. August 1958

• Muddy Waters vcl; Little Walter hca; Pat Hare gtr; Otis Spann pno; Andrew Stephenson bass; George Hunter or Fred Below drums

9140	Walking Thru The Park (Walking In The Park)	Chess 1718, LP1501, LP60006, LP203, LP4000, LP680002, LP8202, LPS6040-6050, SOH LP9032, Cleo LP14983, TR LP2633, BM LP1014, Showcase LP141, Instant LP5017, Chess CD CHD3-80002, CHD9274, Charly CD Red Box 3, Charly CD BM 10

NOTE: This track may have been recorded at the previous session.

MUDDY WATERS
Live at the Free Trade Hall, Manchester, England, Sunday, 26 October 1958

• Muddy Waters vcl, gtr; Otis Spann pno; Graham Burbridge drums; Chris Barber trombone ①; Monty Sunshine clarinet ①; Pat Halcox trumpet ①; Eddie Smith banjo ①; Dick Smith bass ①; Ottilie Patterson vcl ②

Hoochie Coochie Man ①	Krazy Kat LP7405, MW CD 261058, Tomato CD R2 711661
Blow Wind Blow	Krazy Kat LP7405, MW CD 261058, Tomato CD R2 711661
Long Distance Call	Krazy Kat LP7405, MW CD 261058, Tomato CD R2 711661
Baby Please Don't Go	Krazy Kat LP7405, MW CD 261058, Tomato CD R2 711661
Blues Before Sunrise	Krazy Kat LP7405, MW CD 261058, Tomato CD R2 711661
Rollin' Stone (Muddy Waters solo)	Krazy Kat LP7405, MW CD 261058, Tomato CD R2 711661

I Can't Be Satisfied	Krazy Kat LP7405, MW CD 261058, Tomato CD R2 711661
I Feel Like Going Home	Krazy Kat LP7405, MW CD 261058, Tomato CD R2 711661
Walking Thru The Park ①	Krazy Kat LP7405, MW CD 261058, Tomato CD R2 711661
Encore ① ②	Krazy Kat LP7405, MW CD 261058, Tomato CD R2 711661

MUDDY WATERS
Chicago, January 1959

• Muddy Waters vcl; Little Walter hca; Luther Tucker gtr; Otis Spann piano; Andrew Stephenson bass; Francis Clay drums

	Blues Before Sunrise (2 false starts, studio dialogue)	Chess LP680002, LPS6040-6050, CD CHD3-80002, Charly CD Red Box 3
9193	Blues Before Sunrise	Sunnyland LP100, Chess LP680002, LPS6040-6050, Charly CD Red Box 3
9194	Mean Mistreater	Chess 1718, LP9291, LPS6040-6050, DV LP2034, SC LP2, SOH LP9032, Cleo LP14983, TR LP2633, BM LP1014, Showcase LP141, Chess CD CHD9291, Charly CD Red Box 3
9195	Crawlin' Kingsnake	Chess LP1553, LP624474, LP515036, LPS6040-6050, Sunnyland LP100, Python LP19, GL LP8109, Chess CD CHD9299, Charly CD Red 1, Charly CD Red Box 3
	Crawlin' Kingsnake (alt. take)	Chess CHD2-9348

MUDDY WATERS
Live at Carnegie Hall, New York City, Friday, 3 April 1959

• Muddy Waters vcl, gtr; Isaac Washington hca; Otis Spann pno; Al Hall bass; Shep Sheppard drums; Alan Lomax mc

| Hoochie Coochie Man | United Artists LP3050, Capitol CD CPD 8 29375 |
| Goin' Down (Walkin' Through The Park) | United Artists LP3050, Capitol CD CPD 8 29375 |

NOTE: "Goin' Down" is correctly retitled "Walkin' Through The Park" on the Capitol CD. Some sources list James Cotton as the harp player on this session.

MEMPHIS SLIM
Live at Carnegie Hall, New York City, Friday, 3 April 1959

• Memphis Slim vcl, pno; Otis Spann pno ①; Muddy Waters gtr; Al Hall bass; Shep Sheppard drums

Boogie Woogie Memphis (inst.) ①	United Artists LP3050, Capitol CD CPD 8 29375
The Saddest Blues (Rollin' And Tumblin')	United Artists LP3050, Capitol CD CPD 8 29375
How Long	United Artists LP3050, Capitol CD CPD 8 29375

NOTE: "The Saddest Blues" is correctly retitled "Rollin' And Tumblin'" on the Capitol CD.

MUDDY WATERS
Chicago, June 1959

- Muddy Waters vcl; James Cotton hca; Pat Hare gtr; Otis Spann pno; Andrew Stephenson bass; Francis Clay drums; unk. maracas ①

9502	Lonesome Road Blues	Chess LP1444, LP680002, LPS6040-6050, CD CHD3-80002, Charly CD Red Box 3, Charly CD BM 10
9503	Mopper's Blues	Chess LP1444, LPS6040-6050, Charly CD Red Box 3, Charly CD BM 10
9504	Take The Bitter With The Sweet	Chess 1733, LPS6040-6050, SC LP5, Python LP19, Chess CD CHD9291, Charly CD Red Box 3, Charly CD BM 10
	Take The Bitter With The Sweet (false start, studio dialogue)	Chess LP680002, LPS6040-6050, CD CHD3-80002, Charly CD Red Box 3
	Take The Bitter With The Sweet (alt. take)	Chess LP 680002, LPS6040-6050, CD CHD3-80002, Charly CD Red Box 3
9505	She's Into Something ①	Chess 1733, LP680002, LPS6040-6050, SC LP5, Chess CD CHD3-80002, CHD9291, Charly CD Red Box 3, Charly CD BM 10
9506	Southbound Train	Chess LP1444, LP680002, LPS6040-6050, CD CHD3-80002, Charly CD Red Box 3, Charly CD BM 10
9510	Just A Dream (On My Mind)	Chess LP1444, LPS6040-6050, Charly CD Red 1, Charly CD Red Box 3
9511	I Feel So Good	Chess 1748, LP1444, LPS6040-6050, Cleo LP15983, TR LP2632, DV LP2034, Charly CD Red 1, Charly CD Red Box 3
9512	Hey, Hey	Chess LP1444, LPS6040-6050, Charly CD Red Box 3
9513	Love Affair	Chess 1758, LP624801, LPS6040-6050, Charly CD Red Box 3
9514	Recipe For Love	Chess 1739, SC LP2, Charly CD Red Box 3
	Recipe For Love (alt. take)	Chess LPS6040-6050, Charly CD Red Box 3

MUDDY WATERS
Chicago, July–August 1959

- Muddy Waters vcl; James Cotton hca ①; Pat Hare gtr, acoustic gtr ②; Otis Spann pno ①; Andrew Stephenson bass; Willie Smith drums

9639	Baby, I Done Got Wise ①	Chess LP1444, LPS6040-6050, Charly CD Red Box 3
9640	Tell Me Baby ②	Chess 1739, LP1444, LPS6040-6050, Charly CD Red Box 3
9641	When I Get To Thinking ①	Chess 1748, LP1444, LPS6040-6050, Charly CD Red Box 3
9642	Double Trouble ①	Chess LP1444, LP680002, LPS6040-6050, CD CHD3-80002, Charly CD Red Box 3
	Double Trouble (alt. take) ①	Chess CD CHD4-9340

NOTE: Chess LP1444 also issued as Chess LP515029, M. Arch LP723, Pye Int. LP28048, Greenline LP8029. Organ overdubbed on Chess 1748 issue of 9511.

MUDDY WATERS
Chicago, Saturday, 23 April 1960

- Muddy Waters vcl, gtr ①; Little Walter hca; Jimmy Rogers gtr; Otis Spann pno; Willie Dixon 2nd vcl ②; Andrew Stephenson bass; Francis Clay drums

10030	Woman Wanted ①	Chess 1774, LP624801, Python LP19, Charly CD Red Box 3
10031	Read Way Back ②	Chess 1752, SC LP5, Charly CD Red Box 3
10032	I'm Your Doctor	Chess 1752, SC LP5, Charly CD Red Box 3
10033	Deep Down In My Heart ①	Chess LP2057, LP515040, GL LP8010, Sunnyland LP100, Chess CD CHD9180, Charly CD Red Box 3

NOTE: All titles on Chess LPS6040-6050. This issue also has 8 takes of mx 10030, of which only 2 (takes 3 and 8) are complete, and 9 takes of mx 10031, of which only 2 (takes 7 and 9) are complete, plus a complete instrumental take of mx 10031 plus studio dialogue. This material was issued on a bonus LP that was issued with a limited number of the 6040-6050 box sets. Willie Dixon's 2nd vocal on mx 10031 may possibly have been added at a later date.

MUDDY WATERS
Chicago, 7 June 1960

- Muddy Waters vcl, gtr ①; James Cotton hca; Pat Hare gtr; Otis Spann pno; Andrew Stephenson bass; Francis Clay drums

10293	Tiger In Your Tank ①	Chess 1765, LP8202, LP4015, LPS6040-6050, LP9101, Python LP1, LP18, SC LP5, K/G LP8156, Chess CD CHD2-9348, Charly CD Red Box 3
10294	Soon Forgotten	Chess LPS 6040-6050, Charly CD Red Box 3
10295	Meanest Woman	Chess 1765, LP4015, LPS6040-6050, SC LP5, Python LP1, LP19, Chess CD CHD2-9348, Charly CD Red Box 3
10296	I Got My Brand On You	Chess LPS6040-6050, CD CHD2-9348, Charly CD Red Box 3

MUDDY WATERS
Live at Newport Jazz Festival, Newport, RI, Sunday, 3 July 1960

- Muddy Waters vcl, gtr; James Cotton hca; Pat Hare gtr; Otis Spann pno, vcl ①; Andrew Stephenson bass; Francis Clay drums; Langston Hughes mc

	I Got My Brand On You	Chess LP1449, CD CHD31269, Charly CD Red Box 3, Charly CD RB 6
	I'm Your Hoochie Coochie Man	Chess LP1449, CD CHD31269, Charly CD Red Box 3, Charly CD RB 6
	Baby Please Don't Go	Chess LP1449, LP60006, LP203, CD CHD31269, Charly CD Red Box 3, Charly CD RB 6
	Soon Forgotten	Chess LP1449, CD CHD31269, Charly CD Red Box 3, Charly CD RB 6
	I Wanna Put A Tiger In Your Tank	Chess LP1449, LP624801, CD CHD31269, Charly CD Red Box 3, Charly CD RB 6
	I Feel So Good	Chess LP1449, LP680002, CD CHD3-80002, CD CHD31269, Charly CD Red Box 3, Charly CD RB 6
10544	Got My Mojo Working, Part 1	Chess 1774, 133, LP1449, LP8202, Argo LP4027, DV LP2034, M. Arch LP610, Mercury LP25003, GL LP8035, Pye Int. LP28035, Instant LP5011,

	Chess CD CHD31269, Charly CD Red Box 3, Charly CD RB 6
Got My Mojo Working, Part 2	Chess LP1449, CD CHD31269, Charly CD Red Box 3, Charly CD RB 6
Goodbye Newport Blues ①	Chess LP1449, CD CHD31269, Charly CD RED BOX 3, CHARLY CD RB 6

NOTE: Chess LP1449 was also issued as Checker LP6467306, M.Arch LP661, Chess LP4513, LP814, Pye LP34, Barclay LP84093, Chess LP 515039, Chess LP2026, Greenline LP8022. On "Goodbye Newport Blues," Lafayette Thomas can be heard faintly playing guitar.

OTIS SPANN (MUDDY WATERS AND OTIS SPANN – CHARLY)
Live at Newport Jazz Festival, Newport, RI, Sunday, 3 July 1960

• Muddy Waters vcl ①, gtr; James Cotton hca; Pat Hare gtr; Otis Spann pno; Andrew Stephenson bass; Francis Clay drums; Langston Hughes mc

Catfish Blues	JSP LP1070, Charly CD RB 6
Boogie Woogie (inst.)	JSP LP1070, Charly CD RB 6
Slow Blues (inst.)	JSP LP1070, Charly CD RB 6
Jump Blues (inst.)	JSP LP1070, Charly CD RB 6
St. Louis Blues (inst.)	JSP LP1070, Charly CD RB 6

ARBEE STIDHAM
c. 1960–1961

• Arbee Stidham vcl, with Muddy Waters and Willie Dixon (details unknown)

Wee Wee Baby	Doblon LP504117

NOTE: The existence of this session is unsubstantiated.

MUDDY WATERS
New York City, c. January–February 1961

• Muddy Waters vcl, gtr; James Cotton hca ①; Otis Spann pno; unk. bass; poss. Francis Clay or Casey Jones drums

Rock Me (All Night Long) ①	United Artists LP3137, LP1042, LEB LP401, Capitol CD CPD 8 29375, Wolf CD120200
Sunrise Blues (Blow Wind Blow)	United Artists LP3137, LP1042, LEB LP401, Capitol CD CPD 8 29375, Wolf CD120200

NOTE: "Rock Me" was incorrectly titled "All Night Long" on LEB LP401, and "Sunrise Blues" was correctly retitled "Blow Wind Blow" on the Capitol CD.

MEMPHIS SLIM
New York City, c. January–February 1961

• Memphis Slim vcl, pno; Muddy Waters gtr; unk. bass; poss. Francis Clay or Casey Jones drums

John Henry	United Artists LP3137, Capitol CD CPD 8 29375
Stack Alee	United Artists LP3137, Capitol CD CPD 8 29375
How Long	United Artists LP3137, Capitol CD CPD 8 29375
All This Piano Blues (inst.)	United Artists LP3137, Capitol CD CPD 8 29375
Bye Bye Baby	United Artists LP3137, Capitol CD CPD 8 29375
Love My Baby	United Artists LP3137, Capitol CD CPD 8 29375
When The Sun Goes Down	United Artists LP3137, Capitol CD CPD 8 29375

Someday Baby	United Artists LP3137, Capitol CD CPD 8 29375	
Slim's Slow Blues (inst.)	United Artists LP3137, Capitol CD CPD 8 29375	
Gee Ain't It Hard To Find Somebody	United Artists LP3137, Capitol CD CPD 8 29375	

NOTE: United Artists LP3137 was also issued in a stereo version as LP6137.

MUDDY WATERS
Chicago, July–August 1961

• Muddy Waters vcl; Marcus Johnson, Boyd Atkins tenor sax; Matt Murphy gtr; Otis Spann pno; Milton Rector bass; Al Duncan drums

11012	Real Love	Sunnyland LP100, Chess LPS6040-6050, Charly CD Red Box 3
11013	Lonesome Bedroom Blues (Lonesome Room Blues)	Chess 1796, SC LP5, Chess LPS6040-6050, DV LP2034, Chess CD CHD2-9348, Charly CD Red Box 3
11014	Messin' With The Man	Chess 1796, LP624801, LPS6040-6050, Pye Int. EP 44022, Chess CD CHD2-9348, Charly CD Red Box 3
11015	Untitled	unissued

MUDDY WATERS
Chicago, January 1962

• Muddy Waters vcl; A.C. Reed tenor sax; John "Big Moose" Walker organ; unk. gtr; Earnest Johnson bass; Casey Jones drums; female vcl group

U11446	Going Home	Chess 1819, LPS6040-6050, Cleo LP15983, TP LP2632, Charly CD Red Box 3
U11447	Down By The Deep Blue Sea	Chess LPS6040-6050, Charly CD Red Box 3
U11448	Muddy Waters Twist	Chess 1827, LPS6040-6050, Pye Int. EP44010, Charly CD Red Box 3
U11449	Tough Times	Chess 1819, LPS6040-6050, Charly CD Red Box 3

MUDDY WATERS
Chicago, dubbed vcl, Wednesday, 27 June 1962

• Muddy Waters dubbed vcl on instrumental track; Earl Hooker gtr; A.C. Reed tenor sax; John "Big Moose" Walker organ; Lafayette Leake pno; Willie Dixon bass; Bobby Little drums

U11711	You Shook Me	Chess 1827, LP1544, LP4015, LP16500, LPS6040-6050, Bellaphon LP1558, GRT LP903360003, Pye Int. EP44010, Charly CD Red Box 3
	You Shook Me (alt. take)	Chess LP680002, Charly CD Red Box 3

NOTE: Original instrumental track of above recorded Chicago, poss. Wednesday, 3 May 1961, and later issued as:

EARL HOOKER

26-205	Blue Guitar	Age 29106, Red Lightning LP005, P-Vine Special LP9015, Charly LP1134

MUDDY WATERS
Chicago, dubbed vcl, Friday, 12 October 1962

• Muddy Waters dubbed vcl on instrumental track; Earl Hooker gtr; A.C. Reed tenor sax ①;
Jackie Brenston baritone sax ①; John "Big Moose" Walker organ; Earnest Johnson bass; Casey
Jones drums; dubbed percussion ②; bird imitations ③

U11836	You Need Love ②	Chess 1839, LP4015, LPS6040-6050, LP680002, LP316500. Pye Int. EP 44010, Pye Golden Guinea LP0280, M. Arch LP813, Chess CD CHD3-80002, Charly CD Red Box 3
U11837	Little Brown Bird ① ③	Chess 1839, LPS6040-6050, Pye Int. EP44010, Charly CD Red Box 3
U11838	Black Angel ①	unissued

NOTE: Original instrumental tracks of above recorded Chicago, July 1962.

MUDDY WATERS
Chicago, Thursday, 2 May 1963

• Muddy Waters vcl; James Cotton hca; Luther Tucker gtr; Otis Spann pno; Willie Dixon bass;
Willie Smith drums; band vcl ①

U12442	Five Long Years	Chess 1862, LP4015, LPS6040-6050, SC LP5, Chess CD CHD2-9348, Charly CD Red Box 3
U12443	Brown Skin Woman	Chess LPS6040-6050, Charly CD Red Box 3
U12444	Twenty Four Hours	Chess 1862, LPS6040-6050, LP680002, SC LP5, Chess CD CHD3-80002, Charly CD Red Box 3
U12445	Coming Round The Mountain ①	Chess LPS6040-6050, Charly CD Red Box 3
U12446	Let Me Hang Around	Chess LPS6040-6050, Charly CD Red Box 3

MUDDY WATERS
Chicago, Thursday, 6 June 1963

• Muddy Waters vcl, gtr ①; prob. James Cotton hca; prob. Luther Tucker gtr; Otis Spann pno;
prob. Willie Dixon bass; prob. Willie Smith drums

12479	Elevate Me Mama	Chess LPS6040-6050, CD CHD2-9348, Charly CD Red Box 3
	Elevate Me Mama (alt. take)	Chess LP680002, CD CHD3-80002, Charly CD Red Box 3
12480	So Glad I'm Living	Chess LPS6040-6050, LP680002, SOH LP9015, Cleo LP30683, TR LP2633, BM LP1023, Astan LP20028, CD CHD3-80002, Charly CD Red Box 3
12481	My Love Strikes Like Lightning	Chess LPS6040-6050, LP680002, CD CHD3-80002, Charly CD Red Box 3
12482	Early In The Morning	Chess LPS6040-6050, CD CHD2-9348, Charly CD Red Box 3
12483	One More Mile	Chess LPS6040-5050, SOH LP9015, Cleo LP30683, TR LP2633, BM LP1023, Astan LP20028, Chess CD CHD2-9348, Charly CD Red Box 3
12484	Thirteen Highway	Chess LPS6040-6050, CD CHD2-9348, Charly CD Red Box 3
12485	You Don't Have To Go	Chess LPS6040-6050, CD CHD2-9348, Charly CD Red Box 3
	You Don't Have To Go (alt. take)	Chess LP680002, CD CHD3-80002, Charly CD Red Box 3

| 12486 | Things I Used To Do ① | Chess LPS6040-6050, LP660002, CD CHD3-80002, Charly CD Red Box 3 |

BLUES FROM BIG BILL'S
Live at the Copa Cabana, Chicago, Friday, 26 July 1963

• Muddy Waters vcl; Willie Dixon vcl ①; Jarrett Gibson tenor sax; Donald Hankins baritone sax; Otis Spann pno; Buddy Guy gtr, vcl ①; Jack Meyers bass; Fred Below drums

12574	Wee Wee Baby ①	Argo LP4031, Pye Int. EP 44030, Charly CD Red Box 3, Charly CD BM 15
12575	Got My Mojo Working	Argo LP4031, Pye Int. EP 44030, Charly CD Red Box 3, Charly CD BM 15
	Sitting And Thinking	Argo LP4031, Charly CD Red Box 3, Charly CD BM 15
	Clouds In My Heart	Argo LP4031, Charly CD Red Box 3, Charly CD BM 15
	19 Years Old	Argo LP4031, Charly CD Red Box 3, Charly CD BM 15

NOTE: Argo LP4031 was also issued on Chess LP1533, LP2006, LP4558, LP831, LP515041, Greenline LP6004, M. Arch LP724, Barclay LP84116 and Pye Int. LP 28033.

MUDDY WATERS
Chicago, September 1963

• Muddy Waters vcl, gtr; Buddy Guy gtr; Willie Dixon bass ①; Clifton James drums ①

12838	My Home Is In The Delta ①	Chess LP1483, LP515016, LP628622, LP680002, Pye Int. LP28038, Chess CD CHD3-80002, Charly CD Red Box 3
12839	Long Distance ①	Chess LP1483, LP515016, Pye Int. LP26038, Charly CD Red Box 3
12840	My Captain	Chess LP1483, LP515016, Pye Int. LP26038, Charly CD Red Box 3
12841	Good Morning Little School Girl ①	Chess LP1483, LP515016, Pye Int. LP26038, Chess LP680002, CD CHD3-80002, Charly CD Red Box 3
12642	You Gonna Need My Help ①	Chess LP1483, LP515016, Pye Int. LP26038, Chess LP680002, Charly CD Red Box 3
12843	Cold Weather Blues	Chess LP1483, LP515016, Pye Int. LP26038, Chess LP680002, Charly CD Red Box 3
12844	Big Leg Woman	Chess LP1483, LP515016, Pye Int. LP26038, Chess LP680002, Charly CD Red Box 3
12845	Country Boy ①	Chess LP1483, LP515016, Pye Int. LP26038, Chess LP680002, Charly CD Red Box 3
12846	Feel Like Going Home (Muddy solo)	Chess LP1463, LP515016, LP6641047, LP4006, Pye Int. LP28038, Charly CD Red Box 3

MUDDY WATERS / AMERICAN FOLK BLUES FESTIVAL 1963
Jahrhunderthalle, Frankfurt, Germany, Friday, 4 October 1963

• Muddy Waters vcl; Otis Spann pno; Matt Murphy gtr; Willie Dixon bass; Billy Stepney drums; band vcl ①

	Trouble No More	Black Bear LP901
	Five Long Years	Black Bear LP901
	Got My Mojo Working ①	Black Bear LP901

MUDDY WATERS / AMERICAN FOLK BLUES FESTIVAL 1963
The Glocke, Bremen, Germany, Sunday, 13 October 1963

- Muddy Waters vcl, gtr

Captain, Captain	ACT CD 92042, CD 92052, Evidence ECD26100
Catfish Blues	ACT CD 92052, Evidence ECD26100

- Add Otis Spann pno; Matt Murphy gtr; Willie Dixon bass; Billy Stepney drums; band vcl ①

Got My Mojo Working ①	Fontana LP5204, Buddah LP7510, Phillips LP451
Five Long Years	Fontana LP5204, LP885403, Joy LP177, Buddah LP7510, Phillips LP451, L&R LP42023, Evidence ECD26100
In The City (Blow Wind Blow)	ACT CD 92052, Evidence ECD26100
I Feel Like Cryin' (My Home Is In The Delta)	ACT CD 92052, Evidence ECD26100

NOTE: Titles as given on CD; correct titles are in parentheses.

MUDDY WATERS / AMERICAN FOLK BLUES FESTIVAL 1963
Baden-Baden, Germany, October 1963

- Muddy Waters vcl, gtr; Sonny Boy Williamson hca; Otis Spann pno; Matt Murphy gtr; Willie Dixon bass; Billy Stepney drums; band vcl ①

Sonny Boy And Muddy's Mojo (Got My Mojo Working) ①	Black Bear LP903
Captain, Captain (Muddy solo)	Black Bear LP901

MUDDY WATERS / AMERICAN FOLK BLUES FESTIVAL 1963
Poss. Heilbronn, Germany, October 1963

- Muddy Waters vcl, gtr; Otis Spann pno; Matt Murphy gtr; Willie Dixon bass; Billy Stepney drums; band vcl ①

Five Long Years	GSR LP13
Got My Mojo Working ①	GSR LP13
Blow Wind Blow	GSR LP13

MUDDY WATERS
Chicago, Thursday, 9 April 1964

- Muddy Waters vcl, gtr; Otis Spann pno; James "Peewee" Madison gtr; Willie Dixon bass; S.P. Leary drums

13150	The Same Thing	Chess 1895, **LP1501**, LP60006, LP680002, **LP203**, LP4000, LP628622, LP6040-6050, SMP LP850, Chess CD CHD3-80002, CD CHD9274, Charly CD Red Box 3, Charly CD RB 15
13151	You Can't Lose What You Ain't Never Had	Chess 1895, **LP1501**, LP60006, LP68002, **LP203**, LPS6040-6050, Cleo LP14983, SOH LP9032, TR LP2832, BM LP1014, Astan LP20027, Showcase LP141, Chess CD CHD3-80002, CD CHD9274, Charly CD Red Box 3

MUDDY WATERS
Europe, May 1964

• Muddy Waters vcl, gtr; Otis Spann pno; Ransom Knowling bass; Willie Smith drums

Country Boy	LRC CD 9050
Baby Please Don't Go	LRC CD 9050
Hoochie Coochie Man	LRC CD 9050
Sittin' And Thinkin'	LRC CD 9050
(Tiger In Your Tank)	
19 Years Old	LRC CD 9050
Good Looking Woman	LRC CD 29077
(Rollin' Stone)	

NOTE: Titles as given on CDs; the correct titles are in parentheses. "Good Looking Woman" is wrongly credited to Otis Spann on the LRC CD.

OTIS SPANN
London, Monday, 4 May 1964

• Otis Spann pno, vcl, jangle pno ①; Muddy Waters gtr, vcl ③; Eric Clapton gtr ④; Memphis Slim pno ②; Ransom Knowling bass; Willie Smith drums; Jimmy Page gtr ⑤ or overdubbed hca, gtr, bass

DR33230	Natural Days (No Sense In Worrying)	Decca LP4615, Black Cat LP001, SFM LP54, Deram LP1036, SEECD389
DR33231	Meet Me In The Bottom (Mr. Highway Man)	Decca LP4615, Black Cat LP001, SFM LP54, Deram LP1036, SEECD389
DR33232	I Got A Feeling (Everything Gonna Be Alright)	Decca LP4615, Black Cat LP001, SFM LP54, Deram LP1036, SEECD389
DR33233	Keep Your Hand Out Of My Pocket (Crack Your Head)	Decca LP4615, Deram LP1036
DR33234	Sarah Street	Decca LP4615, Black Cat LP001, SFM LP54, Deram LP1036, SEECD389
	Sarah Street (alt. take)	unissued
DR33235	Jangleboogie (Iced Nehi) ①	Decca LP4615, Black Cat LP001, SFM LP54, Deram LP1036, SEECD389
DR33236	Nobody Knows	Black Magic LP9004
DR33237	The Blues Don't Like Nobody (Dollar Twenty Five) ①	Decca LP4615, Black Cat LP001, SFM LP54, Deram LP1036, SEECD389
DR33238	T 99 (Lucky So and So) ①	Decca LP4615, Black Cat LP001, SFM LP54, Deram LP1036, SEECD389
DR33239	My Home Is In The Delta	Ace of Clubs LP1220, Black Cat LP001, MCA LP1862
DR33240	Mojo Rock 'n' Roll ② ③	Decca LP4681, Black Magic LP9004
DR33241	Pretty Girls Everywhere ④	Decca LP4681, LP21, LP387, SFM LP54, Black Magic LP9004, Ace of Clubs LP1220, SEECD389
DR33242	Country Boy	Ace of Clubs LP1220, Black Magic LP9004, SFM LP54, SEECD389
DR33243	Spann's Boogie	Decca LP4615, Black Cat LP001, SFM LP54, SEECD389
DR33244	Stir's Me Up ④ ⑤	Decca 11972, LP4615, LP4681, Black Magic LP9004, SFM LP54, SEECD389
DR33245	I'd Rather Be The Devil	Black Magic LP9004

DR33246	I Came From Clarksdale (Sometimes I Wonder)	Decca LP4615, Black Cat LP001, SFM LP54, Deram LP1036, SEECD389
DR33247	Rock Me Mama (Wagon Wheel)	Decca LP4615, Black Cat LP001, SFM LP54, Deram LP1036, SEECD389
DR33248	Get Out Of My Way	unissued
DR33249	Lost Sheep In The Fold (What Will Become Of Me)	Decca LP4615, Black Cat LP001, SFM LP54, Deram LP1036, SEECD389
DR33250	Keep Your Hand Out Of My Pocket ⑤	Decca LP4615, Black Cat LP001, SFM LP54 SEECD389
DR33251	T 99	unissued
DR39340	You're Gonna Need My Help ① ②	Ace of Clubs LP1220, Black Cat LP001, SFM LP54, SEECD389

NOTE: Personnel as above, plus Spit James gtr; Steve Gregory sax; Bud Beadle sax; Rod Lee tpt overdubbed 1968–1969, and retitled as shown in parenthesis on Deram LP1036. DR33244 has Jimmy Page hca, bass, gtr dubbed on. DR33250 has Jimmy Page gtr dubbed on; not heard on Black Cat issue.

MUDDY WATERS
Chicago, October 1964

• Muddy Waters vcl, gtr ③; J.T. Brown tenor sax ①, clarinet ②; Sam Lawhorn gtr; James Cotton hca; Otis Spann pno; James "Peewee" Madison gtr ④; Milton Rector bass; S.P. Leary drums

13473	My John The Conquer Root ① ④	Chess 1914, 8001, LPS6040-6050, Charly CD Red Box 3
13474	Short Dress Woman ② ④	Chess 1914, 8001, LP680002, LPS6040-6050, CD CHD3-80002, Charly CD Red Box 3
13475	Put Me In Your Lay Away (Put Me On Your Lay Away Plan) ② ③	Chess 1921, LP624801, LP628622, LPS6040-6050, Charly CD Red Box 3

OTIS SPANN
Chicago, Saturday, 21 November 1964

• Otis Spann pno, vcl; Muddy Waters gtr; James Cotton vcl ①, hca; James "Peewee" Madison gtr; Milton Rector bass; S.P. Leary drums; band vcls ②

The Blues Never Die	Prestige LP7391, LP7719, OBGCD 530-2
I Got A Feeling	Prestige LP7391, LP7719, 45-348, OBGCD 530-2
One More Mile To Go ① ②	Prestige LP7391, LP7719, OBGCD 530-2
Feeling Good ①	Prestige LP7391, LP7719, OBGCD 530-2
After Awhile	Prestige LP7391, LP7719, OBGCD 530-2
Dust My Broom ①	Prestige LP7391, LP7719, OBGCD 530-2
Straighten Up Baby ①	Prestige LP7391, LP7719, 45-348, OBGCD 530-2
Come On	Prestige LP7391, LP7719, OBGCD 530-2
Must Have Been The Devil	Prestige LP7391, LP7719, OBGCD 530-2
Lightnin' (inst.)	Prestige LP7391, LP7719, OBGCD 530-2
I'm Ready (no guitar) ①	Prestige LP7391, LP7719, OBGCD 530-2

NOTE: Prestige LP 7391 was also issued on Stateside LP10169 and Ace LP231. Muddy Waters is listed as "Dirty Rivers" on the Prestige release; however, only one guitar can be heard on the recording, presumably Madison, but Muddy can be heard on the band vocal on "One More Mile To Go."

MUDDY WATERS
Chicago, Tuesday, 18 May 1965

- Muddy Waters vcl, gtr; James Cotton hca; Otis Spann pno; prob. Sam Lawhorn, James "Peewee" Madison gtr; Calvin Jones bass; Willie Smith drums

13932	My Dog Can't Bark	Chess 1937, 8019, LPS6040-6050, CD CHD2-9348, Charly CD Red Box 3
13933	Roll Me Over Baby	Chess CD CHD2-9348
13934	Come Back Baby (Lets Talk It Over)	Chess CD CHD2-9348
13935	I Got A Rich Man's Woman	Chess 1937, 8019, LPS6040-6050, BM LP1014, SOH LP9032, Cleo LP14983, TR LP2633, Showcase LP141, Charly CD Red Box 3

MUDDY WATERS
Los Angeles, Thursday, 17 February 1966

- Muddy Waters vcl, gtr

| | I'll Never Be Satisfied | unissued |

NOTE: Recorded at a John Lee Hooker session.

WILLIE MAE "BIG MAMA" THORNTON
San Francisco, Monday, 25 April 1966

- Willie Mae Thornton vcl, drums ①; James Cotton hca; Muddy Waters gtr; Sam Lawhorn gtr; Otis Spann pno; Luther "Georgia Boy Snake" Johnson bass; Francis Clay drums

	I'm Feeling Alright	Arhoolie LP1032, CD305
	Sometimes I Have A Heartache	Arhoolie LP1032, CD305
	Black Rat	Arhoolie LP1032, CD305
	Life Goes On	Arhoolie LP1032, CD305
	Bumble Bee	Arhoolie LP1032, CD305
	Wrapped Tight	Arhoolie LP1032
	Everything Gonna Be Alright ①	unissued
	Gimme A Penny	Arhoolie LP1032, CD305
	Looking The World Over	Arhoolie LP1032
	Big Mama Shuffle	unissued
	My Love	Arhoolie LP1032
	Since I Fell For You	unissued
	I Feel The Way I Feel	Arhoolie LP1032
	Guide Me Home	Arhoolie LP1032

NOTE: "My Love" appears only on the first and third pressings; it is replaced by "Guide Me Home" on the second pressing.

MUDDY WATERS
Chicago, Wednesday, 22 June 1966

- Muddy Waters vcl; James Cotton hca; Otis Spann pno; James "Peewee" Madison, Sam Lawhorn gtr; poss. Calvin Jones bass; Willie Smith drums

| 14628 | Making Friends | Chess 2107, 169559, LP1553, LPS6040-6050, LP680002, GL LP8109, Chess CD CHD9299, CD CHD3-80002, Charly CD Red Box 3 |
| 14629 | That's Why I Don't Mind | Chess CD CHD4-9340 |

	Betty And Dupree	unissued
	Trouble, Trouble	Chess LP68506, CD CHD2-9348
	Black Night	Chess LP680002, CD CHD3-80002
	Trouble In Mind	Chess CD CHD2-9348
	Take My Advice	unissued
	Hard Loser	unissued
	Going Back To Memphis (Memphis Blues)	Chess LP624801, LP628622
	Piney Brown Blues	unissued
	Sweet Little Angel (no hca)	unissued
	Corine, Corina (Coreena)	Chess LP68506

NOTE: "Trouble, Trouble" and "Trouble In Mind" are described as "hornless remixes" on the CD CHD 2-9348 release. Gene Barge tenor sax, unk. alto sax, baritone sax, trumpet, trombone, organ ①, (possibly Pinetop Perkins) dubbed on above session.

Chicago, Thursday, 23 June 1966

14857	Betty And Dupree ①	Chess LP1507, LP4526, CD CHD9286, Charly CD Red Box 3
14658	Trouble ①	Chess LP1507, LP4526, CD CHD9286, Charly CD Red Box 3
14859	Black Night	Chess 169.522, Chess LP1507, LP4526, CD CHD9286, Charly CD Red Box 3
14860	Trouble In Mind	Chess LP1507, LP4526, CD CHD9286, Charly CD Red Box 3
14861	Take My Advice	Chess LP1507, LP4526, CD CHD9286, Charly CD Red Box 3
14862	Hard Loser	Chess LP1507, LP4526, CD CHD9286, Charly CD Red Box 3
14363	Going Back To Memphis	Chess 169.522, Chess LP1507, LP4526, CD CHD9286, Charly CD Red Box 3
14864	Piney Brown Blues ①	Chess LP1507, LP4526, CD CHD9286, Charly CD Red Box 3
14865	Sweet Little Angel ①	Chess LP1507, LP4526, CD CHD9286, Charly CD Red Box 3
14886	Corine, Corina ①	Chess 1973, Chess LP1507, LP4526, CD CHD9286, Charly CD Red Box 3

MUDDY WATERS

15035	See matrix 7589

JOHN LEE HOOKER
New York City, Tuesday, 30 August 1966

• John Lee Hooker vcl, gtr; Muddy Waters, Sam Lawhorn, Luther "Georgia Boy Snake" Johnson gtr; Otis Spann pno; Mac Arnold bass; Francis Clay drums

	I'm Bad Like Jesse James	Bluesway LP6002, LP6061, HMV LP3612, MCA LP204926, BGOCD39
	She's Long, She's Tall (She Weeps Like A Willow Tree)	Bluesway LP6002, HMV LP3612, MCA LP204926, BGOCD39
	When My First Wife Left Me	Bluesway LP6002, HMV LP3612, MCA LP204926, BGOCD39
	Heartaches And Misery	Bluesway LP 6002, HMV LP3612, MCA LP204926, BGOCD39

One Bourbon, One Scotch, One Beer	Bluesway LP6002, HMV LP3612, MCA LP204926, BGOCD39
I Don't Want No Trouble	Bluesway LP6002, HMV LP3612, MCA LP204926, BGOCD39
I'll Never Get Out Of These Blues Alive	Bluesway LP6002, HMV LP3612, MCA LP204926, BGOCD39
Seven Days	Bluesway LP6002, HMV LP3612, MCA LP204926, BGOCD39

NOTE: Although listed on the LP sleeve, George Smith does not play on this session. This session purports to be a live recording at the Cafe Au-Go-Go, but is, in fact, a studio recording with an audience present.

OTIS SPANN
New York City, Tuesday, 30 August 1966

• Otis Spann pno, vcl; George Smith hca ①; Muddy Waters, Luther "Georgia Boy Snake" Johnson, Sam Lawhorn gtr; Mac Arnold bass; Francis Clay drums

Popcorn Man ①	Bluesway LP6003, MCA MCAD-11202, BGOCD221
Brand New House ①	Bluesway LP6003, LP6063, MCA MCAD-11202, BGOCD221
Chicago Blues	Bluesway LP6003, LP6063, MCA MCAD-11202, BGOCD221
Steel Mill Blues	Bluesway LP6003, MCA MCAD-11202, BGOCD221
Down On Sarah Street ①	Bluesway LP6003, LP6063, MCA MCAD-11202, BGOCD221
T'Aint Nobody's Biz-ness ①	Bluesway LP6003, MCA MCAD-11202, BGOCD221
Nobody Knows Chicago Like I Do (Party Blues) ①	Bluesway LP6003, MCA MCAD-11202, BGOCD221
My Home Is In The Delta	Bluesway LP6003, LP6063, MCA MCAD-11202, BGOCD221
Spann Blues ①	Bluesway LP6003, LP6063, MCA MCAD-11202, BGOCD221

NOTE: Bluesway LP6003 was also issued on HMV LP3609, MCA LP204927 and Charly LP106. This session purports to be a live recording at the Cafe Au-Go-Go, but is in fact a studio recording with an audience present.

MUDDY WATERS BLUES BAND
New York City, Saturday, 25 November 1966

• Victoria Spivey vcl ①; George Smith vcl ②, hca; Otis Spann vcl ③, pno, organ; Sam Lawhorn, Muddy Waters gtr; Luther "Georgia Boy Snake" Johnson vcl ④, bass; Francis Clay drums

Chicago Slide	Spivey LP1008
Creepin' Snake ④	Spivey LP1008
Look Out Victoria ②	Spivey LP1008
You Done Lost Your Good Thing Now ③	Spivey LP1008
Take Webster's Word For It ①	Spivey LP1008
Theme	Spivey LP1008
Juke	Red Lightnin LP0024
Take Webster's Word For It (alt. take) ①	Spivey LP1026 Spivey LP1008
Ain't Nobody's Business What I Do ③	Spivey LP1008

Born In Georgia ④	Spivey LP1008
Trouble Hurts ①	Spivey LP1008
Watermelon Man	Spivey LP1008
Old Ugly Man Like Me ②	Spivey LP1008
Gave It All To Me ④	Spivey LP1008
Gave It All To Me (alt. take) ④	Spivey LP1035
Yes Sir! Boss	Spivey LP1009

NOTE: Muddy Waters probably does not play on all tracks. Muddy is listed on sleeve of LP1008 as "Main Stream."

MUDDY WATERS
Live at Newport Folk Festival, Newport, RI, c. 1966–1967

• Muddy Waters vcl, gtr; Otis Spann pno; poss. George Smith hca; James "Peewee" Madison, Luther "Georgia Boy Snake" Johnson gtr; Sonny Wimberley bass; S.P. Leary drums

Nineteen Years Old	Golden Hour LP864, Vanguard LP25-6

SUPER BLUES / LITTLE WALTER (RED LIGHTNIN')
Chicago, January 1967

• Muddy Waters vcl ①, speech ⑤, gtr; Bo Diddley vcl ②, gtr; Little Walter vcl ③, speech ⑤, hca; Otis Spann pno; Buddy Guy gtr; Sonny Wimberley bass; Frank Kirkland drums; Cookie Vee tambourine, backing vcl ④

15498	My Babe ① ② ③ ④	Checker LP3008, Chess CD CHD9168, Charly CD Red Box 8
15499	Hoocher Coocher	unissued
15500	I'm A Man ① ②	Checker LP3008, Chess CD CHD9168, Charly CD Red Box 8, Charly CD BM 26
15501	Blues With A Feeling	unissued
15502	Who Do You Love (omit piano) ① ② ③	Checker LP3008, Chess CD CHD9168, Charly CD Red Box 8, Charly CD BM 26
	Juke Red Lightnin'	EP0027, Charly CD Red Box 8
15503	Juke (alt. mix)	Chess CD CHD9168
15504	Make Love To Me	unissued
15505	Long Distance Call ① ② ③	Checker LP3008, Chess CD CHD9168, Charly CD Red Box 8, Charly CD BM 26
15506	Bo Diddley (omit pno) ② ⑤	Checker LP3008, Chess CD CHD9168, Charly CD Red Box 8
15507	I Just Want To Make Love To You ① ② ③ ④	Checker LP3008, Chess CD CHD9168, Charly CD Red Box 8, Charly CDBM 26
15525	You Don't Love Me ① ② ③ ④	Checker LP3008, Chess CD CHD9168, Charly CD Red Box 8, Charly CD BM 26
15526	You Can't Judge A Book By The Cover ① ②	Checker LP3008, Chess CD CHD9168, Charly CD Red Box 8
15527	Sad Hours	Red Lightnin' EP0027, Charly CD Red Box 8
	Sad Hours (alt. mix)	Chess CD CHD9168

NOTE: Checker LP3008 was also issued as Chess LP2012, LP4529 and Bellaphon LP5534.

MUDDY WATERS
Chicago, 1967

- Muddy Waters gtr ①, vcl; poss. George Buford hca; Otis Spann pno; James "Peewee" Madison, Sam Lawhorn gtr; Sonny Wimberley bass; Willie Smith drums; Pinetop Perkins organ ②

15655	It's All Over ①	Chess LP1553, LP515036, LPS6040-6050, GL LP8109, Chess CD CHD9299, Charly CD Red Box 3
15656	County Jail ②	Chess LP1553, LP624801, LP515036, LPS6040-6050, GL LP8109, Chess CD CHD9299, Charly CD Red Box 3
15657	Two Steps Forward ②	Chess 2107, 169559, LP1553, LP515036, LPS6040-6050, GL LP8109, Chess CD CHD9299, Charly CD Red Box 3
15658	Blind Man ②	Chess LP1553, LP515036, LPS6040-6050, GL LP8109, Chess CD CHD9299, Charly CD Red Box 3

MUDDY WATERS
Chicago, 1967

- Muddy Waters vcl; poss. George Buford hca ①; Otis Spann pno; James "Peewee" Madison, Sam Lawhorn gtr; Earnest Johnson bass; Willie Smith drums; unk. organ ② (poss. Pinetop Perkins)

15840	Find Yourself Another Fool ①	Chess LP1553, LP515036, LPS6040-6050, GL LP8109, Chess CD CHD9299, Charly CD Red Box 3
15841	Kinfolk's Blues ①	Chess LP1553, LP624801, LP 515036, LPS6040-6050, GL LP8109, Chess CD CHD9299, Charly CD Red Box 3
15842	Birdnest On The Ground ②	Chess 2018, LP1553, LP515036, LP680002, LPS6040-6050, GL LP8109, Chess CD CHD3-80002, CD CHD9299, Charly CD Red Box 3
15843	When The Eagle Flies	Chess 2018, LP1553, LP624801, LP515036, LPS6040-6050, GL LP8109, Chess CD CHD9299, Charly CD Red Box 3

THE SUPER SUPER BLUES BAND / HOWLIN' WOLF (LP 624804)
Chicago, September 1967

- Muddy Waters gtr, vcl ①; Bo Diddley gtr, vcl ②; Howlin' Wolf hca, acoustic gtr ⑥, vcl ③; Otis Spann pno; Hubert Sumlin gtr ④; prob. Buddy Guy bass; Frank Kirkland drums; Cookie Vee tambourine, backing vocal ⑤

16224	The Red Rooster ① ② ③ ④ ⑥	Checker LP3010, Chess 169520, CD CHD9169, Charly CD Red Box 8, Charly CD BM 26
16225	Diddley Daddy ① ② ③ ⑤	Checker LP3010, Chess CD CHD9169, Charly CD Red Box 8, Charly CD BM 26
16226	Ooh Baby / Wrecking My Love Life (no pno) ① ② ③ ⑤	Checker LP3010, Chess CD CHD9169, Charly CD Red Box 8
16227	Spoonful ① ③ ④	Checker LP3010, Chess CD CHD9169, Charly CD Red Box 8
16228	Goin' Down Slow ① ② ③ ⑤	Checker LP3010, Chess CD CHD9169, Charly CD Red Box 8, Charly CD BM 26

15229	Sweet Little Angel (Sweet Black Angel) ① ② ③ ⑤	Checker LP3010, Chess LP624804, CD CHD9169, Charly CD Red Box 8
16444	Long Distance Call ① ② ③ ④ ⑤	Checker LP3010, Chess CD CHD9169, Charly CD Red Box 8

NOTE: Checker LP3010 was also issued on Chess LP4537, Chess LP9169 and Bellaphon LP5534. The 159520 issue of mx 16224 is "The Red Rooster Parts 1 and 2"; the credit is Howlin' Wolf, Muddy Waters and Bo Diddley.

LUTHER "GEORGIA BOY SNAKE" JOHNSON WITH THE MUDDY WATERS BLUES BAND (LP781, LP5021); MUDDY WATERS (LP5008, LP90077, LP90099)
New York City, September 1967

• Muddy Waters gtr; George Buford hca, vcl ①; Luther "Georgia Boy Snake" Johnson gtr, vcl ②; Otis Spann pno; Sam Lawhorn gtr; Sonny Wimberley bass; Francis Clay drums

Long Distance Call ②	Douglas LP781, Muse LP5008, CD600630, HB LP90077, LP90098, LP90142, TR LP2545, Vogue CD651 600630
Chicken Shack (inst.)	Douglas LP781, Muse LP5021, CD600630, HB LP90080, LP90099, TR LP2548, LP2584, Vogue CD651 600630
Love n' Trouble ②	Douglas LP781, Muse LP5021, CD600630, HB LP90080, LP90134, TR LP2548, LP2603, Timewind LP50085, Vogue CD651 600630
Mini Dress ②	Douglas LP781, Muse LP5021, CD600630, HB LP90080, TR LP2548, Vogue CD651 600630
Looking For My Baby (no hca) ②	Douglas LP781
Watch Dog ①	Douglas LP781, Muse LP5008, CD600630, HB LP90077, LP90099, LPF4-90111, LP90098, Timewind LP50085, TR LP2545, LP2584, Tran. LP2004, Vogue CD651 600630
Mud In Your Ear (inst.)	Douglas LP781, Muse LP5008, CD600630, HB LP90077, LP90134, LP90098, TR LP2545, LP2603, Timewind LP50085, Vogue CD651 600630
I'm So Glad ①	Douglas LP781 Muse LP5021, CD600630, HB LP90080, TR LP2548, Vogue CD651 600630
Love Without Jealousy ①	Douglas LP781, Muse LP5021, CD600630, HB LP90080, Timewind LP50085, Vogue CD651 600630
Excuse Me Baby (no hca) ②	Douglas LP781, Muse LP5008, CD600630, HB LP90077, LP90134, LP90098, TR LP2545, LP2603, Timewind LP50085, Vogue CD651 600630

NOTE: Douglas LP781 was also issued as Tran. LP188; HB LP90080 also issued as HB LPF4-90111. Muddy Waters probably does not play on all tracks.

OTIS SPANN
New York City, Monday, 20 November 1967

• Otis Spann vcl, pno; Lucille Spann vcl ①; Muddy Waters, Luther "Georgia Boy Snake" Johnson, Sam Lawhorn gtr; George Buford hca; Sonny Wimberley bass; S.P. Leary drums

Heart Loaded With Trouble	Bluesway LP6013, LP6063, MCA MCAD-11202, BGO CD92

Diving Duck	Bluesway LP6013, MCA MCAD-11202, BGO CD92
Shimmy Baby ①	Bluesway LP6013, MCA MCAD-11202, BGO CD92
Looks Like Twins	Bluesway LP6013, LP6063, MCA MCAD-11202, BGO CD92
I'm A Fool ①	Bluesway LP6013, LP6063, MCA MCAD-11202, BGO CD92
My Man ①	Bluesway LP6013, MCA MCAD-11202, BGO CD92
Down To Earth ①	Bluesway LP6013, LP6063, MCA MCAD-11202, BGO CD92
Nobody Knows	Bluesway LP6013, MCA MCAD-11202, BGO CD92
Doctor Blues	Bluesway LP6013, LP6063, MCA MCAD-11202, BGO CD92

NOTE: Bluesway LP6013 was also issued as Stateside LP 10255.

MUDDY WATERS
Washington, D.C., c. 1967–1968

• Muddy Waters vcl, gtr; Paul Oscher hca; Otis Spann pno; Luther "Georgia Boy Snake" Johnson, James "Peewee" Madison gtr; S.P. Leary drums

	Long Distance Call	Smithsonian Institution LP100

MUDDY WATERS
Chicago, February 1968

• Muddy Waters vcl; others unk.

16739	Let's Spend The Night Together	unissued

MUDDY WATERS
Chicago, May 1968

• Muddy Waters vcl; poss. Gene Barge soprano sax ①; unk. flute ②; Phil Upchurch, Roland Faulkner, Pete Cosey gtr; Charles Stepney organ; unk. tambourine ③; unk. harp ④; unk. pno ⑤; Louis Satterfield bass; Morris Jennings drums

17062	I Just Want To Make Love To You	Cadet LP314, Charly CD RB 15
17063	Hoochie Coochie Man ①	Cadet LP314, Charly CD RB 15
17064	Let's Spend The Night Together	Cadet LP314, Bellaphon 18033, Chess 8083, 169538, LP624474, LP628622, Charly CD RB 15
17065	She's Alright ② ③	Cadet LP314, Charly CD RB 15
17066	I'm A Man ④ ⑤	Cadet LP314, Chess 8083, Charly CD RB 15
17067	Herbert Harper's Free Press ③ ⑤	Cadet LP314, Charly CD RB 15
17068	Tom Cat ① ⑤	Cadet LP314, Chess 169538, Charly CD RB 15
17069	Same Thing ⑤	Cadet LP314, Charly CD RB 15

NOTE: Harp in this incidence is the stringed instrument, not a harmonica. Cadet LP314 was also issued on Bellaphon LP6503, Chess LP9283007 and Chess LP4542.

MUDDY WATERS
Live at Newport Folk Festival, Newport, RI, 1968

• Muddy Waters vcl, gtr

	Walking Blues	Vanguard CD 277005
	I Can't Be Satisfied	Vanguard CD 277005

GEORGE SMITH
University of California, Los Angeles, Wednesday, 2 October 1968

• George Smith vcl, hca; Otis Spann pno; Muddy Waters gtr; Sonny Wimberley bass; S.P. Leary drums

Can't Hold Out Much Longer	World Pacific LP21887, Liberty LP83218E, Capitol CD 8 36288

LUCILLE SPANN
University of California, Los Angeles, Wednesday, 2 October 1968

• Lucille Spann vcl; Otis Spann pno; Muddy Waters gtr; Luther Allison gtr; Sonny Wimberley bass; S.P. Leary drums

Love Me With A Feeling	Capitol CD 8 36288

GEORGE SMITH
University of California, Los Angeles, Thursday, 3 October 1968

• George Smith vcl, hca; Otis Spann pno; Muddy Waters gtr; Marshall Hooks gtr ①; Luther "Georgia Boy Snake" Johnson gtr ②; Sonny Wimberley bass; S.P. Leary drums

Juke ①	World Pacific LP21887, Liberty LP83218E, Capitol CD 8 36288
Key To The Highway ①	World Pacific LP21887, Liberty LP83218E, Capitol CD 8 36288
Everything Gonna Be Alright ① ②	World Pacific LP21887, Liberty LP83218E, Capitol CD 8 36288
Tell Me Mama ① ②	World Pacific LP21887, Liberty LP83218E, Capitol CD 8 36288
Last Night ① ②	World Pacific LP21887, Liberty LP83218E, Capitol CD 8 36288
You Better Watch Yourself ① ②	World Pacific LP21887, Liberty LP83218E, Capitol CD 8 36288
West Helena Woman ①	World Pacific LP21887, Liberty LP83218E, Capitol CD 8 36288
Goin' Down Slow	Capitol CD 8 36288
Just A Feelin'	Capitol CD 8 36288

GEORGE SMITH
University of California, Los Angeles, Friday, 4 October 1968

• George Smith vcl, hca; Otis Spann pno; Muddy Waters, Luther "Georgia Boy Snake" Johnson gtr; Sonny Wimberley bass; S.P. Leary drums

My Babe	World Pacific LP21887, Liberty LP83218E, Capitol CD 8 36288
Too Late	World Pacific LP21887, Liberty LP83218E, Capitol CD 8 36288
Mellow Down Easy	World Pacific LP21887, Liberty LP83218E, Capitol CD 8 36288

MUDDY WATERS
BBC 2 TV Broadcast, "Jazz At The Maltings," The Maltings Theatre, Snape, England, Monday, 21 October 1968

• Muddy Waters vcl, gtr; Otis Spann vcl ①, pno; Paul Oscher hca; James "Peewee" Madison, Luther "Georgia Boy Snake" Johnson gtr; Sonny Wimberley bass; S.P. Leary drums; band vcl ②

Blues Riff (inst., incomplete)	Black Bear LP902
Can't Lose What You Ain't Never Had	Black Bear LP902
Bloodstains On The Wall ①	Black Bear LP902
Hoochie Coochie Man	Black Bear LP902
Got My Mojo Working ②	Black Bear LP902
Long Distance Call	Black Bear LP902
Country Boy	Black Bear LP902
Five Long Years (incomplete)	Black Bear LP902

MUDDY WATERS
Live at Salle Pleyel, Paris, France, 4 November 1968

• Muddy Waters vcl, gtr; Otis Spann vcl ①, pno; Paul Oscher hca; James "Peewee" Madison, Luther "Georgia Boy Snake" Johnson gtr; Sonny Wimberley bass; S.P. Leary drums; band vcl ②

Presentation, Andre Francis	France's Concert LP121, FCD 121
Back To The Chicken Shack (inst.)	France's Concert LP121, FCD 121
Train Fare Home	France's Concert LP121, FCD 121
Hoochie Coochie Man	France's Concert LP121, FCD 121
Blow Wind Blow	France's Concert LP121, FCD 121
Long Distance Call	France's Concert LP121, FCD 121
Ring Up ①	France's Concert LP121, FCD 121
Worried Life Blues ①	France's Concert LP121, FCD 121
Got My Mojo Working ②	France's Concert LP121, FCD 121
Got My Mojo Working (encore) ②	France's Concert LP121, FCD 121

MUDDY WATERS
Live at Montreux Jazz Festival, Switzerland, November 1968

• Muddy Waters vcl, gtr; Otis Spann pno; Paul Oscher hca; James "Peewee" Madison, Luther "Georgia Boy Snake" Johnson gtr; Sonny Wimberley bass; S.P. Leary drums

Country Boy	Chess LP680002, CD CHD3-80002

LUTHER JOHNSON WITH THE MUDDY WATERS BLUES BAND (LP789, LPS091, LP9008); MUDDY WATERS (LP90099, LP90077, LPS008)
New York City, 1968

• Muddy Waters gtr; Luther "Georgia Boy Snake" Johnson gtr, vcl ①; James "Peewee" Madison gtr; Paul Oscher hca; Otis Spann pno; Sonny Wimberley bass; S.P. Leary drums

Comin' Home Baby	Douglas LP789, Muse LP5021, HB LP90080, LPF4-90111, TR LP2548, Vogue CD651 600630
Remember Me (no hca) ①	Douglas LP789, Muse LP5021, HB LP90060, LPF4-90111, TR LP2548, Vogue CD651 600630
Natural Wig ①	Douglas LP789, Muse LP5008, HB LP90077, LP 90098, TR LP2545, Vogue CD651 600630
Blues For Hippies ①	Douglas LP789, Muse LP5021, HBLP90080, LPF4-90111, TR LP2548, Vogue CD651 600630
Sting It	Douglas LP789, Muse LP5008, HB LP90077, LP90142, LP90098, TR LP2545, Vogue CD651 600630

Top Of The Boogaloo	Douglas LP789, Muse LP5008, TR LP2545, HB LP 90098, Vogue CD651 600630
Digging My Potatoes ①	Douglas LP789, Muse LP5008, HB LP90077, LP90098, LP90099, LPF4-90111, TR LP2545, LP2584, Timewind LP50085, Vogue CD651 600630
Sad Day Uptown (no hca) ①	Douglas LP789, Muse LP5008, HB LP90077, LP 90098, TR LP2545, Vogue CD651 600630
Evil ①	Douglas LP789, Muse LP5021, HB LP90080, LPF4-90111, TR LP2545, Vogue CD651 600630
Why'd You Do Me (Snake) ①	Douglas LP789, Muse LP5021, HB LP90077, LP 90098, TR LP2545, Vogue CD651 600630
Snake ①	Muse LP5021, HB LP90080, LB90099, LPF4-90111, TR LP2548, LP2584, Vogue CD651 600630

NOTE: Although "Top Of The Boogaloo" is listed on LP90077, it is not on the LP.

OTIS SPANN
Prob. Chicago, 1968–1969

• Otis Spann vcl, pno; Muddy Waters gtr; prob. Willie Dixon bass

Been A Long, Long Time	Testament TCD6001
Look Under My Bed	Testament TCD6001
Tribute To Martin Luther King	Testament TCD6001
Sarah Street	Testament TCD6001
Worried Life Blues	Testament TCD6001

MUDDY WATERS
Chicago, January 1969

• Muddy Waters gtr ①, vcl; Paul Oscher hca; Otis Spann pno ②; Charles Stepney organ ③; Phil Upchurch, Pete Cosey gtr; Louis Satterfield bass; Morris Jennings drums

17581	Screamin' And Cryin' ①	Cadet LP320, Chess 275022
17582	Rolling Stone	unissued
17583	Bottom Of The Sea ③	Cadet LP320, Chess 275022
17584	Honey Bee ①	Cadet LP320, Chess 275022
17585	Plane Fare Home	unissued
17586	Streamline Woman	unissued
17587	Mojo	unissued
17588	My Sweet Man	unissued
17589	Buzzing	unissued
17690	I Am The Blues ②	Cadet LP320, Chess 275022

MUDDY WATERS
Chicago, February 1969

• Muddy Waters gtr ①, vcl; Paul Oscher hca; Otis Spann pno ②; Charles Stepney organ ③; Phil Upchurch, Pete Cosey gtr; Louis Satterfield bass; Morris Jennings drums

17705	Ramblin' Mind ③	Cadet LP320, Chess 275022
17706	Rollin' And Tumblin' ①	Cadet LP320, Chess 275022, Bellaphon 18033
17707	Blues And Trouble ①	Cadet LP320, Chess 275022
17708	Hurtin' Soul ② ③	Cadet LP320, Chess 275022
17709	Need More Woman	unissued

NOTE: Cadet LP320 was also issued on Chess LP4553, LP50017 and Bellaphon LP6503.

MUDDY WATERS
Location and date unknown

• Muddy Waters vcl, gtr; Otis Spann pno ①, lead vcl ②, vcl ③; poss. Sam Lawhorn and James "Peewee" Madison; unknown hca; poss. Calvin Jones bass; poss. Francis Clay or Willie Smith drums

Kansas City ① ②	Testament TCD6001
Tin Pan Alley ① ②	Testament TCD6001
5 Long Years	Testament TCD6001
Live The Life I Love	Testament TCD6001
I Wanna Go Home ① ③	Testament TCD6001
Can't Lose What You Ain't Never Had	Testament TCD6001
High Rising	Testament TCD6001

FATHERS AND SONS
Chicago, Monday, 21 April 1969

• Muddy Waters vcl, gtr; Otis Spann pno; Paul Butterfield hca; Mike Bloomfield gtr; Paul Asbell gtr ②; Donald "Duck" Dunn bass; Sam Lay drums

17782	Sad Letter	unissued
17783	Walkin' Thru The Park ②	Chess LP127, LP8200, LP9100, Charly CD Red 8
17784	Standing Around Crying	Chess LP127, Charly CD Red 8
17785	Live The Life I Love	unissued

FATHERS AND SONS
Chicago, Tuesday, 22 April 1969

• Muddy Waters vcl, gtr; Otis Spann pno; Paul Butterfield hca; Jeff Carp hca ①; Mike Bloomfield gtr; Paul Asbell gtr ②; Donald "Duck" Dunn bass; Phil Upchurch bass ③; Sam Lay drums

17786	Twenty Four Hours	Chess LP127, Charly CD Red 8
17787	Country Boy	unissued
17788	Sugar Sweet ②	Chess LP127, Charly CD Red 8
	Sugar Sweet (alt. take) ②	Chess LP680002, CD CHD3-80002
17789	Forty Days And Forty Nights ②	Chess LP127, Charly CD Red 8
17790	All Aboard ① ③	Chess LP127, LP8200, LP9100, Charly CD Red 8
	All Aboard (alt. take) ① ③	Chess LP680002, CD CHD3-80002
17791	Can't Lose What You Ain't Never Had Chess	Chess LP127, LP8200, LP9100, Charly CD Red 8
17792	I Wanna Go Home	unissued

FATHERS AND SONS
Chicago, Wednesday, 23 April 1969

• Muddy Waters vcl, gtr; Otis Spann pno; Paul Butterfield hca; Mike Bloomfield gtr; Donald "Duck" Dunn bass; Sam Lay drums

17793	Oh Yeah	unissued
17794	Mean Disposition	Chess LP127, , Charly CD Red 8
17795	Blow Wind Blow	Chess LP127, LP8200, LP9100, Charly CD Red 8
17796	I'm Ready	Chess LP127, LP8200, LP9100, Charly CD Red 8
17797	I Feel So Good	Chess 2085, BM LP1006 Astan LP20027
17798	Someday Baby	unissued

FATHERS AND SONS
Live at Super Cosmic Joy Scout Jamboree, Chicago, Thursday, 24 April 1969

- Muddy Waters vcl, gtr; Otis Spann pno; Paul Butterfield hca; Mike Bloomfield gtr; Donald "Duck" Dunn bass; Sam Lay drums; band vcls ①; Buddy Miles drums ②

17799	Hoochie Coochie Man	unissued
17800	Long Distance Call	Chess LP227, LP8200, LP9100, Charly CD Red 8, MCA CHD92522
17801	Baby Please Don't Go	Chess LP127, Bellaphon LP5545, Charly CD Red 8, MCA CHD92522
17802	The Same Thing	Chess LP127, Chess LP16500, Charly CD Red 8, MCA CHD92522
17803	Got My Mojo Working, Part 1 ①	Chess LP127, LP624801, LP60006, LP203, LP628537, Bellaphon LP5545, Charly CD Red 8, MCA CHD92522
17803	Got My Mojo Working, Part 2 ① ②	Chess LP127, LP624801, Bellaphon LP5545, Charly CD Red 8, MCA CHD92522
17804	Honey Bee	Chess LP127, Bellaphon LP5545, Charly CD Red 8, MCA CHD92522

NOTE: Chess LP127 was also issued as Chess LP4556, LP427015, LP50033 and LP22010.

MUDDY WATERS
Chicago, Friday, 11 July 1969

- Muddy Waters vcl; others unk.

17992	Soul Farmer	unissued
17993	Fascination	unissued

MUDDY WATERS
Chicago, c. 1969

- Muddy Waters vcl; Paul Oscher hca; Joe "Pinetop" Perkins pno ①; Sam Lawhorn, James "Peewee" Madison gtr; Sonny Wimberley bass; Willie Smith drums

Mojo	Sunnyland LP 100
Sun Rose This Morning (Goodbye Baby on LEB issue; correct title is Blow Wind Blow) ①	Sunnyland LP 100, LEB LP 401

MUDDY WATERS
Chicago, October 1969

- Muddy Waters vcl; James "Peewee" Madison or Sam Lawhorn gtr; Paul Oscher hca; Joe "Pinetop" Perkins pno; Calvin Jones bass; Willie Smith drums; unk. tenor sax; female vcl group

18253	Going Home	Chess 2085, BM LP1006, Astan LP20027

NOTE: Muddy was hospitalized following a car crash on 27 October, so this song was recorded prior to this date.

MUDDY WATERS
Theresa's Club or Rose and Kelly's Club, Chicago, April–May 1970

- Muddy Waters vcl; Buddy Guy gtr; Paul Oscher hca; unk. bass; poss. Frank Kirkland drums

She's Nineteen Years Old	Red Lightnin LP0055, MAC CD193

| Hoochie Coochie Man | Red Lightnin LP0055, MAC CD193 |
| I Got My Mojo Working | Red Lightnin LP0055, MAC CD193 |

NOTE: Tracks recorded for use in Harley Cokliss's film, *Chicago Blues*. A shortened or possibly alt. take of "Hoochie Coochie Man" may have been used in the film.

MUDDY WATERS
Paris, November 1970

• Muddy Waters vcl, gtr; James "Peewee" Madison, Sam Lawhorn gtr; Carey Bell hca; Joe "Pinetop" Perkins pno; Sonny Wimberley bass; Willie Smith drums

Chicken Shack (band only)	Fan Club CD99
Carrey Shuffle (band only)	Fan Club CD99
After Hours (band only)	Fan Club CD99
Train Fare Home	Fan Club CD99
Honey Bee	Fan Club CD99
Blow Wind Blow	Fan Club CD99
Long Distance Call	Fan Club CD99
Trouble No More	Fan Club CD99
Hoochie Coochie Man	Fan Club CD99
Got My Mojo Working	Fan Club CD99
Goin' Home	Fan Club CD99

MUDDY WATERS
Radio broadcast, Stockholm, November 1970

• Muddy Waters vcl, gtr ①; James "Peewee" Madison, Sam Lawhorn gtr; Joe "Pinetop" Perkins pno; Carey Bell hca; Sonny Wimberley bass; Willie Smith drums

Blow Wind Blow (incomplete)	Black Bear LP903, LEB LP401, MAC CD193
Blow Wind Blow (incomplete; Goodbye Baby on Black Bear issue)	Black Bear LP901, LEB LP401
Hoochie Coochie Man	Black Bear LP901, LEB LP401, Wolf CD120200
Honey Bee ①	Black Bear LP901, LEB LP401, Castle CD MBSCD416/3, Wolf CD120200, MAC CD193
Walking Thru The Park	Black Bear LP901, LEB LP401, Wolf CD120200, MAC CD193
Trouble No More	Black Bear LP903, LEB LP401, Wolf CD120200
Goin' Down Slow	Black Bear LP903, LEB LP401, Wolf CD120200
Got My Mojo Working	unissued

NOTE: "Blow Wind Blow" on the LEB issue plays as a complete track, whereas it is split over 2 LPs on the Black Bear issues.

MUDDY WATERS
Live at Mister Kelly's, Chicago, June 1971

• Muddy Waters vcl, gtr; Paul Oscher hca; James Cotton hca ①; Joe "Pinetop" Perkins pno; James "Peewee" Madison, Sam Lawhorn gtr; Calvin Jones bass; Willie Smith drums

1737	Going Down Slow	Chess LP680002, CD CHD3-80002
1738	Blow Wind Blow	Chess LP50012, LP50006, LP628622, LP515037, CD CHD9338
1739	You Don't Have To Go	Chess LP50012, LP50006, LP628622, LP515037, CD CHD9338
1740	Country Boy	Chess LP50012, LP50006, LP628622, LP515037, LP624801, CD CHD9338

343

1741	Nine Below Zero	Chess LP50012, LP50006, LP628622, LP515037, CD CHD9338
1742	Long Distance Call	Chess CD CHD9338 (see note)
1743	What Is That She Got ①	Chess LP50012, LP50006, LP628622, LP515037, CD CHD9338
1744	She's Nineteen Years Old	Chess CD CHD9338
1745	Stormy Monday	unissued
1746	Strange Woman ①	Chess LP500012, LP50006, LP628622, LP624474, LP515037, CD CHD9338
1747	Boom Boom ①	Chess LP500012, LP50006, LP515037, CD CHD9338
1748	Got My Mojo Working	unissued
1749	Stormy Monday Blues	Chess LP50012, LP50006, LP515037, CD CHD9338
1750	Boom Boom (repeat)	unissued
1751	C.C. Woman	Chess LP50012, LP50006, LP515037, CD CHD9338
1752	She Moves Me	unissued
1753	Rock Me	Chess LP628622
1754	Long Distance Call	unissued (see note)
1755	Mudcat (inst.)	Chess LP50012, LP50006, LP515037, CD CHD9338

NOTE: James Cotton is listed on the sleeve of LP50012 as "Joe Denim." It is not known which version of "Long Distance Call" is issued on Chess CD CHD9338.

MUDDY WATERS
London, Saturday, 4 December 1971

• Muddy Waters gtr ①, vcl; Carey Bell hca; Steve Winwood pno ②, organ ③; Sam Lawhorn, Mick Kelly, Rory Gallagher gtr; Rick Grech bass; Mitch Mitchell drums

Overdubbed New York City, early 1972

• Ernie Royal, Joe Newman tpt; Garnett Brown tb; Seldon Powell tenor sax ⑤

2065	Key To The Highway ②	Chess LP60013, CD CHD9298, Charly CD Red 22
2066	Sad Sad Day ① ③	Chess LP60013, LP50038, CD CHD9298, Charly CD Red 22
2067	Hard Days ①	Chess LP60026, LP50038, Bellaphon LP5545
2068	I'm Gonna Move To The Outskirts Of Town ③	Chess LP60013, CD CHD9298, Charly CD Red 22

MUDDY WATERS
London, Tuesday–Wednesday, 7–8 December 1971

• Muddy Waters gtr ①, vcl; Carey Bell hca ①; Georgie Fame pno ②; unk. organ ③; Sam Lawhorn, Rory Gallagher, Rosetta Green gtr; Rick Grech bass; Mitch Mitchell drums; Herbie Lovelle drums ④

Overdubbed New York City, early 1972

• Ernie Royal, Joe Newman tpt; Garnett Brown tb; Seldon Powell tenor sax ⑤; Rosetta Hightower vcl ⑥

2069	Highway 41 (omit Gallagher, Mitchell) ①	Chess LP60026, LP50038, Bellaphon LP5545
2070	Who's Gonna Be Your Sweet Man When I'm Gone? ① ②	Chess LP60013, LP680002, CD CHD9298, Charly CD Red 22
2071	I'm Ready ③ ④ ⑤	Chess LP60013, CD CHD9298, Charly CD Red 22
2072	Young Fashioned Ways ③	Chess LP60013, CD CHD9298, Charly CD Red 22

2073	Blind Man Blues ② ④ ⑤ ⑥	Chess LP60013, CD CHD9298, Charly CD Red 22
2074	Walkin' Blues (Waters, Lawhorn only)	Chess LP60013, CD CHD9298, Charly CD Red 22
2075	I Almost Lost My Mind ① ② ③	Chess LP60026, LP50038, Bellaphon LP5545
2076	Lovin' Man ①	Chess LP60026, LP50038, Bellaphon LP5545
2077	I Don't Know Why ② ④ ⑤	Chess LP60013, CD CHD9298, Charly CD Red 22

NOTE: Chess LP60013 was also issued on Chess LP6310121, LP2005, LP50002 and Bellaphon LP19097. The organ may have been added at the overdubbing session and may have been played by the producer, Esmond Edwards.

MUDDY WATERS
Chicago, March 1972

• Muddy Waters gtr ①, vcl; James Cotton hca; Joe "Pinetop" Perkins harpsichord ②, pno; James "Peewee" Madison, Sam Lawhorn gtr; Calvin Jones bass; Willie Smith drums

2743	Whiskey Ain't No Good ①	Chess LP50023, CD CHD9319, Charly CD BM 39
2744	Garbage Man	Chess 2143, LP50023, CD CHD9319, Charly CD BM 39
2796	Live Weapon ① ②	Chess LP50023, CD CHD9319, Charly CD BM 39
2797	Someday I'm Gonna Ketch You ①	Chess LP50023, CD CHD9319, Charly CD BM 39
2798	Mother's Bad Luck Child ①	Chess LP50023, CD CHD9319, Charly CD BM 39
2799	Sad Letter ①	Chess LP50023, CD CHD9319, Charly CD BM 39
2800	Funky Butt (inst.) ②	Chess LP50023, CD CHD9319, Charly CD BM 39
2801	Muddy Waters Shuffle	Chess LP50023, CD CHD9319, Charly CD BM 39
2802	After Hours (inst.)	Chess LP50023, CD CHD9319, Charly CD BM 39
	Can't Get No Grindin' (What's The Matter With The Mill or Meal) (band vocals) ②	Chess 2143, LP50023, LP680002, CD CHD9319, Charly CD BM 39

NOTE: Chess LP50023 was also issued on Chess LP50034, LP6310129, LP7002 and Bellaphon LP19868.

MUDDY WATERS
Paris, 1972

• Muddy Waters vcl, gtr; George Buford hca; Joe "Pinetop" Perkins pno; Louis Myers gtr; Calvin Jones bass; Willie Smith drums

	Introduction	Pablo Jazz PACD 5302-2
	Clouds In My Heart	Pablo Jazz PACD 5302-2
	Lovin' Man	Pablo Jazz PACD 5302-2
	County Jail	Pablo Jazz PACD 5302-2
	Hoochie Coochie Man	Pablo Jazz PACD 5302-2
	Blow Wind Blow	Pablo Jazz PACD 5302-2
	Honey Bee	Pablo Jazz PACD 5302-2
	Walking Thru The Park	Pablo Jazz PACD 5302-2
	Rollin' 'n' Tumblin'	Pablo Jazz PACD 5302-2
	Walkin' Blues	Pablo Jazz PACD 5302-2
	Got My Mojo Working	Pablo Jazz PACD 5302-2

MUDDY WATERS
Lausanne, Switzerland, Tuesday, 13 June 1972

• Muddy Waters vcl, gtr; George Buford hca; Louis Myers acoustic gtr

2765	My Pencil Won't Write No More	Chess CD CHD 2-9348
2766	Cold Up North	Chess CD CHD2-9348
2767	Streamline Woman	Chess CD CHD2-9348
2768	Rock Me	Chess CD CHD2-9348
2769	Standin' Around Cryin'	Chess CD CHD2-9348
2770	Hoochie Coochie Man	Chess CD CHD2-9348
2771	Baby Please Don't Go	Chess CD CHD2-9348
2772	You Can't Miss What You Ain't Never Had	Chess CD CHD2-9348
2773	Feel Like Goin' Home (Waters solo)	Chess CD CHD2-9348
2774	Where's My Woman Been	Chess CD CHD2-9348
2775	Rollin' And Tumblin'	Chess CD CHD2-9348

MUDDY WATERS
Live at Montreux Jazz Festival, Montreux, Switzerland, Saturday, 17 June 1972

• Muddy Waters vcl, gtr; George Buford hca; Lafayette Leake pno; Louis Myers gtr; Dave Myers bass; Fred Below drums

2468	Sail On	unissued
2469	Hoochie Coochie Man	unissued
2470	County Jail	Chess LP60015, LP50023, LP4056, Bellaphon LP6559, GL LP26033, LRC CD9050
2471	Long Distance Call	LRC CD9050
2472	Rock Me Baby	LRC CD9050
2473	Trouble No More (Sweet Little Angel)	Chess LP60015, LP50023, LP4056, Bellaphon LP6559, GL LP26033, LRC CD9050
2474	Rosalee (Rosalie)	LRC CD9050
2475	Rollin' And Tumblin' (All Night Long)	LRC CD9050
2476	All I Had Was Gone (Early Morning Blues)	LRC CD9050
2477	Got My Mojo Working	Chess LP60015, LP50023, LP4056, Bellaphon LP6559, GL LP26033

NOTE: The alternative titles in parentheses are those given on the LRC CD9050 release. The correct title of "All I Had Was Gone / Early Morning Blues" is "I Feel Like Going Home."

T-BONE WALKER WITH MUDDY WATERS
Live at Montreux Jazz Festival, Montreux, Switzerland, Saturday, 17 June 1972

• Muddy Waters vcl, gtr; T-Bone Walker vcl, gtr; George Buford hca; Lafayette Leake pno; Louis Myers gtr; Dave Myers bass; Fred Below drums

2478	They Call It Stormy Monday	Chess LP60015, LP50023, LP4056, Bellaphon LP6559, GL LP26033
2543	She Says She Loves Me	Chess LP60015, LP50023, LP4056, Bellaphon LP6559, GL LP26033

KOKO TAYLOR WITH MUDDY WATERS
Live at Montreux Jazz Festival, Montreux, Switzerland, Saturday, 17 June 1972

• Koko Taylor, Muddy Waters vcl; Lafayete Leake pno; Louis Myers gtr; Dave Myers bass; Fred Below drums

| 2501 | I Got What It Takes | Chess LP60015, LP50023, LP4056, Bellaphon LP6559, GL LP26033 |

JOHN SINCLAIR, MUDDY WATERS, LUCILLE SPANN
Live at Ann Arbor Festival, Ann Arbor, MI, Saturday, 9 September 1972

• John Sinclair speech; Muddy Waters speech; Lucille Spann speech

| | Festival dedication to Otis Spann | Atlantic LP502, LP60048 |

MUDDY WATERS
Live at Ann Arbor Festival, Ann Arbor, MI, Saturday, 9 September 1972

• Muddy Waters vcl, gtr; Marcus Johnson alto sax; George Buford hca; Joe "Pinetop" Perkins pno; James "Peewee" Madison, Louis Myers gtr; Calvin Jones bass; Willie Smith drums

| 25832 | Honey Bee | Atlantic LP502, LP60048, LP78131, LP7816971 |

MUDDY WATERS
Unknown date and location

• Muddy Waters vcl; unk. hca, pno, gtrs, bass and drums

| | Got My Mojo Working | Paradise CD Para 1060 |

NOTE: Paradise CD Para 1060 is a John Lee Hooker bootleg CD called *The Night Of The Hook.* The song is credited to Hooker, but it is by Muddy Waters. The location is unknown, but the recording sounds like it was made circa 1970s.

MUDDY WATERS
Live at Lincoln Center, New York City, Friday, 29 June 1973

• Muddy Waters vcl, gtr; George Buford hca; Joe "Pinetop" Perkins pno; Luther "Guitar Jr." Johnson, Bob Margolin gtr; Calvin Jones bass; Willie Smith drums

	Long Distance Call	Buddah LP5144, Blue Moon CDBM 071
	Where's My Woman Been	Buddah LP5144, Blue Moon CDBM 071
	Got My Mojo Working	Buddah LP5144, Blue Moon CDBM 071

NOTE: Buddah LP5144 was also issued on Atlantic LP90003, Intermedia LP5022, Astan LP20039, Blue Moon LP002 and Charly LP34.

MUDDY WATERS
Live, unknown location, poss. 1970s

• Muddy Waters gtr, vcl; poss. Jerry Portnoy hca; Joe "Pinetop" Perkins pno; Bob Margolin, Luther "Guitar Jr." Johnson gtr; Calvin Jones bass; Willie Smith drums

| | Baby Please Don't Go | LEB LP401, Wolf CD120200 |

MUDDY WATERS
Live in Boston, 16 January 1974

• Muddy Waters vcl, gtr; probably Bob Margolin, Luther "Guitar Jr." Johnson gtr; Jerry Portnoy hca; Joe "Pinetop" Perkins pno; Calvin Jones bass; Willie Smith drums

Blow Wind Blow	Blue Knight BKR CD23
Howlin' Wolf	Blue Knight BKR CD23
What's The Matter With The Mill	Blue Knight BKR CD23
Love 'n' Trouble	Blue Knight BKR CD23
Hoochie Coochie Man	Blue Knight BKR CD23
Baby Please Don't Go	Blue Knight BKR CD23
Mannish Boy	Blue Knight BKR CD23
Everything's Gonna Be Alright	Blue Knight BKR CD23
Got My Mojo Working	Blue Knight BKR CD23
Instrumental (Honky Tonk)	Blue Knight BKR CD23
Harmonica Boogie (Off The Wall)	Blue Knight BKR CD23
Garbage Man	Blue Knight BKR CD23

NOTE: The titles are as given on the CD; the correct titles are in parentheses.

MUDDY WATERS
Chicago, Tuesday–Wednesday, 29–30 January 1974

• Muddy Waters gtr ①, vcl; George Buford hca ②; Paul Oscher hca ③; Carey Bell hca ④; Joe "Pinetop" Perkins pno; Luther "Guitar Jr." Johnson, Bob Margolin gtr; Calvin Jones bass; Willie Smith drums

3354	Trouble No More ②	Chess LP60031, Charly CD BM 39
3355	Katie ④	Chess LP60031, Charly CD BM 39
3356	Pinetop Boogie	unissued
3357	Electric Man ④	Chess LP60031, Charly CD BM 39
3358	Rollin' And Tumblin' ① ④	Chess LP60031, Charly CD BM 39
3359	"Unk" In Funk ③	Chess LP60031, Charly CD BM 39
3360	Drive My Blues Away ④	Chess LP60031, Charly CD BM 39
3361	Just To Be With You ④	Chess LP60031, Charly CD BM 39
3362	Everything Gonna Be Alright ②	Chess LP60031, Charly CD BM 39
3412	Waterboy, Waterboy ④	Chess LP60031, Charly CD BM 39

NOTE: Chess LP 60031 was also issued on Chess LP50040, LP91513, GL LP8115 and Bellaphon LP19179.

MUDDY WATERS
Los Angeles, 1974 (from soundtrack of the film *Mandingo*, directed by Richard Fleischer)

• Muddy Waters vcl; unk. banjo, washboard; with orchestra dir. and cond. by Maurice Jarre

        Born In This Time

NOTE: This recording was possibly not issued in LP/cassette/CD form, but it is on film/video sound track.

MUDDY WATERS
Live in Antibes, France, Wednesday, 24 July 1974

• Muddy Waters vcl, gtr; Bob Margolin gtr; Luther "Guitar Jr." Johnson gtr; Joe "Pinetop" Perkins pno, vcl ①; Jerry Portnoy hca; Calvin Jones bass; Willie Smith drums; band vcl ②

Honky Tonk (band only)	France's Concert LPFC116, CD116, Best CD9104
Off The Wall (band only)	France's Concert LPFC116, CD116, Best CD9104
Blow Wind Blow	France's Concert LPFC116, CD116, Best CD9104

Howlin' Wolf	France's Concert LPFC116, CD116, Best CD9104	
Can't Get No Grindin' ②	France's Concert LPFC116, CD116, Best CD9104	
Trouble No More	France's Concert LPFC116, CD116, Best CD9104	
Garbage Man	BRMT 016, France's Concert LPFC116, CD116, Best CD9104	
Hoochie Coochie Man	BRMT 016, France's Concert LPFC116, CD116, Best CD9104	
Baby Please Don't Go	France's Concert LPFC116, CD116, Best CD9104	
Manish Boy	BRMT 016, France's Concert LPFC116, CD116, Best CD9104	
Everything Gonna Be Alright	France's Concert LPFC116, CD116, Best CD9104	
Got My Mojo Workin' ①	France's Concert LPFC116, CD116, Best CD9104	
Got My Mojo Workin' (reprise)	France's Concert LPFC116, CD116,	

NOTE: BRMT 016 is a 12-inch single. The alternative titles on the Best CD are as follows: "Honky Tonk" ("Big Seven Blues"), "Off The Wall" ("Blues Straight Ahead"), "Blow Wind Blow" ("Don't The Sun Look Lonesome") and "Got My Mojo Workin'" ("We've Got Our Mojo Working").

MUDDY WATERS
Bearsville's Studio, Turtle Creek, Woodstock, NY, Thursday–Friday, 6–7 February 1975

• Muddy Waters gtr ①, vcl; Paul Butterfield hca; Bob Margolin gtr; Garth Hudson organ ②, accordian ③, sax ④; Howard Johnson sax ④; Joe "Pinetop" Perkins 2nd vcl ⑤, pno; Fred Carter gtr, bass; Levon Helm drums, bass

4028	Why Are People Like That ②	Chess LP60035, LP50052, LP9283009, Bellaphon LP19277, Chess CDCHD9359
4029	Going Down To Main Street ③	Chess LP60035, LP50052, LP9283009, Bellaphon LP19277, Chess CDCHD9359
4030	Born With Nothing ① ③	Chess LP60035, LP50052, LP9283009, Bellaphon LP19277, Chess CDCHD9359
4031	Caledonia ③ ⑤	Chess LP60035, LP50052, LP9283009, Bellaphon LP19277, Chess CD CHD9359
4032	Funny Sounds ③	Chess LP60035, LP50052, LP9283009, Bellaphon LP19277, Chess CD CHD9359
4033	Love, Deep As The Ocean ① ②	Chess LP60035, LP50052, LP9283009, Bellaphon LP19277, Chess CDCHD9359
4034	Let The Good Times Roll ④	Chess LP60035, LP50052, LP9283009, Bellaphon LP19277, Chess CDCHD9359
4035	Kansas City ② ⑤	Chess LP60035, LP50052, LP9283009, Bellaphon LP19277, Chess CD CHD9359
4036	On My Back	unissued
4037	Untitled	unissued
	Fox Squirrel	Chess CD CHD9359

NOTE: "Caledonia" is retitled "Caldonia" on Chess CHD CD9359.

JOHNNY WINTER
Live, unk. location, 22 March 1976

• Muddy Waters vcl; Johnny Winter vcl, gtr; James Cotton hca; Joe "Pinetop" Perkins pno; Bob Margolin gtr; Charles Calmese bass; Willie Smith drums

Walking Thru The Park	Blue Sky LP34313, LP82141, BGO CD104

MUDDY WATERS
Westport, CT, 4–10 October 1976

• Muddy Waters vcl; Johnny Winter vcl ①, gtr; James Cotton hca; Joe "Pinetop" Perkins pno; Bob Margolin gtr; Charles Calmese bass; Willie Smith drums

Mannish Boy ①	MUDT 1, MUD 1, Blue Sky LP34449, LP25565, CD32357
Bus Driver	Blue Sky LP34449, CD32357, Epic CD4611862
I Want To Be Loved	Blue Sky LP34439, LP255565, Epic LP461186, CD4611862, Blue Sky CD32357
Jealous Hearted Man	Blue Sky LP34449, CD32357, COL CD467892 2
I Can't Be Satisfied (omit Cotton, Perkins, Calmese)	Blue Sky LP34449, LP25565, Epic LP461186, Blue Sky CD32357, CD4611862, COL CD467892 2
I Feel Like Going Home (omit Cotton, Perkins, Calmese)	Blue Sky LP37064, CD ZK37064, COL CD467892 2
The Blues Had A Baby And They Named It Rock And Roll (No. 2)	MUDT 1, Blue Sky LP34449, LP25565, Epic LP461186, Blue Sky CD32357
Deep Down In Florida	Blue Sky LP34449, CD32357
Crosseyed Cat	Blue Sky LP34449, CD32357, COL CD467892 2
Little Girl	MUDT 1, Blue Sky LP34449, CD32357
My Eyes Keep Me In Trouble	Blue Sky LP37064, CD ZK37064, COL CD467892 2

NOTE: Blue Sky LP34449 was also issued as Blue Sky LP 81853 and LP 32357. Blue Sky LP37064 was also issued as Blue Sky LP84918. MUDT 1 is a 12-inch single. "Mannish Boy" on MUD 1 is an edited version.

MUDDY WATERS BLUES BAND
Live in Warsaw, Poland, Friday, 22 October 1976

• Muddy Waters vcl, gtr; Luther "Guitar Jr." Johnson, Bob Margolin gtr; Jerry Portnoy hca; Joe "Pinetop" Perkins pno, 2nd vcl ①; Calvin Jones bass; Willie Smith drums

Junior Shuffle (band only)	Poljazz LP0634, Poljazz LP79, Moon LP007-1, Blues Collection CD011
Floyd's Guitar Blues (band only)	Poljazz LP0634, Poljazz LP79, Moon LP007-1, Blues Collection CD011, Classic CD7511, CDSGP 0150
J Ps Boogie (band only) (G.P.'s Boogie on Moon CD)	Poljazz LP0634, Poljazz LP79, Moon LP007-1, MCD 007-2, Blues Collection CD011
Baby Please Don't Go	Poljazz LP0634, Poljazz LP79, Moon LP007-1, Blues Collection CD011, Classic CD7511, CDSGP 0150
Soon Forgotten	Poljazz LP0634, Poljazz LP79, Moon LP007-1, Blues Collection CD011, Classic CD7511, CDSGP 0150
Corinne Corinna (Corrinna Corrinna on Moon CD)	Poljazz LP0634, Poljazz LP79, Moon LP007-1, MCD 007-2, Blues Collection CD011, Classic CD7511, CDSGP 0150, Blue Knight CD BKR23
Hoochie Coochie Man	Poljazz LP0634, Poljazz LP79, Moon LP007-1, Blues Collection CD011, Classic CD7511, CDSGP 0150
Howlin' Wolf	Poljazz LP0634, Poljazz LP79, Moon LP007-1, Blues Collection CD011, Classic CD7511, CDSGP 0150

Blow Wind Blow	Poljazz LP0635, Poljazz LP80, Classic CD7511, CDSGP 0150, Blue Knight CD BKR23, Moon MCD 017-2
What's A Matter With A Meal (What's The Matter With The Mill)	Poljazz LP0635, Poljazz LP80, Blues Collection CD011, Poljazz LP0635, Poljazz LP80, Poljazz LP0635, Moon MCD 017-2
Kansas City ①	Poljazz LP80, Classic CD7511, CDSGP 0150, Blue Knight CD BKR23, Moon MCD 017-2
Caldonia ①	Blue Knight CD BKR23, Poljazz LP0635, Moon MCD 017-2
Screamin' And Crying'	Poljazz LP0635, Poljazz LP80, Classic CD7511, CDSGP 0150,
Everything Gonna Be Alright	unissued
I Got My Mojo Working	Poljazz LP0635, Poljazz LP80, Classic CD7511, CDSGP 0150
Garbage Man (Gabbage Man on Moon CD)	Poljazz LP0635, Poljazz LP80, Classic CD7511, CDSGP 0150, Moon MCD 017-2
Goin' Down Slow	Blues Collection CD011
After Hours	Blues Collection CD011

MUDDY WATERS BLUESBAND
Dortmund, Germany, prob. 29 October 1976

• Muddy Waters vcl, gtr; Bob Margolin gtr; Luther "Guitar Jr." Johnson gtr, speech ①; Jerry Portnoy hca; Joe "Pinetop" Perkins pno; Calvin Jones bass; Willie Smith drums; Junior Wells vcl, hca ②

Intro (After Hours) (band only) ①	Corinne LP100
Untitled blues no. 1 (Soon Forgotten)	Corinne LP100
Howlin' Wolf Blues	Corinne LP100, Wolf CD120200
Hoochie Coochie Man	Corinne LP100
Untitled blues no. 2 (Blow Wind Blow)	Corinne LP100
What's The Matter (Can't Get No Grindin')	Corinne LP100
Long Distance Call	Corinne LP100, Wolf CD120200
Got My Mojo Workin'	Corinne LP100
Got My Mojo Workin' (first encore)	Corinne LP100
Theme	Corinne LP100
Got My Mojo Workin' (second encore) ②	Corinne LP100

NOTE: This session probably originates from a TV broadcast. The titles are as given on the LP; the correct titles are shown in parentheses.

MUDDY WATERS
Monthey, Montreux, Switzerland, 4 November 1976

• Muddy Waters gtr, vcl ①; Luther "Guitar Jr." Johnson gtr, vcl ②; Bob Margolin gtr; Jerry Portnoy, hca; Joe "Pinetop" Perkins pno, vcl ③; Calvin Jones bass, vcl ④; Willie Smith drums

After Hours (band only, inst.)	Jazz Helvetica CD 02, Landscape CD LS2908
Floyd's Guitar Blues / Blue Lights (band only, inst.)	Jazz Helvetica CD 02, Landscape CD LS2908

Boogie Thing (band only, inst.)	Jazz Helvetica CD 02, Landscape CD LS2908
Chicken Shack (band only, inst.)	Jazz Helvetica CD 02, Landscape CD LS2908
Going Down Slow ①	Jazz Helvetica CD 02, Landscape CD LS2908
What's The Matter With The Mill (Can't Get No Grindin') ①	Jazz Helvetica CD 02, Landscape CD LS2908, MAC CD193
Hoochie Coochie Man ①	Jazz Helvetica CD 02, Landscape CD LS2908
Howlin' Wolf ①	Jazz Helvetica CD 02, Landscape CD LS2908, MAC CD193
Everything's Gonna Be Alright ① ②	Jazz Helvetica CD 02, Landscape CD LS2908, MAC CD193
Theme (band only)	Jazz Helvetica CD 02, Landscape CD LS2908
Dust My Broom ④	Jazz Helvetica CD 02, Landscape CD LS2908, MAC CD193
You Left Me With A Broken Heart ④	Jazz Helvetica CD 02, Landscape CD LS2908
Nothing But Soul ②	Jazz Helvetica CD 02, Landscape CD LS2921
I Got A Mind To Travel ②	Jazz Helvetica CD 02, Landscape CD LS2921
After Hours (band only, inst.)	Jazz Helvetica CD 02, Landscape CD LS2921
Stormy Monday ①	Jazz Helvetica CD 02, Landscape CD LS2921
Walking Blues ①	Jazz Helvetica CD 02, Landscape CD LS2921, Best CD BSTCD9104, MAC CD193
Rollin' And Tumblin' ①	Jazz Helvetica CD 02, Landscape CD LS2921, Best CD BSTCD9104, MAC CD193
Got My Mojo Working ①	Jazz Helvetica CD 02, Landscape CD LS2921
Take A Little Walk With Me ③	Jazz Helvetica CD 02, Landscape CD LS2921
For You My Love ③	Jazz Helvetica CD 02, Landscape CD LS2921

NOTE: Muddy Waters does not play on all tracks.

THE BAND
Live at Winterland, San Francisco, Thursday, 25 November 1976

• Muddy Waters vcl; Paul Butterfield hca; Bob Margolin, Robbie Robertson gtr; Joe "Pinetop" Perkins pno; Richard Manuel, Garth Hudson keyboards; Rick Danko bass; Levon Helm drums

Mannish Boy	Warner Bros. LP3146, LP66076, CD7599-27346-2

MUDDY WATERS
Live at Harry Hope's Club, Chicago, Friday, 18 March 1977

• Muddy Waters vcl, gtr, slide gtr ①; Johnny Winter gtr; Bob Margolin gtr; Luther "Guitar Jr." Johnson gtr; Joe "Pinetop" Perkins pno; Jerry Portnoy hca; Calvin Jones bass; Willie Smith drums

Mannish Boy	Blue Sky LP35712, BGO CD109
She's Nineteen Years Old ①	Blue Sky LP35712, LP25565, Epic LP461186, CD4611862, BGO CD109
Streamline Woman ①	Blue Sky LP35712, BGO CD109, COL CD467892 2
Baby Please Don't Go	Blue Sky LP35712, LP25565, Epic LP461186, CD4611862, BGO CD109

NOTE: Blue Sky LP35712 was also issued as Blue Sky LP83422.

MUDDY WATERS
Live at Nice Jazz Festival, Nice, France, 9 July 1977

- Muddy Waters vcl, gtr; prob. Bob Margolin, Luther "Guitar Jr." Johnson gtr; Jerry Portnoy hca; Joe "Pinetop" Perkins pno, vcl ①; Calvin Jones bass; Willie Smith drums; Dizzy Gillespie trumpet ②

Instrumental (incomplete)	LRC CD9015
Nicest Blues (Back To The Chicken Shack, inst.)	LRC CD9015, Laserlight CD17-102
Harmonica Rockin' (Rocker, inst.)	LRC CD9015, Laserlight CD17-102
Down Broke Down (Can't Get No Grindin')	LRC CD9015, Laserlight CD17-102
Baby Rock And Roll (The Blues Had A Baby And They Named It Rock And Roll)	LRC CD9015, Laserlight CD17-102
So Long (Honey Bee) ②	LRC CD9015, Laserlight CD17-102
Kansas City ②	LRC CD9015, Laserlight CD17-102

NOTE: The titles are as given on the CD; the correct titles are shown in parentheses.

T BONE WALKER WITH THE MUDDY WATERS BLUES BAND
Live prob. at Nice Jazz Festival, Nice, France, July 1977

- Muddy Waters vcl, gtr; Jerry Portnoy hca; Bob Margolin gtr; Luther "Guitar Jr." Johnson gtr; Joe "Pinetop" Perkins pno, vcl ①; Calvin Jones bass; Willie Smith drums

Come Baby (You Don't Have To Go)	LRC Jazz Classics 1003
Hold It (Trouble No More)	LRC Jazz Classics 1003
Little Queenie (Long Distance Call)	LRC Jazz Classics 1003
Kansas City ①	LRC Jazz Classics 1003

NOTE: Although listed on the cassette as "T Bone Walker with The Muddy Waters Blues Band," T-Bone does not appear on these tracks. Titles are as given on the cassette; the correct titles are in parentheses. LRC Jazz Classics 1003 is a cassette issue. These recordings may have appeared on an Italian vinyl issue, details unknown.

MUDDY WATERS BLUES BAND
Live prob. at Nice Jazz Festival, Nice, France, July 1977

- Muddy Waters vcl, gtr; Jerry Portnoy hca; Bob Margolin gtr; Luther "Guitar Jr." Johnson gtr, vcl; Joe "Pinetop" Perkins pno, vcl ②; Calvin Jones bass; Willie Smith drums

Portnoy's Blues (inst.)	LRC Jazz Classics 1007, CD9015, Laserlight CD17-102
Hoochie Coochie Man	LRC Jazz Classics 1007, CD9015, Laserlight CD17-102
Baby Please Don't Go	LRC Jazz Classics 1007, CD9015, Laserlight CD17-102
Kansas City ②	LRC Jazz Classics 1007, CD9015
Luther's Blues (Everything Gonna Be Alright) ①	LRC Jazz Classics 1007, 1003, CD9015, Laserlight CD17-102
Got My Mojo Working	LRC Jazz Classics 1007, 1003, CD9015, Laserlight CD17-102

Key Little Highway	LRC Jazz Classics 1007, Laserlight CD17-102
(Floyd's Guitar Blues, inst.)	

NOTE: Titles are as given on the cassette; the correct titles are in parentheses. LRC Jazz Classics 1003 and 1007 are cassette issues. These recordings may have appeared on an Italian vinyl issue, details unknown.

MUDDY WATERS

Westport, CT, Monday, 31 October–Saturday, 5 November 1977

- Muddy Waters gtr ①, vcl; Walter Horton acoustic hca ②, electric hca ③; Jerry Portnoy acoustic hca ④, electric hca ⑤; Joe "Pinetop" Perkins pno; Johnny Winter gtr ⑥; Jimmy Rogers gtr; Bob Margolin bass; Willie Smith drums

I'm Ready ② ⑤ ⑥	Blue Sky LP34928, LP25565, LP461186, BGO CD108, Epic CD4611862
33 Years ① ③	Blue Sky LP34928, BGO CD108
Who Do You Trust ① ③ ⑥	Blue Sky LP34928, BGO CD108, COL CD467892 2
Copper Brown ① ⑤ ⑥	Blue Sky LP34928, BGO CD108
I'm Your Hoochie Coochie Man ② ⑤ ⑥	MUD 1, Blue Sky LP34928, LP25565, LP461186, BGO CD108, Epic CD4611862
Mamie ① ④	Blue Sky LP34928, BGO CD108, COL CD467892 2
Rock Me ⑤ ⑥	Blue Sky LP34928, BGO CD108
Screamin' And Cryin' ① ③	Blue Sky LP34928, LP25565, LP461186, BGO CD108, COL CD467892, Epic CD4611862
Good Morning Little School Girl ⑤ ⑥	Blue Sky LP34928, BGO CD108

NOTE: Blue Sky LP34928 was also issued as Blue Sky LP82235.

MUDDY WATERS

Masonic Temple, Detroit, Sunday, 27 August 1978

- Muddy Waters vcl, gtr, slide gtr ①; James Cotton hca; Joe "Pinetop" Perkins pno; Bob Margolin gtr; Johnny Winter gtr ②; Charles Calmese bass; Willie Smith drums

Nine Below Zero	Blue Sky LP35712, BGO CD109
Howling Wolf ① ②	Blue Sky LP35712, BGO CD109
Deep Down In Florida ②	Blue Sky LP35712, BGO CD109, COL CD467892 2

NOTE: Blue Sky LP35712 was also issued as Blue Sky LP83422.

MUDDY WATERS

Live recording, poss. at Harry Hope's Club, Chicago 1979

- Muddy Waters vcl, gtr; Luther "Guitar Jr." Johnson gtr, vcl ①; Bob Margolin gtr; Jerry Portnoy hca; Joe "Pinetop" Perkins pno, vcl ②; Calvin Jones bass; Willie Smith drums; band vcls ③

Last Nite (After Hours, inst.)	Charly CD CBL751
Harry's Groove (inst.)	Charly CD CBL751
Instrumental (spoken intros by Perkins, Waters)	Charly CD CBL751
Nine Below Zero	Charly CD CBL751
Baby Please Don't Go	Charly CD CBL751
They Call Me Muddy Waters	Charly CD CBL751
Everything's Gonna Be Alright ①	Charly CD CBL751
Manish Boy	Charly CD CBL751

Lonesome In My Bedroom	Charly CD CBL751
Corrine Corrina	Charly CD CBL751
Kansas City ②	Charly CD CBL751
Caldonia ②	Charly CD CBL751
Long Distance Call	Charly CD CBL751
Hold It (instr.)	Charly CD CBL751
Got My Mojo Working (encore) ③	Charly CD CBL751

NOTE: The titles are as given on the CD; the correct titles are shown in parentheses.

MUDDY WATERS
Live recording, unk. location, prob. 1979

• Muddy Waters vcl, gtr; prob. Luther "Guitar Jr." Johnson gtr; prob. Bob Margolin gtr; prob. Jerry Portnoy hca; prob. Joe "Pinetop" Perkins pno; prob. Calvin Jones bass; prob. Willie Smith drums; band vcls ①

Hoochie Coochie Man	Charly CD CD1257
My Home Is In The Delta	Charly CD CD1257
You Don't Have To Go	Charly CD CD1257
I'm A King Bee	Charly CD CD1257
Baby, Please Don't Go	Charly CD CD1257
Long Distance Call	Charly CD CD1257
Trouble No More	Charly CD CD1257
Got My Mojo Working ①	Charly CD CD1257
Mannish Boy	Charly CD CD1257

MUDDY WATERS
Westport, CT, May 1980

• Muddy Waters gtr ①, vcl; Luther "Guitar Jr." Johnson, Bob Margolin, Johnny Winter gtr; Joe "Pinetop" Perkins pno; Jerry Portnoy hca; Calvin Jones bass; Willie Smith drums

I'm A King Bee ①	Blue Sky LP37064, LP25565, Epic LP461186, CD6411862, Blue Sky CD ZK37064
Too Young To Know ①	Blue Sky LP37064, CD ZK37064, COL CD467892 2
Mean Old Frisco Blues (omit Margolin, Johnson, Portnoy)	Blue Sky LP37064, CD ZK37064
Forever Lonely (omit Portnoy)	Blue Sky LP37064, CD ZK37064, COL CD467892 2
Champagne And Reefer (omit Winter) ①	Blue Sky LP37064, LP25565, Epic LP461186, CD6411862, Blue Sky CDZK37064
Sad Sad Day ①	Blue Sky LP37064, LP25565, Epic LP461186, CD4611862, Blue Sky CD ZK37064
Deep Down in Florida No. 2 ①	Blue Sky LP37064, CD ZK37064
No Escape From The Blues ①	Blue Sky LP37064, BCD ZK37064

NOTE: Blue Sky LP37064 was also issued as Blue Sky LP84918.

MUDDY WATERS
Live at Navy Pier, Chicago, Saturday, 16 August 1980

• Muddy Waters vcl, gtr; George Buford hca; Lovie Lee pno; John Primer, Rick Kreher gtr; Earnest Johnson bass; Ray Allison drums

Clouds In My Heart	XRT LP9301, Sonet LP859

MUDDY WATERS AND THE ROLLING STONES
Checkerboard Lounge, Chicago, Sunday, 22 November 1981

- Muddy Waters vcl ①, gtr ②; Lovie Lee pno, vcl ③; John Primer gtr, vcl ④; Rick Kreher gtr; George "Mojo" Buford hca; Earnest Johnson bass; Ray Allison drums; Mick Jagger vcl ⑤; Keith Richards gtr; Ron Wood gtr ⑥ (Richards and Wood replace Kreher and poss. Primer); Ian Stewart pno (replaces Lee) ⑦; Lefty Diz gtr ⑧, vcl ⑨; Buddy Guy gtr ⑩, vcl ❶; Junior Wells vcl ❷, hca ❸ (replaces Buford); Mick Jones bass ❹ (replaces Johnson)

Unidentified inst.	unissued
You're Gonna Miss Me	unissued
When I'm Gone ④	
Sweet Little Angel ③	Swingin' Pig CD115-2
Flip Flop And Fly ③	Swingin' Pig CD115-2
Introduction (MW speech)	Swingin' Pig CD115-2
Down The Road I Go ① ②	Swingin' Pig CD115-2
Country Boy ① ②	Swingin' Pig CD115-2
County Jail ① ②	Swingin' Pig CD115-2
I'm A King Bee ① ②	Swingin' Pig CD115-2
Someday Baby ① ②	Swingin' Pig CD115-2
Baby Please Don't Go ① ② ⑤ ⑥	Swingin' Pig CD115-2
Hoochie Coochie Man ① ⑤ ⑥	Swingin' Pig LP009, CD115-2
Long Distance Call ① ⑤ ⑥	Swingin' Pig LP009, CD115-2
Mannish Boy ① ⑤ ⑥ ⑨ ① ❶ ❷	Swingin' Pig LP009, CD115-2
Got My Mojo Working ⑥ ⑩ ❷ ❸	unissued
Next Time You See Me ⑥ ⑦ ⑧ ⑩ ❶ ❷	Swingin' Pig LP009, CD115-2
Talkin' About My Woman ⑥ ⑦ ⑧ ⑨ ❷ ❹	Swingin' Pig LP009, CD115-2
Instrumental (based on "Baby Please Don't Go" theme) ⑥ ⑧ ❹	unissued
Clouds In My Heart ① ⑥ ⑧ ❹	unissued
Champagne And Reefer	Swingin' Pig LP009, CD115-2
Instrumental ❸ ❹	unissued
Instrumental	unissued

NOTE: This session originates from a video recording. "Champagne And Reefer" is titled "I'm Gonna Get High," and "Talkin' About My Woman" is correctly titled "Ugly Woman Blues" on LP009; the latter track is incomplete on this LP. The Swingin' Pig LP009 has a U.K. cassette release, titled *Rolling Stones And Muddy Waters – "Blues Jam In Chicago"* (no issue number), on which "Next Time I See Her" is titled "You're A Liar," and "Long Distance Call" is titled "Phone Call." The correct title of "Down The Road I Go" on the CD issue is "You Don't Have To Go." The CD also includes 3 vintage Stones recordings of Muddy Waters songs.

LP INDEX

Equivalents

In the case of the following albums, the original issue only is listed in the discography highlighted in bold text, e.g. Chess LP 1427 ("The Best Of"). Subsequent reissues of these albums are listed below:

Chess LP 203 (double LP) / Muddy Waters / Chess Masters
    Reissued on Chess LP 427005, Chess LP 6641539, Bellaphon LP 5551
Chess LP 1427 / Muddy Waters / The Best Of
    Reissued on Chess LP 9124224, Chess LP 230, Chess LP 801, Chess LP 515038,
    Chess LP 9255, Chess LP 8343, London LP 15152, Pye Int. LP 28040, Greenline LP8044
Chess LP 1501 / Muddy Waters / The Real Folk Blues
    Reissued on Chess LP 4515, Chess LP 515008, Chess LP 9274
Chess LP 1511 / Muddy Waters / More Real Folk Blues
    Reissued on Chess LP 1005, Chess LP 515020, Chess LP 92781

Abbreviations

To conserve space, the following abbreviations have been used: M.W. – Muddy Waters; L.W. – Little Walter; J.R. – Jimmy Rogers; S.B.W. – Sonny Boy Williamson; V.A. – various artists.

The LPs are listed alphabetically by label / number / artist / title / country of issue.

A

Ace LP 231 / Otis Spann / The Blues Never Die / U.K.
Ace of Clubs LP 1220 / V.A. / Raw Blues / U.K.
Argo LP 4026 / V.A. / The Blues Vol. 1 / U.S.A.
Argo LP 4027 / V.A. / The Blues Vol. 2 / U.S.A.
Argo LP 4031 / V.A. / Blues From Big Bill's / U.S.A.
Argo LP 4034 / V.A. / The Blues Vol. 3 / U.S.A.
Argo LP 4042 / V.A. / The Blues Vol. 4 / U.S.A.
Arhoolie LP 1032 / Willie Mae "Big Mama" Thornton / Big Mama Thornton And The
    Chicago Blues Band / U.S.A.
Astan LP 20027 / M.W. / Sweet Home Chicago / Germany
Astan LP 20028 / M.W. / Original Hoochie Coochie Man / Germany
Astan LP 20039 / V.A. / Live At Newport / Germany
Atlantic LP 502 / V.A. / Ann Arbor Blues And Jazz Festival / U.S.A.
Atlantic LP 60048 / V.A. / Ann Arbor Blues And Jazz Festival / Germany
Atlantic LP 90003 / V.A. / The Blues, A Real Summit Meeting / Germany
Atlantic LP 7816971 / V.A. / Atlantic Blues-Chicago / U.S.A.
Atlantic LP 7817131 / V.A. / Blues Box / U.S.A.

B

Barclay LP 84093 / M.W. / At Newport / France
Barclay LP 84116 / V.A. / Folk Festival Of The Blues / France
Barclay LP 84405 / V.A. / The Blues Vol. 1 / France
Bellaphon LP 1558 / V.A. / Pop Origins / Germany
Bellaphon LP 4002 / J.R. / Chicago Bound / Germany
Bellaphon LP 4007 / L.W. / Hate To See You Go / Germany
Bellaphon LP 5534 / V.A. / Super Blues Session / Germany
Bellaphon LP 5545 / M.W. / Blues Blood / Germany
Bellaphon LP 5548 / S.B.W. / Chess Blues Masters / Germany

Bellaphon LP 5551 / M.W. / Chess Blues Masters / Germany
Bellaphon LP 5552 / L.W. / Chess Blues Masters / Germany
Bellaphon LP 6503 / M.W. / Experiment In Blues / Germany
Bellaphon LP 6542 / S.B.W. / This Is My Story / Germany
Bellaphon LP 6559 / V.A. / Blues Avalanche: Montreux / Germany
Bellaphon LP 19097 / M.W. / London Sessions / Germany
Bellaphon LP 19179 / M.W. / "Unk" In Funk / Germany
Bellaphon LP 19277 / M.W. / Woodstock Album / Germany
Bellaphon LP 19868 / M.W. / Can't Get No Grindin' / Germany
Biograph LP 12035 / V.A. / Love Changin' Blues / U.S.A.
Black Bear LP 901 / M.W. / Rare Live Recordings Vol. 1 / U.K.
Black Bear LP 902 / M.W. / Rare Live Recordings Vol. 2 / U.K.
Black Bear LP 903 / M.W. / Rare Live Recordings Vol. 3 / U.K.
Black Cat LP 001 / Otis Spann / Half Ain't Been Told / Holland
Black Magic LP 9004 / Otis Spann / Take Me Back Home / Holland
Blue Moon LP 002 / V.A. / Live At Newport / U.K.
Blue Moon LP 1006 / M.W. / Rollin' Stone / U.K.
Blue Moon LP 1014 / M.W. / Mississippi Rollin' Stone / U.K.
Blue Moon LP 1023 / M.W. / The Original Hoochie Coochie Man / U.K.
Blue Moon LP 10731 / V.A. / Love Changin' Blues / U.K.
Blue Sky LP 25565 / M.W. / Hoochie Coochie Man / U.K.
Blue Sky LP 32357 / M.W. / Hard Again / U.K.
Blue Sky LP 34313 / Johnny Winter / Nothin' But The Blues / U.S.A.
Blue Sky LP 34449 / M.W. / Hard Again / U.S.A.
Blue Sky LP 34928 / M.W. / I'm Ready / U.S.A.
Blue Sky LP 35712 / M.W. / Muddy Mississippi Waters Live / U.S.A.
Blue Sky LP 37064 / M.W. / King Bee / U.S.A.
Blue Sky LP 81853 / M.W. / Hard Again / U.K.
Blue Sky LP 82141 / Johnny Winter / Nothin' But The Blues / U.K.
Blue Sky LP 82235 / M.W. / I'm Ready / U.K.
Blue Sky LP 83422 / M.W. / Muddy Mississippi Waters Live / U.K.
Blue Sky LP 84918 / M.W. / King Bee / U.K.
Blues Classics LP 8 / V.A. / Chicago Blues, The Early 50's / U.S.A.
Blues Document LP 2058 / St Louis Jimmy Oden 1932–1948 / Austria
Blues Document Box DB-01 / V.A. / The Greatest In Country Blues (1927-1956) / Austria
Bluesway LP 6002 / John Lee Hooker / Live At The Cafe Au-Go-Go /U.S.A.
Bluesway LP 6003 / Otis Spann / The Blues Is Where It's At / U.S.A.
Bluesway LP 6013 / Otis Spann / The Bottom Of The Blues / U.S.A.
Bluesway LP 6061 / V.A. / Classic Blues Vol. 2 / U.S.A.
Bluesway LP 6063 / Otis Spann / Heart Loaded With Trouble / U.S.A.
Boogie Disease LP 101-2 / V.A. / Take A Little Walk With Me / U.S.A.
Bounty LP 6031 / M.W. / Down On Stovall's Plantation / U.K.
Buddah LP 5144 / V.A. / The Blues, A Real Summit Meeting / U.S.A.
Buddah LP 7510 / V.A. / Blues Jam / U.S.A.

C

Cadet LP 314 / M.W. / Electric Mud / U.S.A.
Cadet LP 320 / M.W. / After The Rain / U.S.A.
Cadet LP 4042 / V.A. / The Blues Vol. 4 / U.S.A.
Cadet LP 4051 / V.A. / The Blues Vol. 5 / U.S.A.
Charly / S.B.W. / Chess Box 1 / U.K.
Charly LP 34 / V.A. / The Blues – A Real Summit Meeting / U.K.
Charly LP 1062 / Otis Spann / Nobody Knows Chicago Like I Do / U.K.
Charly LP 1134 / Earl Hooker – Magic Sam / Calling All Blues /U.K.

Checker LP 1437 / S.B.W. / Down And Out Blues / U.S.A.
Checker LP 2973 / V.A. / Love Those Goodies / U.S.A.
Checker LP 3004 / L.W. / The Best Of / U.S.A.
Checker LP 3008 / V.A. / Super Blues / U.S.A.
Checker LP 3010 / V.A. / Super Super Blues / U.S.A.
Checker LP 6467306 / M.W. / At Newport / U.K.
Chess LP CS1 / V.A. / Chess Story Vol. 1 / U.S.A.
Chess LP 3-16500 / Willie Dixon / U.S.A. (box set)
Chess LP 127 / M.W. / Fathers And Sons / U.S.A.
Chess LP 202 / L.W. / Chess Blues Masters Vol. 2 / U.S.A.
Chess LP 203 / M.W. / Chess Blues Masters Vol. 3 / U.S.A.
Chess LP 206 / S.B.W. / Chess Blues Masters Vol. 6 / U.S.A.
Chess LP 207 / J.R. / Chess Blues Masters Vol. 7 / U.S.A.
Chess LP 230 / M.W. / The Best Of / New Zealand
Chess LP 407 / J.R. / Chicago Bound / U.S.A.
Chess LP 416 / L.W. / Confessin' The Blues / U.S.A.
Chess LP 417 / S.B.W. / One Way Out / U.S.A.
Chess LP 801 / M.W. / The Best Of / Japan
Chess LP 802 / L.W. / The Best Of / Japan
Chess LP 813 / J.R. / Chicago Bound / Japan
Chess LP 814 / M.W. / At Newport / Japan
Chess LP 817 / S.B.W. / Down And Out Blues / Japan
Chess LP 831 / V.A. / Folk Festival Of The Blues / Japan
Chess LP 1005 / M.W. / More Real Folk Blues / Australia
Chess LP 1427 / M.W. / The Best Of / U.S.A.
Chess LP 1428 / L.W. / The Best Of / U.S.A.
Chess LP 1444 / M.W. / Sings Big Bill / U.S.A.
Chess LP 1449 / M.W. / At Newport / U.S.A.
Chess LP 1483 / M.W. / Folk Singer / U.S.A.
Chess LP 1501 / M.W. / The Real Folk Blues / U.S.A.
Chess LP 1507 / M.W. / Brass And The Blues / U.S.A.
Chess LP 1511 / M.W. / More Real Folk Blues / U.S.A.
Chess LP 1522 / V.A. / Heavy Heads / U.S.A.
Chess LP 1528 / V.A. / Heavy Heads Vol. 2 / U.S.A.
Chess LP 1533 / V.A. / Blues From Big Bill's / U.S.A.
Chess LP 1535 / L.W. / Hate To See You Go / U.S.A.
Chess LP 1539 / M.W. / Sail On / U.S.A.
Chess LP 1544 / V.A. / Pop Origins / U.S.A.
Chess LP 1553 / M.W. / They Call Me Muddy Waters / U.S.A.
Chess LP 2005 / M.W. / London Sessions / U.K.
Chess LP 2006 / V.A. / Folk Festival Of The Blues / U.K.
Chess LP 2012 / V.A. / Super Blues / Italy
Chess LP 2015 / S.B.W. / One Way Out / Italy
Chess LP 2026 / M.W. / At Newport / Italy
Chess LP 2057 / M.W. / Rare And Unissued / U.K.
Chess LP 4000 / M.W. / Chess Masters / U.K.
Chess LP 4001 / S.B.W. / Chess Masters / U.K.
Chess LP 4002 / L.W. / Chess Masters / U.K.
Chess LP 4003 / V.A. / The Blues Vol. 4 / U.K.
Chess LP 4004 / V.A. / Chess Story Vol. 1 / U.K.
Chess LP 4006 / M.W. / Chess Masters Vol. 2 / U.K.
Chess LP 4007 / L.W. / Hate To See You Go / Germany
Chess LP 4008 / J.R. / Chess Masters / U.K.
Chess LP 4010 / V.A. / Chess Masters / U.K.
Chess LP 4011 / L.W. / Chess Masters Vol. 2 / U.K.

Chess LP 4012 / S.B.W. / Chess Masters Vol. 2 / U.K.
Chess LP 4013 / V.A. / Chicago Blues / U.K.
Chess LP 4015 / M.W. / Chess Masters Vol. 3 / U.K.
Chess LP 4053 / V.A. / Chicago Blues Anthology / U.K.
Chess LP 4056 / V.A. / Blues Rock Avalanche / U.K.
Chess LP 4512 / V.A. / The Blues Vol. 5 / U.K.
Chess LP 4513 / M.W. / At Newport / U.K.
Chess LP 4515 / M.W. / The Real Folk Blues / U.K.
Chess LP 4526 / M.W. / Brass And The Blues / U.K.
Chess LP 4529 / V.A. / Super Blues / U.K.
Chess LP 4537 / V.A. / Super Super Blues / U.K.
Chess LP 4542 / M.W. / Electric Mud / U.K.
Chess LP 4553 / M.W. / After The Rain / U.K.
Chess LP 4556 / M.W. / Fathers And Sons / U.K.
Chess LP 4558 / V.A. / Blues From The Copacabana / U.K.
Chess LPS 6040-6050 (11-album box) / M.W. / The Chess Box / Japan
Chess LP 7002 / M.W. / Can't Get No Grindin' / U.K.
Chess LP 7250 / V.A. / Chess Masters Sampler / U.K.
Chess LP 8200 / M.W. – Howlin' Wolf / Muddy And The Wolf / U.S.A.
Chess LP 8202 / M.W. / Rolling Stone / U.S.A.
Chess LP 8203 / V.A. / Wizards From The Southside / U.S.A.
Chess LP 8343 / M.W. / The Best Of / Japan
Chess LP 9100 / M.W. – Howlin' Wolf / Muddy And The Wolf / U.S.A.
Chess LP 9101 / M.W. / Rolling Stone / U.S.A.
Chess LP 9169 / V.A. / Super Super Blues / U.S.A.
Chess LP 9291 / M.W. / Trouble No More / U.S.A.
Chess LP 22010 / M.W. / Fathers And Sons / Italy
Chess LP 50002 / M.W. / London Sessions / France
Chess LP 50006 / M.W. / Live At Mister Kelly's / France
Chess LP 50011 / V.A. / Chicago Blues Anthology / France
Chess LP 50012 / L.W. / Boss Blues Harmonica / France
Chess LP 50012 / M.W. / Live At Mister Kelly's / U.S.A.
Chess LP 50017 / M.W. / After The Rain / France
Chess LP 50020 / S.B.W. / This Is My Story / France
Chess LP 50023 / M.W. / Can't Get No Grindin' / U.S.A.
Chess LP 50023 / V.A. / Blues Avalanche, Montreux, 1972 / France
Chess LP 50027 / S.B.W. / This Is My Story / U.S.A.
Chess LP 50033 / M.W. / Fathers And Sons / U.S.A.
Chess LP 50034 / M.W. / Can't Get No Grindin' / France
Chess LP 50038 / M.W. – Howlin' Wolf / London Revisited / France
Chess LP 50040 / M.W. / "Unk" In Funk / France
Chess LP 50043 / L.W. / Confessin' The Blues / France
Chess LP 50052 / M.W. / Woodstock Album / France
Chess LP 60006 / M.W. / McKinley Morganfield AKA Muddy Waters / U.S.A.
Chess LP 60012 / V.A. / Chicago Blues Anthology / U.S.A.
Chess LP 60013 / M.W. / London Sessions / U.S.A.
Chess LP 60014 / L.W. / Boss Blues Harmonica / U.S.A.
Chess LP 60015 / V.A. / Blues Avalanche, Montreux 1972 / U.S.A.
Chess LP 60026 / M.W. – Howlin' Wolf / London Revisited / U.S.A.
Chess LP 60031 / M.W. / "Unk" In Funk / U.S.A.
Chess LP 60035 / M.W. / Woodstock Album / U.S.A.
Chess LP 68506 / V.A. / Big Blues Vol. 1 / France
Chess LP 427001 / L.W. / France
Chess LP 427004 / S.B.W. / France
Chess LP 427005 / M.W. / France

Chess LP 427012 / J.R. / France
Chess LP 427015 / M.W. / Fathers And Sons / France
Chess LP 515005 / V.A. / Heavy Heads / France
Chess LP 515008 / M.W. / The Real Folk Blues / France
Chess LP 515015 / S.B.W. / One Way Out / France
Chess LP 515016 / M.W. / Folk Singer / France
Chess LP 515020 / M.W. / More Real Folk Blues / France
Chess LP 515029 / M.W. / Sings Big Bill / France
Chess LP 515036 / M.W. / They Call Me Muddy Waters / France
Chess LP 515037 / M.W. / Live At Mister Kelly's / France
Chess LP 515038 / M.W. / Best Of / France
Chess LP 515039 / M.W. / At Newport / France
Chess LP 515040 / M.W. / Rare And Unissued / France
Chess LP 515041 / V.A. / Blues From Big Bill's Copacabana / France
Chess LP 624474 / M.W. / Profile / Germany
Chess LP 624801 / M.W. / Blues Roots Vol. 11 / Germany
Chess LP 624802 / Willie Dixon / Blues Roots Vol. 12 / Germany
Chess LP 624804 / Howlin' Wolf / Blues Roots Vol. 14 / Germany
Chess LP 624805 / L.W. / Blues Roots Vol. 15 / Germany
Chess LP 624807 / J.R. / Blues Roots Vol. 17 / Germany
Chess LP 624825 / V.A. / Heavy Heads / Germany
Chess LP 628537 / V.A. / Black & White Blues / Germany
Chess LP 628622 / M.W. / In Memoriam / Germany
Chess LP 680002 / M.W. / Muddy Waters / U.S.A. (6-LP box)
Chess LP 915313 / M.W. / "Unk" In Funk / U.S.A.
Chess LP 6310121 / M.W. / London Sessions / U.K.
Chess LP 6310129 / M.W. / Can't Get No Grindin' / U.K.
Chess LP 6641047 / V.A. / Genesis One – The Beginnings Of Rock / U.K.
Chess LP 6641125 / V.A. / Genesis Two – Memphis To Chicago / U.K.
Chess LP 6641174 / V.A. / Genesis Three – Sweet Home Chicago / U.K.
Chess LP 6641539 / M.W. / Chess Blues Masters / U.K.
Chess LP 9033417 / S.B.W. / One Way Out / Canada
Chess LP 9124224 / M.W. / The Best Of / France
Chess LP 9283009 / M.W. / Woodstock Album / Holland
Cleo LP 14983 / M.W. / Mississippi Rollin' Stone / Holland
Cleo LP 15983 / M.W. / Rock Me / Holland
Cleo LP 30683 / M.W. / The Original Hoochie Coochie Man / Holland
Club LP (no number) / V.A. / Grab This And Dance Vol. 1 / Spain
Connoisseur Collection LP 130 / V.A. / The Chess Story / U.K.
Corrine LP 100 / M.W. / Live 1976 / Austria

D

Decca LP 21 / Eric Clapton / Steppin' Out / U.K.
Decca LP 387 / Eric Clapton / The Blues World Of / U.K.
Decca LP 4615 / Otis Spann / The Blues Of / U.K.
Decca LP 4681 / V.A. / Blues Now / U.K.
Delmark LP 604 / Junior Wells / Blues Hit Big Town / U.S.A.
Delmark LP 648 / V.A. / The Blues World Of Little Walter / U.S.A.
Deja Vu LP 2034 / M.W. / The Collection / Italy
Deram LP 1036 / Otis Spann / Cracked Spanner Head / U.K.
Doblon LP 504117 / V.A. / Grandes Nombres Del Blues Vol. 2 / Spain
Douglas LP 781 / Luther "Georgia Boy Snake" Johnson With the Muddy Waters Band / U.S.A.
Douglas LP 789 / Luther Johnson With The Muddy Waters Blues Band / U.S.A.

E

Epic LP 22123 / V.A. / Okeh Chicago Blues / U.K.
Epic LP 37318 / V.A. / Okeh Chicago Blues / U.S.A.
Epic LP 461186 / M.W. / Hoochie Coochie Man / U.K.

F

Festival LP 1088 / V.A. / America's Musical Roots / U.S.A.
Fontana LP 5204 / V.A. / American Folk Blues Festival 1963 / U.K.
Fontana LP 885403 / V.A. / American Folk Blues Festival 1963 / Holland
Frances Concert LP FC116 / M.W. / Muddy Waters Live In Antibes 1974 / France
Frances Concert LP FC121 / M.W. / Muddy Waters Live In Paris 1968 / France

G

Golden Hour LP 864 / V.A. / Great Blues Men / U.K.
Greenline LP 6023 / V.A. / The Best Of Blues / Italy
Greenline LP 7002 / M.W. / Can't Get No Grindin' / Italy
Greenline LP 8001 / V.A. / Wizards Of The Southside / Italy
Greenline LP 8004 / V.A. / Folk Festival Of The Blues / Italy
Greenline LP 8006 / S.B.W. / One Way Out. / Italy
Greenline LP 8010 / M.W. / Rare And Unissued / Italy
Greenline LP 8018 / L.W. / The Best Of / Italy
Greenline LP 8022 / M.W. / At Newport / Italy
Greenline LP 8027 / V.A. / The Blues Vol. 1 / Italy
Greenline LP 8029 / M.W. / Sings Big Bill / Italy
Greenline LP 8035 / V.A. / The Blues Vol. 2 / Italy
Greenline LP 8040 / M.W. / Folk Singer / Italy
Greenline LP 8044 / M.W. / The Best Of / Italy
Greenline LP 8105 / V.A. / Knights Of The Keyboard, Chicago Piano Blues 1947–1956 / Italy
Greenline LP 8109 / M.W. / They Call Me Muddy Waters / Italy
Greenline LP 8115 / M.W. / "Unk" In Funk / Italy
Greenline LP 26027 / J.R. / Chess Masters / Italy
Greenline LP 26033 / V.A. / Blues Rock Avalanche / Italy
Greenline LP SAM500 / V.A. / The Rhythm And The Blues / Italy
GRT LP 903360003 / V.A. / Rockbottom / Canada
GSR LP 13 / V.A. / Grande Storia Del Rock Vol. 13 / Italy

H

Happy Bird LP F4-90111 (box set) / V.A. / The Blues Legend / Germany
Happy Bird LP 90077 / M.W. / Mud In Your Ear / Germany
Happy Bird LP 90080 / Luther Johnson With The Muddy Waters Blues Band / Chicken Shack / Germany
Happy Bird LP 90098 / V.A. / The Blues Legends Vol. 2 / Germany
Happy Bird LP 90099 / V.A. / Blues From The Fields Into The Town / Germany
Happy Bird LP 90134 / V.A. / Blues From The Fields Into The Town Vol. 2 / Germany
Happy Bird LP 90142 / V.A. / Blues From The Fields Into The Town Vol. 3 / Germany
Highway 51 LP 100 / V.A. / Decade Of The Blues / U.K.
HMV LP 3609 / Otis Spann / The Blues Is Where It's At / U.K.
HMV LP 3612 / John Lee Hooker / Live At The Cafe Au-Go-Go / U.K.

I

Instant LP 5003 / M.W. / Chicago Blues / U.K.

Instant LP 5011 / Instant Blues / U.K.
Instant LP 5016 / V.A. / Stoned Alchemy / U.K.
Instant LP 5017 / V.A. / White Lightnin' / U.K.
Intermedia LP 5022 / V.A. / Live At Newport / U.S.A.

J

Joy LP 177 / V.A. / Blues Jam / U.K.
JSP LP 1070 / Otis Spann / Rarest Recordings / U.K.

K

Kent-Globe LP 8156 / M.W. / The Best Of / Japan
Krazy Kat LP 820 / V.A. / Alley Special / U.K.
Krazy Kat LP 7405 / M.W. / In Concert / U.K.

L

L&R LP 42023 / V.A. / American Folk Blues Festival 1963 / Germany
Le Roi du Blues LP 2012 / L.W. / Southern Feeling / Canada
Le Roi du Blues LP 2017 / L.W. / Blue Midnight / Canada
Les Editions Blues LP 401 / M.W. / Live 65-68 / France
Liberty LP 83218E / George Smith / Blues With A Feeling, A Tribute To Little Walter / U.K.
London LP 15152 / M.W. / The Best Of / U.K.

M

Marble Arch LP 610 / V.A. / Rhythm And Blues All Stars / U.K.
Marble Arch LP 661 / M.W. / At Newport / U.K.
Marble Arch LP 662 / S.B.W. / Down And Out Blues / U.K.
Marble Arch LP 723 / M.W. / Sings Big Bill / U.K.
Marble Arch LP 724 / V.A. / Festival Of The Blues / U.K.
Marble Arch LP 804 / V.A. / The Blues / U.K.
Marble Arch LP 813 / V.A. / More Rhythm And Blues / U.K.
Marble Arch LP 815 / L.W. / U.K.
Moon LP 007-1 / M.W. / Unreleased In The West / Italy
Muse LP 5008 / M.W. / Mud In Your Ear / U.S.A.
Muse LP 5021 / Luther Johnson With The Muddy Waters Blues Band / Chicken Shack /
    U.S.A.
Muskadine LP 100 / V.A. / On The Road Again / U.S.A.
MCA LP 1862 / V.A. / Standards In Blues And Jazz / U.K.
MCA LP 204926 / John Lee Hooker / Live At The Cafe Au-Go-Go / France
MCA LP 204927 / Otis Spann / The Blues Is Where It's At / France

N

New World LP 261 / V.A. / Straighten Up And Fly Right / U.S.A.
Nighthawk LP 102 / V.A. / Chicago Slickers / U.S.A.

O

Ocean LP 2044 / V.A. / Blues Brothers, 16 RnB Classics / U.K.
Official LP 6043 / Sunnyland Slim / Devil Is A Busy Man / Denmark

P

Phillips LP 451 / V.A. / The Best American Folk Blues Festivals 1963–67 / Holland

Poljazz LP 79 / M.W. / The Warsaw Session Vol. 1 / Poland
Poljazz LP 80 / M.W. / The Warsaw Session Vol. 2 / Poland
Poljazz LP 0634 / M.W. / The Warsaw Session Vol. 1 / Poland
Poljazz LP 0635 / M.W. / The Warsaw Session Vol. 2 / Poland
Polydor LP 236574 / M.W. / Blues Man / U.K.
Prestige LP 7391 / Otis Spann / The Blues Never Die / U.S.A.
Prestige LP 7719 / Otis Spann / The Blues Never Die / U.S.A.
P-Vine Special LP 9015 / Earl Hooker / Blue Guitar / Japan
P-Vine Special LP 9038 / V.A. / Down Home Chicago Blues / Japan
Pye LP 34 / M.W. / At Newport / U.K.
Pye Golden Guinea LP 0280 / V.A. / Rhythm And Blues / U.K.
Pye Int. LP 28030 / V.A. / The Blues Vol. 1 / U.K.
Pye Int. LP 28033 / V.A. / Folk Festival Of The Blues / U.K.
Pye Int. LP 28035 / V.A. / The Blues Vol. 2 / U.K.
Pye Int. LP 28036 / S.B.W. / Down And Out Blues / U.K.
Pye Int. LP 28038 / M.W. / Folk Singer / U.K.
Pye Int. LP 28040 / M.W. / The Best Of / U.K.
Pye Int. LP 28043 / L.W. / U.K.
Pye Int. LP 28045 / V.A. / The Blues Vol. 3 / U.K.
Pye Int. LP 28048 / M.W. / Sings Big Bill / U.K.
Python LP 1 / V.A. / Going Back To Chicago / U.K.
Python LP 6 / Jimmy Rogers – Eddie Taylor / Blues From Chicago Vol. 1 / U.K.
Python LP 12 / M.W. / Real Chicago Blues Of Vol. 1 / U.K.
Python LP 18 / M.W. / Real Chicago Blues Of Vol. 2 / U.K.
Python LP 19 / M.W. / Real Chicago Blues Of Vol. 3 / U.K.
Python LP 20 / L.W. / Little Walter And His Jukes / U.K.
Python LP 21 / V.A. / Blues From The Windy City / U.K.

R

RCA LP 85463 / V.A. / Rock & Roll, The Early Years / U.K.
Red Lightnin LP 005 / V.A. / Blues In "D" Natural / U.K.
Red Lightnin LP 007 / Junior Wells / In My Younger Days / U.K.
Red Lightnin LP 0055 / V.A. / Chicago Blues / U.K.
Roots LP 113002 / V.A. / The Blues Vol. 1 / Holland

S

See For Miles LP 54 / Otis Spann / The Blues Of / U.K.
Showcase LP 141 / M.W. / I Can't Be Satisfied / U.K.
Smithsonian Institution LP100 / V.A. / Music From The Festival Of American Folklife / U.S.A.
Sonet LP 859 / V.A. / Blues Deluxe / U.K.
Spivey LP 1008 / V.A. / The Bluesmen Of The Muddy Waters Chicago Blues Band / U.S.A.
Spivey LP 1009 / V.A. / Encore For The Chicago Blues / U.S.A.
Spivey LP 1026 / V.A. / New York Really Has The Blues Stars Vol. 2 / U.S.A.
Spivey LP 1035 / V.A. / New York Really Has The Blues Stars Vol. 4 / U.S.A.
Stack-O-Hits LP 9015 / M.W. / The Original Hoochie Coochie Man / U.S.A.
Stack-O-Hits LP 9032 / M.W. / Mississippi Rollin' Stone / U.S.A.
Stateside LP 10169 / Otis Spann / The Blues Never Die / U.K.
Stateside LP 10255 / Otis Spann / The Bottom Of The Blues / U.K.
Stylus LP SMP 850 / M.W. / Chess Masters – Muddy Waters / U.K.
Sunnyland LP 100 / M.W. / Vintage Muddy Waters / U.K.
Syndicate Chapter LP 1/2 / M.W. / Back In The Early Days / U.K.
Syndicate Chapter LP 2 / M.W. / Good News / U.K.

Syndicate Chapter LP 4 / L.W. / Thunderbird / U.K.
Syndicate Chapter LP 5 / V.A. / We Three Kings / U.K.

T

Testament LP 2207 / V.A. / Chicago Blues: The Beginning / U.S.A.
Testament LP 2210 / M.W. / Down On Stovall's Plantation / U.S.A.
Timewind LP 50085 / V.A. / The Pure Blues / Holland
Tobacco Road LP 2545 / M.W. / Why'd You Do Me / Germany
Tobacco Road LP 2548 / M.W. & Luther Johnson / Muddy Waters Blues Band Meets Luther
    Johnson / Germany
Tobacco Road LP 2584 / V.A. / What Is This Thing Called Blues / Germany
Tobacco Road LP 2603 / V.A. / What Is This Thing Called Blues / Germany
Tobacco Road LP 2632 / M.W. / I Feel So Good / Germany
Tobacco Road LP 2633 / M.W. / One More Mile / Germany
The Swingin' Pig LP 009 / M.W. & The Rolling Stones / Germany
Transatlantic LP 188 / Luther "Georgia Boy Snake" Johnson With The Muddy Waters Blues
    Band / U.K.
Transatlantic LP 2004 / V.A. / Best Of The Blues / France

U

United Artists LP 1042 / Memphis Slim / Broken Soul Blues / U.K.
United Artists LP 3050 / V.A. / Folk Song Festival At Carnegie Hall / U.S.A.
United Artists LP 3137 / Memphis Slim / Broken Soul Blues / U.S.A.
United Artists LP 6137 / Memphis Slim / Broken Soul Blues / U.S.A.

V

Vanguard LP 25-26 / V.A. / Great Bluesmen / U.S.A.
Vogue LP 60100358 / V.A. / Gospel, Jazz, Blues & Co. / France

W

Warner Brothers LP 3146 / The Band / The Last Waltz / U.S.A.
Warner Brothers LP 66076 / The Band / The Last Waltz / U.S.A.
World Pacific LP 21887 / George Smith / Blues With A Feeling, A Tribute To Little Walter /
    U.S.A.

X

XRT LP 9301 / V.A. / Blues Jam / U.S.A.
Xtra LP 1133 / V.A. / On The Road Again / U.K.

EP INDEX

Checker EP 1437 / S.B.W. / U.S.A.
Chess EP 4008 / V.A. / Chess Mini Masters, The Blues / U.K.
Chess EP 6006 / M.W. / I'm Ready / U.K.
Chess EP 6011 / V.A. / The Blues Vol. 2, Part 1 / U.K.
Chess EP 6022 / The Real Folk Blues Vol. 4 / U.K.
Chess EP 6145011 / V.A. / "Genesis" Box EP / U.K.
London EP 1060 / M.W. / Mississippi Blues / U.K.
Pye Int. EP 44010 / M.W. / U.K.
Pye Int. EP 44022 / V.A. / R&B Showcase Vol. 2 / U.K.
Pye Int. EP 44029 / V.A. / The Blues Vol. 1, Part 1 / U.K.
Pye Int. EP 44030 / V.A. / Festival Of The Blues Vol. 1 / U.K.
Pye Int. EP 44035 / V.A. / The Blues Vol. 1, Part 2 / U.K.
Red Lightnin EP 0027 / Billy Boy Arnold – Little Walter / Superharps / U.K.
Vogue EP 1046 / M.W. / Mississippi Blues / France
XX EP 715 / Junior Wells / U.K.

CASSETTE INDEX

LRC Jazz Classics 1003 / T Bone Walker With Muddy Waters Blues Band / U.S.A.
LRC Jazz Classics 1007 / Muddy Waters Blues Band / U.S.A.

COMPACT DISC INDEX

A

ACT CD 9204-2 / V.A. / American Folk Blues Festival – Lost Tapes Vol. 1 / Germany
ACT CD 9205-2 / V.A. / Blues Giants In Concert – More American Folk Blues Festival 1963 / Germany
Arhoolie CD 305 / Big Mama Thornton / Ball 'n' Chain / U.S.A.

B

Beat Goes On BGOCD 39 / John Lee Hooker / Live At Cafe Au-Go-Go / U.K.
Beat Goes On BGOCD 92 / The Bottom Of The Blues / Otis Spann / U.K.
Beat Goes On BGOCD 104 / Johnny Winter / Nothing But The Blues / U.K.
Beat Goes On BGOCD 108 / M.W. / I'm Ready / U.K.
Beat Goes On BGOCD 109 / M.W. / Muddy "Mississippi" Waters Live / U.K.
Beat Goes On BGOCD 221 / Otis Spann / The Blues Is Where It's At / U.K.
Best CD BSTCD 9104 / M.W. / Muddy Waters / France
Blue Knight CD BKR 23 / M.W. / No Minstrels
Blue Moon CDBM 071 / V.A. / Newport In New York / U.K.
Blue Sky CDSKY 32357 / M.W. / Hard Again / U.S.A.
Blue Sky ZK 37064 / M.W. / King Bee / U.S.A.
The Blues Collection CD 011 / M.W. / Chicago Blues / U.K.

C

Capitol CD 8 29375 / M.W. & Memphis Slim / Chicago Blues Masters / U.S.A.
Capitol CD 8 36288 / Chicago Blues Masters, Vol. 3 / U.S.A.
Castle Communications MAC CD 193 / M.W. / Got My Mojo Working / U.K.

Castle Communications MAC CD 193 / M.W. / Rollin' and Tumblin' / U.K.
Charly CD BM 10 / M.W. / Rock Me / U.K.
Charly CD BM 15 / V.A. / Live Action / U.K.
Charly CD BM 26 / V.A. / The Super, Super Blues Band / U.K.
Charly CD BM 39 / M.W. / Funky Butt / U.K.
Charly CD CBL 751 / M.W. / Muddy Waters – Chicago 1979 / U.K.
Charly CD CDCD 1257 / M.W. / Muddy Waters In Concert / U.K.
Charly CD RB 6 / M.W. and Otis Spann / Live At Newport / U.K.
Charly CD RB 15 / M.W. / Electric Mud And More / U.K.
Charly CD Red 1 / M.W. / Rollin' Stone / U.K.
Charly CD Red 8 / M.W. / Fathers And Sons / U.K.
Charly CD Red 16 / J.R. / That's All Right / U.K.
Charly CD Red 17 / M.W. / Rollin' And Tumblin' / U.K.
Charly CD Red 22 / M.W. / The London Muddy Waters Sessions / U.K.
Charly CD Red Box 1 (4-CD box) / S.B.W. / The Chess Years / U.K.
Charly CD Red Box 3 (9-CD box) / M.W. / The Complete Muddy Waters 1947–1967 / U.K.
Charly CD Red Box 4 (4-CD box) / L.W. / Little Walter, The Chess Years 1952–1963 / U.K.
Charly CD Red Box 8 (12-CD box) / Bo Diddley / The Chess Years / U.K.
Chess CD CHD 2-9342 (double) / L.W. / The Essential / U.S.A.
Chess CD CHD 2-9343 (double) / S.B.W. / The Essential / U.S.A.
Chess CD CHD 2-9348 (double) / M.W. / One More Mile / U.S.A.
Chess CD CHD 2-9357 / L.W. / Blues With A Feeling / U.S.A.
Chess CD CHD 3-80002 (3-CD box) / M.W. / The Chess Box / U.S.A.
Chess CD CHD 4-9340 (4-CD box) / V.A. / Chess Blues / U.S.A.
Chess CD CHD 9116 / S.B.W. / One Way Out / U.S.A.
Chess CD CHD 9168 / Bo Diddley, M.W., L.W. / Super Blues / U.S.A.
Chess CD CHD 9169 / M.W., Bo Diddley, Howlin' Wolf / Super, Super Blues / U.S.A.
Chess CD CHD 9180 / M.W. / Rare And Unissued / U.S.A.
Chess CD CHD 9274 / M.W. / The Real Folk Blues / U.S.A.
Chess CD CHD 9279 / M.W. / More Real Folk Blues / U.S.A.
Chess CD CHD 9286 / M.W. / Brass And The Blues / U.S.A.
Chess CD CHD 9291 / M.W. / Trouble No More / U.S.A.
Chess CD CHD 9298 / M.W. / The London Muddy Waters Sessions / U.S.A.
Chess CD CHD 9299 / M.W. / They Call Me Muddy Waters / U.S.A.
Chess CD CHD 9319 / M.W. / Can't Get No Grindin' / U.S.A.
Chess CD CHD 9330 / V.A. / The Blues Vol. 6: 50's Rarities / U.S.A.
Chess CD CHD 9338 / M.W. / Live (At Mister Kelly's) / U.S.A.
Chess CD CHD 9344 / M.W. / The Complete Plantation Recordings / U.S.A.
Chess CD CHD 9359 / M.W. / The Muddy Waters Woodstock Album / U.S.A.
Chess CD CHD 19106 / S.B.W. / Down And Out Blues / U.S.A.
Chess CD CHD 31268 / M.W. / The Best Of Muddy Waters / U.S.A.
Chess CD CHD 31269 / M.W. / Muddy Waters At Newport / U.S.A.
Columbia COL 467892 2 / M.W. / Blues Sky / U.S.A.
CSI Classic 7511 / M.W. / Muddy Waters In Concert / U.S.A.

D

Document DOCD-5146 / M.W. / First Recording Sessions 1941–1946 / Austria
Document DOCD-5235 / St Louis Jimmy Oden / Complete Recorded Works Vol. 2 / Austria

E

Epic CD 4611862 / M.W. / Hoochie Coochie Man / U.S.A.
Evidence ECD 26100 (4-CD box) / American Folk Blues Festival '62 To '65 / U.S.A.

F

Fan Club CD 99 / M.W. / Goin' Home / France
France's Concert FCD 116 / M.W. / Live In Antibes 1974 / France
France's Concert FCD 121 / M.W. / Live In Paris 1968 / France

I

Interstate Music CD MW 261058 / M.W. / Live In 1958 / U.K.

J

Jazz Helvetica CD 02 / Muddy Waters Chicago Bluesband / Live In Switzerland / France

L

Landscape CD LS 2908 / M.W. / Live In Switzerland 1976 – Vol. 1 / Switzerland
Landscape CD LS 2921 / M.W. / Live In Switzerland 1976 – Vol. 2 / Switzerland
Laserlight CD 17-102 / M.W. / Muddy Waters Blues Band Featuring Dizzy Gillespie / Germany
LRC CD 9015 / M.W. / Muddy Waters / U.S.A.
LRC CD 9050 / M.W. / Hoochie Coochie Man / U.S.A.

M

MCA CHD 2-9372 / J.R. / Jimmy Rogers – The Complete Chess Recordings / U.S.A.
MCA MCAD-11202 / Otis Spann / Down To Earth, The Bluesway Recordings / U.S.A.
Muse CD 600630 / M.W. / Mud In Your Ear / U.S.A.

O

Original Blues Classics OBGCD 530-2 / Otis Spann / The Blues Never Die / U.S.A.

P

Pablo Jazz PACD 5302-2 / M.W. / Muddy Waters – Live In Paris 1972 / U.S.A.
Paradise CD Para 1060 / John Lee Hooker / The Night Of The Hook / U.S.A.
Prestige CDSGP0150 / M.W. / Muddy Waters In Concert / U.S.A.

S

See For Miles SEECD 389 / Otis Spann / The Blues Of Otis Spann Plus . . . . / U.K.
Story Of Blues CD 3508-2 / St. Louis Jimmy Oden / Austria
The Swinging Pig CD 115-2 / M.W. & The Rolling Stones / Sweet Home Chicago / Luxembourg

T

Testament TCD6001 / Otis Spann / Otis Spann – Live The Life / U.S.A.
Tomato CD R2 711661 / M.W. & Otis Spann / Collaboration / U.S.A.

V

Vanguard CD 2-77005 (double) / V.A. / Blues With A Feeling: Newport Folk Festival Classics / U.S.A.
Vogue CD 651 600630 / Muddy Waters' Blues Band / Mud In Your Ear / France

W

Warner Bros. CD 7599-27346-2 (double) / The Band / The Last Waltz / U.S.A.
Wolf CD 120200 / M.W. / Live Recordings 1965–73 / Austria

INDEX